Horizons

Teaching and Learning Resources

Geography 11–14

David Gardner

Roger Knill

John Smith

™ Nelson Thornes

a Wolters Kluwer business

Published in 2006 by:
Nelson Thornes Ltd
Delta Place
27 Bath Road
CHELTENHAM
GL53 7TH
United Kingdom

06 07 08 09 10 / 10 9 8 7 6 5 4 3 2 1

A catalogue record for this book is available from the British Library

ISBN 0 7487 9058 6

Illustrations by Gordon Lawson, Angela Lumley, Richard Morris, David Russell Illustration
Page make-up by Ann Samuel

Printed in Great Britain by Antony Rowe

Acknowledgements

With thanks to the following for permission to reproduce photographs and other copyright material in this book:

Alamy/ Keith Dannemiller: AS 3.1; Getty Images/ Time Life Pictures: AS 6.10 (both); Rex/ Bruce Bailey: AS 6.6; Science Photo Library/ M-Sat Ltd: AS 6.14 (both); John Smith: pp.162, 163, AS 5.17, AS 5.18.

'Tsunami alert system takes shape' (AS 1.5) by Julianna Kettlewell (BBC News science reporter) adapted from the BBC News website, 24.06.05, and reproduced with permission of BBC News at bbcnews.com.

'Students get explosive view of research at volcano site' (AS 1.13, top) adapted from Newswise website (www.newswise.com), 31.07.03, and reproduced with permission.

Website article on Montserrat (AS 1.13, bottom) adapted from NIDES website (www.nides.bc.ca).

'No greed no need' cartoon (AS 2.8) by Tayo Fatunia © Tayo, CartoonArts International/ CWS, and reproduced with permission.

Make Poverty History advert (AS 2.10) reproduced with permission of www.makepovertyhistory.org.

Logos (AS 2.13) reproduced with kind permission of Oxfam, Christian Aid, Practical Action, ActionAid, CAFOD and the Mkwakwani School Project.

'There's nothing free about fair trade' advert (AS 2.15), reproduced with permission of The Co-operative Bank.

Logo and photograph of a Dubble bar (AS 2.16) reproduced with kind permission of Comic Relief.

African debt cartoon (AS 2.20) © Christo, Sega–Sofia, Bulgaria, and reproduced with permission of CartoonArts International/ CWS.

'Can aid do more harm than good?' (AS 2.21) by Henri Astier, adapted from the BBC News website, 27.08.05, and reproduced with permission of BBC News at bbcnews.com.

Cartoon of smuggling workers (AS 3.15) by Margaret Scott and reproduced with permission.

'Immigration, the United States and Mexico' (AS 3.17) by Ambassador Jeffrey Davidow, adapted from www.mexidata.info.

'Migrant workers aid growth at home' (AS 3.17) by Alberto Souviron (BBC News business reporter), 28.03.05, and 'Mexico's tips to enter US safely' (AS 3.18), 6.01.05, both adapted from the BBC News website and reproduced with permission of BBC News at bbcnews.com.

'Proposition 200' (AS 3.18) by Jerry Bowen (CBS News Correspondent), adapted from the CBS News website (www.cbsnews.com) and reproduced with permission.

'SWITCH IT OFF!' label (AS 5.8), adapted brochure 'Climate change is a business issue' (AS 5.9) and logo reproduced with kind permission of the Carbon Trust.

Screenshot and poster thumbnails (AS 5.12) reproduced from the Recycle Now website, with permission.

'Over 2,000 varieties of apples still grown in Britain' (AS 5.14) and logo adapted from a press release from the National Farmers' Retail and Markets Association (FARMA) and reproduced with permission.

Water calculator and water gauge text (AS 5.19) adapted from a Christian Aid leaflet, and reproduced with permission © Christian Aid, 2005.

Logo (AS 6.11) reproduced with kind permission of Survival International.

Every effort has been made to contact copyright holders. The publishers apologise to anyone whose rights have been inadvertently overlooked.

contents

Aims and raising standards

Aims and purpose of Horizons

Horizons is based on the National Curriculum and has used and developed the QCA Scheme of Work for Key Stage 3. Therefore the aims and purpose of Geography outlined in the *Scheme of Work Teacher Guide* (2000) are just as relevant to **Horizons** Geography.

Geography teaching offers opportunities to:

- *stimulate pupils' interest in their surroundings and in the variety of human and physical conditions on the Earth's surface;*
- *foster pupils' sense of wonder at the beauty of the world around them;*

- *help pupils to develop an informed concern about the quality of the environment and the future of the human habitat and thereby enhance pupils' sense of responsibility for the care of the earth and its people.* PAGE 4

These fundamental aims have been fully integrated in **Horizons**. The course has been developed to demonstrate continually to pupils the awe and wonder of the planet, and how we all have a role to play in a sustainable future.

The **Horizons** course has fully embraced the principles that underpin the Key Stage 3 National Strategy, aiming to help teachers to raise standards by strengthening teaching and learning.

Horizons and the four important principles of the Key Stage 3 National Strategy

	Definition	Horizons commitment
Expectations	establishing high expectations for all pupils and setting challenging targets for them to achieve	High expectations and challenging pupil targets are fundamental to **Horizons**. These are outlined in the unit plans and assessment for learning sections of this *Teaching and Learning Resources* guide.
Progression	strengthening the transition from Key Stage 2 to Key Stage 3 and ensuring progression in teaching and learning across Key Stage 3	A genuine attempt has been made in **Horizons** to build on the pupils' Key Stage 1 and 2 Geography experience. Unit 1 of **Horizons 1** is a transition unit, providing an opportunity for schools to develop a benchmark assessment. The 'Remember' boxes used throughout the series encourage pupils to make links to prior learning. The course has developed a carefully considered approach to progression (see pages 10–11).
Engagement	promoting approaches to teaching and learning that engage and motivate pupils and demand their active participation	**Horizons** engages pupils through the use of large, exciting images of the world with real and relevant case studies linked to open-ended and thought-provoking activities. Each unit begins with an opening spread with a strong visual content to stimulate engagement with the new topic, as well as to share the learning objectives. **Horizons** is far more than just a textbook: each unit is supported by a wide variety of electronic resources utilising ICT, video and other media.
Transformation	strengthening teaching and learning through a programme of professional development and practical support	**Horizons** is committed to supporting innovative teaching and learning. Massive support is provided in the *Teaching and Learning Resources* guide and *Electronic Resources CD-ROM* to assist with planning, assessment for learning and the use of topical and fresh resources. **Horizons** integrates current thinking about teaching and learning, planning, literacy, numeracy, thinking skills, ICT, work-related learning and assessment for learning into a practical and coherent geography programme.

The following table shows how **Horizons** is underpinned throughout by the main principles of the Foundation Subjects strand of the Key Stage 3 National Strategy.

The principle	The Horizons action
Focus the teaching	Plan to objectives – each spread and activity in **Horizons** is clearly linked to learning objectives which are provided in the lesson plans. Each unit also begins with a set of learning objectives ('Where are we going?'). These are revisited in the final spread of the unit ('Where are we now?'), which acts as a plenary or review to the unit of work.
Provide challenge	**Horizons** sets clear expectations and provides guidance for teachers and pupils to surpass previous levels of achievement, in the Assessment for Learning section of this *Teaching and Learning Resources* guide.
Make explicit concepts and conventions	Guidance is provided for teachers in the unit and lesson plans on how to question pupils and make clear the geographical ideas and concepts involved in a spread. Each unit includes a major assessment opportunity where examples of answers are modelled to make it clear to pupils how to respond and demonstrate progress.

Structure the learning	**Horizons** has clearly structured the learning. At the medium term, each unit has a starter and a plenary spread. At the short term, each double-page spread in the book is linked to a lesson plan providing ideas for starters and plenaries and a clear lesson structure.
Make learning active	**Horizons** provides tasks in which pupils construct knowledge and develop understanding and skills through problem-solving, investigation and enquiry.
Make learning engaging and motivating	The first spread in each of the book's six units presents a set of dramatic, eye-catching and thought-provoking pictures. Further images are used throughout each unit and these are supported by a range of visual material on the *Electronic Resources CD-ROM*.
Develop well-paced lessons with high levels of interaction	**Horizons** provides activities that encourage pupils to collaborate and share ideas. Displaying the electronic resources on a whiteboard or projector also encourages whole class discussion and group interaction.
Support pupils' application and independent work	**Horizons** uses prompts, frames and scaffolds to support geographical understanding and communication.
Build reflection	**Horizons** is committed to teaching pupils to think about what and how they learn. Each unit concludes with a review and reflection spread ('Where are we now?') and this *Teaching and Learning Resources* guide provides a self-review sheet for each unit of work.

See pages 13–15 for further information on how **Horizons** supports the implementation of the Foundation Subjects strand of the Key Stage 3 Strategy.

Raising standards

GAIN (Geography Advisers and Inspectors' Network) produced an excellent Occasional Paper entitled *Raising Expectations in Geography*.

This paper suggests strategies that help raise standards of geography within the school, both in terms of classroom practice and pupil achievement. It identifies a series of inputs that are fundamental to raising expectations in Geography. These included a resource input:

Raising Expectations: The Resource Input
Geography is a content-rich subject. It requires a good range of imaginative, stimulating and unusual resources in order to motivate pupils. The school, its grounds, and the locality can provide many first-hand learning experiences. People and organisations can also be encouraged to bring reality to the classroom.

Horizons has been developed through careful consideration of such inputs.

Resources for geography can help to raise expectations when:	**Horizons** response
• they are of a high quality in terms of both content and display	Every effort has been made to provide large, varied and exciting resources. To this end, flaps have been provided on the covers of each Pupil Book to allow the use of large resources that are referred to in different sections of the Pupil Book.
• several resources are used in combination to allow pupils to draw information from different evidence bases	The provision of resources on the cover flaps facilitates this, allowing pupils to open the flap and use resources with those on different pages in the Pupil Book.
• the full potential of a text resource is developed by extending or building on the tasks provided	**Horizons** uses real and extended text resources. The pupil activities are often developed in Activity Sheets provided in this *Teaching and Learning Resources* guide, and electronically on the *Electronic Resources CD-ROM*.
• resources are sufficiently open-ended to allow pupils of all abilities to show what they know and can do, and to allow the most able to demonstrate high achievement	**Horizons** has attempted to produce open-ended activities throughout the course.
• school-based resources such as the site, grounds and locality are used effectively to support learning	**Horizons** encourages pupils to engage in fieldwork. In Unit 5 Think – Act on pages 96–99, pupils are encouraged to undertake surveys of refuse disposal and recycling in their local area.
• resources are customised to the individual circumstances of particular pupils or schools	**Horizons** provides a range of activity sheets in this *Teaching and Learning Resources* guide aimed at different pupil abilities. Teachers should be able to develop and adapt these activity sheets to match the needs of their classes.
• pupils have the opportunity to sort and select the resources they will use from a larger pool including ICT resources	**Horizons** provides a wide range of resources which go beyond the Pupil Book, utilising a range of media on the *Electronic Resources CD-ROM* and a dedicated website that can transport pupils to sites linked to each unit of the course.

• resources, including people from the local community, organisations, business and commerce, are used to help develop a 'full' understanding of the local geography/environment/community	Passport to the World is a major theme that underpins **Horizons**, where real people are used in a variety of ways to demonstrate the significant role that geography plays in our lives.
• pupils are encouraged to question resources (i.e. their origin or motivation) and to make judgements about their quality, their purpose, their point of view	From the first unit, **Horizons** encourages pupils to question resources.

Links to the National Curriculum and QCA Scheme of Work

The content of **Horizons** provides full coverage of the topics suggested by the National Curriculum and QCA Scheme of Work but it is not an exact match in terms of the actual content covered in each topic. Unit titles have been changed to suit the overall style and approach of the materials. Also, where it assists the learning process and encourages 'good geography', the order of topics has been varied within the subject.

The following are recurrent themes throughout the **Horizons** series:

- Enquiry learning is embedded throughout the course. Skills of enquiry are addressed directly in each book, with **Horizons 3** providing a continuation to the enquiry process. See page 9 in this *Teaching and Learning Resources* guide for further information.

- Wherever possible, local fieldwork studies are integrated into units, in particular using the school grounds. In **Horizons 3** pupils are encouraged to investigate soil structures and refuse disposal in their local area.

- A core group of countries is used for case study material in the course. The main countries for study are: in **Horizons 1** the UK and Bangladesh; in **Horizons 2** the UK and Spain; in **Horizons 3** Mexico, the USA and Brazil. Different approaches to portraying countries are used in **Horizons** to help to challenge stereotypes.

- Story threads are often provided, using narration of a story to get pupils into the geographical themes. For example, in **Horizons 3** Unit 5 Think – Act, children in LEDCs describe how they earn a living recycling. In Unit 6 Development or Destruction?, poor farmers and rubber tappers describe their life in the rainforest.

- Sustainability and other issues of relevance to pupils and their lives are incorporated into units, aiming to engage pupils and make them feel valued and their opinions respected. See page 31 for further information on coverage of Education for Sustainable Development (ESD).

- Citizenship responsibilities are drawn out of many of these themes, especially on sustainable development. Citizenship coverage in **Horizons 3** is highlighted on pages 27–28 in this guide.

- 'Can the Earth cope?' – where appropriate, **Horizons** focuses on management and environmental issues at local community, national and global scales.

- 'Passport to the World' is an integrated thread throughout **Horizons**. Passport to the World boxes are provided on spreads in the Pupil Book to highlight the relevance of geography to the 'real world', and provide opportunities to link to work-related learning and possible future careers. The final spread in each book is called 'Passport to the World', encouraging pupils to apply their geographical skills outside of school. For example, in **Horizons 3** examples are provided of people who studied geography and now use it in their careers and leisure time.

The remainder of this introductory section to the course explains in detail how **Horizons** links to the National Curriculum, QCA unit plans, and Key Stage 3 Strategy. Significant support for unit planning is provided on the *Planning CD-ROM* provided with this *Teaching and Learning Resources* guide. Here you will find PDF and Word versions of all the unit plans for **Horizons 3**, together with lesson plans for each spread. Electronic versions allow teachers to customise the planning documents to suit the needs of the school and the individual learning requirements of the pupils. Geography departments can therefore use the resources provided in **Horizons** to create their own unique scheme of work.

Further information on the teaching and learning support provided by **Horizons** can be found on the following pages:

Contents	Pages in the TLR
Horizons 3 Content, themes, skills and teaching and learning support	7–8
Enquiry learning	9
Progression	10–11
Differentiation	12
Implementing the Foundation Subjects strand	13–15
Planning	16–19
Using starters and plenaries to structure lessons	20
Support for thinking skills	21
Support for literacy	22–23
Support for numeracy	23
Support for ICT	24–26
Support for citizenship	27–28
Support for the global dimension	29–30
Support for Education for Sustainable Development (ESD)	31
Developing geographical skills	32–33
Passport to the World	34
Assessment for Learning	35–39
End of Key Stage 3 assessment	39–40
Pupil peer- and self-assessment	41–49
Assessing Levels	50–51
Attainment Targets for Key Stage 3	52–53

	Learning Objectives	QCA SoW coverage	NC Pos focus	Geographical skills/resources
1 Tectonics	Learn: • how the internal structure of the Earth affects people living on the surface • to understand how plate movements cause earthquakes and volcanoes • how people live with the threat of earthquakes and volcanoes • to develop an awareness of how places are interdependent through aid.	2 Restless Earth 21 Virtual volcanoes and internet earthquakes	1a–f 2a–g 3a–e 4a, b 5a 6b, i	Extending geographical vocabulary Ground-level photos Aerial photos Satellite images Internet research
2 80:20	Learn: • different definitions of development • world poverty, its causes and why it is unevenly spread • ways of using data to measure and analyse development patterns • what governments, voluntary groups and individuals can do to support development • the importance of sustainable development, and fair trade.	16 What is development?	1a–f 2a, c–g 3a–e 5b 6i	Atlas work Map interpretation Interpret political cartoons Photo interpretation Development compass rose
3 Comparing Countries	Learn to: • ask geographical questions about Mexico and the USA • develop a sequence for investigation • select relevant information in order to aid comparison of two countries • present data effectively to highlight similarities and differences • consider the interdependence of nations.	12 Image of a country 20 Comparing countries	1a–f 2a–g 3a–e 6a	Atlas work Satellite images Describe patterns and processes Thinking skills – mystery Misconceptions
4 Ecosystems	Learn about: • the interactions that take place in all ecosystems • the coral reef ecosystem – how it is threatened, and how it can be conserved • the rainforest ecosystem • the savanna grassland ecosystem and the farming systems that use it • population and food supply in the human ecosystem.	14 Ecosystems	1a–f 2a–f 3a–e 4a, b 5a, b 6e, j	Climate graphs Extending geographical vocabulary Patterns and processes Environmental interrelationships Values and attitudes
5 Think – Act	Learn about: • the influence you have on the environment when you consume • some of the causes and consequences of global warming • 'food miles' and 'ghost acres' • the rubbish problem • what we can all do to reduce the size of our footprints on the global environment.	23 Local actions, global effects	1a–f 2a–f 3a–e 5a, b 6j	Satellite images Fieldwork
6 Development or Destruction?	Learn: • about the global importance of rainforests • what Brazil is like • about the location and size of Brazil • about development in Brazil • about deforestation in the Amazon and how it affects different groups of people and the environment • about sustainable development projects in the Amazon • to conduct an enquiry using ICT, ending with a mock public debate.	23 Local actions, global effects Citizenship 10 Debating a global issue	1a–f 2a–f 3a–e 4a, b 5a, b 6i, j	Enquiry Debate Extending geographical vocabulary Atlas maps Political cartoons Ground-level and aerial photos Satellite images
Passport to the World	Learn about: • work-related learning in geography. Think about how three people who studied geography have used the subject in their working life and in their leisure activities.	24 Passport to the world		

Theme focus	Places	Assessment/Assessment for learning	Fieldwork	ICT	Links	
Tectonic processes and their effects on landscapes and people Enquiry process	Banda Aceh, Indonesia, Indian Ocean Kobe, Japan Bam, Iran Iceland Montserrat	Decision-making exercise: Saving San Sebastian	Possible field trips to sites of ancient volcanoes, e.g. Malvern Hills, Herefordshire	Internet research Using satellite photos PowerPoint presentation Online GIS – Google Earth	Citizenship Thinking skills Problem solving Science – the rock cycle	**1 Tectonics**
Development Enquiry process Using atlas, globes and maps Using ICT to collect and interpret data Human patterns	Mkwakwani, Kenya Niger	Debate and extended writing on how media coverage affected the Niger aid disaster		Internet research Online GIS DTP poster PowerPoint presentation Spreadsheet	Citizenship Development education Global dimension Sustainable development	**2 80:20**
Two countries Enquiry process Using atlas, globes and maps Using ICT to collect and interpret data	USA Mexico Arizona Illinois Yucatán Sonora	Mystery and extended writing: 'Why is John Doe staying in Tucson, Arizona?'	Possible field trips to assess influence of American or Mexican culture in fast-food or retail outlets	Internet research Online GIS PowerPoint presentation Spreadsheet graphical packages	Citizenship Sustainable development Numeracy Interdependence	**3 Comparing Countries**
Ecosystems	Gulf of Aquaba, Jordan Amazon rainforest African savanna Tanzania Serengeti National Park	Produce a display on world ecosystems Pupils to develop own enquiry questions on a chosen system	Soil experiments	Internet	Citizenship Sustainable development Numeracy	**4 Ecosystems**
Environmental issues	UK London Kenya Bangladesh	Design and describe a 'deconstruction plant' in Future World, to explain how industrial products can be designed on principles of reduce, reuse, recycle	Refuse survey in local area	Internet enquiry Presentation DTP poster PowerPoint presentation	Sustainable development Citizenship Science Global dimension	**5 Think – Act**
Environmental issues Development Ecosystems	Brazil Amazon rainforest	Role play/debate Extended writing		Internet Presentation using ICT DPT leaflet, poster PowerPoint presentation	Sustainable development Interdependence Citizenship Global dimension	**6 Development or Destruction?**
					Transition to Key Stage 4 Review of work-related learning contexts in **Horizons** series	**Passport to the World**

Enquiry learning is essential to good geography at all levels and enquiry skills are assessed at Key Stage 3 as well as at Key Stages 4 and 5 where they may form the basis of coursework components of examinations. Therefore the systematic acquisition of these skills is vital if pupils are to be equipped to perform at the highest levels in this subject. **Horizons** offers accessible and graduated enquiry opportunities throughout the course. Pupils are encouraged to ask geographical questions in a range of different exercises and to consider what makes a geographical question powerful. By learning how to ask the right questions about an issue, pupils are better able to obtain the information they require and make sense of increasingly complex issues. *Pupil enquiry is at the heart of the development of the pupil as an independent learner.*

The enquiry process in **Horizons 3** begins in Unit 1 Tectonics, pages 10–11 'Do all earthquakes have the same impact?', where pupils plan their own advanced organiser, and continues on pages 16–17 with 'What can virtual volcanoes tell us?', where pupils question the origin and reliability of the web-based information they research. There are further enquiries throughout **Horizons 3** to ensure continuity and progression in this vital geographical skill. The aim is to encourage pupils to become more skilled in formulating their own questions and route to enquiry.

An enquiry approach then underpins the entire **Horizons** course. The page-spread titles pose an initial question for every topic, to establish an enquiry framework for that module of learning. 'Over to You' activities on each page not only ask questions of the pupils but, equally important, often encourage the pupils to formulate their own questions. This is done to make pupils more active in the enquiry process as the quality of their questioning has a significant impact on the quality of their learning.

Teachers are supported in this process too. The lesson plans on the *Planning CD-ROM* include key questions to frame the learning opportunity and help extend the thinking of pupils throughout the lesson and beyond. They also help to model styles of questioning and offer adaptable templates to extend the questioning repertoire. For further information on using questioning techniques to encourage enquiry learning and support assessment for learning, see pages 36–37 in the Assessment for Learning section of this *Teaching and Learning Resources* guide.

If enquiry learning is essentially about 'finding out' rather than 'being told', then becoming familiar with the enquiry process is clearly important. Developing the pupils' ability to plan their own route to enquiry is key to increasingly independent learning. In **Horizons** there are frequent, well-supported opportunities to investigate geographical issues and in many instances the importance of these enquiries is underlined by their position as the key summative assessment opportunity for the unit.

There is one enquiry-based Assessment Opportunity for each unit, supported by model answers to allow pupils the opportunity to develop their assessment skills by judging the exemplars against the criteria for success. These Assessment Opportunities for **Horizons 3** are highlighted in the teaching and learning resources for each unit on the following pages:

Unit	Activity in Pupil Book	Teaching and Learning Resources guide
Unit 1 Tectonics	Saving San Sebastian DME	pages 60–65
Unit 2 80:20	Niger report	pages 93–97
Unit 3 Comparing Countries	John Doe mystery	pages 126–130
Unit 4 Ecosystems	Ecosystem display	pages 158–164
Unit 5 Think – Act	Recycling action plan	pages 192–198
Unit 6 Development or Destruction?	Deforestation report	pages 226–234

These enquiries are offered at a range of scales and some encourage pupils to use ICT to extend their research horizons beyond the text and classroom resources. See also pages 50–51, the Assessing Levels section, for further information on these Assessment Opportunities.

The Passport to the World theme in **Horizons** further encourages an enquiry approach. The final spread of each book is designed to provide a 'plenary' for the year and to reinforce for pupils the direct relevance of geography to their lives. The 'Passport to the World' spread in **Horizons 3** (pages 124–125) encourages pupils to use their enquiry skills to consider the ways in which their geographical skills could be used in future careers by exploring the lives of various geography pupils who have gone on to use their skills to different ends. For further information on Passport to the World, see page 34 in this *Teaching and Learning Resources* guide.

Progression

Horizons has been designed to enable pupils to show progression through Key Stage 3, and to provide opportunities for teachers to assess their progress and share this progress with pupils.

As **Horizons** is aimed at pupils of all abilities, each unit contains a range of text and activities to meet the individual needs of pupils. However, the range of levels at which each book is aimed moves upwards through Years 7 to 9.

QCA identified the following aspects of progression in Key Stage 3 Geography (*QCA Scheme of Work Teacher Guide* page 21).

	From	To
Vocabulary	using a limited geographical vocabulary	precise use of a wider range of vocabulary
Knowledge of places	geographical knowledge of some places	understanding of a wider range of areas and links between them
Patterns and processes	describing geographical patterns and processes	explaining geographical patterns and processes
Geographical thinking	participating in practical geographical activities	building increasingly abstract models of real situations
Geographical explanation	explaining events and phenomena in terms of their own ideas	explaining these in terms of accepted ideas or models
Investigation	unstructured exploration	more systematic investigation
Map skills	using simple drawings, maps and diagrams to represent geographical information	choosing and using a wide range of conventional maps, diagrams and graphs
Fieldwork	guided practical activities in the field	working independently outside the classroom

The QCA Teacher Guide

The *QCA Teacher Guide* also identifies a series of questions to consider when planning for progression. These have been used in developing **Horizons**.

QCA questions to consider when planning for progression	**Horizons** response
What is known about what pupils have already achieved at Key Stage 2 and how does this affect the pitch of early units?	**Horizons 1** Unit 1 Making Connections is a transition unit between Key Stages 2 and 3 which encourages pupils to share their experiences and develop their understanding of their new school environment. The early units of **Horizons 1** develop important geographical skills that are revisited in later books. Early units of **Horizons 1** allow opportunities for teachers to discuss, value and build on work that has been done in Key Stage 2.
What ideas in geography depend on secure understanding of other ideas?	The basic principles of economic activities introduced in **Horizons 1** Unit 5 Work are developed further in **Horizons 2** Unit 4 España Nueva and extended further in **Horizons 3**.
How can units be sequenced so that earlier work lays the foundations for later work?	**Horizons 1** develops understanding of basic geographical principles such as population, settlement and economic activities which will be developed in different contexts in **Horizons 2** and **3**.
Are there opportunities to revisit and reinforce the ideas that pupils need to understand and which some will find difficult?	**Horizons** provides a number of opportunities to do this, for example weather and climate in the UK is introduced in **Horizons 1** Unit 6 Exploring the UK and revisited in greater detail in **Horizons 2** Unit 3 Weather Interactive. Climate is linked to ecosystems in **Horizons 3** Unit 4 Ecosystems.
When ideas are revisited or reinforced, is it in a different context or using different activities?	**Horizons** reinforces ideas both in different contexts and by using different activities.

QCA questions to consider when planning for progression	Horizons response
How are those pupils who have some competence or expertise beyond the levels expected in particular years challenged?	**Horizons** provides extension activities within the main activities provided in the Pupil Book as well as activity sheets for the more able in the *Teaching and Learning Resources* guide. **Horizons** also allows many opportunities for pupils to ask geographical questions and develop their enquiries, using the resources provided to go beyond the standard activities in the Pupil Book. Greater challenge can also be found in the activities and resources provided on the *Electronic Resources CD-ROM* and dedicated website.
Is there sufficient challenge for pupils in Years 7, 8 and 9?	Challenge is a fundamental principle of **Horizons**, as outlined on page 14 of this guide. Each book in the series has been developed to provide further but appropriate challenges.
Are appropriate expectations required of pupils in their use of language, number and ICT?	**Horizons** has been carefully matched to other strands of the Key Stage 3 Strategy in order to ensure this. An attempt has been made, for example, to match ICT activities to the yearly objectives set out in the ICT Framework.
Does the programme present a coherent experience of geography for those who leave the subject at the end of Year 9?	**Horizons** has been carefully matched to encompass the whole of the National Curriculum Programme of Study for Geography.
Does the programme adequately prepare pupils who continue geography at Key Stage 4?	**Horizons** deliberately emphasises the vocational from the outset of **Horizons 1**. As a result, at the end of Key Stage 3 pupils will have a clear understanding of the relevance of the subject. Indeed the final Passport to the World spread of **Horizons 3** focuses on the requirements of Key Stage 4 Geography as well as on careers that utilise geography qualifications.

Overview of level, progression and themes of each book

Horizons 1 Year 7	Horizons 2 Year 8	Horizons 3 Year 9
• Key Stage 2 to Key Stage 3 transition	• Moving on in geography	• World issues
• Introduction to basic geography	• Less explaining of skills	• Environmental issues
• Explaining skills	• Fieldwork – coasts and weather	• Higher-level skills
• Fieldwork – school grounds	• Enquiry – explaining process	• Preparation for GCSE
• Enquiry – introducing process and asking questions	• More distant places investigated	• Fieldwork – local area
		• Enquiry – pupils deciding process and using it independently

Horizons takes into account Key Stage 2 Geography and aims to build on that rather than dismiss it. The course respects what pupils already know. The transitional Unit 1 Making Connections in **Horizons 1** is very important as an introduction to the course and to Key Stage 3. The lesson plan for each spread on the *Planning CD-ROM* that is included with the photocopiable *Teaching and Learning Resources* guide has a Prior Learning box for the teacher to link the content back to either Key Stage 2 or earlier in Key Stage 3 if relevant.

As indicated above, the difficulty in level of skills, fieldwork and enquiry increases through **Horizons 1–3** to ensure that there is an increase in the level of geographical challenge to pupils; that is, the course aims to provide a 'spiral' progression in skills as well as in content. Teachers and pupils can use the Learning Plans, Attainment Targets and self-assessment forms for each unit (see Introduction to each unit in this guide) to track learning progress through the course.

Differentiation

Differentiation is very important, as pupils have different experiences and make progress at different rates. It is vital, therefore, that classroom teachers differentiate teaching and learning materials to suit pupils' needs. Textbook series cannot provide all the answers for the classroom teacher, but the classroom teacher can adapt the material to suit individual needs.

The authors of **Horizons** have aimed the Pupil Book at a broad band of ability, around the middle of the range. They have tried to make it as accessible as possible by using a variety of resources (maps, photos, diagrams, etc.), by developing a strong narrative line in the text, by using real-life examples, and by including material that is relevant to the lives of young people whenever possible.

So, with skilled teaching, most of the ability range should have access to most of the work in **Horizons**. Nevertheless, it was felt that **Horizons** must adopt strategies to encourage differentiated work within and around the common core of the Pupil Book. This has been done in a wide variety of ways:

- **Horizons** aims to 'scaffold' the learning to support medium to low-ability pupils but also provides additional resources to challenge more able pupils.

- The activities in the Pupil Book open with easier questions to start with but then build on those parts with more difficult questions to stretch higher abilities.

- The Over to You activities in the Pupil Book are also provided on the *Electronic Resources CD-ROM*. This enables the teacher to adapt the activities to suit the individual needs of pupils.

- The *Teaching and Learning Resources* guide for each book provides between 16 and 24 worksheets per unit – approximately 2 per spread – of which 5 are more suited to lower abilities and 5 to higher abilities with 10 as generic activities for all abilities. Some provide extended reading tasks, others provide writing frames to support less able pupils. This approach is explained in greater detail on pages 22–23 of this guide.

- The **Horizons** website provides further ways of developing differentiated strategies using ICT and the impressive potential of the internet to provide activities suited to pupils of all abilities.

- The lesson plans on the *Planning CD-ROM* include a differentiation box, which indicates appropriate strategies for differentiating the content on each spread and highlights which worksheets are appropriate for which level of ability.

- The Attainment Target handouts and self-assessment forms will help teachers and pupils to set different targets for each pupil but can also be customised for different levels of ability or to suit individual pupil needs.

- The variety of types of task set throughout the book – such as problem-solving exercises, role play, decision-making exercises – means that pupils with a variety of different strengths should find opportunities to build on their strengths at various times.

- The range of different types of stimulus material, in the textbook and in the support materials, means that there should be many opportunities for supported self-study, during which all pupils can work at their own pace, developing their potential as far as possible.

The class teacher can develop and build on the differentiation strategies adopted by the authors of **Horizons** to suit the individual learning needs of their pupils. Approaches adopted will be in line with whole school policies and will utilise support staff provision in the school. Strategies will fully utilise the wide range of resources provided in the **Horizons** suite but will also use the good practice, ideas and resources already available in the department. Differentiation will inevitably be embraced through a combination of the following:

• by task	Different pupils are set different tasks, which are set for specific needs using extension tasks.
• through a variety of learning activities	For example, problem solving exercises, role play, decision-making exercises etc. using a wide variety of resources: geography magazines, pamphlets, newspaper cuttings, books, information technology, library, resource packs to set open-ended tasks.
• through varied stimulus materials	This enables self-motivation and direction. Pupils can work at their own pace.
• through supported self-study	Provision of background materials for courses that support specific themes or subjects and enable pupils to work on their own.
• through groupings	Different groupings are arranged in lessons so that pupils of similar ability can work better. At other times pupils of a wide variety of abilities work in one group.

Implementing the Foundation Subjects strand

Horizons is the first course to fully support both the latest National Curriculum guidelines for Key Stage 3 Geography and implementation of the Foundation Subjects strand of the Key Stage 3 National Strategy (now the Secondary Strategy for School Improvement). **Horizons** seeks to provide a range of stimulating resources to engage pupils with a variety of teaching and learning styles. The classroom teacher is supported by well-structured, adaptable plans to ensure that they have the strategies to engender high levels of interest, pace and purpose in their teaching.

The Foundation Subjects strand of the Key Stage 3 Strategy provides a sound pedagogic framework to develop the skills of the classroom practitioner. It builds upon the methods already used by many teachers and helps to extend their repertoire via a range of techniques. The *Training Materials for the Foundation Subjects* folder (DfES 2002) presents the teaching and learning modules as outlined in the table below but it is worth stressing that there are strong links between all of these modules. **Horizons** is designed to provide teachers with plans and resources to help them to start to implement the teaching and learning strategies of the Foundation Subjects strand.

Training modules for the Foundation Subjects strand		Support provided by **Horizons**
Planning and assessment	**Definition and purpose**	**Horizons examples**
Assessment for learning in everyday lessons	All those activities undertaken by pupils and their teachers that provide evidence about the pupils' learning. It implies that the learners and their teacher interpret and *use* that evidence to decide where the pupils are in their learning, where they are going, and how to take the next steps.	The *Teaching and Learning Resources* guide for each unit (e.g. pages 54–86 for Unit 1) identifies key opportunities for Assessment for Learning and contains a wide range of suggestions to allow teachers to apply Assessment for Learning ideas to other learning activities. The teacher notes on Assessment for Learning (see pages 35–39 of this guide) explain in more detail how **Horizons** provides a framework for implementing Assessment for Learning in Key Stage 3 Geography, and resources to support teachers and pupils with its everyday use in lessons.
The formative use of summative assessments	Those activities that use summative assessment in a formative manner. The aim is to draw pupils into the assessment process, often by helping them to recognise the criteria for success as a framework for self-assessment and peer-assessment. It typically involves pupils setting individual targets.	The *Teaching and Learning Resources* guide identifies a summative Assessment Opportunity for each unit (e.g. pages 60–65 for Unit 1). However, it also provides criteria for success and model answers for the activity as well as pupil-friendly level descriptors for the whole unit which will enable pupils and their peers to identify the stage they have reached in their learning and set achievable targets for improvement. See page 38 for more detail on formative use of summative assessments in **Horizons**.
Planning lessons	Lessons should have clear objectives that are challenging yet achievable. To maintain pupil engagement lessons may feature three or more components to ensure pace and progression. Opportunities for Assessment for Learning can be built into lesson activities to encourage reflection. Starters and plenaries put the lesson in the context of prior and future learning, helping pupils to see the 'big picture' and the relevance of the activities.	**Horizons** provides lesson plans for each double-page spread in the Pupil Book. These lesson plans are provided in customisable format on the *Planning CD-ROM* accompanying this guide. They are designed to be amended as required but provide ideas for learning objectives and outcomes, starter activities, links/debriefs and plenaries to reinforce learning. See pages 16–19 for more detail on the planning support provided by **Horizons**.
Teaching repertoire	**Definition and purpose**	**Horizons examples**
Questioning	The role of questioning in promoting higher-order thinking is crucial. Questioning by pupils is a fundamental skill, particularly in geography where it is required in coursework at all levels. An awareness of what makes a 'big', powerful question rather than a small and ineffective one is important if pupils are to develop as independent learners.	**Horizons** provides leading questions at the start of each spread in the Pupil Book, to raise awareness of the power of questioning in geography. A wide range of questioning techniques is employed throughout **Horizons 3** – from the activities on page 47 in Unit 3 Comparing Countries, where pupils are asked to develop questions as their route to enquiry, to Activity Sheet 3.1, where pupils question an image of Mexico, learners are made aware of the power of effective questioning as a learning tool. See pages 36–37 on effective questioning techniques for Assessment for Learning.

Explaining	Teachers are very aware of the power of clear, interesting explanation addressed at the appropriate level. Pupils regularly cite this ability as one of the most important skills in their teachers. By developing a range of methods of explanation and by improving the ability of pupils to articulate their thoughts, teacher and pupils are more able convey their ideas.	Powerful aids to explanation are added through the teacher lesson plans. Analogies are used frequently to encourage links between personal experience and abstract theoretical ideas. For example, activity 1 on page 19 draws a clear analogy to our own responses to danger and the far greater threats experienced by people living in earthquake zones.
Modelling	By demonstrating a technique and by explicitly sharing the conventions, pupils are helped to recognise the components of potentially complex processes and to comprehend the criteria for success.	Exemplars of weaker and stronger responses to assessment tasks provided in the Assessment Opportunities for each unit in this guide are ideal tools for modelling the conventions of good composition to the whole class. For example, you could model how to analyse text by referring to the written model answers provided for the Assessment Opportunity in Unit 1 Tectonics (see pages 64–65).

Structured learning	**Definition and purpose**	**Horizons examples**
Starters	Activities that help focus pupils' attention can take a variety of forms from arresting images, questioning exercises, odd one out activities, mystery objects to drama. The list is endless but the common aim is to get pupils thinking about the topic or issue that is to follow. The opportunity to exemplify the lesson objectives or link to previous learning is clear.	A wide range of starter activities are suggested in **Horizons**, with at least one option provided for each spread in the lesson plans on the *Planning CD-ROM*. These seek to combine raising engagement and addressing aspects of the learning objectives that are to follow. For example, the first activity in Unit 3 Comparing Countries asks pupils to assign deliberately ambiguous photos to either Mexico or the USA as a starter. This activity challenges their perceptions and raises again the issue of our acceptance of stereotypical images, before they go on to explore what really characterises these two countries. See also notes on using starters and plenaries on page 20.
Plenaries	Plenaries may involve a teacher summing up what has been learned during the lesson, putting that learning in the context of the big picture and indicating what is coming next. Successful use of the plenary necessitates a variety of approaches. Activities planned to encourage pupils to express their understanding, views and emotions are likely to involve participants and test their understanding – an essential part of assessment *of* and *for* learning.	A wide range of plenary activities is offered, with at least one option for each lesson plan. These seek to reinforce learning by addressing aspects of the lesson objectives and setting what has been learned in the bigger picture. For example, the plenary task on page 19 for the 'How much can prediction and prevention help?' spread asks pupils to choose between two contentious statements concerning the role of technology in preventing disasters. This facilitates a discussion about how we rely on technology to enable us to live in parts of the world previously thought to be too dangerous.
Challenge	Pupils of all abilities need to face challenge if they are to develop their skills and understanding. The challenge should be achievable and may be scaffolded to produce a step-by-step progression where appropriate.	**Horizons** aims to ensure high levels of accessibility to activities for all pupils whilst increasingly challenging them to test their knowledge, skills and understanding. The Over to You sections are made progressively more challenging from the initial to final activities. There are also suggestions in the lesson plans for ways in which teachers and pupils can use the Pupil Book material in more challenging ways. For example, in Unit 3 Comparing Countries, Activity Sheet 3.20 offers the chance for a high-level discussion concerning what really matters when comparing the attributes of different countries. The opinion line encourages pupils to become more aware of their own value judgements when they are evaluating complex issues such as levels of development and affluence.
Engagement	We learn most effectively when we are interested in the topic, have a desire to go on and learn more and can use our existing knowledge to achieve something that is challenging but manageable. Improving levels of engagement depends upon factors as diverse as classroom layout or reward systems but in the context of this series it is addressed in terms of teaching and learning. Activities and strategies that	The regular use of whole-class starters, main activities and pupil-centred plenaries encourages engagement for all pupils. Pair- and group-work opportunities are suggested in the Over to You sections and highlighted in the *Teaching and Learning Resources* guide. Many activities, such as activity 5 on page 97, offer the 'hook' of personal involvement. In this case, pupils are asked to work out their family's wastage of resources. This is deliberately personal to establish the link between the actions of the individual and those of the family, nation or continent.

support all pupils in making progress necessarily involve those pupils in the learning process. In short, they are involved in the way the lesson develops rather than being merely 'passengers' who are able to opt out of a passive experience.

Using visual materials from the *Electronic Resources CD-ROM* on whiteboards and digital projectors, if available, will also help to add a stimulating extra dimension to lessons and engage pupils further in the learning.

Knowledge and learning	Definition and purpose	**Horizons** examples
Principles for teaching thinking	Thinking skills provide opportunities for pupils to reflect on their learning. Intelligence may be defined as the capacity to learn and these strategies aim to improve the individual pupil's abilities in terms of general, specific and metacognitive thinking. Higher-level performance in all National Curriculum subjects requires many abilities, including the ability to see patterns in data, solve problems, make links with other topic areas and work effectively with others. All of these are directly addressed by teaching thinking skills and enable pupils not only to become better geographers, but also to be able to transfer their learning to overcome difficulties posed by new situations.	The lesson plans in **Horizons**, particularly the links/debriefs and plenaries sections, suggest strategies for teachers to encourage pupils to make explicit the learning they have experienced and to identify the transferable skills they have acquired. For example the Mystery activity on pages 60–61 of Unit 3 Comparing Countries 'Why is John Doe staying in Tucson, Arizona?' asks pupils not only to decide on a possible solution to the mystery from a range of information but also to think about how they work together to modify their ideas throughout the activity. See page 21 for more detail on thinking skills support provided by **Horizons**.
Thinking together	Group work is well established in most geography classrooms but is often activity or task driven. Thinking together uses talk not only to share information but to work together to make sense of the information. Two or more pupils can solve problems more effectively together than on their own, if they are given direction and ground rules for interaction. Teachers and pupils can engage critically and constructively with each others' ideas. All pupils have an opportunity to contribute, speculate and refine their ideas in a way that encourages reasoned argument.	Group work and pair work are well supported in both **Horizons** Pupil Books and *Teaching and Learning Resources* guides. The lesson plans for each spread, and the opportunities for Assessment for Learning suggested for each unit (e.g. pages 88–89 in this guide for Unit 2), suggest group activities. They also encourage thinking together and exploratory talk by providing opportunities for peers to test and refine their ideas. Resources such as the assessment template for an oral discussion (see page 48 of this guide) can also be used as a vehicle for pupils to understand the dynamics of group discussion and to analyse and improve their personal contributions.
Reflection	Metacognition or 'thinking about thinking' involves pupils considering not only what they have learned but how they learned it. This requires a language of thinking if pupils are to effectively articulate their understanding. Such skills are eminently transferable and may help unblock potential barriers to learning in the future. Modelling of group and then whole class contributions is important if the process of reflection is to become a regular component of lessons.	**Horizons** builds this into the lesson planning by suggesting teaching strategies that require pupils to externalise the thinking processes they have gone through. For example, in activity 3 on page 13 of Unit 1 Tectonics, pupils must reflect on what they currently understand so that they can place the labels in likely locations on the photo. Having to justify these choices requires them to reflect on what they really do understand about volcanoes.
Big concepts and skills	Geography lessons are often characterised by a pronounced focus on the acquisition of knowledge and skills; both are vital to a sound understanding of the subject. It is less common for the emphasis to fall upon the larger patterns that characterise the distinctiveness of learning in geography. Yet these higher-order procedural skills and concepts underpin high-level performance in the subject. Furthermore, recognition of these patterns helps to demystify, organise and simplify the mass of information and tasks that pupils encounter.	**Horizons** seeks to highlight the key procedural skills (e.g. asking relevant questions) and concepts (e.g. countries have similarities and differences) and helps pupils connect their activities (e.g. What do we need to know about these places? on pages 46–47 of **Horizons 3** Pupil Book) to answer big geographical questions (e.g. A continent divided?).

These principles for teaching and learning in the Foundation Subjects strand are consistent with the rest of the Strategy but in particular they recognise the importance of thinking skills and Assessment for Learning in helping pupils to reach higher levels of attainment and become more independent learners.

Planning

Horizons aims to provide comprehensive planning support for teachers, informed by the National Curriculum Programme of Study and the QCA Key Stage 3 Scheme of Work, and incorporating the teaching and learning ideas from the Foundation Subjects strand of the Key Stage 3 National Strategy. **Horizons** has been written to interpret the National Curriculum, QCA Scheme of Work and Key Stage 3 Strategy in a flexible manner to match teachers' own planning and is meant to be supplemented by their own resources.

The overall structure of the **Horizons** course offers a coherent and flexible programme of study for Key Stage 3 Geography that fulfils all the knowledge, skills and understanding requirements of the National Curriculum (see 'Longer-term planning' below). Teachers can use, adapt and augment the content in the three books to create their own schemes of work for Years 7 to 9. Medium and short-term plans for each unit of work in **Horizons** are then provided on the *Planning CD-ROM* for customising and printing (see below for exemplars of these unit and lesson plans). While these plans are designed to provide comprehensive and coherent support that addresses the complex requirements of the modern classroom, they can be amended as desired to fit the individual needs of each teacher and school.

Longer-term planning

All the geography material in **Horizons** is organised in units that cover the National Curriculum requirements and QCA Scheme of Work units. Consequently, much of the planning structure is already in place if required for Key Stage 3 Geography. The content plan for each book in the *Teaching and Learning Resources* guide provides a quick overview of the topics, skills and themes to be covered in that book (see pages 7–8 for more detail on **Horizons 3**) and, combined, these offer teachers a comprehensive long-term plan for delivering geography in Years 7, 8 and 9.

Horizons 1, 2 and **3** probably offer more than is necessary to cover Key Stage 3 Geography and you may wish to rationalise some of the options. Some units provide obvious alternatives; for example, **Horizons 3** Unit 2 80:20 and Unit 5 Think – Act both contain opportunities for extended enquiry into sustainability development issues. It is possible to rationalise these enquiries as there will not be time for most classes to do all of them.

Some of the broader aspects of the National Curriculum often addressed through Geography, such as Citizenship and Education for Sustainable Development, are also integrated within the **Horizons** scheme of work where appropriate (see pages 27–28 and 31 respectively for further information). Some are covered in individual units, such as Unit 6 Development or Destruction? in **Horizons 3**, which explores environmental issues in Brazil. Others are integrated within topics such as Unit 4 Ecosystems, which has a strong sustainability theme.

All departments will have more up-to-date and more local resources with which they will be able to augment or replace the sources offered in **Horizons**.

Medium-term planning

Each unit in **Horizons** is designed to fit within the bigger picture of the overall aims and structure of the course. Each unit begins with opportunities for pupils to connect with prior learning by means of an overview and stimulus material. In addition clear objectives are given to support teaching and learning and to promote assessment. The variety of activities in each unit aims to incorporate innovative approaches to teaching whilst maintaining a level of accessibility that ensures the promotion of positive achievement and inclusive approaches to learning.

The review section at the end of each unit supports assessment and target setting while encouraging pupils to reflect on their learning. The aim of developing transferable skills is paramount in these sections. Individual lesson plans include guidance about how to teach each topic, as well as further suggestions for starters, questioning and plenaries (see 'Short-term planning' on pages 18–19).

There is a blank template for a unit plan provided on the *Planning CD-ROM* to enable teachers to create their own unit plans in this format.

Unit plans are provided on the *Planning CD-ROM* for each unit in **Horizons**. There are a number of useful features:

- **About the unit** This feature gives an overview of the unit and sets out which aspects of the Programme of Study are tackled. Together with **prior learning** and **future learning**, it will help in making decisions about long-term planning. These two components can be tailored to the individual needs of your class.

- **Language for learning** supports language and literacy activities, offering a point of reference and a list of suggested vocabulary.

- **Learning objectives** are set out inside each unit plan. In **Horizons** they are found on the first page of each unit so that the message about what pupils will learn about is shared and understood by all. These are also provided for each spread on the individual lesson plans (see sample).

- **Teaching activities** provide guidance for organising activities and are meant to act as ideas to be amended as the classroom teacher deems necessary. They are designed to offer structured support rather than being a pre-scriptive strait-jacket. Your resources, videos, activities and teaching strategies should be incorporated where you see fit. Suggestions for **teaching strategies** and **resources** for each spread are provided in greater detail on the individual lesson plans (see sample).

- **Learning outcomes** is an important section which shows what pupils might be expected to learn in relation to the objectives. They could be useful as a support to formative assessment, and form a basis for the end-of-lesson review session. These are also provided for each spread on the individual lesson plans (see samples on pages 17–19).

Horizons 3 Unit 1 Tectonics UNIT PLAN Geography Year 9

About the unit

In this unit, pupils learn about the patterns and processes associated with earthquakes and volcanic activity. They contrast the impact of this type of activity on more and less economically developed countries (MEDCs and LEDCs). Explaining the how they are related to Earth structure and plate tectonic activity helps to develop a deeper understanding of these phenomena.

Key aspects

Geographical enquiry and skills

Pupils will learn:
- to ask geographical questions
- to collect/record/present evidence
- to appreciate values and attitudes
- to communicate appropriately
- to use atlases and maps
- to use secondary evidence
- to interpret maps, diagrams and graphs
- to communicate, including using ICT

Knowledge and understanding of places

Pupils will:
- locate places and environments
- describe and explain physical and human features
- explore interdependence and global citizenship

Knowledge and understanding of environmental change and sustainable development

Pupils will study:
- environmental change and management

Expectations

At the end of this unit

most pupils will:
- describe the distribution patterns of earthquakes and volcanic activity and identify their link with the Earth's active zones
- describe how the Earth's active zones are related to Earth structure and plate movements
- describe the physical and human effects of volcanic eruptions and begin to explain their different impacts in MEDCs and LEDCs
- describe the reasons for the level of devastation of some earthquakes and explain how people try to minimise their effects
- begin to explain why people choose to live in these zones and suggest some ways in which people living in active zones attempt to reduce damage from tectonic hazards
- suggest suitable geographical questions and use a range of geographical skills to help investigate earthquakes and volcanoes
- use primary and secondary sources of evidence and communicate their findings using appropriate vocabulary

some pupils will not have made so much progress and will:
- describe and compare the location of some earthquakes and volcanic activity and recognise that they coincide with the Earth's active zones
- begin to describe how the Earth's active zones are related to the structure of the Earth
- describe some of the effects of volcanic eruptions and compare and offer explanations on why their impacts in MEDCs and LEDCs may be different
- understand that some earthquakes are more devastating than others and offer some reasons why people choose to live in these zones
- describe some of the ways people living in active zones attempt to reduce damage from tectonic hazards
- use skills and sources of evidence to respond to a range of geographical questions about earthquakes and volcanoes
- begin to use appropriate vocabulary to communicate their findings

Horizons 3 © Nelson Thornes Ltd 2006

---

some pupils will have progressed further and will:
- describe and begin to explain the distribution patterns of earthquakes and volcanic activity and their relationship with the Earth's active zones
- describe and begin to explain how Earth structure and plate movements may cause earthquakes and volcanoes to occur
- describe and begin to explain the physical and human effects of volcanic eruptions and why their impact differs in MEDCs and LEDCs
- offer explanations as to why people choose to live in these zones and begin to explain how they defend themselves against tectonic hazards
- suggest relevant geographical questions and select and use appropriate skills and ways of presenting information
- select information and sources of evidence in their investigations of earthquakes and volcanoes and present their findings both graphically and in writing

Prior learning

It is helpful if pupils have:
- used an atlas index
- carried out research using a range of sources, e.g. the internet, CD-ROMs, libraries
- drawn plans and maps at a variety of scales
- used world maps (of different projections) and globes
- some knowledge of countries with different levels of economic development

Language for learning

Through the activities in this unit pupils will be able to understand, use and spell correctly words such as:

active andesite basalt bilateral and multilateral aid cause constructive margin convection current critically evaluate crust destructive margin dormant earthquake effect emergency relief evacuation extinct igneous intensity lava less economically developed country liquefaction magma magnitude more economically developed country natural hazard plate tectonics rhyolite slip (passive) margin subduction zone tsunami vent volcanism volcano voluntary aid

Speaking and listening – through the activities pupils could:
- identify the main points of a task, TV programme, etc

Reading – through the activities pupils could:
- follow the sequence of actions, processes or ideas being described

Horizons 3 © Nelson Thornes Ltd 2006

Writing – through the activities pupils could:
- introduce, develop and conclude pieces of writing appropriately
- use information and persuasive styles of writing

Assessment for learning

See pages 55–56 of Horizons 3 Teaching and Learning Resources guide for support with assessment for learning in this unit.

Resources

Resources include:
- lesson plans from Horizons 3 Teaching and Learning Resources CD-ROM
- activity sheets from Horizons 3 Teaching and Learning Resources guide
- electronic resources on the Horizons 3 Electronic Resources CD-ROM

Future learning

The relationships between tectonically active zones, landscape and people are also touched on in Horizons 2 Unit 3 Comparing Countries. The topic of hazards is covered in most GCSE examination syllabuses and is a popular option in many AS and A2 courses.

Links

The activities in this unit link with:
- the theme of physical geography covered in Horizons 1 Unit 3 Rivers, Horizons 2 Unit 1 Coasts and Horizons 2 Unit 5 Limestone, although there are clear links with Horizons 1 Unit 2 People and Horizons 1 Unit 6 Exploring the UK.
- mathematics: handling data and representation
- ICT: using internet news sites
- key skills: working with others, improving own learning and performance
- citizenship: global community
- science scheme of work: Unit 8H The rock cycle

2

LEARNING OBJECTIVES PUPILS SHOULD LEARN	POSSIBLE TEACHING ACTIVITIES	LEARNING OUTCOMES PUPILS	POINTS TO NOTE
Is your world moving you? (pages 4–5)			
• To establish prior knowledge of natural hazards. • To analyse evidence of tectonic hazards. • To suggest factors affecting the location of tectonic hazards.	Establish prior knowledge by diamond ranking a selection of statements about earthquakes and volcanoes. Enable pupils to identify their starting points in terms of knowledge as well as highlighting some areas of new knowledge they will be encountering. Use a scatter graph to differentiate between truly natural hazards and those with a significant human cause. Analyse photographs to determine the threat from earthquakes and volcanoes. Help pupils to consider what determines how likely people are to be affected by earthquakes and volcanoes. These initial thoughts will be revisited later on to allow pupils to recognise how their perceptions have changed.	• Use diamond ranking to create a starting point record of current understanding of tectonics. • Classify hazards on a human-natural continuum graph. • Analyse photographic evidence. • Suggest at least three factors affecting susceptibility to tectonic hazards.	Citizenship: this activity provides pupils with an opportunity to reflect on the world as a global community and the political, economic, environmental and social implications of this. Language for learning: this provides pupils with an opportunity to structure paragraphs to develop points using evidence and additional facts. Number of lives lost may be printed in figures or drawn as graphs. If graphed, there is an opportunity for links to be made with mathematics (data handling and representation).

Horizons 3 © Nelson Thornes Ltd 2006

3

Short-term planning

Horizons is the first Key Stage 3 series to offer detailed short-term, individual lesson plans to help the teacher and pupils to focus on very specific objectives and learning activities for each lesson. These short-term plans for each spread are provided on the *Planning CD-ROM*. They are closely linked to activity sheets and electronic resources as well as assessment strategies. The plans provide support that is fully in keeping with QCA and Key Stage 3 Strategy initiatives and the aim is to offer a wide range of progressive learning experiences over the course of each book. However, they are fully customisable and can be altered to incorporate the classroom teacher's existing materials and strategies.

Apart from the components already mentioned in the medium-term planning section on page 16, some of the most innovative features include the use of individual lesson objectives, starters and plenaries (see also 'Using starters and plenaries to structure lessons' on page 20). These three components are the key to establishing a continuous thread through the lesson that informs pupils of the purpose and establishes the context, excites their curiosity and finally asks them to consider what they have learned and what they need to find out next. By this means the bigger picture is set out and pupils are less likely to view lessons as disconnected or irrelevant sessions.

A blank template for a lesson plan is provided on the *Planning CD-ROM* to enable teachers to create their own lessons plans in this format.

Horizons 3 Unit 1   LESSON PLAN

Tectonics

How much can prediction and prevention help?

Pages 18–19

SUBJECT:	LESSON:	WEEK:
DATE:	TEACHER:	CLASS:

LEARNING OBJECTIVES:	LEARNING OUTCOMES:
Pupils should learn:	Pupils:
• To describe some of the ways prediction can reduce the impact of earthquakes and eruptions.	• Identify the most appropriate prediction methods for volcanic eruptions and earthquakes.
• To understand some of the ways in which the damage caused by natural hazards can be prevented.	• Explain how and why some methods of prediction and precaution need to be managed at a local, national or international scale.
• To consider which forms of prediction and prevention are the responsibility of local, national or international organisations.	• Produce an extended piece of writing to predict the effect of changes in technology on the prediction of tectonic hazards in the future.

PRIOR LEARNING:	KEY VOCABULARY:
Pupils should be aware from work earlier in the unit that countries and international organisations cooperate to help warn of impending natural disasters.	Contingency fund
	Evacuation
	Gas detectors
	Geophysical survey
	Precaution
	Prediction
	Satellite remote sensing

RESOURCES FROM HORIZONS:	OTHER RESOURCES:
Activity Sheet 1.15.	
Electronic resources on the *Horizons 3 Electronic Resources CD-ROM*.	

TEACHING STRATEGIES

Learning Structure	Actions and Resources	Notes
Preparation	Photocopy Activity Sheet 1.15 and cut out the cards to distribute to pupils.	
Starter	Give everyone in the class a method or explanation card of prediction and precaution techniques. Tell all pupils that they have to ask one pupil at a time to say what is on their card and try to find a method/explanation match. When they think they have, they should write down the method/explanation pair of statements and return to their seats. In their groups, pupils should collate their results (they should use the diagrams on pages 18–19 to get a deeper understanding of the methods in their group). Ask pupils to decide which methods they think could be used: • for both an earthquake and an eruption • for prediction (to tell when the event will happen) and for precaution (to be ready to help people after the event) • to help a poor country, but which you may assume only a rich country could afford Read out the correct pairs of statements and award one point for each achieved by the group. Pupils can gain extra points by explaining their answers to activities 4a–c.	Divide the class into four groups. Tell them they will be given a card which they need to find a corresponding explanation or method card for. They should ask their peers one at a time using partner voice. If they cannot find a match, ask them to move on to the next pupil. This activity helps pupils process a lot of information in a short period of time and encourages them to explain their decisions. Suggested time: 10 minutes
Activity	Complete activities 1 and 2. Note that the idea is to try to get pupils to imagine the panic involved when	Suggested time: 10 minutes

	experiencing an earthquake and having to make decisions quickly that could affect life and death, so keep to the short time frames.	
Link	What did pupils choose and why? Which items would help in the long term and which in the short term? Stress the link from personal choices to the choices a country would have to make on behalf of many citizens.	Planning time, information, advice and previous experience all help individuals or countries to deal with hazards more effectively. Suggested time: 5 minutes
Activity	Complete activities 3 and 4. Pupils should think back to the starter and consider which techniques are more expensive and need coordinated effort.	Pupils should be encouraged to speculate that the scale of the problem may require resources that are beyond local communities and at times beyond one nation to deal with. Suggested time: 10 minutes
Activity	Complete activity 5. Before pupils start to write their answers for this activity, ask one in each pair to adopt position a or b as outlined in the question. They should come up with three reasons or statements to support that position. Each pair should take turns to read out their initial arguments to each other. The active listener should try to think of a counter argument to each of the reasons if possible. The pair should then team up with another pair and repeat the exercise, this time with two people defending each position.	Suggested time: 15 minutes
Plenary	Draw a large Venn diagram on the board and label the circles Volcanic eruptions and Earthquakes. Revisit the method cards on Activity Sheet 1.15 by asking pupils to come to locate each method for prediction and precaution on the diagram. Finally, ask them to shade those methods which they	Suggested time: 10 minutes

	think are only really affordable by richer nations.	

DIFFERENTIATION:

The starter could be made more accessible by asking pupils to do this in pairs or by colour-coding the cards into four categories to reduce the search options.

KEY QUESTIONS:
- How can we predict an earthquake or an eruption?
- Why are some of these methods not available to the countries that need them?
- Should countries in safe areas help those in tectonic hazard zones?

ADDITIONAL POINTS TO NOTE:

HOMEWORK IDEA:

Finish activity 5.

FUTURE LEARNING:

The impact of aid on recovery from natural hazards is dealt with in the next spread.

REMINDERS FOR NEXT TIME:

ANSWERS:

Using starters and plenaries to structure lessons

Starters and plenaries frame the lesson and present it as a manageable and contextualised whole to pupils who may, or may not, be motivated when they enter the classroom. These components require time management as much as any part of a lesson does; they are not 'bolt-ons' to existing activities. Pace and challenge are frequently identified from a wide variety of classroom-based research as key components of successful lessons.

The use of starters, phase links, debriefing and plenaries can provide additional impetus and challenge to lessons, thereby maintaining interest more effectively. They are a major support to interactive whole-class teaching as they require pupil involvement and provide a platform that values pupil contributions. Transferable learning and skills also need to be identified and highlighted for pupils; these are some of the best opportunities in a lesson to pose questions, celebrate ideas and look forward to the next challenge.

The lesson plans for each spread in **Horizons** suggest starters and plenaries as well as links and debriefs that can be used as teaching strategies to help structure pupils' learning and maintain pace and challenge.

Starters

Starters activities are designed to help focus pupils' attention on the learning objectives and/or topic at the beginning of the lesson. They provide a crisp and focused start to the learning. The activities and lesson plans in **Horizons** seek to offer a wide range of starter activities, from arresting images, questioning exercises, odd one out activities and mystery objects to drama. This list is not meant to be exhaustive and is intended to complement and not replace existing practice. The aim is to get pupils thinking about the topic or issue that is to follow rather than what happened to them on the way to school (unless this is relevant!). Where possible, the opportunity to exemplify the lesson objectives or link to previous learning is a desirable objective. This helps to familiarise pupils with the later parts of the lesson whilst establishing the links with prior learning that will foster engagement and frame the activities to come.

Plenaries

The more pupil-centred plenaries are, the more engaged pupils are likely to be and the greater the opportunity for them to assess their own learning. Whilst plenaries may also involve a teacher summing up what has to be learned during the lesson, putting that learning in the context of the big picture and indicating what is coming next, this should not become the sole means of concluding a lesson. A plenary that revisits the objectives by stating boldly 'we covered objective A when we did activity B' is less likely to have a long-term benefit to learning – or engagement for that matter. The more varied the plenaries are the less chance there is of pupils becoming complacent, which is why a variety of strategies is utilised throughout the **Horizons** lesson plans.

Plenaries are part of a review process that seeks to explore, digest and understand the information encountered during learning. Without review, 40% of information can be lost within 5–10 minutes of it being encountered. They are also significant in helping pupils to make sense of what they have learned beyond the immediate recall level. They can help to illustrate the 'thinking about thinking' or metacognition that is essential if pupils are to identify the transferable skills they have developed. Whilst the content of a lesson may be reflected in short-term or modular objectives, longer-term or background objectives will seek to develop skills and understanding. This is a good opportunity to make explicit the development in those gradually acquired skills.

Plenaries do not have to come at the end of a lesson. Some may be more appropriate at the end of a key activity during the lesson where clarification of process or pupil thinking is imperative. This is especially so where school lesson duration is unusually short or long. In **Horizons** the plenaries are presented at the end of lesson plans as this is an important time for evaluating progress, placing the learning in the context of the bigger picture and signposting the next steps on the journey. However, this is not intended as being prescriptive and if the teacher identifies a need to present plenaries or starters at alternative points of the lesson then they can customise the lesson plans to facilitate personalised planning.

Starters, plenaries and multiple intelligences

The work of Howard Gardner on multiple intelligence theory widely informs current educational thinking. Understanding the role of these intelligences in determining the way we learn is seen by many educationalists as a fundamental prerequisite to adapting lesson planning to the needs of the individual. On a simplistic level, we may have preferred learning styles, e.g. visual learners can best access new information and processes if they can see what something looks like or how it works. While as many as nine intelligences have been identified, the visual, kinaesthetic and auditory (VAK) intelligences – and therefore preferred learning styles – are generally identified as being crucial to a balanced plan of learning experiences.

Whilst all pupils share a mixture of the multiple intelligences, they may have one style that dominates, e.g. visual learning. If the learning style they are most predisposed towards is not encountered in the way they are taught, they may struggle to access the ideas, information and processes they encounter; they will have to process or transform the information to make sense of it. Whilst acknowledging the need to experience some learning in their preferred style, pupils also need to develop their abilities in the other learning styles. To this end a range of visual, auditory and kinaesthetic learning styles is encouraged throughout **Horizons** and in particular during starters and plenaries in the lesson plans. Here more active, pupil-centred learning is highlighted in a way that we believe will encourage greater engagement and reflection on what has been learned and how this fits into the big picture.

Support for thinking skills

- The key idea behind the thinking skills approach is that pupils have to *learn how to think*.
- To do this they need to be aware of *ways of thinking*.
- Then they need to learn *when to use* these ways of thinking.

All this means that pupils have to go through a structured process in which they are made aware of their thinking skills. They should know that this is giving them a set of 'thinking tools' that can be used to help them learn more efficiently in future. They need to be conscious of this process so that they know:

- what they are doing
- why they are doing it and
- when they should apply that skill in future.

Horizons provides a set of thinking skills exercises, some of which are detailed in the table, right. However, if pupils are to use them to the best advantage these exercises need to be used in a carefully structured way. In particular, lessons should be planned which involve pupils in knowing, before the exercise starts, that they are working on a particular skill.

Then, after they have worked through the exercise, they must discuss what they have done. By being made fully aware of that process they are more likely to be able to apply it to similar situations in future.

Finally, they need to think about the types of situation for which that skill is suited. By doing this they should become more conscious of applying what they have learned. In fact, it is the debriefing session, after working through the skill, that is the most fundamental part of the development of the thinking skills approach.

More details about each of the thinking skills listed in the table on this page are provided in the lesson notes for the relevant pages.

Thinking skills exercise	Pages/*Activity Sheets*
Advanced organiser	11, 47, *1.14*, *3.4*
Ask the expert	*4.13*, *4.14*
Collective memory	*1.11*, *1.12*
Concept mapping	9, 33, *2.9*
Decision-making exercise	19, 22, 79, *1.20*
Development compass rose	24, 31, 43, 109, *2.1*, *3.3*
Diamond sorting	*1.1*, *1.2*, *2.6*, *2.7*
Goals and targets	*2.11*, *2.12*
Interrogating photos	65, 73, *1.4*, *2.2*, *3.4*, *6.6*
Living graph	77, *1.8*, *4.10*
Looking for patterns	27, *6.5*
Mind map	23, 71, 85, 119, *6.15*
Modelling/predicting	19, 103
Mystery	60, *2.16*, *2.17*, *3.19*, *4.11*, *4.12*
Opinion line	41, 46, *2.18*, *3.20*
Prioritising	21, 34, 37, 43, *6.13*
Questioning stereotypes	62
Relational diagram	*1.10*
Role-play/debate	81, 123, *4.15–4.17*, *6.17–6.20*
Sequencing	*1.7*
Storyboarding	41
System diagram	69, *4.4*
True or false?	9
Using a timeline	14, 35, 56, *1.16*
Venn diagram	17, 45, 79, *1.3*, *2.5*, *3.16*
5Ws	109, *2.2*, *6.6*

The DfES publication 'Learning Styles and Writing in Geography for the Key Stage 3 National Strategy' (ref: DfES 0380/2002) opens with the following diagram linking learning styles to particular classroom techniques.

It then goes on to state:

This overview of learning styles starts with 'VAK' (visual, auditory and kinaesthetic), but also has 'interpersonal', and 'intrapersonal' from Howard Gardner's multiple intelligences (see P20 of this book for further references) because reflection and collaboration have always seemed so important to language development. This doesn't aim to be a comprehensive guide; just a way in to thinking about learning and writing.

The writers of **Horizons** have been conscious of two conflicting pressures while writing the series. We were aware that:

- pupils ought to be given the biggest range of experience possible – to allow them to learn in a variety of different ways and to find the ones that were most suitable for them
- textbooks should not shackle classroom teachers to particular styles, but should leave them free to opt for the learning style best suited to the needs of their class at a particular moment within their course.

Therefore we have tried to use the biggest possible variety of resource material within the Pupil Books, and to suggest a range of approaches to that material in the Over to You activity sections. However, we do not prescribe how teachers and pupils should use the resources and activities in their classrooms.

For instance, it would be quite unnecessary to state, in the Pupil Book, where there are opportunities for pupils to 'hear text read'. We also feel that to offer detailed suggestions for classroom drama in the Pupil Book could lead to those pages being completely ignored by many!

Instead, we offer a variety of *suggested* teaching and learning styles in the unit plans, lesson plans and the opportunities for assessment for learning sections of this *Teaching and Learning Resources* guide. Some of these references are given in the table, right.

In addition to providing activities and suggestions for classroom organisation we have tried to ensure that the text and illustrations in the Pupil Book encourage the development of literacy. We have tried to:

- write in a style that is accessible, and yet makes demands on the average reader

- provide case studies and narrative, which should gain the pupils' attention through their concentration on the real world – the real world of pupils of the age range in Years 7–9
- support the text with a wealth of photos, statistics, maps, diagrams, etc.
- provide 'Key Words!' boxes to introduce pupils to new, technical vocabulary
- back this up with a glossary containing the meanings of all technical words
- provide a whole variety of ways of supporting writing, both in the Pupil Book and in the worksheets that can be used with the text. These are provided in hard copy, so that they can immediately be used by teachers, and they are also available electronically, so that they can be adapted to the needs of particular classes and individuals. They are also designed as templates on which teachers can, if necessary, base their own worksheets for other parts of the course.

Some types of support are listed in the table that follows. This table is not exhaustive, even of the techniques to support literacy that are included in the book. Moreover, we leave it to individual teachers and departments to develop the work to fit the learning styles listed above. These are described in more detail in the DfES document cited at the top of this page.

	Pages/*Activity Sheets*
Help with reading	
Distillation from text	15, 23
Analysing and highlighting text	*1.5, 1.13, 3.17, 6.12*
Reading cartoons	*2.8, 2.10, 3.15*
Help with writing	
Structured writing with key words	13, 25, 71, *4.18*
Structured writing	9, 41, 45, 49, 61, 65, *1.9, 2.4, 2.11, 2.19, 2.21, 3.4, 3.18, 5.2, 5.4, 6.13*
Sentence completion	13, 15, 71
Writing for a specific audience	37, *5.8, 5.9, 6.10*
Choosing words/using words	13
How to describe distributions	7, 51, 53
Writing a report	17, 47, *1.20*
Writing a comparison	17, 41, 45, 49, 51, 53
Structuring an argument	11, 19, 121, 123
Empathic writing	79, 81, 93, 95, 105, 119, *6.10*
Storyboarding	41
Writing captions	*1.7*
Drawing and captioning cartoons	*2.8, 2.20, 3.15*
Annotating diagrams	*6.3, 6.16*
Biography	35
Expressing and justifying opinions	81, 101
Summarising	111, 115

Help with speaking and listening

Taking part in a discussion (pairs)	31, 33, 37, 47, 85, 108, 109, 115, *1.1, 1.8, 1.17, 2.6, 2.8, 2.9, 2.20, 6.6, 6.10, 6.13*
Taking part in a discussion (group)	33, 83, 87, 89, 101, 105, 115, *1.12, 1.18, 2.13, 2.20, 4.2, 5.18*
Taking part in a discussion (whole class)	91, 97, 99, 103, 113, 123, *1.15, 2.6, 2.14*
Family discussion homework task	*5.19, 5.20*
Discussion of key questions	47, 99, *5.1*
Planning a presentation	55, 67, 105, 123
Making a presentation to the class	83
Discussion in a DME	19, 22, 79
Ask the expert	*4.13, 4.14*
Reporting back to whole school	37, 91
Working together on fieldwork	97, 99
Questionnaire interviewing	99
Discussion/empathising	39, 93
Role play	*4.15–4.17*
Taking part in a debate	*6.17–6.20*
Using cartoons	33, 117
Creating mind movies	109

Support for numeracy

As with literacy, support for work in numeracy has been built in to all parts of the **Horizons** course. Throughout their work it is expected that pupils should become confident in working with numbers, shapes, transformations of space, abstract thought and generalisations, estimation and so on.

Many of the skills that have to be taught in Key Stages 2 and 3 Geography have a very specific numeracy link. Pupils have to collect, sort, present and analyse data. These processes all involve work with number and concepts of numeracy. The use of data to produce tables, charts, graphs and maps are all excellent examples of the links between geography and numeracy.

One particularly close link between the two subjects is through the use of Ordnance Survey maps. This work involves pupils in the use and understanding of scale, use of symbols, estimation, representation of height by contours and spot heights, transformation of a 3-dimensional shape into a 2-dimensional representation, and so on. Some of the work with OS maps that is particularly closely linked to numeracy is listed in the following table, but more examples can be found in the geographical skills section on pages 32–33 of this guide.

	Pages/*Activity Sheets*
Collecting primary data	97, 99, 102, *4.5, 4.6, 5.20*
Collecting and using statistics	30, 87, 99, 102, *5.2, 5.4*
Presenting data	97, 99, 102
Analysing data	79, 87, 95, 97, 99, 102
Grouping and mapping data sets	*6.8, 6.9*
Using statistics in conclusions	33, 37, 55, 59, 63, 97, 102, *2.4*
Estimating and calculating	*5.19*
Ranking	27, 28, 31, 35, 41, 43, *1.1, 1.2, 2.6, 2.7, 6.13*
Comparing size and scale	*3.2, 3.20, 6.2*
Comparing satellite and map images	*6.7*
Drawing and using bar graphs	75, *1.3*
Drawing and using line graphs	51, 75, 78, *3.9, 4.10*
Drawing and using triangular graphs	52, *3.10*
Drawing and using pie charts	*6.2*
Analysing climate graphs	70, 73, 83, *3.14, 4.9, 4.20*
Analysing population pyramids	*3.8*
Map scales	54, 107, *5.15, 5.16*
Map directions	55
Averages	52
Looking for trends in statistics	77, 79, 87
Predicting trends from statistics	63, 81, 87, *5.2, 5.4*
Comparing trends on graphs	88
Venn diagrams	17, 45, 79, *1.3, 2.5, 3.16*
Using percentages	97
Using map transformations	28
Choosing graph techniques	95
Systems diagrams	69
Auditing	91
Budgeting	*1.20*
Measuring development	25, 26, 28, 30, 111
Choropleth maps	26
Spreadsheets	30
Chart creation	31
Relational diagrams	*1.10*
Looking for patterns in distributions	*3.6, 3.8, 3.11, 3.12, 3.13, 6.5, 6.8, 6.9*

At Key Stage 3 there are statutory requirements to use ICT in all subjects. The Key Stage 3 National Strategy has now provided a framework for ICT, which gives practical advice on meeting the National Curriculum requirements for ICT capability. The framework provides the following guidance about the cross-curricular use of ICT:

To be properly effective, dedicated ICT curriculum time in Key Stage 3 has to be supplemented by significant opportunities for pupils to apply and develop their ICT capability in other subjects, as the National Curriculum requires.

Guidance about using ICT in Geography is provided in the Key Stage 3 Strategy Guide, *ICT Across the Curriculum – ICT in Geography* 09-2004 DfES Ref 0194-2004G:

Pupils will come to geography lessons with expectations about how they might apply ICT to move their own learning forward. Geography teachers will not need to teach ICT capability but can exploit new opportunities for pupils to apply and develop the capability that they already have, to enhance their learning in geography. Consequently, the focus of the lesson remains firmly rooted in geography and teachers are not burdened with the need to teach ICT.

It goes on to say that geography teachers will need to know:

which parts of ICT capability offer significant opportunities for teaching and learning in geography and how they can be incorporated into existing schemes of work... The use of ICT needs to be purposeful and to add value to the teaching and learning of geography and should not be seen simply as a bolt-on It needs to be carefully integrated into geography lessons, with a clear rationale for its use.

The statutory requirements of the National Curriculum for Geography (2000) include these statements:

Pupils should be given opportunities to apply and develop their ICT capability through the use of ICT tools to support their learning in all subjects. Pupils should be given opportunities to support their work by being taught to:
a find things out from a variety of sources, selecting and synthesising the information to meet their needs and developing an ability to question its accuracy, bias and plausibility
b develop their ideas using ICT tools to amend and refine their work and enhance its quality and accuracy
c exchange and share information, both directly and through electronic media
d review, modify and evaluate their work, reflecting critically on its quality, as it progresses.

Horizons provides a wide range of opportunities for using ICT. Schemes of work for each unit identify ICT opportunities. Each *Teaching and Learning Resources* guide provides at least one major ICT activity linked to the units in the Pupil Book. Wherever possible these major ICT activities will be linked to the ICT National Curriculum orders and the ICT Framework, thus demonstrating the whole-school role geography can play regarding ICT. Over the whole **Horizons** course a full range of software and approaches will be used to develop pupils' ICT capability and enhance the quality of their geography experience.

Horizons 3 Unit 2 80:20 provides an opportunity to contribute to pupils' ICT capability and enhance their geographical understanding of development. Pages 30–31 further develop the use of ICT in the enquiry process from the weather enquiry on pages 56–57 of **Horizons 2**. Again, pupils and teachers are given the option of either using data provided in a spreadsheet or researching their own data using an online GIS at the World Bank website. The use of ICT in this instance allows pupils to interrogate a large data set quickly, providing greater time and flexibility to analyse the geographical patterns, thus the ICT enhances the geography. The activities also allow pupils to develop their ICT capability in a real context. They are required to sort their data using the spreadsheet tools, which is a more effective means of interrogating the data. They can also use the spreadsheet to chart their findings. They can write up their findings using a word processing program into which they can export the charts from their spreadsheet.

A further major opportunity for using ICT is provided in on pages 122–123 of **Horizons 3** Unit 6 Development or Destruction? This review spread pulls together the unit in the form of a geographical enquiry leading to a mock public meeting. Different groups of pupils represent the views of different groups of people in the Amazon rainforest. ICT is used for researching the viewpoints from interest group websites and presenting the information in a variety of ways for the public meeting.

Presentation approaches for the enquiry using ICT
It is suggested that each group considers a standard design for each presentation element, including a key question, logo or slogan incorporated into each element.

Leaflet using DTP – this could be a six-panel leaflet outlining the views of the group. The leaflet could be copied and given out to the rest of the class.	**PowerPoint presentation** created by each group to outline the key points of the group's presentation. This needs to link to the leaflet and classroom display.	**Classroom display** using DTP and presentation software to produce banners, posters and slides from the presentation.	**Spreadsheet and charts** presenting data researched on the internet to support the views of the group. These charts can be inserted into the leaflet, presentation and classroom display.

The mock public meeting could provide the foundation of a collaboration between the geography and ICT departments in school, with pupils working in lessons for both subjects. In ICT lessons, pupils could develop their presentations to a standard design.

The ICT framework goes on to identify a checklist for teachers to determine whether use of ICT in their subject is appropriate. The authors of **Horizons 3** have incorporated the checklist below in utilising ICT activities to enhance geographical skills, knowledge and understanding.

Key checklist questions – will use of ICT...

...allow pupils to investigate or be creative in ways not possible otherwise?	...give them access to information not otherwise readily available?
...engage them in the selection and interpretation of information?	...help them to think through and understand important ideas?
...enable them to see patterns or behaviours more clearly?	...add reliability or accuracy to measurements?
...enhance the quality of their presentations?	...save time, for example, spent on measuring, recording or writing?

To ensure good progression in the ICT objectives taught in other subjects, the use of ICT needs to be planned carefully into departmental schemes of work. Teachers of other subjects should be familiar with the knowledge, skills and understanding pupils have been taught in ICT and should be aware of the range of ways in which they can support and help to develop pupils' use of ICT.

The yearly teaching objectives for Years 7, 8 and 9, as set out in the ICT framework, are central to pupils' achievement in ICT. They identify for each year the core of

what pupils should know, understand and be able to do in ICT.

The objectives are set out year by year to help identify progression. Each year includes objectives for the themes:
• finding things out
• developing ideas and making things happen
• exchanging and sharing information.

Objectives for reviewing, modifying and evaluating work as it progresses are integrated throughout the themes.

Use of ICT across the curriculum – themes	Geography PoS	Examples of use of ICT in **Horizons 3**
Finding things out	1c – collect, record and present evidence 1c – ICT opportunity: pupils could use a *digital camera* to record appropriate images to support fieldwork 2b – select and use appropriate fieldwork techniques To select and use secondary sources of evidence including ICT-based sources	*Unit 1 Tectonics* Advanced organiser research using the internet to find information about earthquakes in Japan and Iran: pages 10–11 *Unit 2 80:20* Internet research on the Human Development Report website: page 29 activity 11 Development enquiry using ICT – research data using online GIS: pages 30–31 Internet research for political cartoons: Activity Sheet 2.8 Internet research about a chosen aid agency: Activity Sheet 2.13 Activity to investigate the 'Make Poverty History' website: pages 34–35 Research on the Fairtrade website: pages 38–39 *Unit 3 Comparing Countries* Internet research about the physical and climatic aspects of the USA and Mexico: page 49 activity 4 Internet research about census data for the populations of the USA and Mexico: pages 50–51 Internet research about Arizona and Illinois in the USA, and Yucatán and Sonora in Mexico: page 55 activities 4 and 5 Internet research about trade between the USA, Mexico and the UK: page 57 activity 5; page 59 activity 4 Advanced organiser research using the internet to find information about the USA and Mexico: Activity Sheet 3.4 *Unit 4 Ecosystems* Research images from websites to produce an illustrated diary of a photo safari in the Serengeti National Park: page 79 activity 7 *Unit 5 Think – Act* Research information on the internet on climate change in specific countries: page 87 activity 3 Internet research about Antarctic: Activity Sheets 5.6 and 5.7 Internet research about recycling: page 99 activity 2 *Unit 6 Development or Destruction?* Conduct a search on the internet for images of rainforests: page 105 activity 4

Search for images of Brazil on the internet: page 109 activity 7
Research images of tribal people in the Amazon: page 113 activity 6
Find the latest satellite images of the Amazon rainforest: page 117 activity 3
Investigate the Rainforest Action Network website: page 117 activity 4
Research a viewpoint about the rainforest using websites: pages 122–123

| Developing ideas and making things happen | 2e – draw maps and plans at a range of scales… and to select and use appropriate graphical techniques to present evidence on maps and diagrams [for example, pie charts…], including ICT [for example, using *mapping software* to plot the distribution of shops and services in a town centre]

2g – decision-making skills, including using ICT [for example, by using a *spreadsheet* to help find the best location for a supermarket] | *Unit 1 Tectonics*
Use hazard prediction and precaution data on a spreadsheet to calculate costs within budget limits: pages 23–24
Unit 2 80:20
Development enquiry using ICT – interrogate development data in a spreadsheet, sort and chart data: pages 30–31
Unit 3 Comparing Countries
Use population data to plot line graphs of Mexico/USA population change with appropriate annotation: page 51 activity 4
Use climate data to plot line and bar graphs: Activity Sheet 3.14
Unit 4 Ecosystems
Select illustrations from websites to illustrate a diary: page 79 activity 7
Unit 5 Think – Act
Create a recycling database: page 99 activity 3
Use tools on the Recycle Now website to design posters: Activity Sheet 5.12
Investigate the Energy Saving Trust website: Activity Sheet 5.13
Unit 6 Development or Destruction?
Create charts to present evidence about rainforests: pages 122–123 |
| Exchanging and sharing information | 1f – communicate in ways appropriate to task and audience [for example, by using *desktop publishing* to produce a leaflet]

2f – communicate in different ways, including using ICT [for example, by writing a report about an environmental issue, exchanging fieldwork data using *email*] | *Unit 1 Tectonics*
Create a presentation using PowerPoint to test a hypothesis: page 17 activity 3
Create a PowerPoint presentation to explain how world aid agencies contribute to the Indonesian tsunami aid programme: page 21 activity 4
Unit 2 80:20
Development enquiry using ICT – present findings of enquiry, producing a word processed report incorporating charts from spreadsheet: pages 30–31
Create a world poverty campaign poster using DTP: Activity Sheet 2.10
Create a presentation to class about a chosen aid agency: Activity Sheet 2.13
Use PowerPoint or DPT to develop an aid campaign: page 37 activity 5
Create a storyboard about sustainable development using PowerPoint: page 41 activity 5
Unit 3 Comparing Countries
Produce a word-processed and DTP augmented report to compare the USA and Mexico: pages 46–47
Produce PowerPoint presentations about Arizona and Illinois in the USA, and Yucatán and Sonora in Mexico: page 55 activities 4 and 5
Unit 5 Think – Act
Create a PowerPoint presentation for your local farmers' market: page 93 activity 6
Unit 6 Development or Destruction?
Create PowerPoint presentations of rainforest images and play back to a partner: page 105 activity 4 |

The **Horizons** *Electronic Resources CD-ROM* fully integrates the Pupil Book into electronic learning when used with a data projector and/or interactive whiteboard, providing a major opportunity to extend geographical learning.

The website plays a vital role for schools using the geography course. At a practical level the site keeps any weblinks referred to in the Pupil Book and *Teaching and Learning Resources* guide up to date. As URLs or web addresses change regularly, the website ensures that pupils and teachers do not have to waste time searching the internet for new URLs.

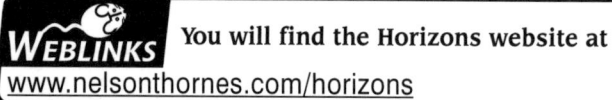

WEBLINKS You will find the Horizons website at
www.nelsonthornes.com/horizons

Support for citizenship

The importance of citizenship

Citizenship gives pupils the knowledge, skills and understanding to play an effective role in society at local, national and international levels. It helps them to become informed, thoughtful and responsible citizens who are aware of their duties and rights. It promotes their spiritual, moral, social and cultural development, making them more self-confident and responsible both in and beyond the classroom. It encourages pupils to play a helpful part in the life of their schools, neighbourhoods, communities and the wider world. It also teaches them about our economy and democratic institutions and values; encourages respect for different national, religious and ethnic identities; and develops pupils' ability to reflect on issues and take part in discussions.

NC CITIZENSHIP ORDERS

Geography clearly makes a major contribution towards citizenship. The QCA Scheme of Work for citizenship includes two schemes that demonstrate the teaching of citizenship through geography: Unit 10 Debating a global issue and Unit 18 Developing your school grounds. The scheme also includes a leaflet identifying citizenship opportunities through geography in Key Stage 3. The QCA Schemes of Work for Geography Key Stage 3 also demonstrate these links. Indeed the Teacher Guide to the schemes states that:

geography can play a significant part in promoting citizenship through for example,

- *Developing pupils' knowledge and understanding of the institutions and systems that influence their lives and communities, and how to participate in decision making, for example, in relation to a local planning issue.*
- *Providing opportunities for pupils to reflect upon and discuss topical, social, environmental, economic and political issues.*
- *Developing pupils' knowledge and understanding about diverse national, regional, and ethnic identities in the United Kingdom and the wider world*
- *Developing pupils' understanding of the world as a global community and the issues and challenges of global interdependence and responsibility.*

Horizons 3 develops a number of links to citizenship. Some are major sections that are in themselves worthy of inclusion in a whole-school citizenship programme; others can be used by the Geography department as a starting point for further development.

Several units in **Horizons 3** can be utilised to make a major contribution to your school's citizenship programme, most notably Unit 2 80:20, Unit 5 Think – Act and Unit 6 Development or Destruction?, which all encourage pupils not only to understand what is happening locally and globally but also to engage and make a contribution to resolve both environmental and economic issues. Indeed, Unit 6 Development or Destruction? has developed the QCA citizenship/geography scheme 10 Debating a global issue.

Book unit	Geography activity	Citizenship PoS		
Unit 1 Tectonics	Pages 20–21 How can aid reduce the damage?	**1**	Pupils should be taught about:	
		f)	the work of community-based, national and international voluntary groups	
		2	Pupils should be taught to:	
		a)	think about topical political, spiritual, moral, social and cultural issues, problems and events by analysing information and its sources, including ICT-based sources	
		b)	justify orally and in writing a personal opinion about such issues, problems or events.	
Unit 2 80:20	Pages 34–35 80:20 – What can be done?	**1**	Pupils should be taught about:	
	Pages 36–37 80:20 – What can I do?	**f)**	the work of community-based, national and international voluntary groups	
	Pages 38–39 Fair trade?	**g)**	the importance of resolving conflict fairly	
	Pages 42–43 Where are we now?	**h)**	the significance of the media in society	
		i)	the world as a global community, and the political, economic, environmental and social implications of this.	
Unit 3 Comparing Countries	Pages 56–57 How are Mexico and the USA connected?	**1**	Pupils should be taught about:	
	Pages 58–59 How are these countries linked to the UK?	**g)**	the importance of resolving conflict fairly	
	Pages 60–61 Mystery: Why is John Doe staying in Tucson, Arizona?	**h)**	the significance of the media in society	
		i)	the world as a global community, and the political, economic, environmental and social implications of this	
	Pages 62–63 Where are we now?	**2**	Pupils should be taught to:	
		a)	think about topical political, spiritual, moral, social and cultural issues, problems and events by analysing information and its sources, including ICT-based sources	
		b)	justify orally and in writing a personal opinion about such issues, problems or events	
		c)	contribute to group and exploratory class discussions, and take part in debates	

		3	Pupils should be taught to:
		a)	use their imagination to consider other people's experiences and be able to think about, express and explain views that are not their own.
Unit 4 Ecosystems	Pages 78–79 Can the savanna ecosystem be conserved? Pages 80–81 Animals, people or sustainable ecosystems?	**1** **i)**	Pupils should be taught about: the world as a global community, and the political, economic, environmental and social implications of this
		2 **a)**	Pupils should be taught to: think about topical political, spiritual, moral, social and cultural issues, problems and events by analysing information and its sources, including ICT-based sources
		b)	justify orally and in writing a personal opinion about such issues, problems or events
		c)	contribute to group and exploratory class discussions, and take part in debates
		3	Pupils should be taught to:
		a)	use their imagination to consider other people's experiences and be able to think about, express and explain views that are not their own.
Unit 5 Think – Act	Pages 84–85 Think about your global footprints … Act locally to reduce them Pages 86–87 What is global warming? Pages 88–89 What is causing global warming? Pages 90–91 How can we cut carbon emissions? Pages 92–93 How does our food affect the environment? Pages 94–95 Are food miles only about energy? Pages 96–97 Rubbish – what's the problem? Pages 98–99 Rubbish – what's the solution? Pages 100–101 Where there's muck, is there brass? Pages 102–103 Where are we now?	**1** **c)**	Pupils should be taught about: central and local government, the public services they offer and how they are financed, and the opportunities to contribute
		f)	the work of community-based, national and international voluntary groups
		i)	the world as a global community, and the political, economic, environmental and social implications of this
		2 **a)**	Pupils should be taught to: think about topical political, spiritual, moral, social and cultural issues, problems and events by analysing information and its sources, including ICT-based sources
		b)	justify orally and in writing a personal opinion about such issues, problems or events
		c)	contribute to group and exploratory class discussions, and take part in debates
		3 **a)**	Pupils should be taught to: use their imagination to consider other people's experiences and be able to think about, express and explain views that are not their own
		b)	negotiate, decide and take part responsibly in both school and community-based activities
		c)	reflect on the process of participating.
Unit 6 Development or Destruction?	Pages 112–113 What is life like for tribal people? Pages 116–117 Is the rainforest being destroyed? Pages 118–119 What are the consequences of deforestation? Pages 120–121 Can the rainforest be developed sustainably? Pages 122–123 Where are we now?	**1** **f)**	Pupils should be taught about: the work of community-based, national and international voluntary groups
		g)	the importance of resolving conflict fairly
		i)	the world as a global community, and the political, economic, environmental and social implications of this
		2 **a)**	Pupils should be taught to: think about topical political, spiritual, moral, social and cultural issues, problems and events by analysing information and its sources, including ICT-based sources
		b)	justify orally and in writing a personal opinion about such issues, problems or events
		c)	contribute to group and exploratory class discussions, and take part in debates
		3	Pupils should be taught to:
		a)	use their imagination to consider other people's experiences and be able to think about, express and explain views that are not their own.
Passport to the World	Pages 124–125	**1** **i)**	Pupils should be taught about: the world as a global community, and the political, economic, environmental and social implications of this
		2 **a)**	Pupils should be taught to: think about topical political, spiritual, moral, social and cultural issues, problems and events by analysing information and its sources, including ICT-based sources
		b)	justify orally and in writing a personal opinion about such issues, problems or events.

Support for the global dimension

In March 2005, the DfES published a booklet called *Developing the Global Dimension in the School Curriculum*. Its purpose was to show how, in a global society, the global dimension can be integrated into both the National Curriculum and the wider life of schools.

In the booklet, the global dimension was defined as follows:

The global dimension incorporates the key concepts of global citizenship, conflict resolution, diversity, human rights, interdependence, social justice, sustainable development and values and perceptions. It explores the interconnections between the local and the global. It builds knowledge and understanding, as well as developing skills and attitudes.

The publication identified the following eight key concepts underlying the idea of the global dimension to the curriculum:

- global citizenship
- conflict resolution
- social justice
- values and perceptions
- sustainable development
- interdependence
- human rights
- diversity.

The booklet explains that these eight concepts provide a framework for thinking about the global dimension and building it into the curriculum. They are all important and interrelated but, in different contexts, different concepts take a more central position and underpin the others. The concepts can also help with planning and evaluation.

While no school or teacher will address each equally, the concepts are interconnected and an integrated approach is essential.

Although geography clearly has a vital role to play in developing the global dimension, the booklet maintains that its successful development requires a whole-school approach, ideally including the development of partnerships with schools in other countries. It is also important to provide opportunities for pupils to take action to change things. These can be linked to school assemblies and displays around the school, encouraging pupils to support charities and organisations committed to reducing the impact of world poverty. Such approaches have greater meaning for pupils and provide greater capacity for understanding if they evolve from the curriculum. **Horizons** adopts such approaches in several units, most notably in **Horizons 3** Unit 2 80:20 and Unit 5 Think – Act. Indeed, in **Horizons 3** Unit 2 80:20 a real-life school partnership between Raincliffe School in Scarborough and Mkwakwani School in Kenya is used as a starting point to encourage pupils and schools to develop their own partnerships.

Throughout the **Horizons** series, opportunities for whole-school approaches and joint projects between subjects have been developed. Unit 6 Development or Destruction? in **Horizons 3** offers the potential for considerable collaboration and curriculum coverage, including many of the concepts that underpin the global dimension. These links are shown in the diagram below.

The diagram on page 30 summarises how the whole **Horizons** series integrates the concepts that underpin the global dimension.

Geography
1a–f Undertaking geographical enquiry
2a–g Developing geographical skills
3a–e Knowledge and understanding of places
4a–b Knowledge and understanding of patterns and processes
5a–b Knowledge and understanding of environmental change and sustainable development
6j Environmental issues

Citizenship/global citizenship
1i The world as a global community
2a–c Developing skills of enquiry and communication
3 Use their imagination to consider other people's experiences

ICT
1a–c Finding things out
3a–c Exchanging and sharing information
4a–d Reviewing, modifying and evaluating work as it progresses

Horizons 3 Curriculum links for Unit 6 Development or Destruction?

Key skills/skills framework
This unit makes a major contribution to key skills. Pupils have to successfully work together using ICT to produce a joint presentation, developing their communication skills.

Literacy
Pupils are required to scan read the text when researching the topic, and edit, draft and redraft the information. Pupils then make oral presentations to an audience.

Sustainable development
Pupils identify that current rates of deforestation are unsustainable. They investigate a range of sustainable development projects in the Amazon rainforest as a viable future for the region and the planet.

Conflict resolution
Pupils investigate a range of conflicting groups of people in the Amazon rainforest. They represent the views of four conflicting groups and debate the issues to attempt to resolve conflict.

Interdependence
Pupils investigate the consequences of deforestation in the Amazon basin on different groups of people at a variety of scales from local to global.

Underlying the notion of a global dimension to the curriculum are eight key concepts. **Horizons** has integrated these concepts throughout the course, as shown below.

Social justice

Understanding the importance of social justice as an element in both sustainable development and the improved welfare of all people.

Geography: showing how the level of development in different countries is related to quality of life.

Horizons 1 Unit 2 pages 30–35
Unit 6 pages 116–117
Horizons 3 Unit 1 pages 20–21
Unit 2 pages 24–63
Unit 3 pages 44–63
Unit 6 pages 104–123

Conflict resolution

Understanding the nature of conflicts, their impact on development and why there is a need for their resolution and the promotion of harmony.

Geography: explaining how conflicting demands on an environment arise and the difficulties these conflicts can cause.

Horizons 2 Unit 6 pages 118–121
Horizons 3 Unit 2 pages 24–43
Unit 3 pages 60–61
Unit 4 pages 80–81
Unit 5 pages 84–103
Unit 6 pages 104–123

Global citizenship

Gaining the knowledge, skills and understanding of concepts and institutions necessary to become informed, active, responsible citizens.

Geography: inspiring pupils to think about their own place in the world and the rights and responsibilities to other people; studying issues of global significance.

Horizons 1 Unit 1 pages 4–5; 12–17
Unit 2 pages 30–35
Unit 6 pages 120–121
Horizons 2 Unit 4 pages 68–83
Horizons 3 Unit 2 pages 24–25; 32–43
Unit 5 pages 84–103
Unit 6 pages 104–123

Diversity

Understanding and respecting differences and relating these to our common humanity.

Horizons 1 Unit 2 pages 28–37
Unit 6 pages 106–111
Horizons 2 Unit 2 pages 32–35
Unit 4 pages 64–83
Horizons 3 Unit 2 pages 24–43
Unit 3 pages 44–63
Unit 4 pages 64–83
Unit 6 pages 104–123

Values and perceptions

Developing a critical evaluation of representations of global issues and an appreciation of the effect these have on people's attitudes and values.

Geography: studying LEDCs and localities through analysis of sources such as photos and texts, and raising consciousness of the way these shape pupils' and others' views.

Horizons 1 Unit 1 pages 4–5; 16–17
Unit 2 pages 30–37
Unit 4 pages 76–81
Horizons 2 Unit 2 pages 32–35
Horizons 3 Unit 2 pages 24–43
Unit 3 pages 44–63
Unit 6 pages 104–123

Sustainable development

Understanding the need to maintain and improve the quality of life now without damaging the planet for future generations.

Geography: teaching the principles of sustainable development, and explaining the positive and negative effects of developments on the environment and on people.

Horizons 2 Unit 4 pages 80–81
Unit 6 pages 120–121
Passport to the World pages 124–125
Horizons 3 Unit 2 pages 40–41
Unit 4 pages 78–81
Unit 5 pages 84–103
Unit 6 pages 104–123

Interdependence

Understanding how people, places, economies and environments are all inextricably interrelated, and that choices and events have repercussions on a global scale.

Geography: explaining why places and people are interdependent.

Horizons 1 Unit 1 pages 4–5; 12–17
Unit 5 pages 96–97
Horizons 2 Unit 4 pages 64–83
Unit 2 pages 24–43
Unit 4 pages 64–83
Horizons 3 Unit 1 pages 4–24

Unit 2 pages 30–37
Unit 6 pages 120–121
Unit 6 pages 104–123
Unit 3 pages 44–63
Unit 5 pages 84–103
Unit 6 pages 104–123

Human rights

Knowing about human rights including the UN Convention on the Rights of the Child.

Horizons 3 Unit 2 pages 34–37
Unit 6 pages 112–113; 122–123

Support for Education for Sustainable Development (ESD)

The QCA web page on Education for Sustainable Development, or ESD (www.nc.uk.net/esd/index.htm) opens with the following statement:

Education for sustainable development (ESD) is an approach to the whole curriculum and management of a school, not a new subject. It has its roots in environmental education and development education. As a result, many of the building blocks of education for sustainable development are already present in every school.

Quite obviously geography has always provided many of the building blocks that can go to make up ESD. The web page recognises this by stating:

Geography is a focus within the curriculum for understanding and resolving issues about the environment and sustainable development. It can inspire pupils to think about their own place in the world, their values, and their rights and responsibilities to other people and the environment.

Horizons accepts this definition wholeheartedly and tries to provide even more of the 'building blocks', so ESD is integrated throughout the course, just like support for literacy, numeracy and so on.

The QCA web page describes the elements that go to make up ESD. These can be broken down as in the table below. In the **Horizons 1** and **2** *Teaching and Learning Resources* guide, page references were given in the table to show where the concepts, skills, etc. were dealt with. However, in **Horizons 3**, these aspects of ESD are interwoven throughout the whole book. Therefore, page references have not been provided for any aspects as ESD is fundamental to the whole course.

a Key concepts	(i)	interdependence
	(ii)	citizenship and stewardship
	(iii)	needs and rights of future generations
	(iv)	diversity
	(v)	quality of life
	(vi)	sustainable change
	(vii)	uncertainty and precaution
b Skills	(i)	critical thinking
	(ii)	finding information
	(iii)	weighing evidence
	(iv)	presenting rational argument on issues
c Personal and social development	(i)	an awareness of the needs of others
	(ii)	an appreciation of diverse viewpoints
d Global dimension	(i)	issues are investigated at a local, national and global scale
	(ii)	pupils are helped to understand the impact of the global dimension on their own lives
e Systems approach		the interactions between economic, social and environmental systems
f Range of viewpoints and opinions		exposure to many different ideas and views helps pupils to develop an awareness of the complexity of sustainable development issues, and helps them to develop their own attitudes towards such issues
g Futures		pupils are encouraged to consider possible and preferred futures

Developing geographical skills

The skills that should be developed during Key Stage 3 Geography are described in detail on the National Curriculum website at www.nc.uk.net

These can be summarised as:

1 In undertaking geographical enquiry, pupils should be taught to:

   a ask geographical questions and identify issues

   b suggest appropriate sequences of investigation

   c collect, record and present evidence

   d analyse and evaluate evidence and draw and justify conclusions

   e appreciate how people's values and attitudes, including their own, affect contemporary social, environmental, economic and political issues, and to clarify and develop their own values and attitudes about such issues

   f communicate in ways appropriate to the task and audience.

2 In developing geographical skills, pupils should be taught:

   a to use an extended geographical vocabulary

   b to select and use appropriate fieldwork techniques and instruments

   c to use atlases and globes, and maps and plans at a range of scales, including Ordnance Survey maps at 1:25 000 and 1:50 000

   d to select and use secondary sources of evidence, including photographs (including vertical and oblique aerial photographs), satellite images and evidence from ICT-based sources

   e to draw maps and plans at a range of scales, using symbols, keys and scales and to select and use appropriate graphical techniques to present evidence on maps and diagrams, including using ICT

   f to communicate in different ways, including using ICT

   g decision-making skills, including using ICT.

Obviously, many of these skills are generic and pupils are encouraged to use them throughout the book. Skills are integrated throughout **Horizons 3** and the rest of the series. The teaching and learning of skills follows a spiral approach with skills being introduced in early parts of the series and then being reinforced and developed later on. For example, Unit 1 of **Horizons 1** introduces techniques such as:

- describing photographs   on pages 4–5
- field sketching   on pages 10–11
- using grid references   on pages 18–19.

These skills are revisited, used and developed throughout **Horizons 2** and **3**.

The authors of **Horizons** felt that it was important that skills were totally integrated into pupils' work and not separated out. However, to give teachers some idea about the breadth of skills covered, the table below shows where specific skills are introduced in **Horizons 3**. The numbering system is used as listed in the National Curriculum document (left).

In **Horizons 3** pupils are encouraged to be more independent in using the skills they have developed earlier in the series. In particular, they should be encouraged to use them in extended enquiry work, such as on pages 11, 83, 99 and 123.

1 Enquiry skills	Pages/*Activity Sheets*
a Asking questions	11, 17, 24, 31, Unit 3, 65, 83, 97, 99, 101, 103, 109, 115, *1.4, 1.5, 2.1, 2.2, 3.3, 6.6*
b Planning an enquiry	11, 17, 31, 46, 83, 97, 99, 103, 122, *5.6, 5.13, 5.20, 6.17–6.20*
c Collecting data	11, 17, 31, 39, 46, 49, 53, 57, 65, 73, 83, 87, 97, 99, 103, 122, *1.13, 2.13, 3.4, 3.17, 3.18, 4.5, 4.6, 5.2, 5.4, 5.6, 5.13, 5.20, 6.17–6.20*
Presenting data	11, 17, 31, 46, 53, 65, 73, 83, 87, 97, 99, 103, 122, *2.13, 4.5, 4.6, 5.20, 6.17–6.20*
d Analysing data	11, 17, 31, 46, 53, 55, 57, 65, 73, 77, 79, 83, 87, 97, 99, 103, *2.13, 4.5, 4.6, 5.2, 5.4, 5.20, 6.17–6.20*
Writing conclusions	11, 17, 31, 46, 51, 53, 57, 63, 65, 73, 77, 79, 83, 87, 97, 99, 101, 103, 123, *2.13, 3.17, 3.18, 4.5, 4.6, 5.2, 5.4, 5.20, 6.17–6.20*
Evaluation	11, 17, 31, 53, 63, 77, 79, 83, 87, 97, 99, 101, 103, 123, *2.13, 6.17–6.20*

Opportunities for enquiry skills **e** and **f** are intrinsic to many aspects of the work in **Horizons**.

2 General geographical skills

Skill	Pages/*Activity Sheets*
b Fieldwork skills	39, 97, 99, 102, *5.20*
c Using atlases/atlas maps	5, 7, 11, 15, 17, 26, 43, 67, 75, 83, 87, 107, *1.9, 2.3, 2.4, 2.5, 4.19, 6.4, 6.5, 6.8*
d Using latitude and longitude	11
Describing photos	65, 70, 73, 75, 83, 101, *2.1, 2.2, 4.7, 4.13, 4.14, 4.18, 6.6*
Comparing photos	83, 119
Photo analysis and labelling	24, 31, 33, 45, 108, *3.1, 3.3, 6.16*
Using map scales	107, *5.15, 5.16*
Linking photos to maps	83, *6.7*
Using satellite images	44, 87, 106, 111, 115, 117, *6.7, 6.14*
e Completing/labelling diagrams	7, 71, *1.18*
Using maps at different scales	53, 106
Using map transformations	29
Describing mapped distributions	7, 49, 97, 107, *3.5, 3.6, 3.8, 3.11, 3.12, 3.13, 6.8*
Using climate maps	49, 75, 83, 87, *5.2, 5.4, 5.5*
Drawing climate graphs	75, *3.14*
Analysing climate graphs	75, *3.14, 4.8, 4.20*
Using climate statistics	51, 53, 75, 83
Drawing and using line graphs	51, 117, *3.9, 4.10*
Drawing and using triangular graphs	*3.10*
Analysing diagrams	73, *4.3, 4.4, 5.10, 5.11, 6.3*
Analysing population pyramids	*3.7*
g Decision-making skills	19, 22, 79

Other skills

Skill	Pages/*Activity Sheets*
Looking for trends in statistics	63, *3.7*
Using percentages	97
Ranking data	27, 28, 31, 35, 41, 43, *6.13*
Diamond ranking	*1.1, 2.6*
Averages	53
Drawing and using Venn diagrams	17, 45, 79, *1.3, 2.5, 3.16*
Using a timeline	35, 57, 77, *1.16*
Using an opinion line	*2.18, 3.20*
Using statistics in descriptions	37, 51, 95, *2.4, 2.21, 3.14, 5.2, 5.4, 6.2, 6.8*

Skill	Pages/*Activity Sheets*
Predicting future environments	87, 103, 117
Development indexes	29, 111
Development compass rose	*2.1*
Designing and carrying out a questionnaire	99
Matching captions	*1.7, 1.15, 2.11, 4.7, 4.8, 5.10, 6.3*
Living seismograph	*1.8*
Relational diagram	*1.10*
3-D model making	*1.19*
Analysing soil	*4.5, 4.6*

Opportunities for skills **a** and **f** are intrinsic to many aspects of the work in **Horizons**.

The ICT skills mentioned in **2e** and **2f** of the National Curriculum document are listed on pages 25–26 of this *Teaching and Learning Resources* guide.

Passport to the World

Geography has to survive in an education marketplace that is becoming more and more vocationally oriented.

Geography can never become a purely vocational subject. There are very few jobs for 'geographers'.

However, geographers have always known that their subject is an excellent way of starting to prepare for a whole variety of jobs. Many recruiters in a wide range of fields insist that geography is an excellent preparation for employment. Although people can complain and joke about geography's failure to teach about the location of capital cities, the recruiters still say that geography prepares people to:

- think
- solve problems
- see different sides of arguments
- understand the environment
- move beyond specialisation to see links between topics
- appreciate a world view, or a continental view
- use ICT and appreciate its importance in everyday working life

and so on.

Of course, as teachers of the subject we have always known that, but have we got the idea over to our Key Stage 3 pupils? Or have they seen geography as 'just a school subject'?

Has it then been too easy for pure vocational subjects to come along at the start of Key Stage 4 and sell themselves as new, relevant, exciting and, most importantly, as the key to good employment prospects?

And do we only start to emphasise the vocational benefits of studying geography in a last-ditch attempt to counter the appeal of the vocational subjects?

In **Horizons** we have made a very deliberate attempt to emphasise the vocational value of the subject right from the outset of Key Stage 3. This is done in a number of ways:

- Wherever possible the real work element of studies is emphasised. For instance:
  - links between geography and work in conservation are mentioned in Unit 4 Ecosystems
  - opportunities for work in development are mentioned in Unit 2 80:20 and Unit 6 Development or Destruction?
  - links between geography and work in disaster management are mentioned in Unit 1 Tectonics.
- In many places we have included 'Passport to the World' boxes. These contain little asides, drawing out the vocational aspects of the geography being studied. For example, on page 77 in Unit 4 Ecosystems is the box seen above right.

PASSPORT TO THE WORLD

Would you like to work in a National Park like Serengeti? It is obviously fair that local people have first choice of the jobs available, but you could gain experience of work like this by volunteering to work with an organisation like VSO or Farm Africa. They prefer volunteers who can offer some useful skills, so the best time to apply is when you have finished your higher education, but you could start thinking and planning now.

- The last unit in each of the three **Horizons** books is also called 'Passport to the World'. This tries to achieve a number of different but linked objectives:
  - it provides a plenary page as a 'farewell to the key stage', and perhaps even to geography as a separate subject
  - it suggests how geography at GCSE and A level helps prepare people for a wide range of courses and jobs
  - it shows how those jobs can either use geography directly or link to the subject indirectly
  - it also emphasises how a study of geography can lead on to a particular interest in travel, and all the opportunities that travelling presents to broaden experience and understanding of the world.

In addition, throughout the series **Horizons** has encouraged pupils to expand their horizons by using the internet for:

- practical purposes, such as downloading maps for a variety of uses
- helping with research into topics being studied
- discovery and exploration of the world.

We have tried to ensure that **Horizons** emphasises the practical nature of geography – showing that the subject is, indeed, a Passport to the World.

In fact it can be seen as:

- a Passport to the World of Work
- a Passport to the World of Leisure
- a Passport to the World of Tourism
- a Passport to the Cyberworld
- a Passport to life outside school.

Assessment for Learning

Assessment for Learning is a key part of the Key Stage 3 National Strategy. **Horizons** provides resources to help implement these strategies and offers suggestions to support associated changes in teaching styles and marking. These notes are designed as a brief introduction to Assessment for Learning and are not meant as an exhaustive or prescriptive framework. Although, by its nature, Assessment for Learning informs all aspects of the lesson, these notes aim to indicate where specific Assessment for Learning opportunities exist within lessons, so that teachers can help pupils to determine what they have learned and what they need to do next to improve upon current performance. Suggestions concerning teaching styles (e.g. questioning) and marking strategies are offered as a sample of good practice and may be employed as the teacher sees fit.

Horizons also supports Assessment *of* Learning (see Assessing Levels section on pages 50–51) and encourages the formative use of summative assessment (see below) to ensure that pupils and teachers make best use of the summative assessment process to identify areas for improvement in future work.

Further information on Assessment for Learning can be found on the QCA website (www.qca.org.uk/ages3-14/afl/294.html), from the Assessment reform group (www.assessment-reform-group.org.uk/), and in the Key Stage 3 Strategy 'Assessment for Learning' folder, a DfES publication (HMSO). Assessment for Learning reflects the work of Black and William in 'Inside the Black Box' (Black, P. and William, D. in *Inside the Black Box: raising standards through classroom assessment*) which can also be read on the QCA website.

- *Assessment **for** learning is also termed **formative assessment** and involves pupils and teachers identifying the next steps they need to take to be successful in their work.*

- *Assessment **of** learning is also known as **summative assessment** and focuses on determining where the pupil is in terms of expected learning.*

- *Summative assessment can have a formative context if it is used to identify the areas of performance that are currently weak and to inform the next steps on the route to improvement. This is termed the **formative use of summative assessment**.*

Most geography departments are well organised in terms of summative assessment, particularly at end-of-unit or end-of-stage testing. However, they are often deemed to be less secure when it comes to formative assessment in everyday lessons where the main focus is on giving effective feedback and helping pupils plan their next steps. As assessment for learning aims to help pupils identify where they are in their learning, and to help the teacher set appropriate curriculum targets for future learning, it plays a key role in improving pupil achievement.

Assessment for learning should:
- *be embedded in the teaching and learning and not a separate task;*
- *involve sharing lesson objectives with pupils;*
- *aim to help pupils to know the standards they are aiming for;*
- *involve pupils in peer and self assessment;*
- *provide feedback to pupils so that they recognise their next steps in learning and how to take them;*
- *involve pupils and teachers reviewing and reflecting on assessment data and information.*

Adapted from Assessment for Learning: beyond the black box, Assessment Reform Group (1999)

Although some aspect of Assessment for Learning is a component of most lessons, whether it is referred to by that term or not, *effective* Assessment for Learning must be planned as a part of the lesson structure. Pupils must understand the aim as well as the process if they are to be purposefully engaged in assessing their own progress. Assessment for Learning is not a process that is simply done *to* pupils as it necessarily requires their active participation and informed judgements. For instance, the key components of peer and self-assessment are dependent upon the participants (teachers *and* pupils) understanding the criteria for success and being able to identify tangible next steps to high-level performance. Whilst Assessment for Learning is much more than a series of techniques, it is possible to identify components or methods of teaching which engender the kind of active engagement with the assessment process that is likely to result in pupils being able to understand:

- where they are in their learning
- where they need to be, and
- what they have to do to get there.

Horizons has been designed to provide opportunities and suggest methods of teaching that will support teachers aiming to implement more effective Assessment for Learning. Ideas and resources are provided in the Pupil Books, *Teaching and Learning Resources* guides and on the *Electronic Resources CD-ROMs* that can be used or adapted by teachers to suit their own needs. These are referred to in the outlines below of the following components that may form part of an overall Assessment for Learning strategy:

- Strategies for early lessons in Key Stage 3
- Strategies in everyday lessons
- Questioning techniques
- Peer and self-assessment
- Formative use of summative assessments
- Marking and feedback strategies.

Throughout the **Horizons** Pupil Books there are many activities that lend themselves to Assessment for Learning and there are key summative assessments set up so that pupils can use the outcomes formatively to set targets for their next assessment. Many of these opportunities are identified on the opportunities for Assessment for Learning pages for each unit in this guide (see pages 55–56 for Unit 1, pages 88–89 for Unit 2, pages 121–122 for Unit 3, pages 153–154 for Unit 4, pages 187–188 for Unit 5 and pages 221–222 for Unit 6).

Strategies in everyday lessons

- Actively **share learning objectives** of a lesson with pupils by stating them explicitly or writing them on the board, flipchart, OHT or electronic whiteboard. These should be in child-friendly language to ensure that pupils understand what this learning experience is about. **Horizons** provides learning objectives for each double-page spread on the lesson plans (for teachers) and on PowerPoint slides on the *Electronic Resources CD-ROM* that may be customised and printed onto OHTs or projected onto a whiteboard (for pupils). The more actively these can be addressed, the more they are likely to be understood and their relevance to different parts of the lesson realised. Asking pupils to remember what the last lesson objectives were and to guess all or part of this lesson's objectives will help to engage some. Giving the objectives in mixed-up order and asking pupils which should come first could help get across the elements of progression planned for the lesson.

- Establish the **criteria for success** (assessment criteria) for a task in advance and share these with the pupils. Although the learning objectives explain the purpose of the lesson, the criteria for success should explain what the pupils need to do during any activity in language they can understand. This is essential if pupils are to judge their own work or that of peers. They also serve as guidance for setting targets for improvement. Again, these criteria may be written on the board, flipchart, worksheet, OHT or whiteboard. **Horizons** does not attempt to provide the criteria for success for every exercise in the Pupil Books as these may vary according to how the teacher uses these activities. Suitable criteria for success for any activity can be derived by studying the question and referring to the answers section on the lesson plan. For example, in 'What can virtual volcanoes tell us?' in Unit 1 Tectonics (pages 16–17), activity 3 asks pupils to plan a Microsoft PowerPoint report comparing two volcanoes. The criteria for success for the report should signal to the pupils what their report must contain. It may contain other things but these are the focus of the exercise. For example:

  Your work should include:
  1 *An annotated map locating your volcanoes.*
  2 *An explanation of why both areas are prone to volcanic eruptions.*
  3 *An evaluation of the effects of eruptions on both locations.*

- The **plenaries and debriefs** in the lesson plans suggest ways in which the lesson can be managed to give pupils time to think about what they have learned and how this may be applied in later learning in geography and beyond. When a particular skill has been developed that is more of a long-term objective (as opposed to the content-related aspects of the lesson) this should be drawn out and highlighted. For example, in 'Is your world moving you?' in Unit 1 Tectonics (pages 4–5), activity 3 asks pupils to identify the factors that they think determine whether people living in different parts of the world are at risk from earthquakes and/or volcanoes or not. This is a big question that is revisited several times during the unit.

- Self-esteem is easily damaged by constant reference to seemingly unattainable goals, so **Horizons** helps the teacher identify small steps to enable pupils to see their progress, thus building confidence and self-esteem. It does this by offering graduated tasks and opportunities for the pupil, with peers and teachers, to identify achievable 'next steps'.

- A significant part of the strength of Assessment for Learning approaches is that they give pupils more of the **ownership of the learning process**. This can be further encouraged by providing pupils with the information they need to set their next targets for improvement and to help them prepare for reviews of progress by identifying points they want to discuss. It can also be developed during Year 9 by regularly providing the class with model answers and analysing them.

- A wall display, possibly based on pupil work from a previous year, could be used at the start of Key Stage 3 to illustrate what pupils are aiming for as a benchmark for success. Annotating pieces of work can highlight what the key components of work in progess or successful finished products actually look like so that pupils learn to recognise these criteria and understand what they need to do to succeed. Seeing previous work used constructively in this way can also help to reinforce to pupils that thier work is valued.

- These strategies are not just for everyday lessons, however. Each unit in **Horizons** provides an Assessment for Learning framework and documentation to help pupils to set themselves learning targets for each unit and to review their progress against these targets as well as to self-assess their overall performance in the unit. This Assessment for Learning framework is outlined in more detail on the Assessment for Learning pages for each unit (see pages 55–56 for Unit 1, for example).

Questioning techniques

According to research, the average time teachers wait for an answer from a pupil in Britain is 0.9 seconds. This probably reflects a preponderance of closed and/or recall-based questions. Certainly these questions are useful ways of establishing knowledge and help to inject pace into lessons. However, higher levels of performance in Key Stage 3 require pupils to do more than recall and to this end **Horizons** utilises a wide range of questioning techniques which encourage a mix of question styles. More open-ended questions offer greater accessibility for a wider range of pupils and provide more opportunities for participation and testing of ideas.

The QCA guidance on Assessment for Learning (see www.qca.org.uk/ages3-14/afl) identifies a range of types of questions that are effective in providing assessment opportunities:

- *Why is … an example of … ?*
- *How can we be sure that … ?*
- *What is the same and what is different about … ?*
- *Is it ever/always true/false that … ?*
- *How do you … ?*

- *How would you explain … ?*
- *What does that tell us about … ?*
- *What is wrong with … ?*
- *Why is … true?*

www.qca.org.uk/ages3-14/afl/296.html

Horizons aims to raise awareness of the power of questioning in geography and to encourage an enquiry approach. Hence each double-page spread in the Pupil Book starts with a leading question. For example: *What are coral ecosystems like?* (Unit 4 Ecosystems, pages 66–67) or *How can we cut carbon emissions?* (Unit 5 Think – Act, pages 90–91).

In each case this leading question sets the scene for the two-page spread and frames the ensuing activities. At the end of the Over to You section, pupils should be able to answer the leading question. This is another way in which **Horizons** aims to link the pupils' thinking with the big questions that provide the structure for each unit.

Alongside specific questioning activities in the Pupil Book, such as activity 1 on page 47 of Unit 3 Comparing Countries – where pupils formulate questions as part of their route to enquiry – there are activity sheets dedicated to improving questioning techniques, such as Activity Sheet 3.3 What questions do we need to ask?

As a further support to teachers, key questions to test understanding and add extra challenge are provided in most lesson plans as suggestions of the kind of questions that teachers, or preferably pupils, should raise during that lesson. The aim is to make the pupils think about what they have learned and to test their understanding.

e.g. **Key questions**:

1 Why did so many rural migrants think they would have a better life in Mexico City?
2 How can the rate of population increase be falling if the population total is still rising?
3 Who is responsible for housing all the migrants?

The questioning strategies suggested in **Horizons** are meant to augment rather than replace the teacher's repertoire. Further effective questioning strategies (such as the no hands-up rule, mixing conscripts and volunteers and allowing for 'thinking time') are outlined in the Foundation Subjects folder ref. DfES 0350/2002.

Peer- and self-assessment

Peer- and self-assessment can be readily integrated into **Horizons** lessons and encourage greater pupil understanding of, and engagement with, the learning process. Peer-assessment is often seen as a developmental stage on the way to self-assessment which requires more independence. However, **Horizons** contains self-assessment techniques that are sufficiently well structured to allow pupils to assess their work in either individual Assessment Opportunities or over a whole unit against criteria for success or learning objectives (outlined in the Introduction to each unit in this guide, e.g. page 54 for Unit 1). The sections on opportunities for Assessment for Learning in each unit, e.g. pages 221–222 for Unit 6, outline some of the opportunities where peer-assessment is encouraged by the nature of the activity.

Where group work is employed, the peer- and self-assessment templates on pages 43–49 offer a convenient and adaptable framework to support pupils as they assess not only their collaborations in a wide range of activities but also how effectively they have managed the group work process. In the right-hand column the pupils identify what they will do to improve the next time they engage in a similar activity. This process is at the heart of effective Assessment for Learning.

Part of a completed exemplar for group work self-assessment:

How well did you…	1	2	3	4	5	Next time…
	Not very well			Very well		
Discuss what the task required before starting?			✔			We will have to think more about what is needed for a well structured presentation.
Listen to the views of everybody in the group?			✔			We will make sure everyone has a say.
Share the tasks out fairly between the group?		✔				Someone else will take a turn to choose who does what.
Check your progress against the criteria for success?		✔				This will happen during the lesson – not just at the end.

Peer-assessment tasks involve talk focused on the assessment criteria which encourages greater understanding of the activity being undertaken. For example, in Unit 3 Comparing Countries, on page 49 activity 1 pupils are asked to describe the topography of USA and Mexico from the physical geography map provided. A simple peer-assessment opportunity could involve pupils selecting their best descriptive sentence from the completed answers, swapping their work with their partner and assessing it against the criteria. The pupils can then check to see if it is the best description in their view. If they agree they can suggest an improvement for the selected description. If they disagree they can explain why another description is better. The pupils could amend their work accordingly. To reinforce the learning they could work out the key characteristics of a good geographical description, first as a pair and then as a class. The teacher could help them to link their ideas to the accepted criteria (e.g. clarity, specific factual detail, and comparison between different photos and/or parts of photos).

An alternative is to get pupils to devise their own criteria and mark scheme by asking them to say what they think a good written description of a photo should have.

Pupils could use the teacher's criteria to peer- or self-assess a piece of work before handing it in, by writing their feedback comments on the form and/or grading the work. Their evaluation can be judged by the teacher who could add formative comments. A variation on this might involve the pupils using the criteria to peer- or self-assess a piece of work after the teacher has marked it, but before they have given the grade and formative comments. Pupils are then more engaged in determining why the discrepancies in pupil and teacher grades exist and what they need to do to improve. See also the notes on 'Marking and feedback strategies' on page 38.

Assessment sheets for peer- and self-assessment of activities

The notes on 'Organising your group work assignments' (page 41) are specially written for pupils to introduce them to the fundamental principles of group work and also to point out the ways in which the Assessment Sheets can be used, whether as 'criteria for success' at the start of an exercise or as a framework for evaluation on completion. Page 42 offers a completed example of a generic group work self-assessment for modelling if required.

The Assessment Sheets provided are as follows:

Group Work Activity (generic)	page 43
Investigation or Enquiry	page 44
Poster Activity	page 45
Presentation Activity	page 46
Decision-making Exercise or Role-play Activity	page 47
Oral Discussion	page 48
Mystery Activity	page 49

These Assessment Sheets are also provided in Word on the *Planning CD-ROM*. This enables teachers to customise the templates to suit their own needs or the needs of their pupils. The criteria can be adapted or reduced to make the process more accessible for any pupils who need extra support. Alternatively the templates can be adapted to suit the particular activity that pupils are undertaking. For example, the Assessment Sheet for a Presentation Activity includes criteria for assessing both the preparation and delivery of a presentation. However, if teachers want pupils to assess only the actual presentation itself, the questions on planning and considering the audience can be deleted from the template. Once they are familiar with the process, pupils can be asked to decide for themselves which criteria are relevant for the particular activity in hand.

It is worth noting that these Assessment Sheets also provide a convenient vehicle for recording performance in non-written work, such as collaborative working and oral discussion, to include in a pupil's portfolio for Key Stage 3 Geography. These sheets can provide written evidence to contribute to the end-of-stage assessment of their individual level of attainment.

The formative use of summative assessment

The Assessment Opportunities in each unit in **Horizons** provide the main summative assessments, but there is a wide variety of activities that may be used as summative assessment opportunities. While the assigning of grades to such work is a regular component of monitoring progress within a subject, it does not in itself necessarily help the pupil to identify how to improve. There are many opportunities to use the summative assessment process in a more formative manner that does enable pupils to identify what they need to do to get better.

The Assessing Levels section on pages 50–51 explains how the main Assessment Opportunity activities can be used for summative assessment in each unit. However, the Assessment Opportunity sheets for these activities (e.g. pages 60–65 for Unit 1) also allow pupils to set their targets, record their levels and, possibly in conjunction with the Attainment Targets for that topic (e.g. pages 58–59 for Unit 1) or a relevant Assessment Sheet (see above), identify which aspects of their work they must concentrate on to be more successful in subsequent assignments. This is a more formative use of a summative assessment. By asking pupils to mark their work before the teacher does or before grades are released (as outlined above in peer and self-assessment) the pupils are justifying their marks in a way that encourages them to relate what they have written to the criteria for success. Over time this reinforces the need to keep those criteria in mind whilst constructing answers. Where the teacher's grade differs from the pupil grade, the latter has the responsibility to use the criteria and teacher comments to determine why this is the case and to set targets to reflect this.

Marking and feedback strategies

Marking policies vary from school to school and **Horizons** clearly cannot suggest how pupil's work should be marked. However, the role of both marking and feedback in maintaining progress in learning is too important to ignore. In particular the more formative use of marking and feedback as a means of clarifying what the pupil needs to do next and/or as a way of helping the pupil to determine what they do or do not know, is inextricably linked with the Assessment for Learning agenda.

A lot of marking reiterates the pupils' summative achievement represented by the grade and does little in terms of pointing the way forward for the pupil.

> *Well done Martin. You have compiled a well-structured argument using a wide range of sources. Your work is well presented, covering many of the main issues.*

or

> *You have missed the point of the question and failed to cover the important issues. You must do something about your presentation, and particularly your spelling.*

There is a growing amount of research evidence to suggest that marking with grades tells the pupil little about how to improve; and marking with grades and comments results in the learner valuing the grade and largely ignoring formative comments. Marking that is largely summative in nature has a tendency to confirm the self-image of a learner ('I always do badly – what's the point?' or 'I always do well enough – what's the point?'). By separating the grade from the feedback, the pupil is required to read feedback before knowing the grade and is thus more likely to act upon the formative comments that help them define their next steps. Alternatively, teachers can be very clear in the layout of the feedback *which part* confirms/justifies the grade (summative) and *which part* aims to help pupils improve their work (formative); pupils are encouraged to concentrate on the latter.

The use of constructive feedback using phrases such as:
'You might find it will help if you … '
'One thing I'd like you to do … '

'For your next description … '
'Next time see if you can add … '

provides a useful way to structure the next steps to ensure improvement.

Formative feedback may often take the part of questions to encourage the self-assessment process:

- 'Which of the three photos was most like the source and why … ?'
- 'Are meanders only found near the mouth … ?'
- 'In which photo was erosion more important than deposition … ?'

All encourage the pupil to think about their answers again and, if they are linked to an expectation that replies will be used – perhaps to re-evaluate the grade of work – such questions do tend to be answered.

End of Key Stage 3 assessment

The advice and support offered throughout **Horizons 1**, **2** and **3** should enable teachers to make reliable and accurate assessments of pupil attainment. This is particularly supported by the levelling of the end of unit assessment opportunity exercises. These may involve peer- and self-assessment but are also designed to allow teachers to make judgements concerning the levels pupils are working at. The variety of assessment tasks has been specifically chosen to cover all of the attainment targets in Key Stage 3 geography as outlined in the specification.

Each assessment highlights certain aspects within the attainment targets to help clarify the teaching and assessment focus. This can help to judge work indicative of specific levels of attainment for the aspect(s) of geography covered (see the criteria for success for each assessment). By separating out these aspects, they become easier for pupils to understand and, for the teacher, planning for progression is made simpler. However, when looking across a range of work from one pupil and considering what judgement to make at the end of the key stage, it is necessary to use the level description as a whole and to make a best-fit judgement.

The statutory requirement to determine a 'final' end of key stage National Curriculum level towards the end of Year 9, usually ready by May, means that teachers must reflect on the levelled assignments recorded so far and use them in part or in whole to assign a level. This final summative judgement of the full range of pupil attainment should consider evidence from a variety of activities, some of which may come from other class work, oral, group or fieldwork experiences that are not specifically the subject of the end of unit assessments. However, as indicators of levels of attainment, the end of unit assessments are extremely useful and can help to chart progression and inform the overall National Curriculum level for each pupil.

The units are presented in a logical manner to support progression of skills, knowledge and understanding through the key stage. While it is possible to follow the teaching and assessment schedule as outlined in the **Horizons** schemes of work, it is recognised that,

because of time constraints, some teachers may decide to cover and assess only some of the units and/or assessments on offer in the **Horizons** schemes of work.

Teachers may also:

- decide early on in Year 9 if the current range of completed assessments reflects adequately the full range of pupil attainment
- select Year 9 topics and assessments to ensure a balanced portfolio of assessed work, which will cover all the necessary targets to enable pupils to access the higher levels.

The table on page 40 shows which themes in the attainment targets are covered best by which assignments.

While the **Horizons** assessments offer a wide range of assessment opportunities, there is flexibility for teachers to determine what is best for their classes. However, time constraints may mean that it is not possible to cover and assess every unit in **Horizons**. Therefore, some **Horizons 3** units may be taught after the overall end of key stage level has been assigned. These units may contain aspects of geography and assessment opportunities the teacher feels have a higher priority than others. For example, if it is felt that pupils have not had sufficient opportunities to demonstrate their knowledge, skills and understanding of environmental change and sustainable development, Unit 2 80:20, Unit 5 Think – Act or Unit 6 Development or Destruction? might be more suitable for assessment than Unit 3 Comparing Countries, the assessment opportunity for which is focused more on enquiry skills. These are important considerations as there is evidence from Ofsted that pupils often receive lower levels for their assessed assignments than their overall work deserves. One of the key reasons may be the result of 'capping', whereby the setting of some assessment tasks, with an emphasis on lower-order skills, prevents pupils from demonstrating their full abilities. For example, if higher levels of attainment include requirements to demonstrate the ability to ask geographical questions and show independence in planning enquiry work, there must be opportunities for pupils to be assessed on these aspects of their work.

By using the **Horizons** schemes of work and assessments flexibly, teachers can plan for progression and coverage in terms of skills, knowledge and understanding of the main aspects in geography. They will derive end of key stage judgements of pupil performance that not only reflect the full range of attainment but that also support and inform learning in the process.

Theme	Horizons 1						Horizons 2						Horizons 3					
	Unit 1	Unit 2	Unit 3	Unit 4	Unit 5	Unit 6	Unit 1	Unit 2	Unit 3	Unit 4	Unit 5	Unit 6	Unit 1	Unit 2	Unit 3	Unit 4	Unit 5	Unit 6
	Fieldwork enquiry	DME/persuasive letter	Photo analysis	Comparing floods UK/Bangladesh	Employment structures and development	Tour of the UK	How do coastal defences affect people?	New supermarket location DME/report writing	How do you use ICT for enquiry?	How has Spain changed?	Limestone walk	Surfing mystery/discursive writing	Saving San Sebastian DME	Niger report	John Doe mystery	Ecosystem display	Recycling action plan	Deforestation report
Enquiry and skills	S	S	S	M	M	S	M	S	S	M	M	S	S	M	S	M	M	M
Knowledge of places	S	S	L	M	M	S	S	S	S	S	S	L	L	S	L	S	S	S
Knowledge of patterns and processes	L	M	S	S	S	L	S	M	L	S	S	M	M	M	M	S	S	S
Environmental change and sustainable development	L	M	M	M	L	L	M	L	L	L	M	L	L	S	L	S	S	S

S	Strong focus
M	Medium focus
L	Low focus

Group Work

Organising your group work assignments

When you are involved in group work you need to think carefully about the task. What is it the task or question wants you to do? One of the best ways of deciding this is to imagine what your finished project will be like. It doesn't matter if you are preparing a written answer, a talk or a poster; the 'end product' should be clearly visible in your mind. Once you have the final version in sight you can think about how you are going to get there, step by step.

Think of it as a recipe! Imagine a loaf of bread, just out of the oven, crusty and still warm. It's the finished item but how did it get to look like that?

- Ingredients – flour, water, yeast, butter, salt, sugar, milk powder.
- Mixing – ingredients added together, in order, with some like the yeast being involved very early on.
- Kneading – being worked on until all the ingredients have blended.
- Proving – given time to rise but being assessed to check for problems as well.
- Cooking – in a pre-heated oven and in a bread tin, to shape the bread into the loaf shape that most people like.

A skilled baker can make this look easy. But it isn't magic. It is a series of actions or processes done at the right time and in the right order. It depends upon selecting the right ingredients or components. The final product is there for all to judge or assess, but what we don't see is the small judgements or assessments the baker made along the way. The criteria for success (shape, taste, colour etc.) were all in the baker's head but he/she followed the recipe or instructions and checked them regularly. This was especially true when the baker did it the first time.

Think about your task as a group.
- What are the components of the task (e.g. title, introduction, tables, paragraphs, options, annotated images, speakers' notes, conclusion)?
- What will you need to find out (e.g. background facts or detailed information on specific issues)?
- How long have you have got to complete – what will you have done in 10 minutes in a single lesson task? Or by the end of each lesson if it is a longer project?
- Who will be responsible for what? Often, there is no need for everyone to do the same task, and it may be useful to give specific tasks to each person.
- How will you know when each task is finished – what will it look like?
- How will you decide what is the best way to present your work?
- What will you do to make it even better next time?

Your teacher may give you an Assessment Sheet *before* a group work task or *after* you have completed a group work exercise. You need to know if you are assessing yourself or your peers (classmates).

- If you receive it **before starting** you can use the comments in the left-hand column as pointers as to what you will need to do when you start.
  e.g. If the evaluation question is 'How well did you … Listen to the views of everybody in the group?' – then you know you will need to plan opportunities for everyone to have their say during the exercise.
- If you receive it **after finishing** you can use the comments in the left-hand column as pointers as to judge how well you did these tasks.
  e.g. If the evaluation question is 'How well did you… Discuss what the task required before starting?' – then you can judge how well you did this. If it wasn't done very well then you can decide what you will need to change to make sure it's better next time.

With a self-assessment sheet you will concentrate on your contribution to the group work. With a peer-assessment sheet you should reflect on how well the group worked together. You may not do everything right straight away but being realistic about what you have achieved will help you to decide on the next steps.

You may not need to use all of the comments in the left-hand column for every group work task. Your teacher will tell you which ones are applicable.

Assessment Sheet
Group Work Activity

Activity: _Saving San Sebastian DME_

Date: _6/6/06_   Marker: _Dan Tyler_

Who are you assessing?   Yourself ✔   Classmate ☐   Group ✔

How well did you ...	Not very well — 1	2	3	Very well — 4	5	How will you improve next time?
Discuss what the task required before starting? (criteria for success)			✔			We will have to think more about what is needed for a well structured presentation.
Listen to the views of everybody in the group?			✔			We will make sure everyone has a say.
Share out the tasks fairly between members of the group?		✔				Someone else will take a turn to choose who does what.
Check your progress against the criteria for success?		✔				This will happen during the lesson — not just at the end.
Think about the process and explain or justify your choices?				✔		We will justify all decisions.
Evaluate your finished work?	✔					We will have to give more time to this.
Express your own ideas and points of view?			✔			I need to contribute to each part of the exercise.
Explain your own ideas and points of view?		✔				Some of my ideas must be more clearly explained.
All contribute to any presentation of the group's work to the class?			✔			Different tasks will be given to people in the group to get experience.
Personally contribute to any presentation or discussion?				✔		I did the Introduction this time, but will help to draw things together in the conclusion next time.

What did you enjoy most about this piece of work?

Putting together the display for the presentation and trying to convince others why our route was best.

What do you think is the main lesson you will learn from this piece of work?

Use the display to support what you say – but talk to the audience not the display!

Any other comments?

Talk slowly and clearly. Don't assume the audience know anything – try to convince them.

Assessment Sheet

Group Work Activity

Activity: [   ]

Date: [   ] Marker: [   ]

Who are you assessing? Yourself [ ] Classmate [ ] Group [ ]

How well did you ...	Not very well 1	2	3	4	Very well 5	How will you improve next time?
Discuss what the task required before starting? (criteria for success)						
Listen to the views of everybody in the group?						
Share out the tasks fairly between members of the group?						
Check your progress against the criteria for success?						
Think about the process and explain or justify your choices?						
Evaluate your finished work?						
Express your own ideas and points of view?						
Explain your own ideas and points of view?						
All contribute to any presentation of the group's work to the class?						
Personally contribute to any presentation or discussion?						
What did you enjoy most about this piece of work?						
What do you think is the main lesson you will learn from this piece of work?						
Any other comments?						

Assessment Sheet

Investigation or Enquiry

Activity:

Date: Marker:

Who are you assessing?   Yourself [ ]   Classmate [ ]   Group [ ]

How well did you ...	Not very well 1	2	3	4	Very well 5	How will you improve next time?
Discuss what the task required before starting?						
Share out the tasks or roles fairly between members of the group?						
Check your progress against the criteria for success?						
Discuss the aims of the enquiry as a group?						
Discuss the steps and methods to use in the enquiry?						
Collect the information (primary and secondary evidence)?						
Present your findings?						
Analyse the results as a group?						
Describe and explain your feelings?						
Offer a conclusion to the enquiry?						
Evaluate the whole investigation?						
Express your own ideas and points of view?						
Explain your own ideas and points of view?						
All contribute to any presentation or discussion?						
What did you enjoy most about this piece of work?						
What do you think is the main lesson you will learn from this piece of work?						
Any other comments?						

Assessment Sheet

Poster Activity

Activity: [   ]

Date: [   ]   Marker: [   ]

Who are you assessing?   Yourself [ ]   Classmate [ ]   Group [ ]

How well did you ...	Not very well 1	2	3	Very well 4	5	How will you improve next time?
Discuss what the task required before starting?						
Share out the tasks fairly between members of the group?						
Plan the layout of the poster before starting?						
Plan the content of the poster before starting?						
Consider what is required for your audience (e.g. your class, the whole school or other people)?						
Make sure the design elements fitted the task (e.g. title, aim/intro, bullets points)?						
Make sure that all the text was readable by the rest of the class?						
Choose eye-catching images?						
Lay out the parts so that they follow a sequence?						
Check your progress against the criteria for success?						
Evaluate your finished work?						
Express your own ideas and points of view?						
Explain your own ideas and points of view?						
All contribute to any presentation or discussion?						
What did you enjoy most about this piece of work?						
What do you think is the main lesson you will learn from this piece of work?						
Any other comments?						

Assessment Sheet

Presentation Activity

Activity:

Date: Marker:

Who are you assessing?   Yourself ☐   Classmate ☐   Group ☐

How well did you ...	Not very well 1	2	3	Very well 4	5	How will you improve next time?
Discuss what the task required before starting?						
Share out the tasks fairly between members of the group?						
Plan the structure of the presentation before starting?						
Plan the content of the presentation before starting?						
Consider what is required for your audience (e.g. your class, the whole school or other people)?						
Prepare your speaker's notes?						
Make sure that all the speeches addressed the task?						
Check your progress against the criteria for success?						
Speak clearly and confidently?						
Start with a clear introduction to explain what you were presenting?						
Present the components so that they follow a logical sequence?						
Offer a conclusion to sum up your ideas?						
Answer any questions from the class or teacher?						
Express your own ideas and points of view?						
All contribute to any presentation or discussion?						
What did you enjoy most about this piece of work?						
What do you think is the main lesson you will learn from this piece of work?						
Any other comments?						

Assessment Sheet

Decision-making Exercise or Role-play Activity

Activity:

Date: Marker:

Who are you assessing?   Yourself ☐   Classmate ☐   Group ☐

How well did you ...	Not very well 1	2	3	4	Very well 5	How will you improve next time?
Discuss what the task required before starting?						
Share out the tasks or roles fairly between members of the group?						
Check your progress against the criteria for success?						
Discuss the problem or situation as a group?						
Explain the problem or situation at the start?						
Discuss all the options as a group?						
Outline the advantages and disadvantages of each option?						
Use the opinions of the group to choose the best option?						
Justify your choice by offering points *for* as well as points *against*?						
Offer a conclusion to sum up your ideas?						
Answer any questions from the class or teacher?						
Express your own ideas and points of view?						
Explain your own ideas and points of view?						
All contribute to any presentation or discussion?						
What did you enjoy most about this piece of work?						
What do you think is the main lesson you will learn from this piece of work?						
Any other comments?						

Assessment Sheet

Oral Discussion

Activity:

Date: Marker:

Who are you assessing?   Yourself ☐   Classmate ☐   Group ☐

How well did you ...	Not very well 1	2	3	4	Very well 5	How will you improve next time?
Discuss what the task required before starting?						
Make sure that everyone took part in the discussion?						
Listen to the views of everybody in the group?						
Ask questions about the comments you heard from members of the group?						
Revise your comments in the light of group comments?						
Check your progress against the criteria for success?						
Stay focused on the main issue being discussed?						
Evaluate your discussion?						
Express your own ideas and points of view?						
Explain your own ideas and points of view?						
All contribute to any whole class discussion or presentation to others?						
What did you enjoy most about this piece of work?						
What do you think is the main lesson you will learn from this piece of work?						
Any other comments?						

Assessment Sheet

Mystery Activity

Activity:

Date: Marker:

Who are you assessing?   Yourself ☐   Classmate ☐   Group ☐

How well did you ...	Not very well			Very well		How will you improve next time?
	1	2	3	4	5	
Discuss what the mystery question was about before starting?						
Read the information on the cards before deciding on an answer?						
Share out the tasks fairly between members of the group?						
Work as a group to decide on the most and least relevant pieces of information?						
Listen to each other when discarding information?						
Use the opinions of the group to construct a possible solution?						
Justify your solution by offering evidence in support as well as accepting that some evidence did not fit your theory?						
Offer a conclusion to sum up your ideas?						
Answer any questions from the class or teacher?						
Revise your ideas following comments from others?						
Express your own ideas and points of view?						
Explain your own ideas and points of view?						
All contribute to any presentation or discussion?						
What did you enjoy most about this piece of work?						
What do you think is the main lesson you will learn from this piece of work?						
Any other comments?						

Other pages in this *Teaching and Learning Resources* guide show how the National Curriculum descriptions of the Levels of Attainment can be used as part of a formative assessment process. For instance, you can see how parts of the Level descriptors, or adaptations of the descriptors, can be used for that process in Unit 1 Tectonics on pages 58–65 in this guide.

However, that was not the use for which the Level descriptions were written. They were designed for summative assessment at the end of each Key Stage. Some people think that is still the main or even the only place where they should be used.

In **Horizons** we feel sure that it is possible to use the Level Statements in far more varied and constructive ways than was originally intended. To do this, though, we felt it was necessary to put the Level Statements through two processes:

- First we *deconstructed* the Level Statements – largely for the benefit of teachers.
- Then we *translated* them – mainly for the pupils' benefit.

Deconstructing the Levels

When the time comes to make the final summative assessment for the Key Stage, teachers are advised to read the Level Statements as a whole, and to match pupil performance to the full statements. However, during the course it is important that teachers, parents and pupils know what is being achieved, and what targets still need to be set. At some times teachers will need to aim work at particular elements of the statements. Most lessons, and most parts of **Horizons**, are aimed at particular elements, rather than aiming generally at the statements as a whole.

The table on pages 52–53 shows the Level Criteria for Key Stage 3 broken down into separate elements. Readers should be able to follow elements across the table, through the Levels, and see how each element develops.

The first main division is into *Enquiry and Skills* and *Places and Environments*. Places and Environments has been further subdivided into *Environmental management* and *Places*. It is hoped that this subdivision will allow teachers to analyse each piece of work that their pupils do, and to see how it contributes to their overall progress through the Levels of Attainment.

Translating the Levels

As stated above, the Level Statements can be useful for teachers, pupils and parents, but even teachers find them difficult to work with in their original form. If pupils and their parents are to make real use of them, the statements need translating. **Horizons** does this in the *Teaching and Learning Resources* for each unit.

The Level Statements relevant to each unit are provided in the Learning Plan for each unit (see page 57 for an example). These have been translated into more pupil-friendly language. They can be used to give pupils a medium-term objective for their work on that unit.

Then these statements have been adapted and made even more pupil friendly in the specific Assessment Opportunity for each unit. Pages 61–62 show one example of Level Statements adapted to fit one particular set of activities in the book. Whilst pupils are working through this set of activities they can use the specific Level Statements to assess their work and to set themselves targets for improvement.

To translate the Statements into pupil-friendly language we:

- changed the person to whom they were addressed: 'pupils' became 'I' throughout
- changed the verb structure so that statements become 'can do' statements of achievement
- shortened and simplified sentences
- concentrated on specific outcomes instead of generalisations.

How do pupils use the Level Statements?

Pupils can use these simplified versions of the statements in several ways. The following two uses are clearly linked to aspects of the **Horizons** Pupil Book:

- the fuller statements, given in the Learning Plan, to set medium-term targets for the unit
- the reduced statements, given in the Assessment Opportunity, to set short-term targets for a particular piece of work.

Having targeted objectives in their work, and being aware of the way they can progress through the Levels, should help pupils. Progress should be much easier than when they are working in the dark trying to work their way through Levels which they may not know and which they probably do not understand.

How do teachers use the Level Statements?

There is a lot of help for teachers on using the Level Statements for summative assessment. Of particular importance is the National Curriculum in Action (NCA) website at www.ncaction.org.uk/. This can provide a lot of help with using the Level Statements for assessment. The geography section states:

- *You will arrive at judgements by taking into account strengths and weaknesses in performance across a range of contexts and over a period of time, rather than focusing on a single piece of work.*

- *A single piece of work will not cover all the expectations set out in a Level description. It will probably provide partial evidence of attainment in one or two aspects of a Level description. If you look at it alongside other pieces of work covering a range of contexts you will be able to make a judgement about which level best fits a pupil's overall performance.*

- *... when you are looking across a range of work from one pupil and considering what judgement to make, it* *is necessary, and indeed easier, to use the Level description as a whole.*

- *At Key Stage 3, much of the information about a pupil's performance will be based on knowledge of their work in Year 9. However ... it may be necessary to give some consideration to significant achievements displayed in earlier work from Year 7 or 8.*

In other words, right from the start of Key Stage 3 you can start looking for evidence that could be used to support your decisions on pupil achievement at the end of the Key Stage. Some pieces of work might provide crucial evidence of attainment in some aspects of the Level Statements. You will only make your final decision much later, but good work in key areas might need to be saved towards the pupil's portfolio for assessment.

Equally important throughout Key Stage 3 is looking for evidence that might help your recording and reporting of progress. You might be asked to do this for parents, for whole-school record-keeping, or just for departmental purposes. Whatever your purpose, **Horizons** provides opportunities and guidance on assessing levels in at least one piece of work in every unit of the series (see the list of Assessment Opportunities for **Horizons 3** below).

Each assessed piece of work is matched against parts of the targets set out in the table on pages 52–53. The NCA website advises teachers to focus on the holistic view when making the end of Key Stage assessment of a pupil's progress level but, when planning what material to assess during the Key Stage, it is important to check exactly which parts of the statements are being covered by each piece of assessed work. That is the only safe way to make sure that a balanced final assessment can be made.

How does Horizons help you make your assessments?

The *Teaching and Learning Resources* guides for **Horizons** have detailed advice on levelled assessment for one piece of work in every unit in each book. The Assessment Opportunities for **Horizons 3** are as follows:

Unit	Activity in Pupil Book	*Teaching and Learning Resources Guide*
Unit 1 Tectonics	Saving San Sebastian DME	pages 60–65
Unit 2 80:20	Niger report	pages 93–97
Unit 3 Comparing Countries	John Doe mystery	pages 126–130
Unit 4 Ecosystems	Ecosystem display	pages 158–164
Unit 5 Think – Act	Recycling action plan	pages 192–198
Unit 6 Development or Destruction?	Deforestation report	pages 226–234

In each case **Horizons** provides:

- introductory advice for pupils to explain how they can be helped to attain their best possible level in the assessed piece of work
- extracts from the NC Attainment Statements, expressed in terms that are addressed to pupils, showing what is being assessed
- advice for pupils on target setting for the assessed piece of work
- model answers, sometimes linked to the Levels, but usually just showing examples of good work, better work, and then even better work! These can be modelled by teachers at the start of the activity to help pupils set their targets, or be used by pupils as part of a self- or peer-assessment exercise.

In each unit the process of assessment is described in detail. A large amount of support is provided for both pupils and teachers. It would be impractical to use *all* of this material with any one class. Teachers will obviously need to pick and choose from what is on offer. Many teachers will feel that they need to adapt and develop the material, tailoring it to their own particular needs. However, it is hoped that the material will provide a very useful starting point for assessment, giving support to both pupils and teachers where it is needed.

Attainment Targets for Key Stage 3

		Level 2 Pupils:	**Level 3** Pupils:	**Level 4** Pupils:	**Level 5** Pupils:
Places and Environments	**Places**	• show their knowledge, skills and understanding in studies at a local scale • describe physical and human features of places, and recognise and make observations about those features that give places their character • show an awareness of places beyond their own locality	• show their knowledge, skills and understanding in studies at a local scale • describe and compare the physical and human features of different localities and offer explanations for the locations of some of these features • are aware that different places may have both similar and different characteristics	• show their knowledge, understanding and skills in studies of a range of places and environments, at more than one scale and in different parts of the world • begin to recognise and describe patterns and to appreciate the importance of wider geographical location in understanding places • recognise and describe physical and human processes • begin to understand how these processes can change the features of places, and how these changes can affect the lives and activities of people living there	• show their knowledge, understanding and skills in relation to studies of a range of places and environments, at more than one scale and in different parts of the world • describe and begin to explain geographical patterns and physical and human processes • describe how these processes can lead to similarities and differences in the environments of different places and in the lives of people who live there • recognise some of the links and relationships that make places dependent on each other
	Environmental management	• express views on the environment of a locality and recognise how people affect the environment	• offer reasons for some of their observations and judgements about places and environments • recognise how people seek to improve and sustain environments	• understand how people can both improve and damage the environment • explain their own views and the views that other people hold about an environmental change	• suggest explanations for ways in which human activities cause changes in the environment and the different views that people hold about them • recognise how people try to manage environments sustainably
Enquiry and Skills		• carry out simple tasks and select information using resources that are given to them • use this information and their own observations to ask and respond to questions about places and environments • begin to use appropriate geographical vocabulary	• use skills and sources of evidence to respond to a range of geographical questions • begin to use appropriate vocabulary to communicate their findings	• drawing on their knowledge and understanding, suggest suitable geographical questions for study • use a range of geographical skills, drawn from the Key Stage 2 or Key Stage 3 Programme of Study, to help them investigate places and environments • use primary sources of evidence in their investigations and communicate their findings using appropriate vocabulary	• drawing on their knowledge and understanding, select and use appropriate skills and ways of presenting evidence to help them investigate places and environments • explain their own views and begin to suggest relevant geographical questions and issues • select information and sources of evidence, suggest plausible conclusions to their investigations and present their findings both graphically and in writing

Level 6 Pupils:

- show their knowledge, understanding and skills in studies of a wide range of places and environments at various scales, from local to global, and in different parts of the world

- describe and explain a range of physical and human processes and recognise that these processes interact to produce the distinctive characteristics of places

- describe ways in which processes operating at different scales create geographical patterns and lead to changes in places

- appreciate the many links and relationships that make places dependent on each other

---

- recognise how conflicting demands on the environment may arise and describe and compare different approaches to managing environments

- appreciate that different values and attitudes, including their own, result in different approaches that have different effects on people and places

---

- drawing on their knowledge and understanding, suggest relevant geographical questions and issues and appropriate sequences of investigation

- select a range of skills and sources of evidence and use them effectively in their investigations

- present their findings in a coherent way and reach conclusions that are consistent with the evidence

Level 7 Pupils:

- show their knowledge, understanding and skills in studies of a wide range of places and environments at various scales, from local to global, and in different parts of the world

- describe interactions within and between physical and human processes and show how these interactions create geographical patterns and help change places and environments

---

- understand that many factors, including people's values and attitudes, influence the decisions made about places and environments, and use this understanding to explain the resulting changes

- appreciate that the environment in a place, and the lives of the people who live there, are affected by actions and events in other places

- recognise that human actions, including their own, may have unintended environmental consequences and that change sometimes leads to conflict

- appreciate that considerations of sustainable development affect the planning and management of environments and resources

---

- with growing independence, draw on their knowledge and understanding to identify geographical questions and issues and establish their own sequence of investigation

- select and use accurately a wide range of skills

- evaluate critically sources of evidence, present well-argued summaries of their investigations and begin to reach substantiated conclusions

Level 8 Pupils:

- show their knowledge, understanding and skills in studies of a wide range of places and environments at various scales, from local to global, and in different parts of the world

- offer explanations for interactions within and between physical and human processes

- explain changes in the characteristics of places over time, in terms of location, physical and human processes, and interactions with other places

- begin to account for disparities in development and understand the range and complexity of factors that contribute to the quality of life in different places

---

- recognise the causes and consequences of environmental issues and understand a range of different views about them and different approaches to tackling them

- understand how considerations of sustainable development can affect their own lives as well as the planning and management of environments and resources (they use examples to illustrate this)

- drawing on their knowledge and understanding, show independence in identifying appropriate geographical questions and issues, and in using an effective sequence of investigation

- select a wide range of skills and use them effectively and accurately

- evaluate critically sources of evidence before using them in their investigations

- present full and coherently argued summaries of their investigations and reach substantiated conclusions

1 Tectonics

Unit 1 of the Pupil Book is supported by:

- photocopiable activity sheets and assessment for learning materials in this *Teaching and Learning Resources* guide on pages 55–86

- customisable unit and lesson plans on the accompanying *Planning CD-ROM* attached to the inside front cover of this guide

- visual resources, presentations and interactive activities on the *Electronic Resources CD-ROM* using the Just Click teaching solution.

Just Click!

In this section of the *Teaching and Learning Resources* guide you will find:

Pages 55–56... have a list of opportunities for **Assessment for Learning** in this unit. One example is provided for each double-page spread. These ideas are based on activities in the Pupil Book, but each activity needs some development if it is to be used as an Assessment for Learning opportunity. Most of the suggestions involve pupils in assessment of their own work, in peer-assessment, or in some other form of discussion of the work either before or after it is attempted. All these suggestions are intended to increase pupils' awareness of what characterises good work, and of how their own work can be developed and improved.

The suggestions here are not intended to be prescriptive. Rather they provide teachers with opportunities that we feel fit the best practice of Assessment for Learning, and which target pupils' learning – an increasingly important area of focus under the new Ofsted inspection framework.

Page 57... is a **Learning Plan** for pupils, which gives them a copy of the learning objectives for the unit – copied from page 4 of the Pupil Book – and provides opportunities for pupils to assess their prior learning and set their targets for the whole unit, using the Attainment Targets on pages 58–59 as criteria for success. There is an opportunity at the end of the unit for pupils to re-assess their level against the Attainment Targets before completing the final self-assessment form (How far have I travelled?) on page 66.

Pages 58–59... give pupils a summary of the **Attainment Target** statements, adapted from the National Curriculum level descriptors, which are relevant to their work in this unit. Pupils can use the levels as criteria for success to set themselves learning targets for the unit and check their progress using the Learning Plan on page 57. They have also been divided into two sections, *Places and Environments* and *Enquiry and Skills*. Pupils should be able to see what it is that allows their work to move from one level to the higher level. These Attainment Targets can also be used to provide further support if required for pupils setting and reviewing their targets in the Assessment Opportunity for this unit (see below).

Pages 60–63... are also written for pupils. They describe the **Assessment Opportunity** on pages 22–23 of the Pupil Book. If teachers decide to use this exercise to assess the level at which pupils are working, these pages can be used to help guide pupils through that exercise. They should also help pupils to set targets for the exercise, to assess their own work and to set new targets for subsequent work. This will enable teachers and pupils to benefit from making formative use of the Assessment Opportunity. (Note that this differs from the Learning Plan on page 57 which provides Assessment for Learning support for the whole unit rather than an individual assessment.) Alternatively, teachers can use these pages as a mark scheme to help them to assess the individual performance of pupils and build a portfolio of assessments to track their progress during Key Stage 3 Geography.

Pages 64–65... provide **Model Answers** for the Assessment Opportunity on pages 22–23 of the Pupil Book. These model answers can be used in a variety of ways. Teachers can display them as models of good practice for whole-class discussion, or pupils could look at them before they start to write their own answers. However, they are really intended to support the self- or peer-assessment process before pupils analyse their own work. The aim is to demonstrate the need to offer supporting information/explanation for each point made when answering the question as well as the need for balance when constructing an argument. Pupils can identify where the writer has successfully addressed the question and/or where they fail to address it. Pupils will be better able to identify the specific actions they must take to produce better-quality answers. This will help them to assess their own work or the work of peers. This process is further supported by the Assessment Sheets on pages 43–49.

Page 66... is a **Self-Assessment Sheet** (How far have I travelled?) that can be used to complement the Learning Plan on page 57 or as an alternative form of self-review for the unit to be filled in by pupils at the end of the unit. This form is not linked to the Attainment Targets for the unit, but reviews progress against the learning objectives and enables pupils to record their personal impressions and achievements during the unit, providing them with a more subjective opportunity for self-assessment than the levelled approach adopted by the Learning Plan.

Pages 67–86... consist of photocopiable **Activity Sheets** to support the material in the Pupil Book.

*All of these resources and activities are also available on the **Planning CD-ROM** in either Word or PDF for teachers to print out if preferred or to display on whiteboards or projectors for whole-class discussion. They can also be customised to suit individual needs and, if required, saved with the other **electronic resources** for the unit using the facility to 'add your own resources' in the Just Click teaching solution.*

1 Tectonics
Assessment for Learning

The following suggestions are intended to show how the material in Unit 1 of **Horizons 3** provides opportunities for teachers and pupils to assess their work as they go along, and to improve their learning as a result of that assessment. It must be stressed that these are only a few of the ways in which the material in the Pupil Book can be used. The techniques could be used as they are outlined here, but teachers will probably find that it is more helpful to use these as starting points and to develop their own ideas to suit their own circumstances.

Before you get started

There is an integral Assessment for Learning framework provided for Unit 1 (and every unit in **Horizons**):

- The unit opens on pages 4–5 of the Pupil Book with the learning objectives for the unit (Where are we going?). The lesson plans on the *Planning CD-ROM* then include learning objectives and outcomes for each spread in turn (supported by pupil-friendly versions in PowerPoint on the *Electronic Resources CD-ROM*).

- The unit ends on pages 22–23 of the Pupil Book with a plenary spread to review and evaluate the unit (Where are we now?), particularly in light of the learning objectives from the opening spread.

- The Learning Plan and Attainment Targets for the unit on pages 57–59 in this *Teaching and Learning Resources* guide provide pupils with the opportunity to set individual learning targets at the start of the unit and to review their progress against these targets at the end. The final self-assessment sheet (How far have I travelled?) on page 66 then offers pupils a more subjective review of their progress during the unit.

Teachers can use or adapt all or some of these resources to set and review goals and involve pupils in their own learning. Further resources on the *Electronic Resources CD-ROM* provide activities for initial assessment of prior learning at the start of the unit to help teachers to diagnose strengths and weaknesses for each topic and for checking and testing knowledge and understanding during and at the end of the unit. All these resources will provide teachers with further evidence to help structure and focus the learning programme.

Pages 4–5

Pupils can share their ideas on what determines the likelihood of tectonic danger in activity 3, identifying any similarities and differences in their current perceptions. They should come back to these questions at the end of the unit to see if their ideas have changed. The starter based on Activity Sheets 1.1 and 1.2 allows them to establish prior knowledge via a diamond ranking exercise. The Venn diagram exercise on Activity Sheet 1.3 can be replicated on the board and gives pupils the opportunity to explain their classification of the hazards and the rest of the class a chance to justify their own decisions at the same time. Activity Sheet 1.4 encourages pupils to think more deeply about images from hazard zones and the annotated outcomes may be compared to identify the range of ideas and big picture links between peers.

Pages 6–7

The starter exercise in the lesson plan allows the opportunity for pupils to explain the answers. This is supported further by Activity Sheet 1.6. Activities 2 and 4 are ideally suited to peer-assessment and the suggested mini debrief would provide an excellent opportunity for pupils to contribute and refine their thoughts. The plenary on Activity Sheet 1.7 asks pupils to test each other's understanding of plate movement and encourages them to write additional captions to the sequences. A comparison of the best suggestions for additional captions would help to broaden the class understanding of these interconnected tectonic sequences.

Pages 8–9

The starter and Activity Sheet 1.8 encourage pupils to speculate using the living graph strategy. This is made easier if the diagram is reproduced on the board to allow for comparisons to be made. Pupils can share their thoughts on activities 1 and 2 and activity 3 could be used by pairs of pupils to identify their best sentences relating to criteria indicated in the hints section.

Pages 10–11

This spread is based on a report comparing two major earthquakes in different countries. Pupils could be encouraged to decide on the criteria for success for a good final report. Comparing which categories of information are given and which might be added during the web searches would help pupils to think about how their final products could be improved as they progress. Activity Sheet 1.10 could be given as an extension exercise or homework and allows pupils to compare and justify the way each of them has related the key words and phrases.

Pages 12–13

The starter and Activity Sheets 1.11 and 1.12 require pupils to work together to recreate a volcano benefits and dangers diagram. The lesson plan explains the debrief by exploring the strategies used to record and recreate. All aspects of this exercise encourage discussion of which aspects of their learning were effective and which could be improved. The plenary should ideally involve pupils sharing their understanding of the technique used and the knowledge gained.

The words generated by activity 1 should be explored in class discussion to determine how volcanic settings can generate such widely different responses. Activity 3 encourages pupils to speculate using the living photo strategy. This is made easier if photo C is reproduced on the board to allow for comparisons to be made. Activity 4 could involve pupils reading out their rough versions on the volcanic sequence while their peer actively listens and suggests an additional fact or aspect to help them improve.

Pages 14–15

Activities 1, 2 and 4 are suited to peer-assessment and Activity Sheet 1.13 is based on a text-marking exercise that should provide opportunities for pupils to compare how they have classified the effects and solutions to different stages of a sequence of volcanic eruptions.

Pages 16–17

The starter involves comparing photos A and B, two volcanic scenes in Iceland and Montserrat. Pupils should be encouraged to compose lists of similarities and differences prior to comparing with peers. By replicating the Venn diagram in activity 1 on the whiteboard, pupils can be invited to lead the discussion and explain their decisions.

Activities 2 and 3 could involve peer-assessment of search or report criteria prior to commencing the activity proper. A pupil-led plenary could ask for pupils to volunteer aspects of their investigation planning while others identify the advantages and potential improvements to the plan. This is supported by Activity Sheet 1.14.

Pages 18–19

Activity Sheet 1.15 encourages pupils to actively find a definition for a key word. They must be able to explain why these two cards are linked. Activity 1 is best accomplished in pairs. Ask pupils to list their most valued items on the board and then to classify them as aids to long- and short-term survival. Pupils should be encouraged to demonstrate how the following factors might have affected their decisions: planning, time, information, advice, previous experience. Class derivation of the criteria for success for activity 5 will allow peer-assessment of the initial efforts in answer to these tasks. As this activity invites pupils to provide evidence to prove or disprove one of two hypotheses, their thinking behind how they selected appropriate evidence to support their arguments should form part of the plenary and be used to identify the key characteristics of successful answers

Pages 20–21

Activity Sheet 1.16 charts the progress of delivering aid to a disaster zone. Done in pairs or small groups on large sheets of paper, these timelines could be displayed around the walls of the classroom for peers to assess according to agreed class criteria and suggestions made for improvement. Activity 2 encourages pupils to look at not what was done but what could be done first. When they have justified their own disaster relief plan, pupils should return to their timeline for the Asian tsunami and compare the actions taken with what they consider to be the most appropriate shorter- and longer-term actions. Activity 4 should provide a range of presentations to be assessed at a later date.

Pages 22–23

The decision-making exercise can be used as a summative assessment opportunity for this unit. However, the Assessment Opportunity on pages 60–65 in this *Teaching and Learning Resources* guide provides criteria for success, model answers and a process for target setting and reviewing that enables teachers and pupils to make formative use of this assessment. These activities are supported by Activity Sheets 1.18, 1.19 and 1.20.

The activities on page 23 of the Pupil Book are ideally suited to peer- and self-assessment as pupils initially develop a basic memory map into a personalised one. They can explain what makes their final diagram more effective as a memory aid and compare with partners to give extra ideas. Pupils then create a new version from scratch on a different topic but using the same memory mapping rules they have acquired in the first exercise. This will help them to review their own learning by encouraging them to look back over their work in this unit and transform the information most important to them.

1 Tectonics

Learning plan

What are my learning objectives for this unit?

I aim to learn:

✓ how the internal structure of the Earth affects people living on the surface

✓ to understand how plate movements cause earthquakes and volcanoes

✓ how people live with the threat of earthquakes and volcanoes

✓ to develop an awareness of how places are interdependent through aid.

Read the Attainment Targets for this unit on pages 58–59 and tick any statements that you feel refer to you. *Places and Environments* covers *what you know* about the topic and *Enquiry and Skills* covers *what you can do*.

Using these statements for this unit, decide what level you are overall at this stage:

Level [ ]

What level do you think you can achieve by the end of this unit?

Level [ ]

What are you going to concentrate on to achieve this level? A good place to start might be any statements on pages 58–59 that you have not ticked:

[ ]

At the end of the unit, read the Attainment Targets again and tick in a different colour any *new* statements that refer to you. Then decide what level you are now:

Level [ ]

If you have improved, well done! What evidence can you show for this improvement? What or who do you think particularly helped you to improve your level?

[ ]

If you have stayed the same, better luck next time! What do you think you could have done differently to help improve your levels? What will you do next time to progress further?

[ ]

1 Tectonics

My Attainment Targets for this unit

These Attainment Targets show you the different levels that you can aim for in this unit. They are divided into two parts:

- **Places and Environments** (which covers what you know about the topic)
- **Enquiry and Skills** (which covers what you can do).

You can decide your overall level by checking which statements refer to *what you know* and those that refer to *what you can do*. You can use these Attainment Targets as your criteria for success during the Tectonics unit.

Level 3

Places and Environments

- ☐ I can describe where volcanoes and earthquakes occur.
- ☐ I can describe and give some reasons for the location of the tectonically active places in the world.
- ☐ I can describe some of the similarities and differences between the effects of volcanoes and earthquakes in different countries.
- ☐ I can describe some of the ways people manage hazards to reduce the effect on people.

Enquiry and Skills

- ☐ I can select and use some information from maps, photographs and written sources to find out how different parts of the world are affected by hazards.
- ☐ I can use appropriate geographical vocabulary to describe volcanoes and earthquakes.

Level 4

Places and Environments

- ☐ I can describe and begin to explain the location of volcanoes and earthquakes.
- ☐ I can describe and begin to explain some of the similarities and differences between the effects of volcanoes and earthquakes in different countries.
- ☐ I can describe and begin to explain some of the ways people manage hazards to reduce the threat to human life.
- ☐ I can recognise that people hold different views on how tectonic hazards should be managed.

Enquiry and Skills

- ☐ I can select and use some information from a variety sources to explain patterns of volcanic and earthquake activity.
- ☐ I can use maps, diagrams and photographs to explain how volcanoes and earthquakes affect people and their environments.

Level 5

Places and Environments

- ☐ I can describe and explain why some places experience more volcanoes and earthquakes than others.
- ☐ I can describe and explain some of the similarities and differences between the effects of volcanoes and earthquakes in different countries.
- ☐ I can describe and explain how people and countries act to manage the threat to human life from hazards.
- ☐ I can suggest reasons why people may hold different views on how tectonic hazards should be managed.

Enquiry and Skills

- ☐ I can suggest geographical questions about volcanoes and earthquakes.
- ☐ I can collect data from a range of sources to investigate volcanoes and earthquakes.
- ☐ I can select appropriate skills and ways of presenting to help me compare different places affected by volcanoes and earthquakes.
- ☐ I can present my findings with a conclusion.

1 Tectonics

My Attainment Targets for this unit

Level 6

Places and Environments

- ☐ I can use a range of examples from regional to international level to describe and explain why some places experience more volcanoes and earthquakes than others.

- ☐ I can describe and explain the effects of volcanoes and earthquakes in different countries and how this may be linked with levels of development.

- ☐ I can describe and explain how people locally and internationally try to manage hazards to reduce the threat to human life.

- ☐ I can explain why people may hold different views on how tectonic hazards should be managed and how these views may conflict.

Enquiry and Skills

- ☐ I can suggest geographical questions as part of my investigations.

- ☐ I can collect data from a wide range of sources to investigate a variety of tectonic hazards.

- ☐ I can select an appropriate range of skills to compare and contrast different places in different tectonic settings.

- ☐ I can present the findings of my investigations in a logical way and reach conclusions consistent with the evidence.

Level 7

Places and Environments

- ☐ I can use a wide range of examples from local to global level to describe and explain why some places experience more volcanoes and earthquakes than others.

- ☐ I can describe how physical, human and economic factors interact to determine how volcanoes and earthquakes affect people differently in different countries.

- ☐ I can explain how people in some countries interact to try to manage hazards to reduce the threat to human life.

- ☐ I can explain why decisions about managing tectonic hazards are influenced by people's views and attitudes and may have far-reaching consequences.

Enquiry and Skills

- ☐ I can show independence to identify tectonic issues to investigate, ask geographical questions and follow and establish my own sequence of enquiry.

- ☐ I can use accurately a wide range of skills and sources of evidence.

- ☐ I can evaluate critically most sources of evidence, present well-argued summaries of my investigations and begin to reach conclusions that are clearly based on evidence.

Level 8

Places and Environments

- ☐ I can use a wide range of examples at all scales from different parts of the world to describe and explain why some places experience more volcanoes and earthquakes than others.

- ☐ I can offer explanations for the interactions within physical, human and economic factors that determine how volcanoes and earthquakes affect people differently in countries at different levels of development.

- ☐ I can explain how people in different countries interact to try to manage hazards to reduce the threat to human life.

- ☐ I can understand a range of views and attitudes on the management of tectonic hazards and why decisions may have far-reaching consequences.

Enquiry and Skills

- ☐ I can show a high level of independence to identify tectonic issues to plan, investigate and make justified decisions.

- ☐ I can select independently a wide range of techniques and skills to collect and analyse data.

- ☐ I can evaluate critically sources of evidence, present well-argued summaries of my investigations and begin to reach conclusions that are clearly based on evidence.

On page 22 you are asked to write a report following a decision-making exercise on how to reduce the impact of a likely volcanic eruption on Pico Magdalena. Your report should follow the order shown below and should include diagrams or annotated sketch maps to indicate what you would do and where.

You have been appointed as minister in charge of disaster relief in a country on the west coast of South America. Hazard Control Surveys have informed you that a volcanic event is likely within one year at Pico Magdalena in the western section of your province. The important agricultural towns of San Sebastian (population 3000) and Villa Solana (population 1500) lie at the foot of the volcano, close to the main highway and the railway connecting the capital, Peragua, with the major port of Pacifico.

You have been put in charge of reducing the impact of the eruption if it happens. You have a very limited budget (US$ 1 million) to spend, and only a small team of workers. Table B on page 22 below shows the cost of the various methods of prediction and precaution you could use. You need to produce a report urgently, outlining for central government your intended prediction/precaution schemes. Don't go over budget!

Your final report must include:

- a brief description of the problem

- an annotated map showing exactly where you will locate/implement your chosen methods

- a table showing the methods you have chosen and the costs involved

- an explanation of how your scheme will work, and its limitations.

Before you start this activity, look at the **Criteria for success** sheet. Set yourself a target level to aim for in this Assessment Opportunity. Write this level in the box on the target setting sheet. Explain how you intend to obtain this level.

Once you have finished the activity, look again at the Criteria for success and assess your answers. You could also compare your answers with model answers. Write your level in the box and explain how you achieved this level.

Then set yourself a target for improvement in your next assessment. Explain what you need to do to improve next time. Try to set yourself specific tasks to work on.

1 Tectonics

Criteria for success

A **Level 3** answer may	• describe the prediction and precaution methods you have chosen
	• indicate where they will be located
	• begin to explain why the methods and their locations will help reduce the damage
	• give an indication of the costs of the plan.
A **Level 4** answer may	• describe in more detail the prediction and precaution methods you have chosen
	• clearly indicate where they will be located and why
	• explain how the methods and their locations will help reduce the damage
	• show how the budget has been used and the costs of the various methods used
	• suggest some limitations of the scheme.
A **Level 5** answer may	• describe in detail the prediction and precaution methods you have chosen and explain why others were not used
	• clearly indicate where they will be located and why those locations are suitable
	• explain how each method will help reduce the specific kinds of damage and indicate any limitations
	• explain how the costs show an effective use of the budget, and indicate how the scheme will help in the short and long term
	• suggest how some people may have different views about the scheme
	• offer a conclusion based on evidence in your report.
A **Level 6** answer may	• describe in detail then explain clearly the prediction and precaution methods you have chosen and why others were not used
	• explain how each method and its location will help reduce the specific kinds of damage
	• explain how the costs show an effective use of the budget
	• recognise that conflicting demands on the environment may be managed in different ways
	• suggest what the limitations of your scheme are and indicate why some people will benefit more than others.
A **Level 7** answer may	• explain and justify your chosen location for the prediction and precaution methods you have chosen and say why others were not used
	• explain in greater detail how each method and its location will help reduce the specific kinds of damage
	• explain how the costs show an effective use of the budget and indicate how it might be altered if more funds were available
	• recognise that conflicting demands on the environment may be managed in different ways but these need to be sustainable
	• explain the limitations of your scheme and suggest possible future improvements.

A **Level 8** answer may	• fully explain and justify your chosen prediction and precaution methods for limiting damage to the area
	• compare and contrast the site locations for the methods chosen and explain how the impact on people and the environment affected your decision
	• show that you have critically evaluated the evidence available
	• recognise that dealing with conflicting demands on the environment must be planned and managed sustainably
	• suggest ways in which the changes may be made to suit most groups of people.

1 Tectonics

My target setting

I want to make progress in geography, working on the decision-making exercise on how to save San Sebastian in the event of a volcanic eruption.

When I do the activity on page 22, I aim to obtain:

Level

To do this I will need to:

Answer these questions when you have completed the activity on page 22:

In this Assessment Opportunity I obtained:

Level

Explain how you obtained this level:

When I do my next Assessment Opportunity, I aim to obtain:

Level

To do this I will need to:

1 Tectonics

Model answers

A This is a good basic answer that was written by a pupil who had completed the activity on page 22. This is not the full answer but a sample from the report.

I would concentrate on blocking the lava channels because I think lava could come down the valley towards San Sebastian. By damming the river valley with blocks dropped by helicopter at the place marked (1) on my plan, you could stop some of the lava at least. Before that you could build barriers higher up near where I have marked (2) on the plan. The idea here is that you would turn the lava away onto another path before it got to the valley. Another thing would be to have lots of volunteers and paramedics ready to help the injured and those too old to get away in time. You can see in my costs table that these methods use up all my budget. My idea is to deal with it when it happens and not to waste money predicting things that might not happen. Some bad points would be:

a) the scheme won't work very well if the lava keeps coming for more than a week or so;

b) there's not enough money to help Villa Solano, so they will have to get out fast. It might be a good idea to move everybody to a much safer place but as this costs $3 million it's not really an option.

B This is a better answer, which achieves a higher level than the first one (A).
- Read it carefully, and try to see why this is better than the first answer.
- Try to see how it meets new parts of the criteria for success.
- Try to see how you could use ideas from this work to improve your own work.

This report suggests the following actions are taken:

Predictions: it is suggested that a geophysical survey team ($50 000) and hazard mapping survey ($10 000) are used close to the summit and areas nearby to give warning of when the eruption is likely and where the lava is most likely to flow. Warning will not be enough on its own – as we cannot afford to move everyone out of the area it is necessary to do some things to help them when Pico Magdalena finally blows.

Precautions: the barrier walls and diversionary channels located at (A) and (B) on the map should help deflect the lava and ash or mudflows (lahars) from San Sebastian and Villa Solano ($300 000). This could be backed up by emergency measures such as having volunteer rescue teams ($100 000) and safe food and water supplies, perhaps at a rest centre ($300 000). They would be stationed at (C) and (D). If money were kept in reserve to have emergency helicopters, they could block the channels of lava and perhaps ferry helpers around ($200 000). Any spare money could be used to help warning and evacuation systems but these might be limited ($50 000).

Although this isn't ideal, it does give a good balance between preparing for the disaster and dealing with the effects. It cannot please everyone and in particular if the government wants the main road and rail links kept open it will need to provide more money. Repeated eruptions might require an observatory and, in the long term, evacuation.

C This is an even better answer, which achieves a higher level than (A) or (B).

- Read it carefully, and try to see why this is better than the previous answers.
- Try to see how it meets new parts of the criteria for success.
- Try to see how you could use ideas from this work to improve your own work.

When choosing the best methods to defend against a volcanic eruption, there are four main factors to consider.

The first is to predict the areas that are likely to be affected.

A map was included here.

Map A shows the area that is most likely to be affected by lava and pyroclastics. The valleys are very dangerous as there seems to be some evidence that debris has travelled down here in the past.

The second factor is to consider the human aspect and especially where people live. San Sebastian has most people (population 3000) and Villa Solano has 1500. With a total of 4500 people concentrated into two towns, this is where much of the plan will focus. The roads and rail are important but they can be rebuilt so are not as important as people.

The third factor is to select the right methods of protection for this area. Some are too expensive for the region to achieve on its own.

A table was included here.

The symbols on the table and map show where the following methods should be located. Satellite monitoring and geophysical surveying (A and B

on the map) would cost a total of $350 000 but would give most warning of an imminent eruption, which should save lives. Barrier walls and diversionary lava channels at (C) on the map will add $300 000 but will help protect the two main towns and may even save the road and rail links for a while, which could help disaster relief in the event of an eruption. Semi-trained rescue teams and rest centres supported by evacuation routes – marked at (D) on the map – would help those who had some warning ($350 000). This would just balance the budget.

The fourth factor would be the longer term. The budget alone isn't ever going to be enough. The government should seek help from neighbouring countries and the global community if the disaster lasts longer than predicted. The scheme above will not save everyone but a government is not on its own when dealing with a large eruption. Disaster relief organisations like Oxfam and international aid like the G8 countries can help to rescue people in the short term and rebuild the region in the long term.

1 Tectonics

How far have I travelled?

In this unit my **Learning Objectives** were to learn:

- how the internal structure of the Earth affects people living on the surface
- to understand how plate movements cause earthquakes and volcanoes
- how people live with the threat of earthquakes and volcanoes
- to develop an awareness of how places are interdependent through aid.

My progress in this unit

How well have I achieved my objectives?	Okay							Excellent
Enquiry and Skills:								
to annotate photographs, diagrams and maps effectively								
to use the internet to investigate earthquakes and volcanoes								
to be able to ask questions to find out about earthquakes and volcanoes in different parts of the world								
to devise a volcano eruption management plan								
Places and Environments:								
to be able to explain why some places have more volcanoes and earthquakes than others								
to know how the internal structure of the Earth and the movement of the plates are linked								
to understand why tectonic hazards have a greater effect on some places than others								
to identify and explain how wealth, aid and cooperation can affect the ability of a country to recover from a tectonic hazard								

Shade the bars to show how far you think you have made progress in this unit.

The part of this unit that I enjoyed the most was …

because …

The part of this unit that I needed most help with was …

because …

The piece of work that I am most pleased with is …

because …

The aspect of this unit that will be most useful to me in future is …

because …

Any other comments?

1·1

What do you know already? 1

1. Cut out statements A–P below.

2. In pairs, take turns to read out the statements to each other. Listen to the words and make a note of any unfamiliar words.

3. Decide which statements you are most familiar with and be prepared to listen to the explanations of your partner.

4. Using the diamond shape on sheet 1.2, put the statements you are most sure about near the top and the ones you are least sure about towards the bottom.

5. When you are satisfied with the order, stick them into your book.

6. Colour each statement to show how well you think you understand it. Use *green* for **sure**, *orange* for **fairly sure** and *red* for **unsure**.

 You will come back to this classification at the end of the unit to see how many more of these facts you are sure of. You will need to colour them again to record your new level of understanding.

A There are no active volcanoes in the UK.

B Volcanoes can be grouped into active, dormant and extinct.

C Hot-spot volcanoes can occur anywhere, even in ocean plates.

D Basalt lava erupts at about 1000–12 000°C and is very runny.

E Thicker, cooler lava often leads to explosive eruptions.

F Pyroclastic flows from volcanoes can travel downhill at over 200 kph.

G Lava is called magma when it is still in the ground.

H An earthquake is the result of a sudden release of energy.

I Most volcanoes occur near plate margins.

J The Earth's crust is divided into a series of plates.

K Plates move around the Earth driven by convection currents in the mantle.

L Many earthquakes occur near fault lines.

M The UK regularly experiences earthquakes.

N All earthquakes are followed by aftershocks.

O Vulcan was the ancient god of fire.

P There are volcanic rocks in the Lake District, Northumberland and Snowdonia National Parks.

1·2 What do you know already? 2

Use this diamond shape for the statements on sheet 1.1.

Most sure

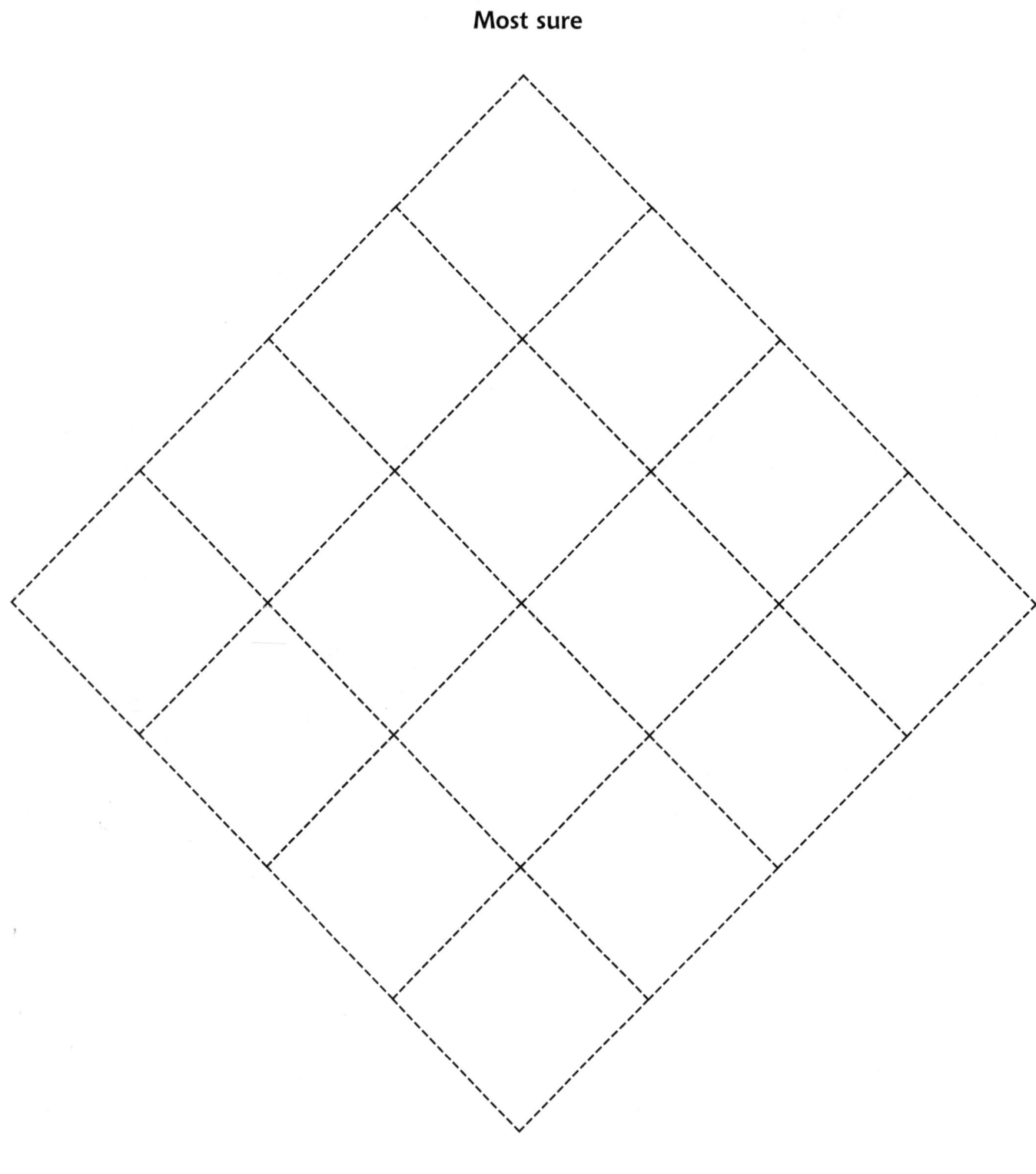

Least sure

1·3 Natural hazards or human mistakes?

1 Read the list of hazards below. Classify each hazard by writing the relevant letter in the right place in Venn diagram A.

A) **Motorway pile-up in fog**

C) **Earthquake that kills no one**

B) **Avalanche that kills three skiers**

D) **Volcanic eruption under the sea**

E) **Famine in Ethiopia**

F) **Drought in the Sahel**

G) **Landslide of a cliff-top house**

H) **Aircraft struck by lightning in a hurricane**

I) **Aircraft crash after seagulls caught in engines**

J) **Riverside houses destroyed by flooding**

K) **Shipwreck off Hebrides in a storm**

L) **Bush fire in Portuguese scrubland**

M) **Indian Ocean tsunami**

N) **Natural gas explosion in block of flats that kills 20 residents**

O) **Three-day blizzard that kills sheep**

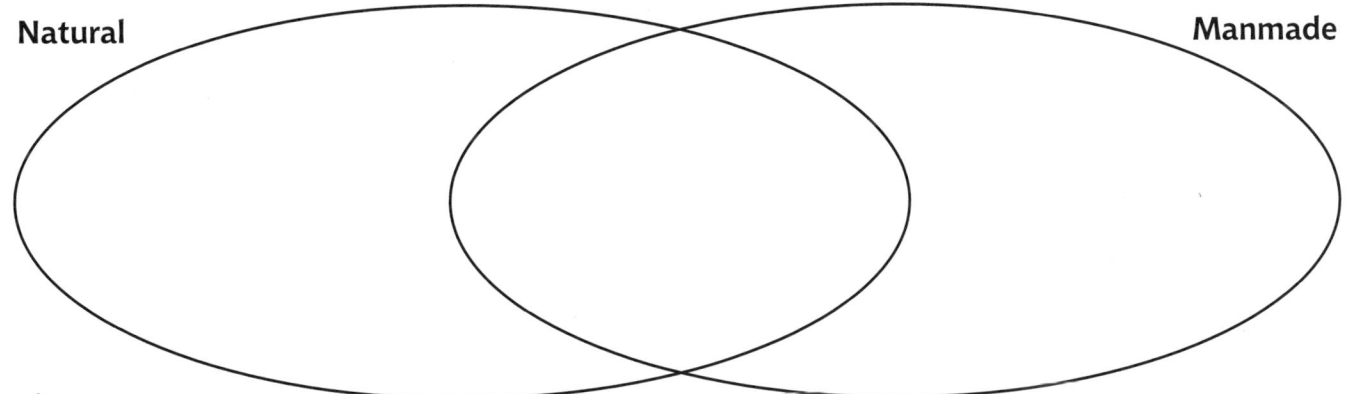

Natural · Manmade

A Venn diagram

2 Study graph B.

a Which of the natural hazards you identified in activity 1 do you think we should care about? Explain your answer.

b Are there any natural hazards in which the potential death toll cannot be reduced by humans?

Scale and frequency of disasters throughout the world **B**

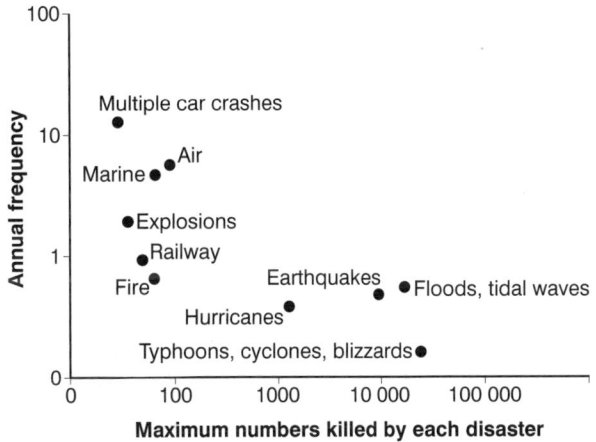

By making links between what we see in a picture and what we know about the place, we have a much better chance of understanding the 'bigger picture'. For example, imagine you are asked to study a photo of your local high street jammed with traffic in the early evening. Possible responses might be:

• What can I see in the picture? Many cars, stationary buses, pedestrians waiting to cross the road.

• What do I know about the 'bigger picture'? It is rush hour, the busiest time of the day. Many journeys are made at this time – accident figures are a concern for the council. Some people want the street to be pedestrianised.

• What links explain the connection between the factors shown in the photo or suggest solutions to the problems? Congestion is a result of many journeys being made at the same time, so staggering work and school times could ease congestion. Pedestrianising the street would reduce accident figures for school pupils.

Study photo B on page 4 of your textbook. Write notes around the sketch below to help you see the 'bigger picture'.

What do I know about the 'bigger picture'?

What can I see in the picture?

1·5 Tsunami responses

Tsunami alert system takes shape

By Julianna Kettlewell
BBC News science reporter

Six months after the 26 December tsunami, which swept away a myriad of futures, many homes still remain crumpled and lives shattered.

People are working tirelessly to build a tsunami early warning system.

'We have made a lot of progress. I think by the anniversary we will look back and think, "My god, did we really do all that in a year?"', said Robert Owen Jones, climate change director for the Australian government.

'On 26 December there weren't any arrangements in place for the Indian Ocean. Now we have the system mapped out, we have lots of plans and money allocated by countries to develop the capabilities. There is no comparison.'

The tsunami early warning system for the Indian Ocean can be seen as a two-tier operation. Firstly, there is the hi-tech network of ocean monitoring technology, which will feed back into an international web of early warning centres. And secondly, there is the low-tech community response drill, which will take an emergency warning to every hawker on the beach.

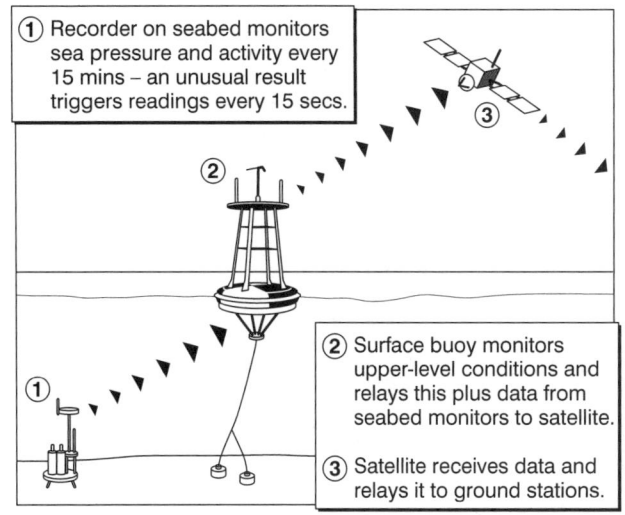

① Recorder on seabed monitors sea pressure and activity every 15 mins – an unusual result triggers readings every 15 secs.

② Surface buoy monitors upper-level conditions and relays this plus data from seabed monitors to satellite.

③ Satellite receives data and relays it to ground stations.

HIGH-TECH EQUIPMENT

The hi-tech system will be shared by 27 countries around the Indian Ocean. Each country is to set up a tsunami warning centre to receive information from the pressure gauges, seismographs and wave sensors that will survey the ocean basin. Many countries have already begun work on their centres.

Some countries have gone a step further. On Monday, Thailand opened a hi-tech national disaster centre. 'We can broadcast to all TV and radio stations in Thailand,' said Col Anutat Bunnag, deputy executive director of Thailand's National Disaster Warning Centre. 'Every station will switch from normal programmes to warning centre programmes, and we can send text messages to all mobile phones. We could warn people within 20 minutes if another tsunami took shape today.'

The next stage will be to install a series of pressure gauges – each worth about $300 000 (£160 000) – which sit under the sea and monitor the weight of water on top of them. By 2006, when the whole system should be complete, the Indian Ocean will host several million dollars' worth of equipment. However, according to Mr Owen Jones, cost should not be a stumbling block.

LOW-TECH RESPONSE

Technology might be the most expensive part of the early warning system, but taking the alert to every fisherman and beach dweller is by far the hardest.

'I have just been to Sri Lanka and the response there was very good,' said Mr Schaar of the International Red Crescent.

'The government used existing telecommunications systems and the network of police stations along the coast to warn people. It was very effective – people did evacuate fast. People are scared about the possibility of another earthquake and they are very much on their toes. There is a great risk that this could happen again soon. But we can be confident that people would react differently today.'

Adapted from the BBC News website (news.bbc.co.uk), 24 June 2005

1 Read the article above. Underline solutions that need international cooperation in red and any ways in which a country could help itself in *blue*.

2 Write a paragraph to explain why countries should cooperate to solve the problems caused by tsunamis in the Indian Ocean.

3 Why must international cooperation be supported by measures taken at home in each country?

Tectonics

1·6 Shaking beliefs

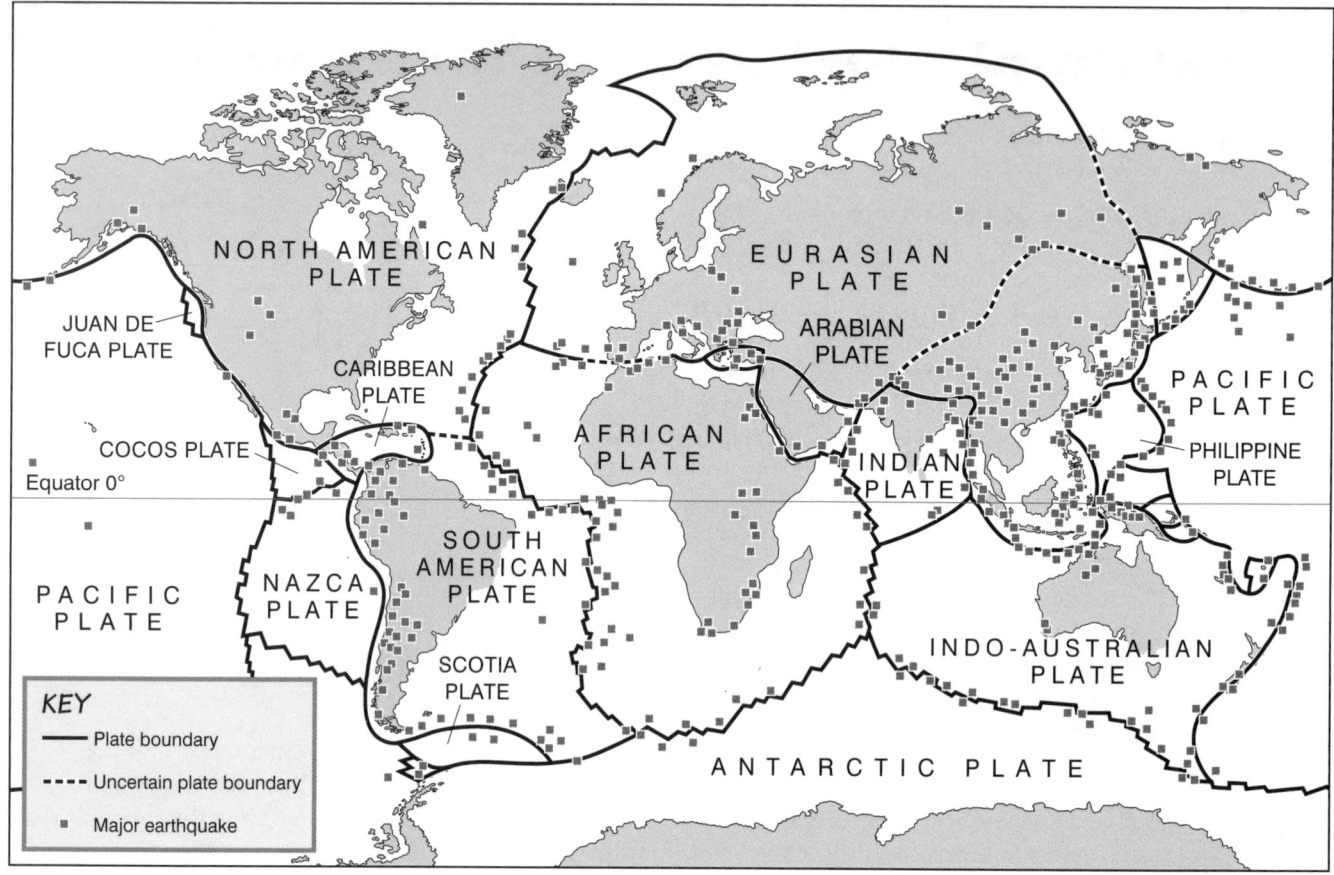

KEY

— Plate boundary

--- Uncertain plate boundary

■ Major earthquake

Read the statements below, which are about earthquakes. Fill in the table by adding ticks in the right places. Find evidence from the map to back up your decisions.

Statement	True	False	Map evidence
Most earthquakes are in the northern hemisphere			
All earthquakes happen at plate margins			
Some earthquakes occur at constructive plate margins			
All earthquakes happen in hot parts of the world			
Earthquakes always happen in less economically developed countries (LEDCs)			
Some areas experience few earthquakes			

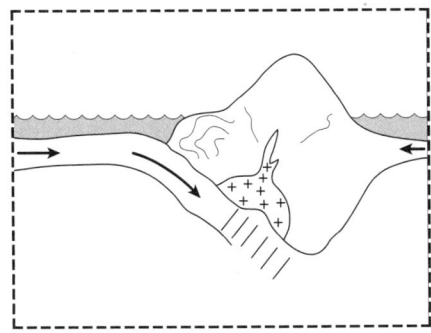
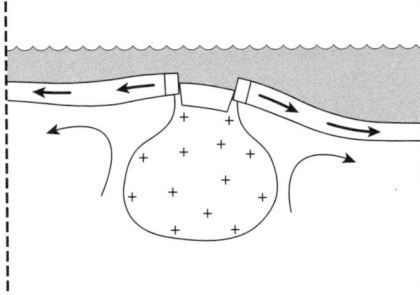
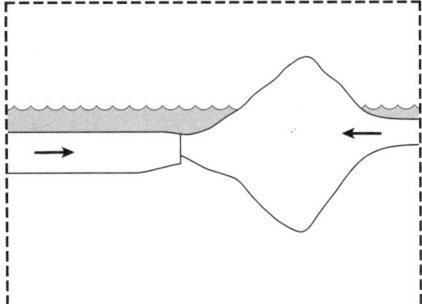

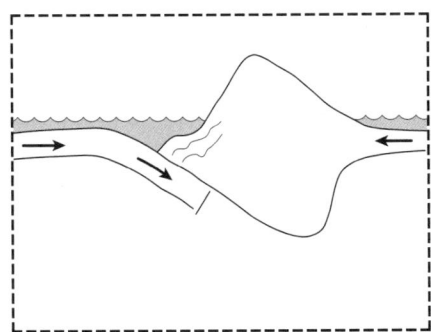
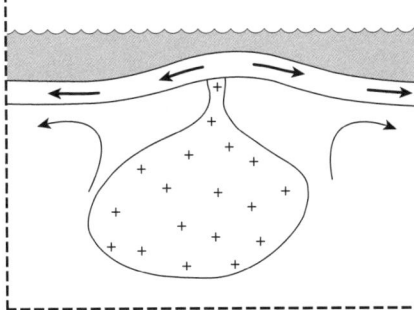
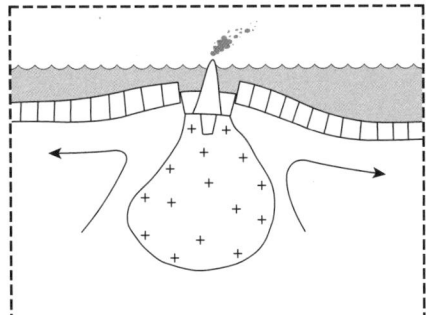

The sketches above represent the stages in:

- the creation of new crust at a constructive plate margin
- the destruction of crust at a destructive plate margin.

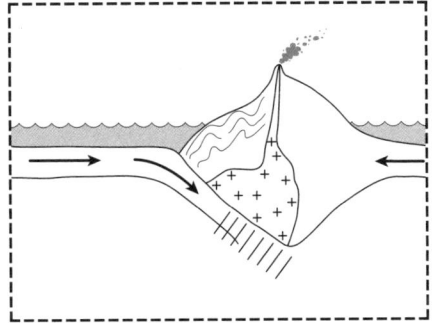
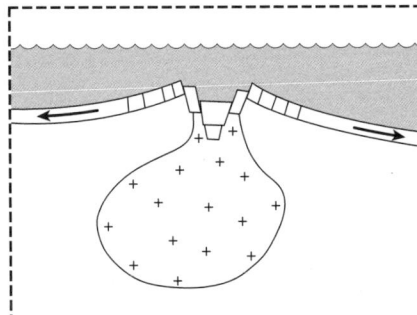

1 Cut out the sketches and arrange them in two sequences, one showing the creation of a crust and the other the destruction of a crust.

2 Cut out the captions below and add them to the appropriate sketches.

3 Mark on the sketches where you think earthquakes and volcanoes might occur.

4 Write three extra captions to explain what happens to link any two sketches.

As the plates pull apart, a rift valley appears.	A section of the crust falls back into the magma chamber.	Volcanoes appear in the rift valley. Some may grow to form islands.	The heat from the magma chamber up-domes the crust.
As they collide, the oceanic crust is subducted beneath the continental crust.	The magma from the melting crust rises through the land mass to form volcanoes.	As the oceanic crust slides beneath the continental crust, friction causes partial melting.	Convection currents push oceanic and continental crusts towards each other.

1·8 Living earthquakes

see pages 8–9 in your Horizons Book 3

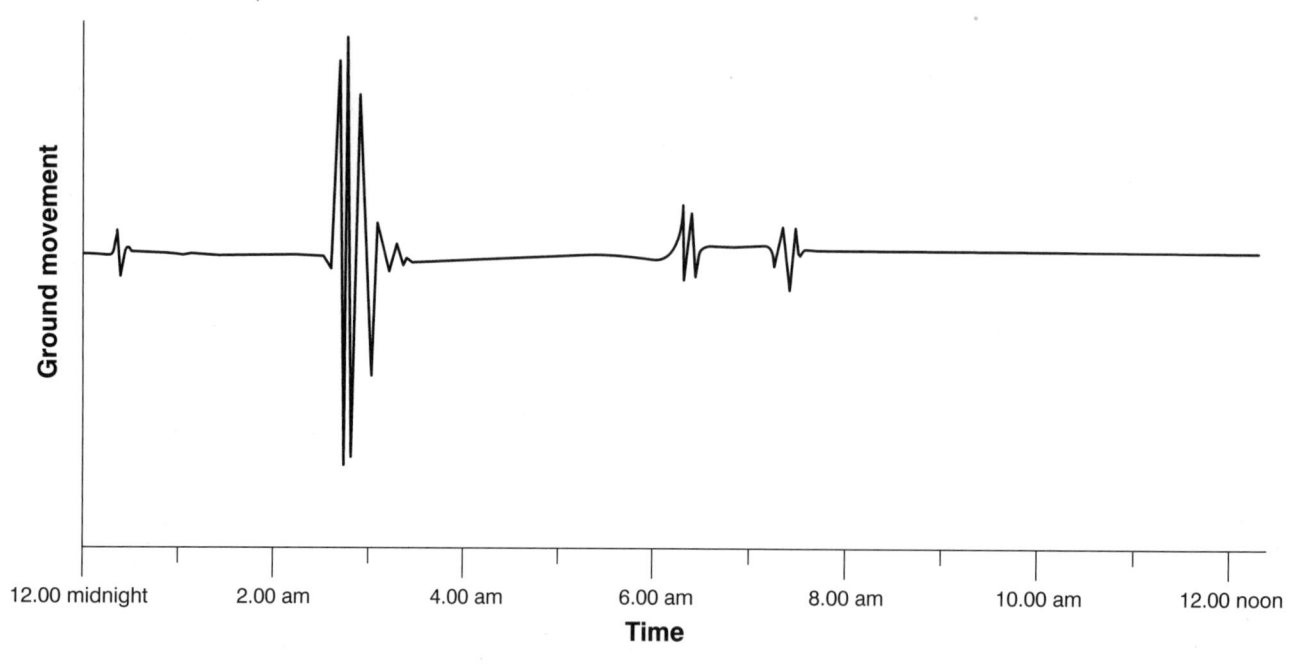

1 Read the quotes below. Write the relevant letter for each quote where you think it best fits the seismograph above.

A I would like to express the sincere sympathy of the government.

B Breaking news on 24-7 TV: reports are coming in of a possible earthquake in the capital region.

C We can't get the bodies out.

D I think we should try that new restaurant tomorrow.

E Get downstairs now!

F We should have built stronger homes.

G I need an ambulance. My wife is badly injured.

H I don't know where my children are!

I Rescuers were further hampered by aftershocks in the bay area.

J This is worrying. Should we issue a general alert?

K This hospital's A & E department is full. Please airlift these casualties to another hospital.

L Keep out of these houses. They're unsafe and there are likely to be aftershocks.

M Thank goodness I remembered my earthquake drill.

N Did you feel something? I'm going to check outside.

O Put the army on standby!

2 Compare your choices with a partner and explain the reasons for any differences between your graphs.

3 Suggest why the death toll was reported as 1000 at 12 noon, 5000 on the evening news and 17 593 in the official report six months later.

1·9 Talking tsunamis

These diagrams show how the Indian Ocean tsunami occurred.

1 Copy the writing frame below, or use your own words, to explain how the tsunami happened.

2 Read your explanation to a partner and listen to their version. Compare your explanations and discuss the best parts of each.

> The cause of the tsunami was
> _____
> _____
>
> The plates that collided were
> _____
> _____
>
> The plates were closing towards each other at _____ mm per year.
>
> As the _____ plate subducted beneath the _____ plate, pressure built up.
>
> The pressure caused movement along the faults running along the subduction zone until
> _____
> _____
> _____
>
> The sudden movement transferred energy from the rocks to the
> _____
>
> In deep water, the waves could reach speeds of up to _____ kph.
>
> As the waves approached shore, they slowed because
> _____
> _____
>
> This pushed the breaking wave higher until
> _____
> _____

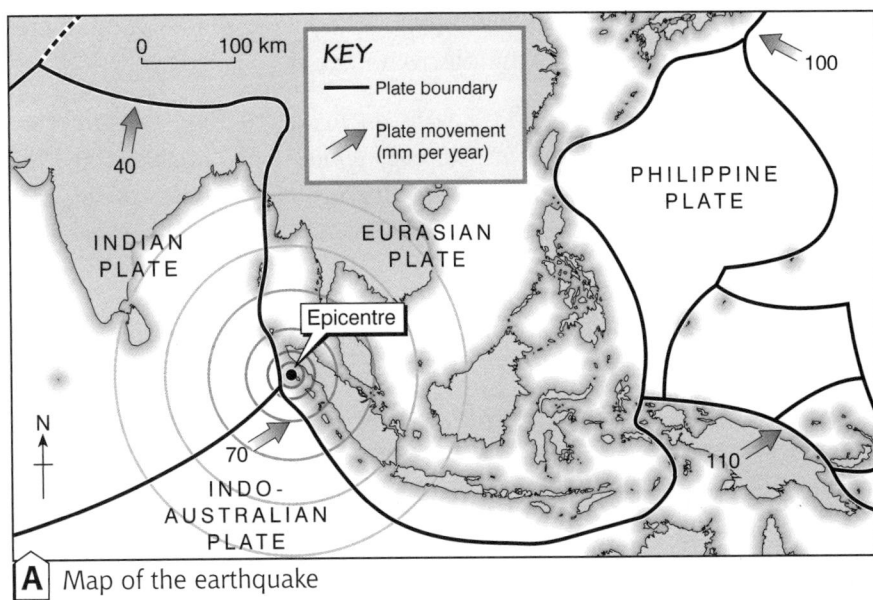

A Map of the earthquake

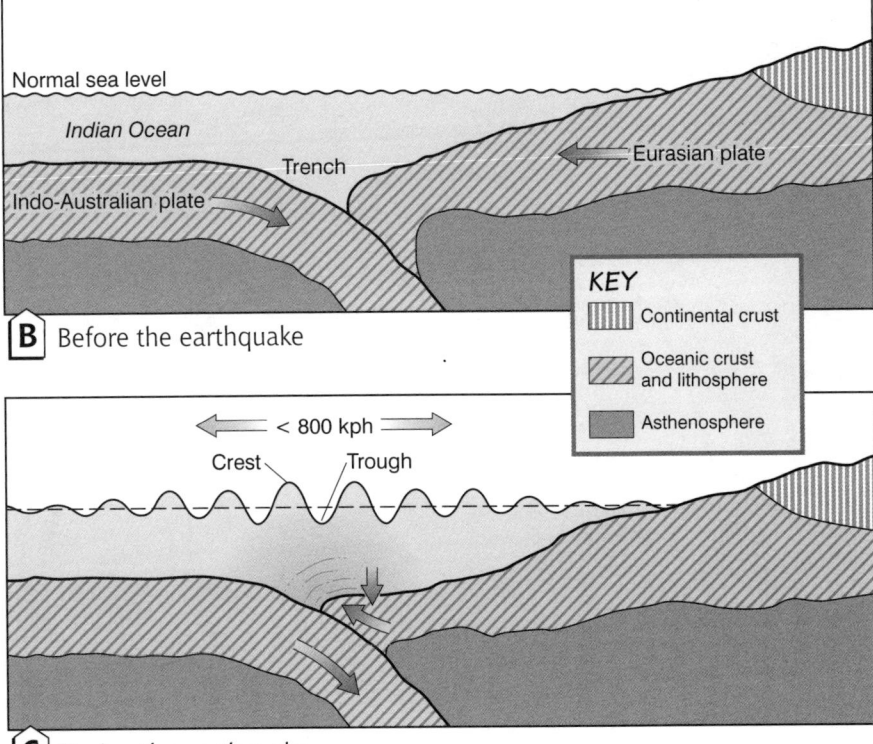

B Before the earthquake

C During the earthquake

D Tsunami waves hitting land

1·10 Earthquake relational diagrams

The relational diagram below has been started by a Year 9 pupil. Here she explains why she has drawn the diagram like this:

Plate tectonics is the theory that covers all things relating to plates, so I put the plates shape inside the plate tectonics shape. I know ocean crust makes up parts of some plates, so I put this shape inside the plates one. I wasn't sure if all destructive margins involved only ocean crust, so I overlapped these two shapes.

Add the following words to complete the earthquake relational diagram.

shock waves	seismometer	evacuation	epicentre	focus	deaths

Indonesia	continental crust	UK	USA	early warning system

Banda Aceh	tsunami	earthquake	aftershock	Eurasian plate

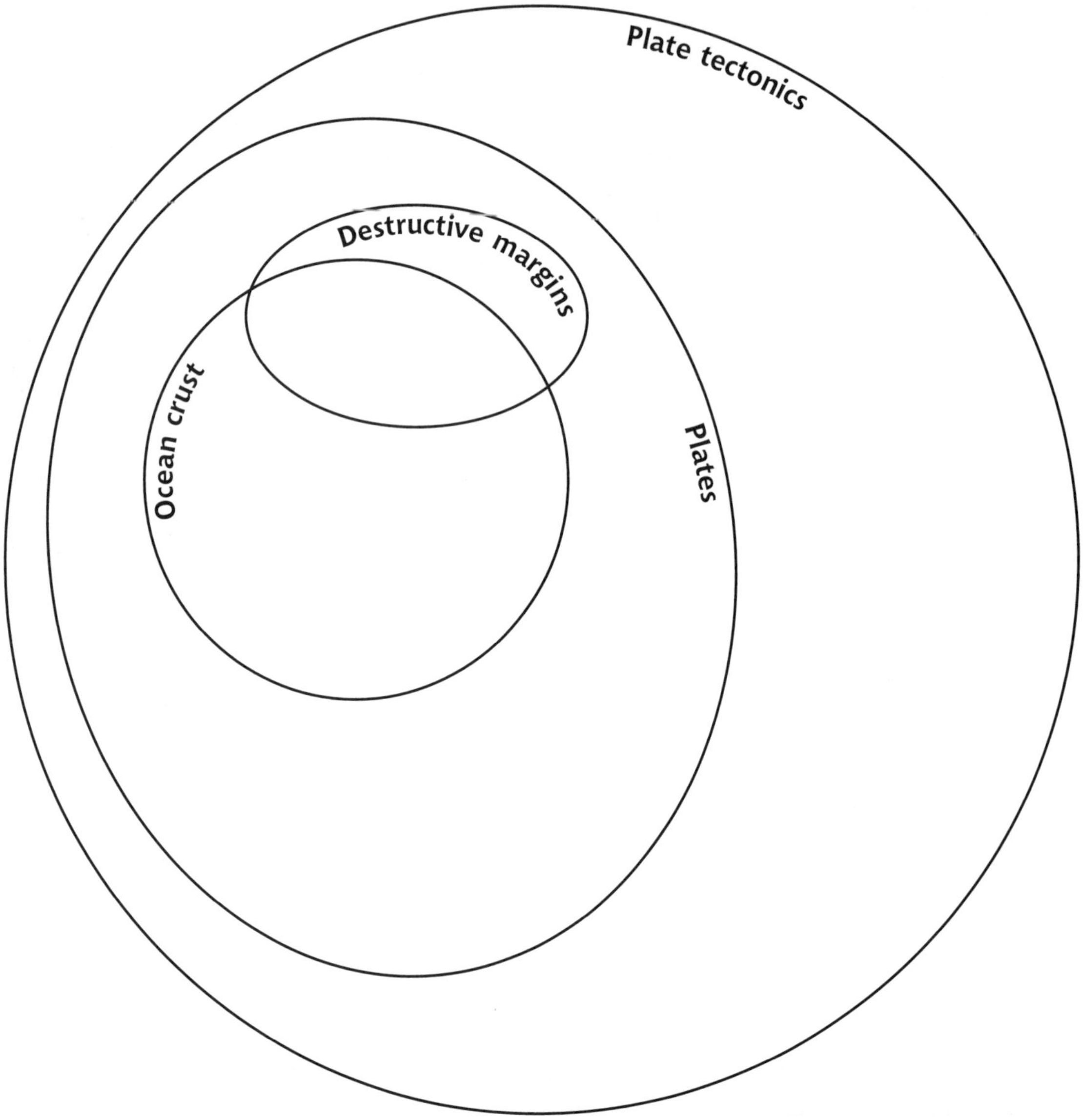

Plate tectonics

Destructive margins

Ocean crust

Plates

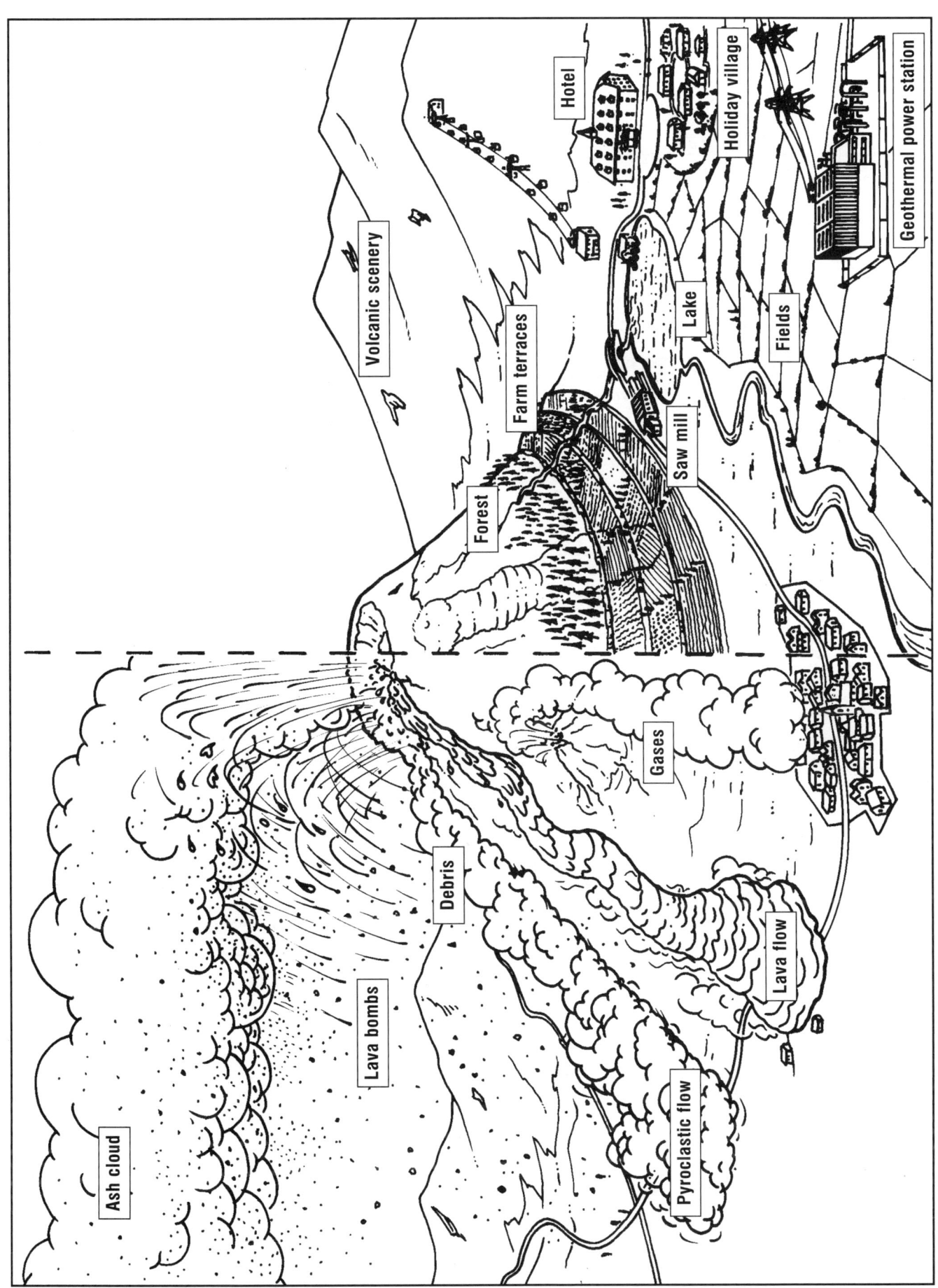

Hotel

Holiday village

Geothermal power station

Volcanic scenery

Lake

Farm terraces

Fields

Saw mill

Forest

Gases

Debris

Lava flow

Lava bombs

Pyroclastic flow

Ash cloud

1·12 Collective memory 2

In groups, work together to redraw the diagram your teacher shows you. Use the space below.

1. The first person in your group will be asked to look at the diagram for 20 seconds.

2. They should tell the other team members what to draw, but must not draw themselves.

3. Repeat steps 1 and 2 for all team members, then go round once more until everyone has had a chance to view and describe the diagram twice.

 Think carefully about your strategy for completing this task. You will each have only two viewings and limited time to study the diagram. What will each team member need to do to avoid repetition?

(1·13) Monserrat memories

Reports of natural disasters come from a variety of sources. They take different viewpoints depending on the story they are trying to convey.

Read the articles on this sheet. One is from a newspaper and the other is from an amateur website.

[1] As you read the text, underline it as follows: red for effects that were an immediate threat to human life, orange for effects that were a possible threat to safety and green for precautions taken by people to reduce damage or harm.

[2] What were the main threats to human life in these two eruptions?

[3] What other effects might cause disruption to the community and local surroundings?

[4] **a** What did people do to reduce the risk of damage?

b Why were the methods used different in each article?

Students get explosive view of research at volcano site

A University of Arkansas professor and his students got an unexpected close-up view of an erupting volcano as they conducted research this summer. They were conducting research on the Caribbean island of Montserrat when the Soufrière Hills volcano erupted, about three miles from where they were staying.

During the day two students could see ash clouds billowing above the mountain. They got to a spot where they could see the flows meet the ocean. Geysers of water flashed upwards as the gas hit the ocean. Later, a rain storm turned the ash cloud into a mud bath, and they had to stop often to refill the windscreen wiper fluid because they could not see out of the window.

Back at the villa, the conditions worsened. They did not hear the explosion, which occurred between 11 and 11.30 pm, but they knew what had happened.

'You could hear rocks hitting the roof, which started leaking,' the students reported. Everyone picked up pots to put on their heads for protection should the rocks start coming through the roof. Lightning produced by the ash clouds flashed continuously and the air smelled sulphurous. Finally, the eruption subsided and the students fell asleep around 3 am.

The next day they awoke to a moon-like landscape, with everything covered in a uniform layer of grey. They saw residents digging themselves out from underneath another eruption that dumped about 12.5 cm of ash in about $1\frac{1}{2}$ hours.

'What was once lush and green was dead and looked like a war zone,' said a student. 'It was like we had gone to another country overnight.'

Adapted from the Newswise website (www.newswise.com), 31 July 2003

August 3, 1997

Pyroclastic flows from Soufrière Hills volcano on Montserrat have reached the capital city of Plymouth. Many homes and businesses can be seen burning from several miles away. Fire fighters have been unable to stop these flames which threaten to consume the entire city. Flows in Gages Valley have also caused fires in Gages Village. These flows generated ash plumes which reached elevations of over 15 000 ft (4500 m). Ashfalls occurred in Isles Bay, Ole Towne, Salem and several other areas west of the volcano.

In the wake of this event and a June 25 event which left 10 dead and nine others missing, the British government is considering permanently relocating all of Montserrat's citizens off the island.

Adapted from website (www.nides.bc.ca/Assignments/Scavenge/Montserrat.htm)

1·14 Virtual volcanoes advanced organiser

Use this organiser to compare and contrast two volcanoes. You need to visit a number of websites to collect information about each volcano. Some areas to compare are given in the organiser below. Add extra categories you feel are relevant.

WEBLINKS You will find a link to the websites you need at www.nelsonthornes.com/horizons

VIRTUAL VOLCANOES – ADVANCED ORGANISER			Notes
TASK: To compare and contrast two volcanoes			
Category	**Volcano A**	**Volcano B**	
Name			
Location			
Plates involved			
Type of margin or hot spot			
Type of volcano			
Major eruptions			
Effects			
Solutions			

CONTENTS CHECKLIST – the final report must contain these things:

1

2

3

4

5

STAGES – the different parts of this report must be ready by these dates:

1	2	3	Final

SELF-EVALUATION – the strengths of this piece of work are:

1	2	3	4

SELF-ASSESSMENT – my report could be improved by:

1	2	3	4

DATA SOURCES – record where you obtained your information:

Web addresses	Texts	Papers	Other

Tectonics

1·15 Prediction and precaution

You will need to enlarge this sheet to A3.

Cut out the cards below so that each pupil has a method or an explanation card. Each pupil must find the person with the correct method to match their explanation or vice versa.

1 Go round the class to find the person with the correct method or explanation card to match your card.

2 When you have found your matching card, bring the result to the rest of the class.

3 As a class, collate your results.

4 Which methods do you think could be used:

   a for both an earthquake and an eruption?

   b for prediction or precaution?

   c to help a poor country?

Method cards	Explanation cards
Geophysical survey using seismometers	If lava threatens an inhabited area, channels may be dug to divert it to a safer area.
Gas detectors	Shock waves can occur before a major earthquake or eruption. As the magma chamber rises before an eruption, the ground may tremor.
Laser reflectors, tilt and creep meters	Deformation or movement of the ground can be detected by satellite photography and changes in heat/energy emissions can be located.
Hydrological survey	Earthquakes may involve movement along fault lines. Volcanoes may experience bulging as they build towards eruption.
Satellite remote sensing	Water levels may rise or fall as the ground is deformed before an earthquake.
Magnetometers and electrical resistivity meters	Money is set aside solely for use in a disaster situation.
Diversionary lava channels	Teams of trained rescuers remove people trapped by a disaster and deliver medical care.
Blocking lava channels	The chemistry of gases released just before an eruption changes and may help predict how close the main eruption is.
Sediment traps and dykes	Organised and known routes are practised to allow people to escape from a danger area.
Emergency rest, shelter and feeding centres	Even minute changes in the earth and atmosphere can be detected by animals such as dogs, geese and cattle.
Evacuation routes	Temporary housing, food and fresh water centres set up to help evacuees recover.
Emergency rescue and paramedics	Pyroclastic flows and lahars (mud/ash flows) may be impeded by digging traps to slow the flow of materials in valleys.
Communication warning systems	Deformation of the ground before an earthquake produces changes in the density and electrical resistance of the ground.
Contingency fund	Helicopters may be used to drop large concrete blocks into lava channels to make it flow elsewhere.
Erratic animal behaviour	Warnings and advice delivered by television, radio, phone or visits from wardens.

Tectonics

1·16 Tsunami aid timeline

see pages 20–21 in your Horizons Book 3

1 Draw a timeline similar to the one below to show the events on the right.

   a Use a large blank sheet of paper and draw a vertical line down the middle of it.

   b Write the events involving aid agencies or unaffected countries to the left of the line.

   c Write the events involving affected countries to the right of the line.

You will need to decide which facts to include and which to leave out.

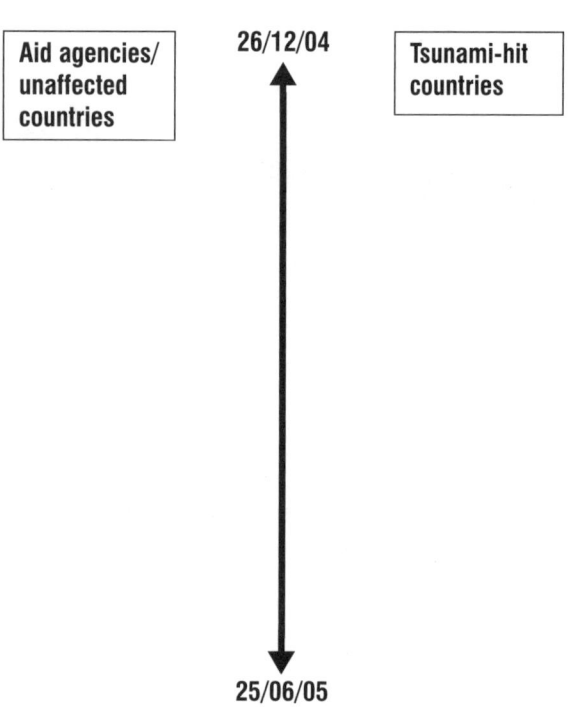

Aid agencies/ unaffected countries   26/12/04   Tsunami-hit countries

25/06/05

2 When you have completed your timeline:

   a circle in *red* the three most important events involving affected countries and explain why you have chosen them.

   b circle in *green* the three most important events involving aid agencies or unaffected countries and explain why you have chosen them.

3 Identify an event where estimated figures changed over time and suggest why this may have happened.

4 How does your timeline help to illustrate the idea that people need to 'think global, act local'?

DECEMBER 2004

26 0059 GMT Earthquake occurs

26 0114 GMT Tsunami warning centre issues first bulletin

26 0130–0700 GMT Sumatra hit by 10 m high waves; Thailand hit – people drowned in hotel rooms; Sri Lanka hit – 1500 washed away in train carriages; Maldives flooded; Somalia on East African coast hit; some tsunami deaths in South Africa 8000 km away ten hours after the earthquake

27 Survivors hunt for relatives; mortuaries overflowing; millions turn to internet for news; 27 000 assumed dead

28 Death toll 50 000; international disaster teams begin to arrive; BBC reports from Banda Aceh; some tourists begin to arrive home from disaster area

29 Death toll 77 000; aid efforts gather pace; need for clean water, body bags, food and medical supplies

30 Death toll 114 000; UK public donates £25 m in 24 hours to aid appeal; UK government increases its donation to £50 m, making it the largest international contributor

31 Death toll 124 000; Thai authorities warn that 6000 may be dead

JANUARY 2005

1 Monsoon rains add to Sri Lankan victims' woes; warnings of disease outbreaks

2 UN warns death toll is likely to top 150 000

3 US president makes appeal to raise money for victims

4 Airport accident blocks Aceh aid effort after cargo plane crashes into cow on runway

5 US secretary of state visits Aceh province to assess the extent of aid needed

6 International aid conference held in Jakarta to discuss how to get aid to victims; promising to work together to rebuild communities, they agree to build an early warning system to guard against future disasters

MARCH 2005

28 Powerful earthquake hits 160 km south of 26 December 2004 earthquake at Nias off coast of Indonesia

JUNE 2005

25 Final tsunami death toll estimated at more than 200 000 in 13 countries; about $13 bn (£7 bn) pledged in aid from around the world; pace of rebuilding slow and thousands of people remain homeless; UN estimates $9 bn needed over five years to rebuild the region

---

1·17 Volcanic words

see pages 22–23 in your Horizons Book 3

You will need to enlarge this sheet to A3.

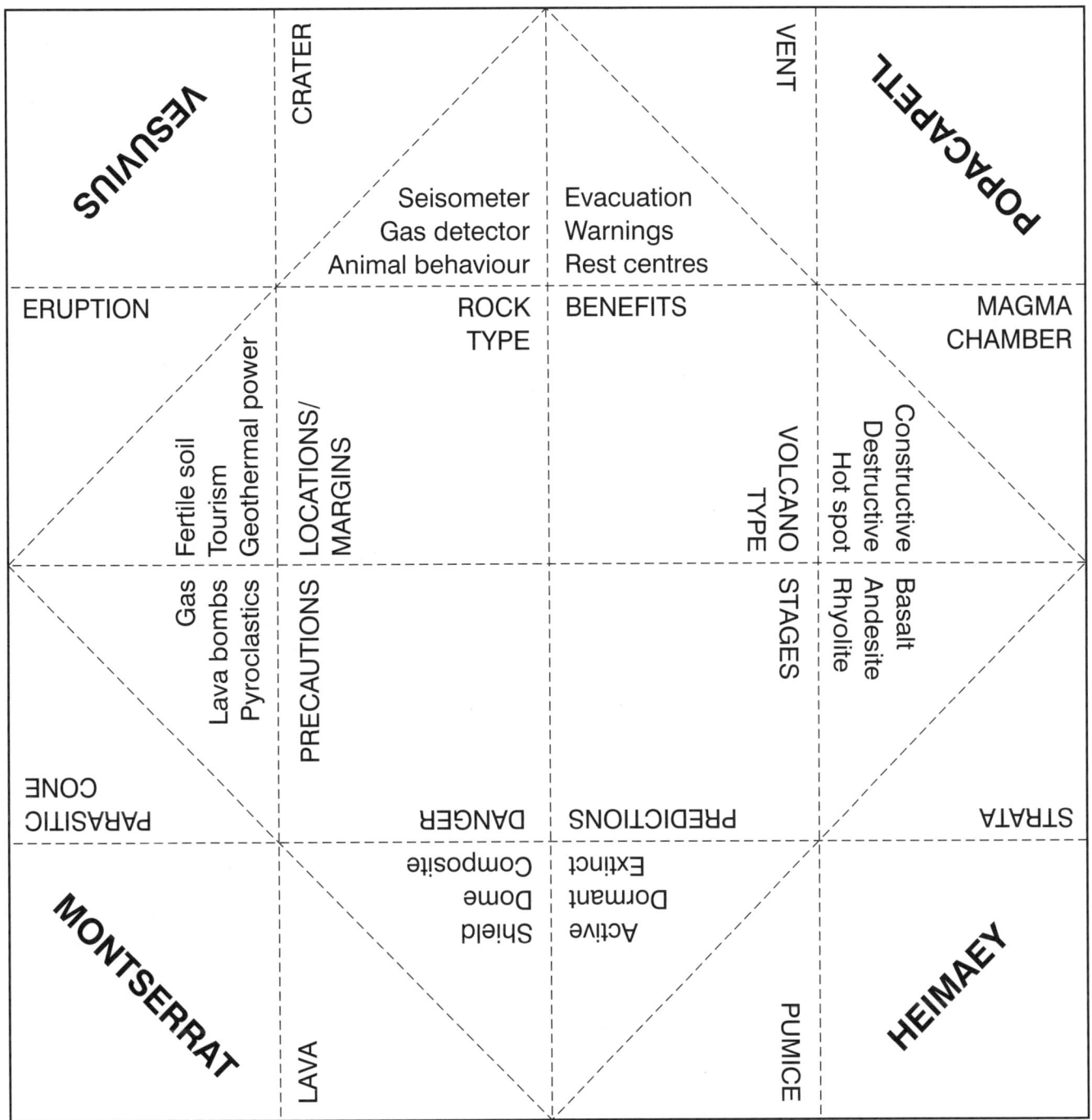

1 In pairs, carefully cut out and fold the paper snap game above.

2 One of you will be the operator and the other will be the player.

3 The player chooses one of the four volcanoes. The operator uses the paper snap to count the number of letters in the volcano's name.

4 The player chooses one of the four terms and explains its meaning to the operator.

5 If the player is correct, lift the flap to see which three-word combinations are inside. The player has to decide what these three words are all examples of. The answers are given on the bottom layer but not in the correct places.

83

1·18 Saving San Sebastian 1

Use the model on sheet 1.19, enlarged to A3.

[1] In small groups, carefully cut out the model along all the cut lines.

[2] Fold along the lines indicated.

[3] Use colour pencils to make the land use clearer and a fine-liner pen to mark on any symbols. All shading and colouring should be done before the model is constructed.

[4] Use glue on the flaps to construct the model.

[5] Stick the model onto a sheet of A2 sugar paper or display paper. This will allow you to annotate your comments around the outside, similar to the example below.

Ideas for features to include in your group display:

- A statement of the causes of the problems.
- A key to show what your symbols mean.
- Zones marked on the map to show which areas are dangerous and which are safer.
- Annotations to say why you located your solutions where you did.
- A table of costs to show how you have spent the funds available.
- Bullet points to highlight the points you want your audience to read as you are giving your presentation.
- Diagrams to show how the solutions might work.
- Concluding remarks.

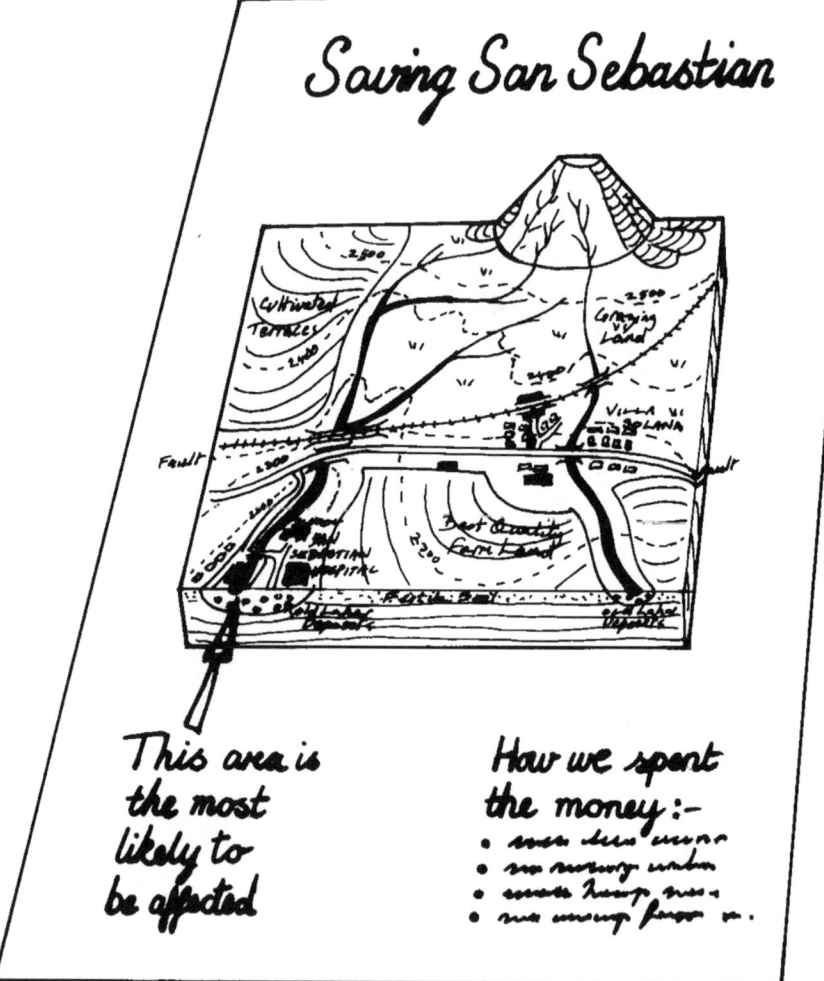

 This display is an aid to your presentation. Your writing should be concise and easy to read from a few metres away.

1·19 Saving San Sebastian 2

You will need to enlarge this sheet to A3.

— — — cut

— – — – fold

·:·:·:· glue

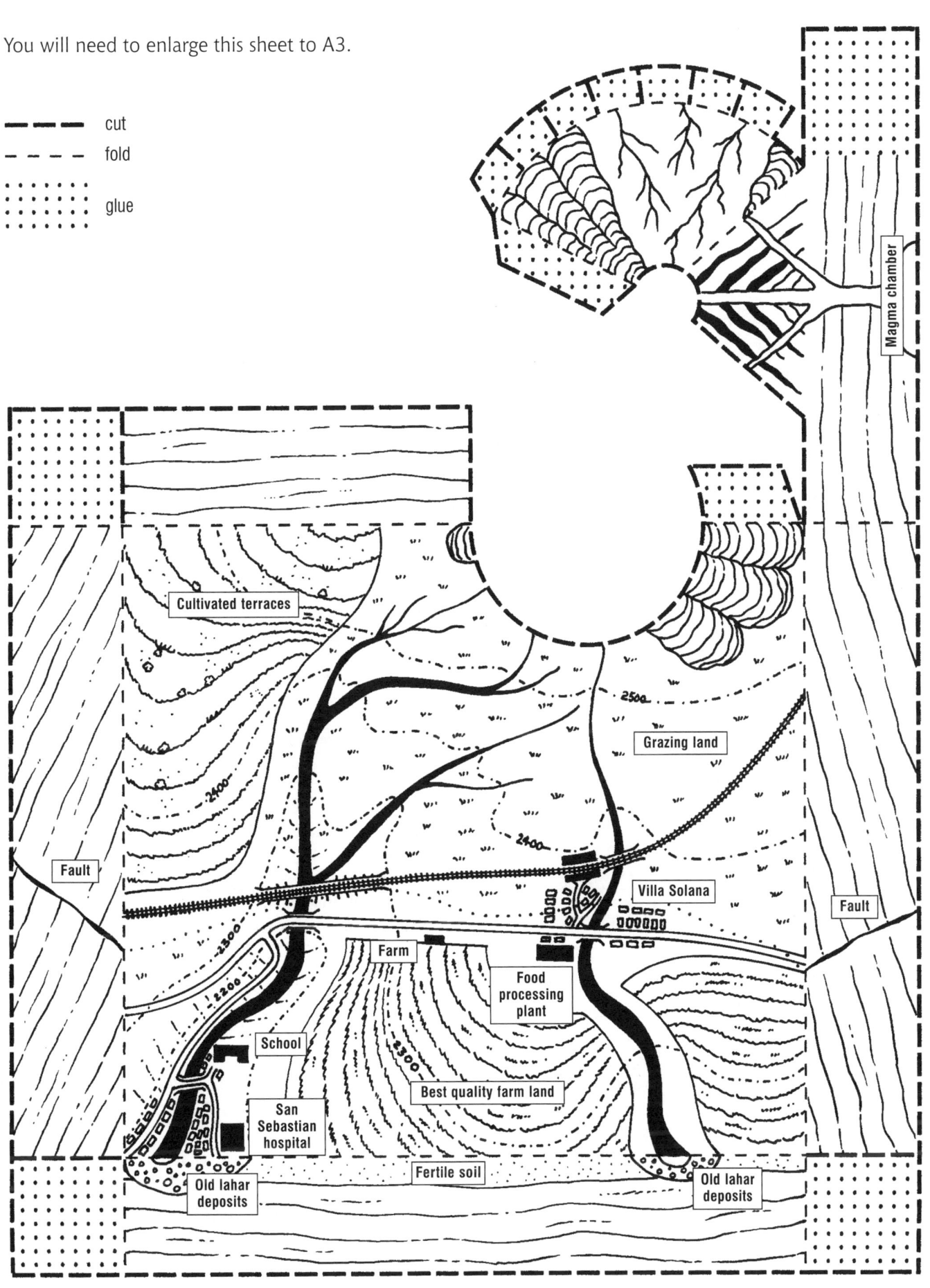

Magma chamber

Cultivated terraces

2500

Grazing land

2400

Fault

Villa Solana

Fault

2300

Farm

Food processing plant

School

2200

2300

San Sebastian hospital

Best quality farm land

Fertile soil

Old lahar deposits

Old lahar deposits

1·20 Reducing the impact of a volcanic eruption

You have been appointed as minister in charge of disaster relief in a country on the west coast of South America. Hazard Control Surveys have informed you that a volcanic event is likely within one year at Pico Magdalena in the western section of your province. The important agricultural towns of San Sebastian (population 3000) and Villa Solana (population 1500) lie at the foot of the volcano, close to the main highway and the railway connecting the capital, Peragua, with the major port of Pacifico.

You have been put in charge of reducing the impact of the eruption if it happens. You have a very limited budget (US$ 1 million) to spend, and only a small team of workers. The table below shows the cost of the various methods of prediction and precaution which you could use. You need to produce a report urgently, outlining for central government your intended prediction/precaution schemes. Don't go over budget!

	US$ (thousands)	Symbol
Predictions		
Hazard mapping	10	
Geophysical survey team (per year)	50	
Satellite monitoring (per year)	300	
Permanent observatory	500	
Precautions – emergency		
Damming lava channels – helicopter (per week)	200	
Paramedic relief/rescue squad (per year)	500	
Semi-trained volunteer rescue teams (per year)	100	
Estimated cost to compensate businesses on evacuation (per month)	100	

	US$ (thousands)	Symbol
Precautions – structural		
Barrier walls (per km)	200	
Diversionary lava channels	100	
Precautions – behavioural		
Education/evacuation drills	5	
Evacuation routes and warning systems	50	
New rest/relief centres	200	
Emergency food and water supplies	100	
Relocate all inhabitants in new towns and re-route road and rail	3000	

Your final report must include:

- a brief description of the problem
- an annotated map showing exactly where you will locate/implement your chosen methods. Design symbols for each method using the table above. Colour-coding land use and landscape features will help you to categorise information and identify high/low risk areas
- a table showing the methods you have chosen and the costs involved
- an explanation of how your scheme will work, and its limitations.

Unit 2 of the Pupil Book is supported by:

- photocopiable activity sheets and assessment for learning materials in this *Teaching and Learning Resources* guide on pages 88–119

- customisable unit and lesson plans on the accompanying *Planning CD-ROM* attached to the inside front cover of this guide

---

- visual resources, presentations and interactive activities on the *Electronic Resources CD-ROM* using the Just Click teaching solution.

In this section of the *Teaching and Learning Resources* guide you will find:

Pages 88–89... have a list of opportunities for **Assessment for Learning** in this unit. One example is provided for each double-page spread. These ideas are based on activities in the Pupil Book, but each activity needs some development if it is to be used as an Assessment for Learning opportunity. Most of the suggestions involve pupils in assessment of their own work, in peer-assessment, or in some other form of discussion of the work either before or after it is attempted. All these suggestions are intended to increase pupils' awareness of what characterises good work, and of how their own work can be developed and improved.

The suggestions here are not intended to be prescriptive. Rather they provide teachers with opportunities that we feel fit the best practice of Assessment for Learning, and which target pupils' learning – an increasingly important area of focus under the new Ofsted inspection framework.

Page 90... is a **Learning Plan** for pupils, which gives them a copy of the learning objectives for the unit – copied from page 24 of the Pupil Book – and provides opportunities for pupils to assess their prior learning and set their targets for the whole unit, using the Attainment Targets on pages 91–92 as criteria for success. There is an opportunity at the end of the unit for pupils to re-assess their level against the Attainment Targets before completing the final self-assessment form (How far have I travelled?) on page 98.

Pages 91–92... give pupils a summary of the **Attainment Target** statements, adapted from the National Curriculum level descriptors, which are relevant to their work in this unit. Pupils can use the levels as criteria for success to set themselves learning targets for the unit and check their progress using the Learning Plan on page 90. They have also been divided into two sections, *Places and Environments* and *Enquiry and Skills*. Pupils should be able to see what it is that allows their work to move from one level to the higher level. These Attainment Targets can also be used to provide further support if required for pupils setting and reviewing their targets in the Assessment Opportunity for this unit (see below).

Pages 93–95... are also written for pupils. They describe the **Assessment Opportunity** on pages 42–43 of the Pupil Book. If teachers decide to use this exercise to assess the level at which pupils are working, these pages can help to guide pupils through that exercise. They should also help pupils to set targets for the exercise, to assess their own work and to set new targets for subsequent work. This will enable teachers and pupils to benefit from making formative use of the Assessment Opportunity. (Note that this differs from the Learning Plan on page 90 which provides Assessment for Learning support for the whole unit rather than an individual assessment.) Alternatively, teachers can use these pages as a mark scheme to help them to assess the individual performance of pupils and build a portfolio of assessments to track their progress during Key Stage 3 Geography.

Pages 96–97... provide **Model Answers** for the Assessment Opportunity on pages 42–43 of the Pupil Book. These model answers can be used in a variety of ways. Teachers can display them as models of good practice for whole-class discussion, or pupils could look at them before they start to write their own answers. However, they are really intended to support the self- or peer-assessment process before pupils analyse their own work. The aim is to demonstrate the need to offer supporting information/explanation for each point made when answering the question as well as the need for balance when constructing an argument. Pupils can identify where the writer has successfully addressed the question and/or where they fail to address it. Pupils will be better able to identify the specific actions they must take to produce better-quality answers. This will help them to assess their own work or the work of peers. This process is further supported by the Assessment Sheets on pages 43–49.

Page 98... is a **Self-Assessment Sheet** (How far have I travelled?) that can be used to complement the Learning Plan on page 90 or as an alternative form of self-review for the unit to be filled in by pupils at the end of the unit. This form is not linked to the Attainment Targets for the unit, but reviews progress against the learning objectives and enables pupils to record their personal impressions and achievements during the unit, providing them with a more subjective opportunity for self-assessment than the levelled approach adopted by the Learning Plan.

Pages 99–119... consist of photocopiable **Activity Sheets** to support the material in the Pupil Book.

*All of these resources and activities are also available on the **Planning CD-ROM** in either Word or PDF for teachers to print out if preferred or to display on whiteboards or projectors for whole-class discussion. They can also be customised to suit individual needs and, if required, saved with the other **electronic resources** for the unit using the facility to 'add your own resources' in the Just Click teaching solution.*

Assessment for Learning

The following suggestions are intended to show how the material in Unit 2 of **Horizons 3** provides opportunities for teachers and pupils to assess their work as they go along, and to improve their learning as a result of that assessment. It must be stressed that these are only a few of the ways in which the material in the Pupil Book can be used. The techniques could be used as they are outlined here, but teachers will probably find that it is more helpful to use these as starting points and to develop their own ideas to suit their own circumstances.

Before you get started

There is an integral Assessment for Learning framework provided for Unit 2 (and every unit in **Horizons**):

- The unit opens on pages 24–25 of the Pupil Book with the learning objectives for the unit (Where are we going?). The lesson plans on the *Planning CD-ROM* then include learning objectives and outcomes for each spread in turn (supported by pupil-friendly versions in PowerPoint on the *Electronic Resources CD-ROM*).

- The unit ends on pages 42–43 of the Pupil Book with a plenary spread to review and evaluate the unit (Where are we now?), particularly in light of the learning objectives from the opening spread.

- The Learning Plan and Attainment Targets for the unit on pages 90–92 in this *Teaching and Learning Resources* guide provide pupils with the opportunity to set individual learning targets at the start of the unit and to review their progress against these targets at the end. The final self-assessment sheet (How far have I travelled?) on page 98 then offers pupils a more subjective review of their progress during the unit.

Teachers can use or adapt all or some of these resources to set and review goals and involve pupils in their own learning. Further resources on the *Electronic Resources CD-ROM* provide activities for initial assessment of prior learning at the start of the unit to help teachers to diagnose strengths and weaknesses for each topic and for checking and testing knowledge and understanding during and at the end of the unit. All these resources will provide teachers with further evidence to help structure and focus the learning programme.

Pages 24–25

Pupils can share their ideas on what the basic needs to live are using a 'think, pair and share' succession of groupings, identifying any similarities and differences in their current perceptions. Activities 3 and 4 give many opportunities to share personal perceptions against the group or collective idea of the norm. Similarly, the development compass rose activities in 5, 6 and 7 ask pupils to raise their own questions before comparing with peers and testing the effectiveness of their questions and answers.

Pages 26–27

Activities 4, 5 and 6 are ideally suited to peer-assessment as pupils can compare the key features of their descriptions in 4 and 5 while in 6 pairs or groups could take turns to name one reason why using GDP may not always be the best indicator of development. Other pairs or groups can be encouraged to be involved with this exercise by actively listening to the general point before being asked to find a named example where this point is demonstrated.

Pages 28–29

By assigning each pair of pupils a different country to consider for activities 2 and 6, pupils will be able to describe their own impressions and suggest if they conflict with preconceptions. Pupils can share their initial descriptions on activity 10 and decide what the best features of their answers are. This could lead them to consider what must feature in a good description of a thematic map, e.g. direction, distance, specific names, comparisons, numerical data.

Pages 30–31

This spread is based on an ICT investigation of development criteria. A starter could involve rephrasing the question in step 1 of the investigation plan 'How can I tell if a country is less economically developed?' Pupil suggestions could be a good starting point in establishing criteria for success for useful search and sorting criteria for the spreadsheet exercise in activities 1 and 2. Comparing which countries pupils have selected in activity 3 is a good way of deriving a class consensus while asking pupils to justify their choices. Activities 13 and 14 are both ideally suited to pair and share activities, perhaps with notes of improvement suggestions stuck to the board to raise the awareness of others.

Pages 32–33

The starter could involve reading Nelson Mandela's speech and asking pairs of students to come up with their three worst effects of world poverty. The class can share and justify their ideas on what are the worst aspects of poverty. They can then use activity 2 to decide which are the major causes of poverty based on their work in activities 3 and 4. The plenary should ideally involve pupils linking the messages from the cartoon to the bigger messages they have derived from the lesson as a whole.

Pages 34–35

Activity 1 asks pairs of students to rank the Millennium Development Goals according to how they perceive their importance. These could be compared and a class tally taken to determine the top five. Justifications on why they are important and which order they should be tackled in should highlight how interconnected these aims are. Activity 3 involves creating a biography from a timeline. Pairs of pupils should take turns to explain their timeline tables while observers suggest improvements. The alternative biographies should be talked through and questioned during pupil-led plenaries.

Pages 36–37

The starter involves comparing the consequences to the individual, family and community of not going to school. By showing a three-circle Venn diagram on the board (individual, family and community), pupils can be invited to classify the consequences on the diagram. Activities 2 and 3 ideally suit pupil plenaries.

To help pupils focus in activity 4, which involves writing a report concerning how a new school has benefited from aid and changed over time, pairs of pupils could suggest what a finished report might include, linking physical change to improved prospects, limitations and future possibilities. The final activity suggests a presentation to the whole school, which would give additional opportunities to develop presentation skills and determine which are the key ingredients for a successful talk.

Pages 38–39

Activity 2 offers four 'Fantastic Facts' to be considered. Pupils can be asked to select the one they think is the most surprising for them and explain why. This is best accomplished as a 'think, pair and share' activity. By asking pupils to then decide which is the fact most likely to be easy to solve in the short term by their actions, the outcomes are further classified. Activity 5 invites pupils to plan what they could do in their own lives. This should lead to an evaluation of the options, beginning with a class consensus on the golden rules for an effective fair trade strategy, e.g. number of people involved, size of market, value of goods sold, number of goods sold, sustainability (how long, how easy it would be to continue), who makes the decisions.

Pages 40–41

A starter activity could be centred on tapping into what pupils already think they know about sustainable development (activities 1 and 2). By asking them to write their definitions on the board in groups before they read the text, pupils can consider the different range of scales encountered when defining the meaning of the word. Activity 4 encourages pupils to look at images of sustainable and unsustainable development. The opinion line activity encourages them to rank the disparate projects and justify their choices. By referring back to the definitions of sustainability listed during the suggested starter, pupils can refine their ideas of what the word means and then consider again the implications of dealing with change in a sustainable manner.

Pages 42–43

The classification exercise in activity 2 based on information about Niger is ideally suited to peer- and self-assessment as pupils initially develop a basic table then assign short-term/long-term and important/less important attributes to a variety of causes. Pupil-led plenaries should be used to encourage pupils to explain their thinking behind the decisions they have made.

Activity 7 is based around a class debate that leads to an extended piece of writing on the effect of media coverage on aid to disasters like Niger and can be used as a summative assessment opportunity for this unit. However, the Assessment Opportunity on pages 93–97 in this *Teaching and Learning Resources* guide provides criteria for success, model answers and a process for target setting and use of this assessment.

2 80:20

Learning plan

What are my learning objectives for this unit?

I aim to learn about:

✓ different definitions of development

✓ world poverty, its causes and why it is unevenly spread

✓ ways of using data to measure and analyse development patterns

✓ what governments, voluntary groups and individuals can do to support development

✓ the importance of sustainable development, and fair trade.

Read the Attainment Targets for this unit on pages 91–92 and tick any statements that you feel refer to you. *Places and Environments* covers *what you know* about the topic and *Enquiry and Skills* covers *what you can do.*

Using these statements for this unit, decide what level you are overall at this stage:

Level ____

What level do you think you can achieve by the end of this unit?

Level ____

What are you going to concentrate on to achieve this level? A good place to start might be any statements on pages 91–92 that you have not ticked:

At the end of the unit, read the Attainment Targets again and tick in a different colour any *new* statements that refer to you. Then decide what level you are now:

Level ____

If you have improved, well done! What evidence can you show for this improvement? What or who do you think particularly helped you to improve your level?

If you have stayed the same, better luck next time! What do you think you could have done differently to help improve your levels? What will you do next time to progress further?

2 80:20

My Attainment Targets for this unit

Level 3

Places and Environments

☐ I can begin to describe the pattern of worldwide poverty.

☐ I can describe and give some reasons for the differences in development throughout the world.

☐ I can begin to describe some of the ways developing countries may be supported.

Enquiry and Skills

☐ I can select and use some information from maps, photos and written sources to find out how developed different parts of the world are.

☐ I can use appropriate data to describe how developed countries are.

Level 4

Places and Environments

☐ I can describe the differences in the pattern of worldwide poverty.

☐ I can describe and give reasons for the differences in development throughout the world.

☐ I can begin to describe some of the ways governments, voluntary groups and individuals can support development in other countries.

Enquiry and Skills

☐ I can select and use some information from a range of different sources to find out how developed different parts of the world are.

☐ I can select and use appropriate data to describe how developed countries are.

Level 5

Places and Environments

☐ I can describe the variations in development worldwide.

☐ I can give reasons for the differences in development throughout the world.

☐ I can describe some of the ways governments, voluntary groups and individuals can support development in other countries.

☐ I can suggest reasons why people may hold different views on how differences in development should be managed.

Enquiry and Skills

☐ I can suggest geographical questions about development.

☐ I can select and use information from a range of different sources to investigate development issues.

☐ I can select and use appropriate data to describe how developed countries are.

☐ I can present my findings with a conclusion.

Level 6

Places and Environments

☐ I can use a range of examples from regional to international level to describe and explain why some places are more developed than others.

☐ I can describe a range of ways governments, voluntary groups and individuals can support development in other countries.

☐ I can suggest reasons why people may hold different views on how differences in development should be managed and how these views may lead to conflict.

Enquiry and Skills

☐ I can suggest geographical questions as part of my investigations.

☐ I can collect data from a wide range of sources to investigate a variety of development issues.

☐ I can select an appropriate range of skills to compare and contrast places at different stages of development.

☐ I can present the findings of my investigations in a logical way and reach conclusions consistent with the evidence.

Level 7

Places and Environments

☐ I can use a wide range of examples at local to global level to describe and explain why some places are more developed than others.

☐ I can describe a range of ways governments, voluntary groups and individuals interact to support development in other countries.

☐ I can explain why decisions about managing development are influenced by people's views and attitudes that may have far-reaching consequences.

Enquiry and Skills

☐ I can show independence to identify issues to investigate, ask geographical questions and follow my own sequence of enquiry.

☐ I can use accurately a wide range of skills and sources of evidence.

☐ I can select an appropriate range of skills to compare and contrast places at different stages of development.

☐ I can evaluate critically most sources of evidence, present well-argued summaries of my investigations and begin to reach conclusions that are clearly based on evidence.

Level 8

Places and Environments

☐ I can use a wide range of examples at all scales from different parts of the world to describe and explain why some places are more developed than others.

☐ I can offer explanations for the interactions within physical, human and economic factors that determine how developed countries are.

☐ I can explain how people in different countries interact to try to manage differences in levels of development.

☐ I can understand a range of views and attitudes on the management of development issues and why decisions may have far-reaching consequences.

Enquiry and Skills

☐ I can show a high level of independence to identify issues to investigate, and make justified decisions.

☐ I can independently select a wide range of techniques and skills to collect and analyse data.

☐ I can evaluate critically most sources of evidence, present well-argued summaries of my investigations and begin to reach conclusions that are clearly based on evidence.

On page 43 in activity 7b you are asked to produce an extended piece of writing on the effect of the media on the Niger famine, following on from a debate based on what you have learned during this unit and reflecting on the two extracts provided.

Your final report must include:

- a brief description of the problems faced by Niger
- a description of how the disaster is portrayed in the media
- an explanation of how the media affects the views, attitudes and actions of people, countries and governments
- suggestions of the limitations of media coverage
- a conclusion.

Before you start this activity, look at the **Criteria for success** sheet. Set yourself a target level to aim for in this Assessment Opportunity. Write this level in the box on the target setting sheet. Explain how you intend to obtain this level.

Once you have finished the activity, look again at the Criteria for success and assess your answers. You could also compare your answers with model answers. Write your level in the box and explain how you achieved this level.

Then set yourself a target for improvement in your next assessment. Explain what you need to do to improve next time. Try to set yourself specific tasks to work on.

A **Level 3** answer may	• describe some of the effects of the Niger famine • describe some of the causes of the Niger famine • give some examples of how the media has helped Niger.
A **Level 4** answer may	• describe in more detail and begin to explain the effects of the Niger famine • begin to explain some of the causes of the Niger famine • give examples of how the media has helped increase aid to Niger • describe some of the ways the media may not help.
A **Level 5** answer may	• describe in more detail and explain the effects of the Niger famine • explain some of the causes of the Niger famine • give examples of how the media has affected people's attitudes about giving aid to Niger • begin to explain some of the ways media coverage can have a negative effect on the aid some countries receive.
A **Level 6** answer may	• explain the main causes and effects of the Niger famine and suggest how they may be linked • give a range of examples to explain how the media has affected the amount of aid Niger has received from individuals, countries and governments • explain some of the limitations of media coverage in helping countries.
A **Level 7** answer may	• explain a wide range of effects and causes of the Niger famine and explain how they are linked • give a wide range of examples to explain how the media has affected the amount of aid Niger has received from different sources • explain some of the links between how the media affects attitudes and decisions from individual to government level • explain a range of the limitations of media coverage in helping countries.
A **Level 8** answer may	• explain the full range of effects and causes of the Niger famine and explain how they are linked • give a full range of examples to explain how the media has affected aid to Niger from different sources • explain the links between how the media affects attitudes and decisions from individual to government level • explain a wide range of the limitations of media coverage in helping countries.

My target setting

I want to make progress in geography, in my written report on the Niger famine.

When I do activity 7b on page 43, I aim to obtain:

Level

To do this I will need to:

Answer these questions when you have completed activity 7b on page 43:

In this Assessment Opportunity I obtained:

Level

Explain how you obtained this level:

When I do my next Assessment Opportunity, I aim to obtain:

Level

To do this I will need to:

2 80:20

Model answers

A This is a good basic answer that was written by a pupil who had completed activity 7b on page 43.

The way the media has reported disasters like the Niger famine has a big effect on how people think about it in other countries. For example, people get upset when they see pictures of dying children on the television or in the newspaper. This may make them want to give some money or take part in fund-raising activities for charity. That can be a good thing because countries like Niger will get money to help them out.

A problem is that if people see too many images they start to lose interest and may stop giving money. They can also see images of a different disaster like the Kashmir earthquake of 2005 and give their money to that instead. If Niger needs a regular supply of help, this may not be good for them because new schools need funds for more than one year.

The media doesn't cause the problem. That seems to be caused by climate change like the rains failing, swarms of locusts and people being driven to do desperate things like selling their animals or tools. The media can play a big part in deciding which disaster we see on the television and which one we want to give our money to. The problem is we don't give until there is a disaster – we don't care enough when problems are starting.

B This is a better answer, which achieves a higher level than the first one (A).
- Read it carefully, and try to see why this is better than the first answer.
- Try to see how it meets new parts of the criteria for success.
- Try to see how you could use ideas from this work to improve your own work.

The media has a big part to play in how we react to disasters but it doesn't cause them in the first place. The Niger famine has been caused by the rains failing, which happens all over the Sahel. It is probably down to climate change. This may also have helped the locust swarms that ate a lot of the crops. In these difficult times, people were forced to do things that probably made things worse like eating their animals, selling their farming equipment or moving away completely and crowding other areas. These things mean they cannot farm successfully even when the rains do come back.

The media is the only way most of us gets to know about these events, so it should get credit for raising our awareness. It is often when there has been a lot of media coverage like when Comic Relief is on the television that people get upset and pay money to charities or get involved in fun runs and collections.

The other way the media helps is that it makes people ask questions of their government and sometimes embarrasses it into giving more money than it had planned to. Some people think this happened with Live Aid in 1985 and the Live 8 events in 2005.

In other ways the media doesn't help. If it's not your disaster that is on the news, you won't get sympathy or money from people. Also, it gives a false impression of countries and shows them as if they can't help themselves. Eighty per cent of people in the UK think the same countries are always 'failing' as if they don't try or as if we are better. There may be lots of schemes to improve things and make good use of aid money from governments but it doesn't look impressive on television.

If we were more interested in other people in different countries, we might hear more about what they do instead of horror stories. Perhaps we get the media we want.

C   This is an even better answer, which achieves a higher level than (A) or (B).

- Read it carefully, and try to see why this is better than the previous answers.
- Try to see how it meets new parts of the criteria for success.
- Try to see how you could use ideas from this work to improve your own work.

The media influences our views, attitudes and how we react to disasters like the Niger famine. It can make us angry, ashamed and even persuade us to give money or raise funds ourselves. It doesn't cause the problems of places like Niger, but it can affect how we respond to such disasters and that isn't always in the interests of that country.

The Niger famine has been caused by the rains failing, which in turn causes crops to fail. It is probably down to climate change, which could also explain the locust swarms that attacked crops. It is a problem faced by about 8 million people in the Sahel in countries like Mali and Chad. In Niger, where 82% of the population are subsistence farmers, this is a serious problem that has led to 3.6 million people going hungry. With 40% of all children undernourished, there is real fear for the future. Because they are desperate, people have been forced to eat leaves and even their own animals. Some sold their farming equipment or moved away completely and overcrowded other areas. As a result, they cannot farm successfully even when the rains do come again. In this way the natural problem has human causes as well.

The media is the main way we find out about Niger – we just wouldn't know if we didn't see it on television or in the papers. Big media events like Comic Relief affect masses of people. They may be upset but they also give money to charities and aid organisations or get involved in sponsored runs or other events. People not normally interested in how much aid the UK gives to the developing world want to help and may put pressure on the government to help more, such as with Live Aid in 1985 and the Live 8 events in 2005.

Government aid is usually predictable and dependable. The media may make us concerned but if the pictures from Niger aren't as exciting as the next tsunami ones, we lose interest or at least send our money elsewhere. New schools like Mkwakwani in Kenya and hospitals need dependable funding for a long time.

Some 80% of people in the UK think most developing countries are in a 'permanent state of disaster'. Some people think that they can only survive if 'better' countries like the UK bale them out. The media may encourage us to think this way. Schemes to improve things in the long run using local people and aid money from governments just aren't as newsworthy. Perhaps the media gets us interested in disaster relief rather than long-term support to help others help themselves.

The media shows us some of the reality, perhaps as much as we can take. Would we switch off the TV if we knew the truth? If we were more interested before things get bad enough to show on TV, we could have solved the hunger problem for $1 a day and not waited until it costs $20 per child. If the media could get the richer 80% of the world to give more to the poorer 20%, it would make an even bigger impact.

2 80:20

How far have I travelled?

In this unit my **Learning Objectives** were to learn about:

- different definitions of development
- world poverty, its causes and why it is unevenly spread
- ways of using data to measure and analyse development patterns
- what governments, voluntary groups and individuals can do to support development
- the importance of sustainable development, and fair trade.

My progress in this unit

How well have I achieved my objectives?	Okay								Excellent
Enquiry and Skills:									
to read photographs, diagrams and maps effectively									
to select appropriate data to analyse development issues									
to be able to ask questions using a development compass rose									
to use spreadsheets to analyse development data									
to search websites for additional development data									
Places and Environments:									
to know why development may have different definitions									
to be able to describe the uneven pattern of world poverty									
to understand why some regions suffer from poverty more than others									
to understand the ways in which governments, voluntary organisations and individuals can support development									
to know how sustainable development can support poorer countries, e.g. with Fairtrade									

Shade the bars to show how far you think you have made progress in this unit.

The part of this unit that I enjoyed the most was ...

because ...

The part of this unit that I needed most help with was ...

because ...

The piece of work that I am most pleased with is ...

because ...

The aspect of this unit that will be most useful to me in future is ...

because ...

Any other comments?

see pages 24–25 in your Horizons Book 3

Development compass rose

Use two copies of this development compass rose to complete activities 5–7 on page 25 of your textbook.

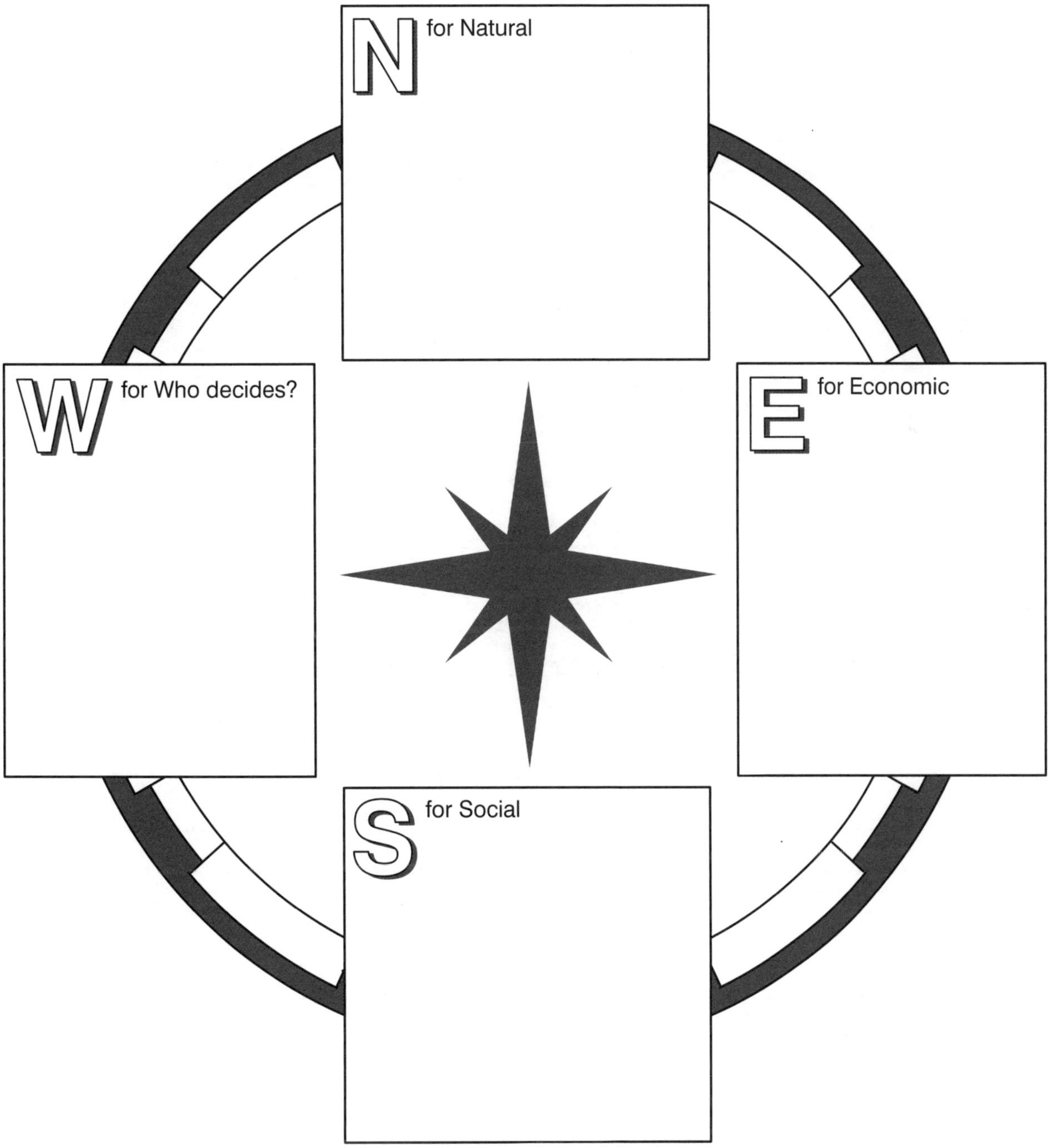
N for Natural
W for Who decides?
E for Economic
S for Social

<table>
<tr><td>

What?

_____
_____
_____
_____

</td><td>

Who?

_____
_____
_____
_____

</td><td>

When?

_____
_____
_____
_____

</td></tr>
</table>

<table>
<tr><td>

Why?

_____
_____
_____
_____
_____

</td><td>

Where?

_____
_____
_____
_____
_____

</td></tr>
</table>

1 Compare the sketch above with photo A on page 24 of your textbook.

2 Label the key geographical features shown on the sketch.

3 Answer the 5Ws questions around the sketch.

2·3 Can I locate places on a world map?

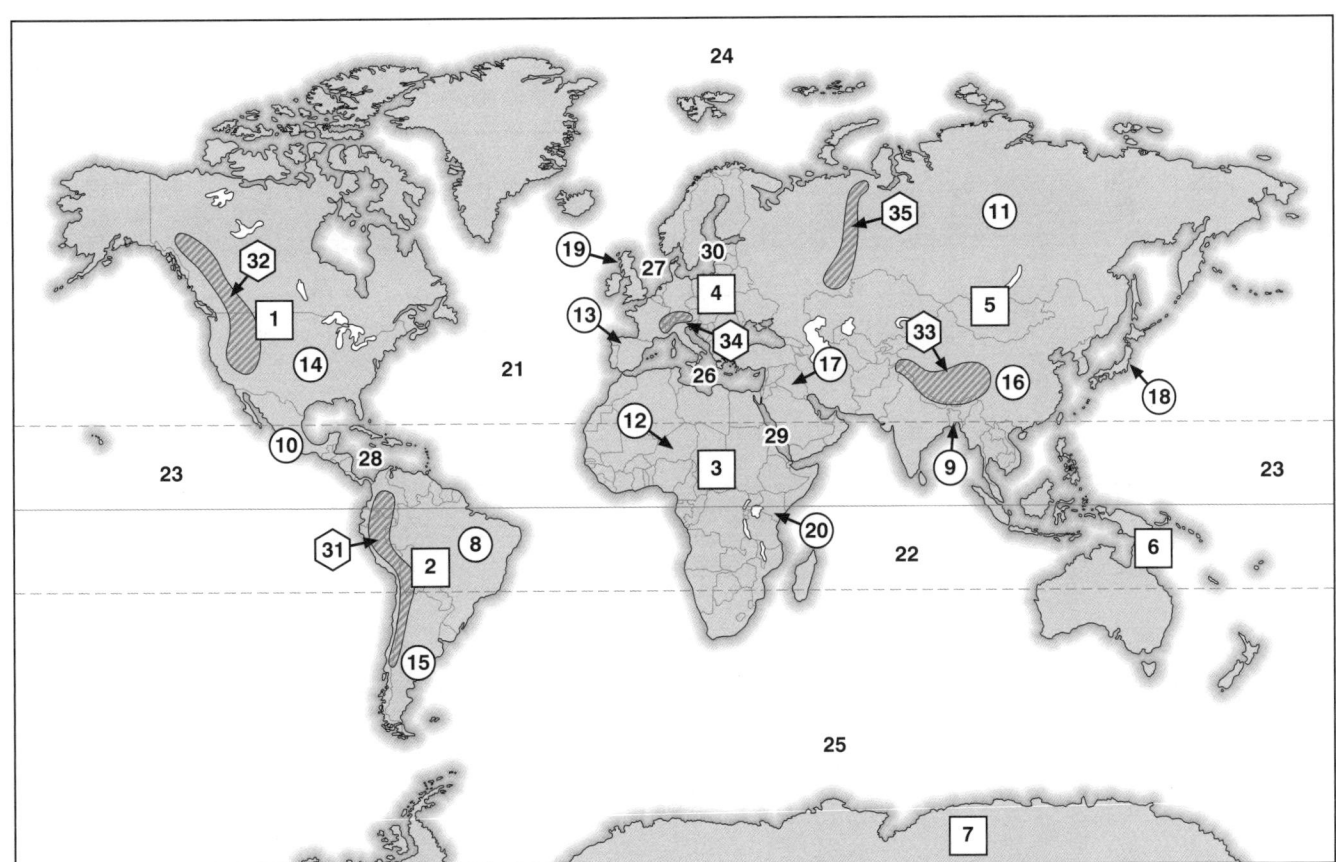

Study the map of the world.

1 Name continents 1–7.

2 Name countries 8–20.

3 Name seas and oceans 21–30.

4 Name mountain ranges 31–35.

Can I locate places on a world map?

Total score: /35

Compare your score and performance with the statements in the table below.

Score	✓	
30–35		I can locate places on a world map. No problem!
20–29		I can locate most places, but need to top-up my knowledge with an atlas.
10–19		I can locate some places on a world map, but need to improve my overall knowledge with an atlas.
1–9		I need to spend time finding the location of places using an atlas or back cover resource F.

2·4 Analysis of world GDP

Use the writing frame below to help you draft an analysis
of map A on pages 26–27 of your textbook.

The world map on pages 26–27 of textbook shows the GDP for each country of the world.
GDP is _____

_____

It is possible to identify a pattern to the world distribution of GDP bands shown on the map.
The highest GDP band countries are concentrated in _____

_____

_____

_____

The lowest GDP band countries are concentrated in _____

_____

_____

_____

The middle band countries are concentrated in _____

_____

_____

_____

The UK's GDP band is _____

_____

_____

Different terms have been used when referring to countries and their level of development.
These include _____

_____

_____

_____

_____

_____

There are disadvantages in using GDP as a measure of development. These include

_____

_____

_____

_____

_____

_____

102

see pages 28–29 in your Horizons Book 3

Comparing proportional world maps

Complete the Venn diagram to show how the two proportional maps on page 28 of your textbook are similar and how they differ.

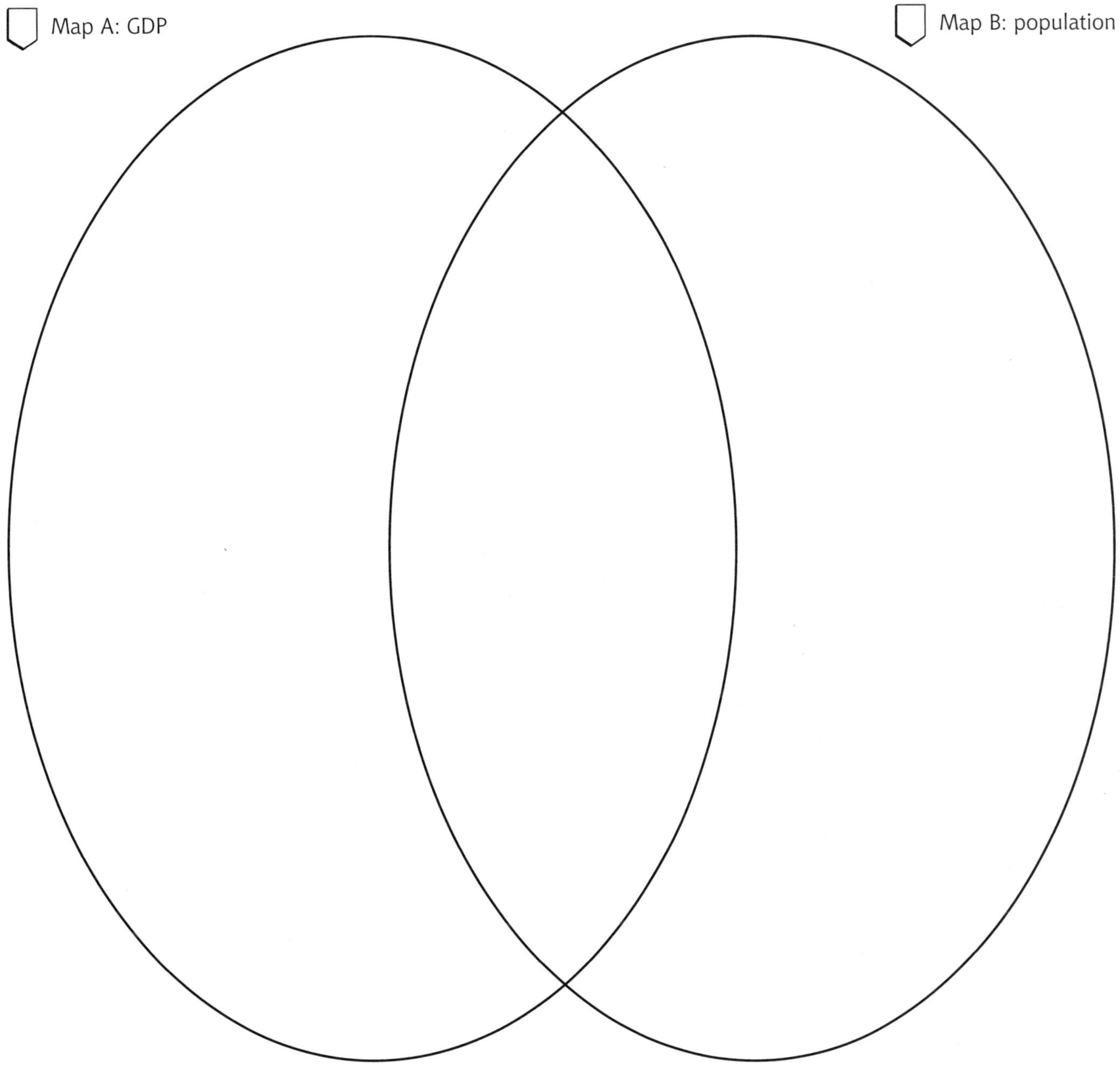
Map A: GDP
Map B: population

2·6 80:20

What is development? 1

The evaluation section of your development enquiry asked you to consider your understanding of development. This diamond ranking activity can help with this.

1 Cut out the statements below.

2 In pairs, take turns to read out the statements to each other.

3 Use the diamond on sheet 2.7 to rank each statement. The statement you think is the most important should be placed at the top, and the statement you think is the least important should be placed at the bottom.

4 Compare your diamond with your partner.

5 Carry out a whole-class discussion to work out the best-fit diamond for the whole class.

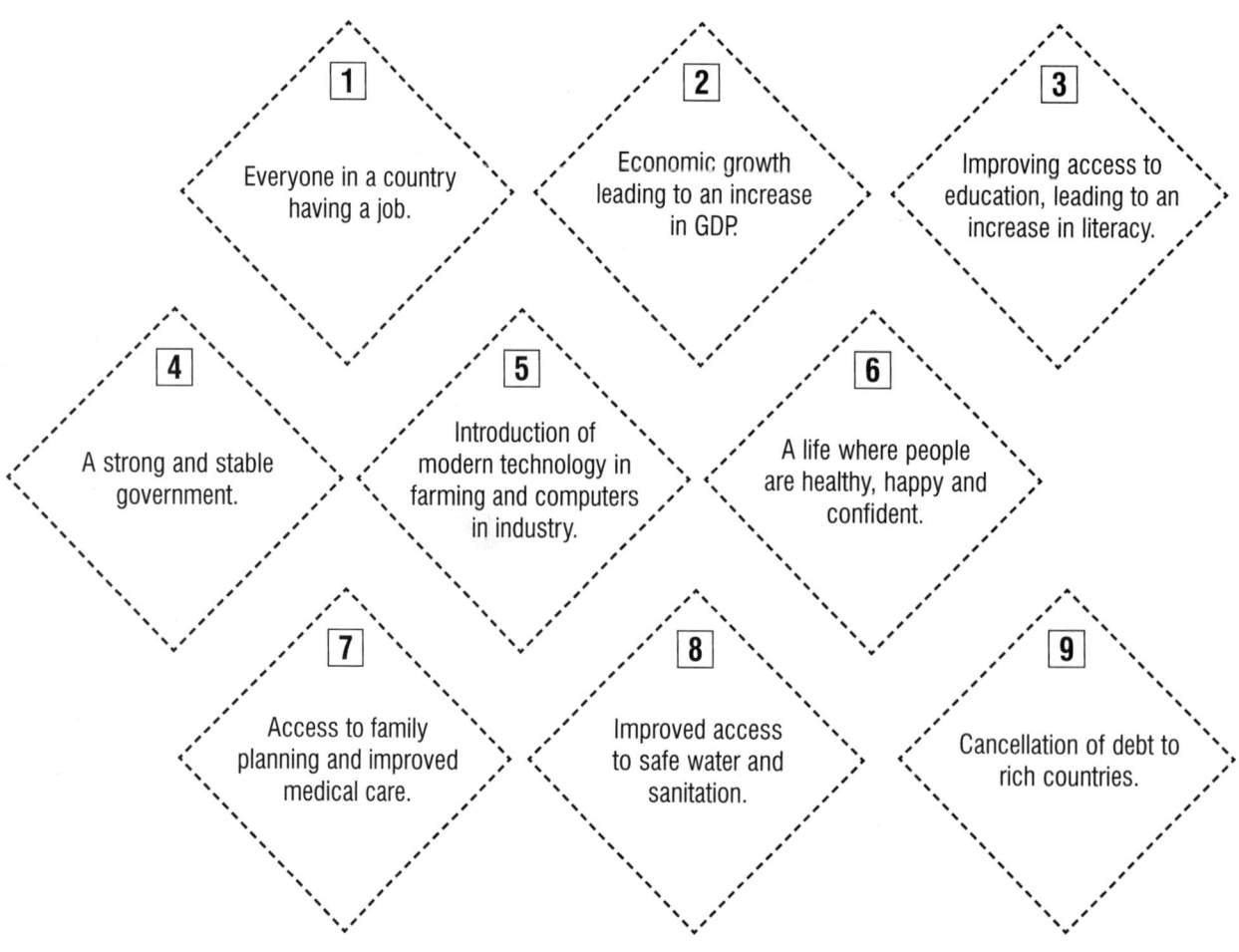

1 Everyone in a country having a job.

2 Economic growth leading to an increase in GDP.

3 Improving access to education, leading to an increase in literacy.

4 A strong and stable government.

5 Introduction of modern technology in farming and computers in industry.

6 A life where people are healthy, happy and confident.

7 Access to family planning and improved medical care.

8 Improved access to safe water and sanitation.

9 Cancellation of debt to rich countries.

What is development? 2

Use this diamond shape for the statements on sheet 2.6.

Most important

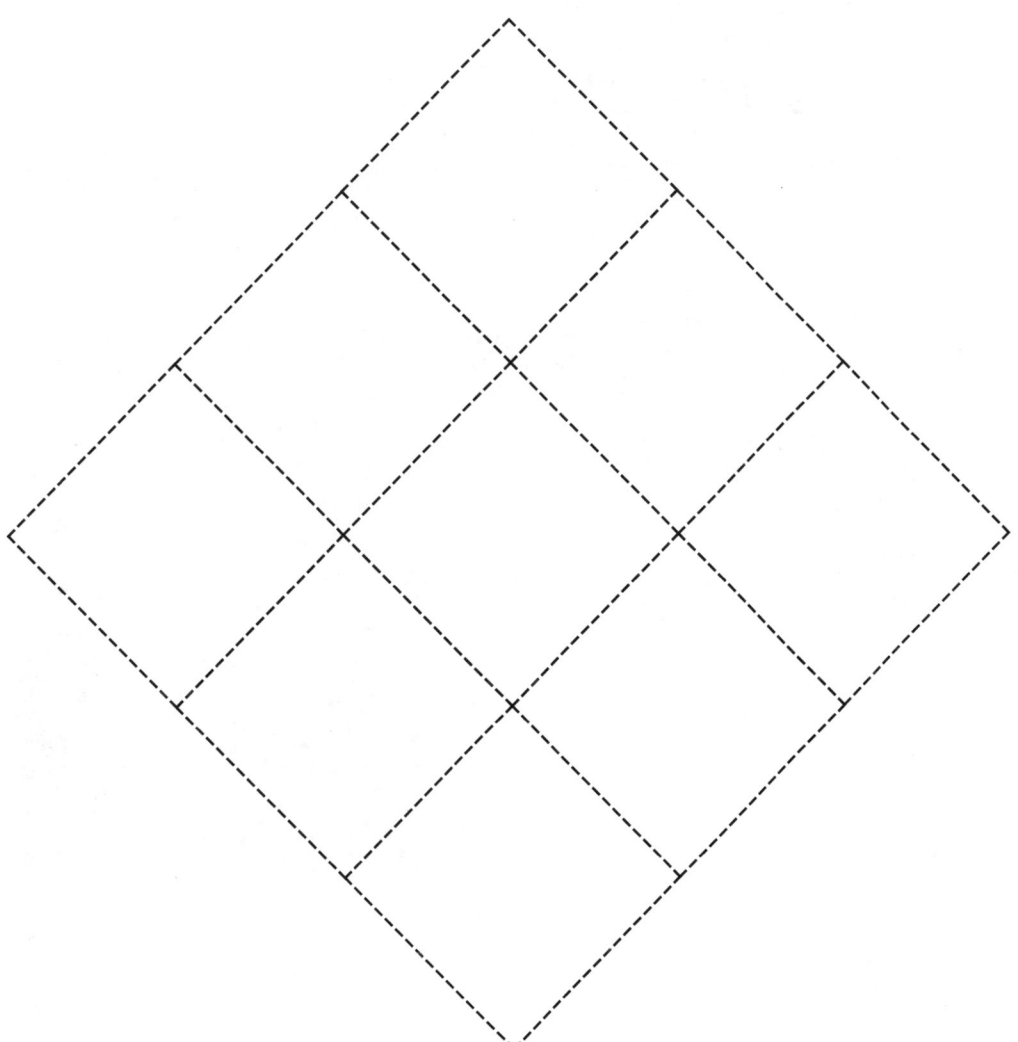

Least important

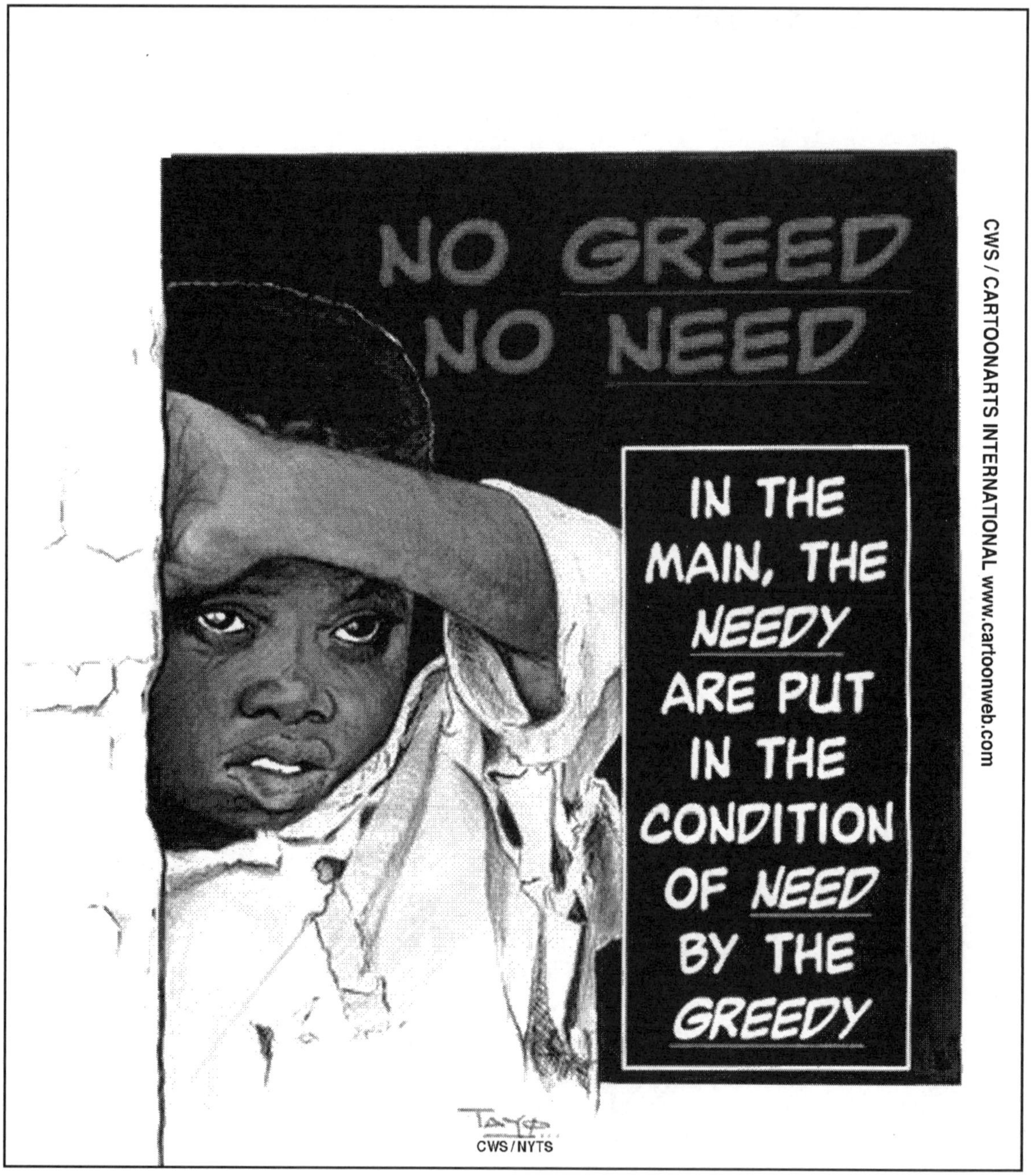

Study the cartoon.

1 What point about the cause of poverty is the cartoonist making?

2 How has the cartoonist tried to get across this message?

3 This cartoon is available on a cartoon website. Visit the site and search for another cartoon about world development.

4 Print the cartoon you have chosen.

5 In pairs, compare cartoons and discuss what views they represent.

6 Draw your own cartoon to show one of the causes of poverty. Your work could form a classroom display.

WEBLINKS You will find a link to the cartoon website at
www.nelsonthornes.com/horizons

2·9 Concept mapping the causes of poverty

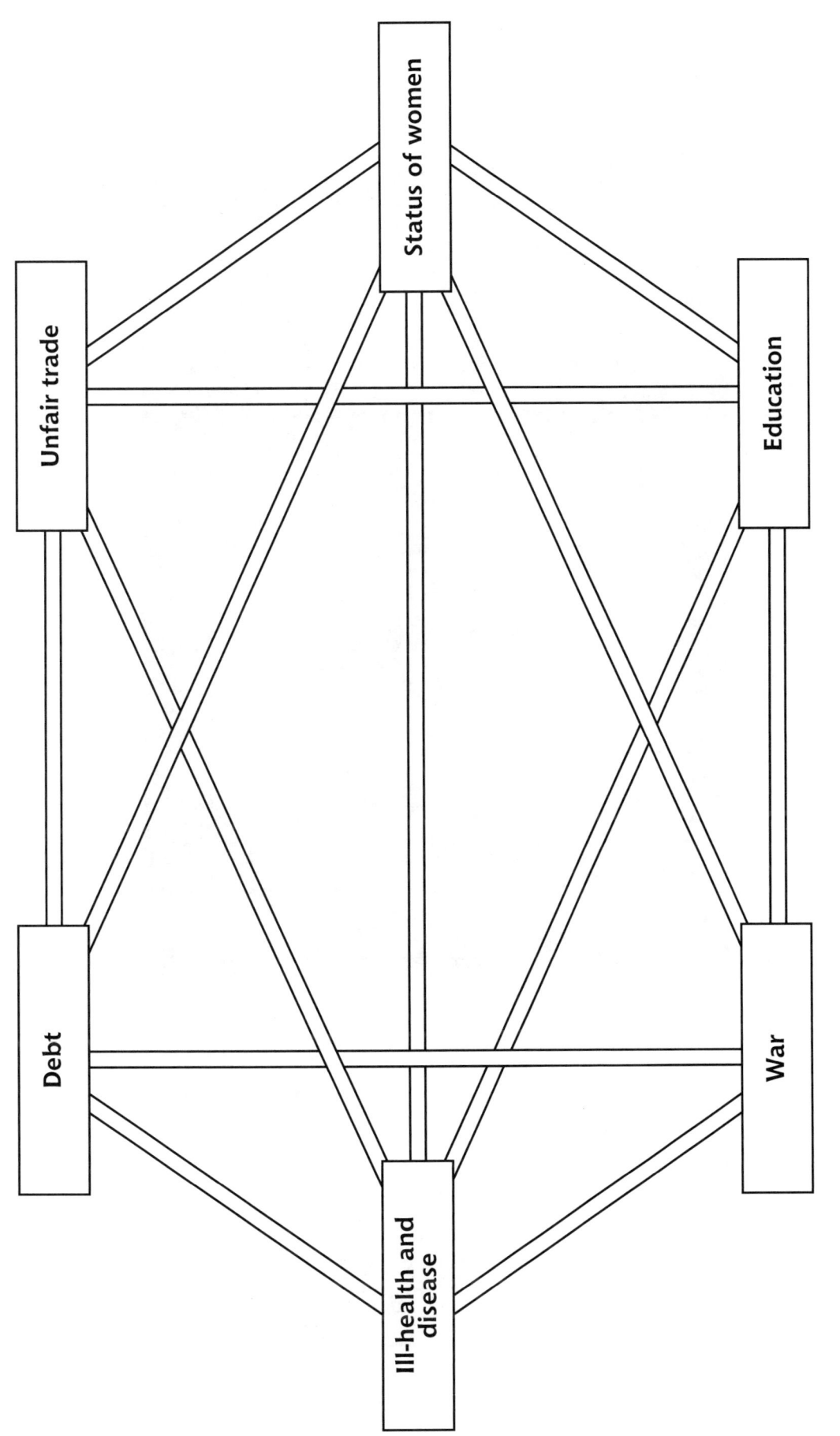

This concept map will help you find connections between the main causes of world poverty.

1 Write a label along each connection to explain the link.

2 Colour in *red* the lines that you think form the main connections.

3 Discuss with a partner what you think are the three main causes of poverty. Shade these boxes *red*.

4 Write a paragraph to explain your choices of the main causes of world poverty.

This advert appeared in national newspapers on 29 March 2005 during the build-up to the G8 world summit in Edinburgh.

1. Which organisation placed the advert in the national press?

2. a To which world issue is the advert referring?

   b How has the advert been designed to draw people's attention to this issue?

   c Explain how successful you think the advert is at drawing attention to the issue.

3. a How many people does the advert say live on less than 53p a day?

   b How can world leaders improve things for 70% of the world's population?

   c What does the advert encourage readers to do?

4. The advert includes a website address. Go to the website and find out other ways that the organisation campaigns against world poverty.

5. Create your own campaign advert, highlighting the plight of people who live on less than 53p a day. You could use a desktop publishing or word processing program to create your advert.

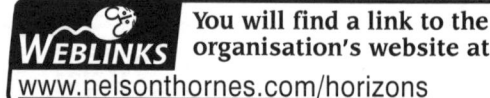

WEBLINKS You will find a link to the organisation's website at www.nelsonthornes.com/horizons

80:20

2·11 Millenium Development Goals and targets 1

The Millenium Development Goals (MDGs) and their targets (below and on sheet 2.12) have been mixed up. There are 8 goals and 18 targets in total.

1 Cut out all the cards.

2 Find the MDGs and colour them in *red*.

3 Match the targets to their goals.

4 Discuss your choices with a partner and make any changes if necessary.

5 Your teacher will provide you with a list of the goals and their targets for you to check your choices against.

6 Stick the goals and their targets in your book.

7 Write a paragraph to explain which targets you feel are:
 a the most important
 b the most likely to be achieved by 2015
 c the least likely to be achieved by 2015.

8 a Which targets did you find the most difficult to match to their goals?
 b Explain why you found this difficult.
 c Why might these difficulties make these targets difficult to achieve?

WEBLINKS You will find a link to the Millenium Development Goals website at www.nelsonthornes.com/horizons

Achieve significant improvement in lives of at least 100 million slum dwellers, by 2020.	Achieve universal primary education.	Address the least developed countries' special needs. This includes tariff- and quota-free access for their exports; enhanced debt relief for heavily indebted poor countries; cancellation of official bilateral debt; and more generous official development assistance for countries committed to poverty reduction.
Address the special needs of landlocked and small island developing States.	Combat HIV/AIDS, malaria and other diseases.	Deal comprehensively with developing countries' debt problems through national and international measures to make debt sustainable in the long term.
Develop a global partnership for development.	Develop further an open trading and financial system that is rule-based, predictable and non-discriminatory, including a commitment to good governance, development and poverty reduction – nationally and internationally.	Eliminate gender disparity in primary and secondary education preferably by 2005, and at all levels by 2015.

Ensure environmental sustainability.	Ensure that all boys and girls complete a full course of primary schooling.	Eradicate extreme poverty and hunger.
Halt and begin to reverse the incidence of malaria and other major diseases.	Halt and begin to reverse the spread of HIV/AIDS.	Improve maternal health.
In cooperation with pharmaceutical companies, provide access to affordable essential drugs in developing countries.	In cooperation with the developing countries, develop decent and productive work for youth.	In cooperation with the private sector, make available the benefits of new technologies – especially information and communications technologies.
Integrate the principles of sustainable development into country policies and programmes; reverse loss of environmental resources.	Promote gender equality and empower women.	Reduce by half the proportion of people living on less than a dollar a day.
Reduce by half the proportion of people who suffer from hunger.	Reduce by half the proportion of people without sustainable access to safe drinking water.	Reduce by three quarters the maternal mortality ratio.
Reduce by two thirds the mortality rate among children under five.	Reduce child mortality.	

The 'Make Poverty History' organisation is a UK alliance of charities, trade unions, campaign groups and celebrities which work together to overcome world poverty and injustice. Each of these organisations has its own campaigns and support projects.

As students at Raincliffe School in Scarborough discovered, there are also local campaigns started up by inspired individuals such as Suzanne Mehmet. Each organisation has a mission statement, focusing on specific countries and on particular aspects of the Millenium Development Goals.

 **WEBLINKS**

You will find links to the websites you need at
www.nelsonthornes.com/horizons

1. Your class will be divided into groups. Each group will investigate a website.

2. Each group can investigate one of the organisations suggested above or find a suitable one themselves.

3. Find out the following information about your chosen organisation:
   a. Aims or mission statement.
   b. An outline of the campaigns it is involved in.
   c. Countries and regions being supported.
   d. Methods of support provided.

4. Produce an information leaflet about the organisation to summarise your findings. You could use a desktop publishing program to create the leaflet.

5. Prepare a short presentation to be made to the rest of the class about your chosen organisation. Distribute copies of your group's leaflet as part of this presentation.

6. As a class, discuss the merits of each organisation, with a view to adopting the most worthy campaign for a class- or whole-school support programme, such as Raincliffe School's support of the Mkwakwani School Project.

Start a school aid campaign

The students at Raincliffe School in Scarborough have been successful in raising awareness in their local community to support students at Mkwakwani School in Kenya.

As a class, investigate how to help people in LEDCs. Promote your ideas to encourage whole-school support of an aid campaign.

Research information about your chosen campaign using the internet. Copyright-free images and text from websites can be included in your posters and leaflets

Ask representatives from your class to talk to the school council, headteacher and/or school governors about your aid campaign in order to get support

Produce posters and banners promoting your campaign. Display them around the school (remember to get permission from your headteacher first)

Ideas for school-based aid campaign activities

Identify how the school will support the aid campaign – the ideas used by Raincliffe School on page 37 will get you started. A group of students needs to work with teachers on this

Make a presentation in school assembly. Create a Microsoft PowerPoint presentation to outline your ideas for an aid campaign. You could also produce a leaflet using DTP to give out during assembly

Arrange a guest speaker. It may be possible for a representative from the aid agency to visit your school to talk to your class or whole-year groups in assembly

---

2·15 Trade justice

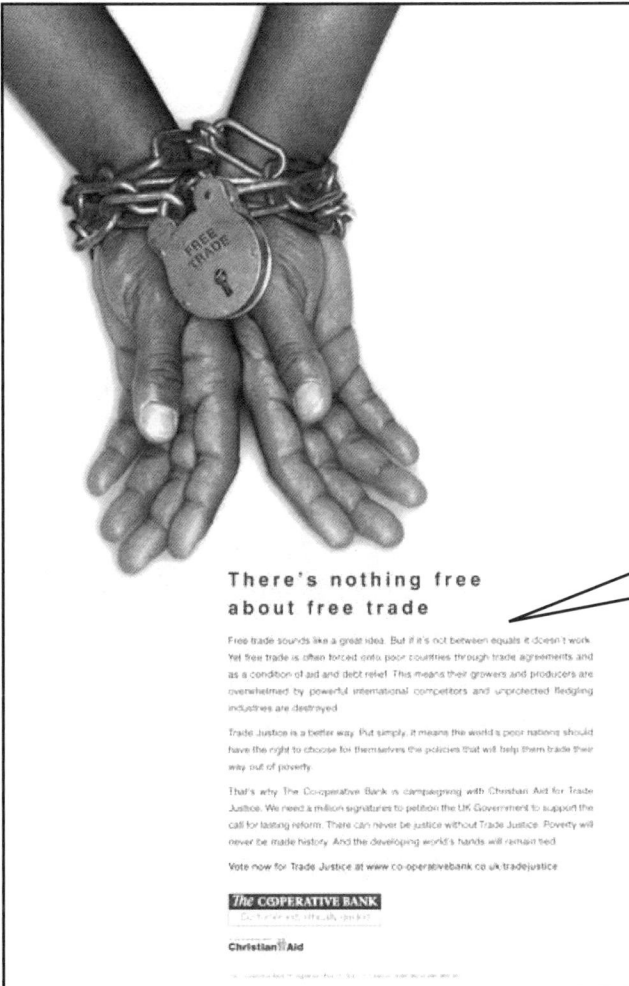

There's nothing free about free trade

Free trade sounds like a great idea. But if it's not between equals it doesn't work. Yet free trade is often forced onto poor countries through trade agreements and as a condition of aid and debt relief. This means their growers and producers are overwhelmed by powerful international competitors and unprotected fledgling industries are destroyed.

Trade Justice is a better way. Put simply, it means the world's poor nations should have the right to choose for themselves the policies that will help them trade their way out of poverty.

That's why The Co-operative Bank is campaigning with Christian Aid for Trade Justice. We need a million signatures to petition the UK government to support the call for lasting reform. There can never be justice without Trade Justice. Poverty will never be made history. And the developing world's hands will remain tied.

Vote now for Trade Justice at www.co-operativebank.co.uk/tradejustice

Study the advert.

1 Why is there 'nothing free about free trade'?

2 How does the advert portray free trade?

3 What is trade justice?

4 Why does the advert claim that 'poverty will never be made history'?

In October 2000, Comic Relief teamed up with 45 000 cocoa farmers in Ghana, West Africa, and the Day Chocolate Company, to launch the Dubble chocolate bar. All the facts set out below and on sheet 2.17 help to explain why Comic Relief did this.

1 Cut out the cards and rearrange them to help you organise your thinking about this question. It may help to arrange them into similar or related groups or into columns. Try to think of headings for these groups or columns.

2 When you have sorted the facts and worked out why Comic Relief got involved with Dubble, you will have to justify your story by explaining how the facts support your viewpoint. You may need to ignore some pieces of evidence if you think they are not relevant to your explanation.

WEBLINKS You will find links to the websites giving more information about Dubble Bars and Comic Relief at
www.nelsonthornes.com/horizons

A	B	C
Cocoa farmers are some of the poorest people in the world and many of them earn on average about £160 a year.	Cocoa farmers depend on selling their beans to pay for the essential things in life, including boots to protect their feet from the scorpions that live among the cocoa trees.	Children in the UK can use their power as consumers by buying Dubble bars and helping to end poverty.
D	**E**	**F**
Fairtrade gives LEDC producers the chance to build a better future by guaranteeing a fair and stable price for their products, all year, every year.	The UK has one of the highest consumption levels of chocolate in the world.	Cocoa has been grown in Ghana since the mid-nineteenth century and is vital to the Ghanaian economy.

G

The cacao tree takes four to five years to produce its first crop and can reach up to 15 metres in height.

H

Many cocoa farmers do not make enough money from selling their beans and cannot afford food, medicine, clean water or schooling for their children.

I

In 1993 a small group of cocoa farmers in Ghana realised that by working together they could earn more money.

J

Fairtrade is not about charity: it is about paying a fair price for the products we use, eat and wear.

K

Ten million Dubble bars have been sold in five years.

L

Kuapa Kokoo, a co-operative of over 45 000 cocoa farmers in Ghana, has been able to build new water wells and schools from sales of Dubble bars.

M

Until the mid-1970s Ghana was the largest cocoa bean producer in the world.

N

Cocoa beans are the product of the cacao tree, a tropical plant that thrives only in hot, rainy climates of 20°C or more.

O

When the world market price for cocoa fell dramatically in the 1970s, the Ghanaian economy went into crisis.

P

Ghanaian farmers pooled their resources and set up their own company called Kuapa Kokoo, which means 'good cocoa farmer' in their local language.

Q

The farmers own a third of Kuapa Kokoo's shares, which means they also have a say in how the chocolate is produced and sold.

R

Fairtrade means you can change the world at the supermarket checkout.

S

Comic Relief and Divine Chocolate launched a children's competition to come up with the name and wrapper for the first Fairtrade product for young people – Dubble!

T

The rules of world trade are stacked in favour of the most powerful countries and their businesses.

2·18 80:20
Images of sustainable development: opinion line

1 Study photos A–H on pages 40–41 of your textbook and write the letter of each photo along the opinion line below. Arrange each letter according to its level of sustainability or unsustainability.

2 Using the lines below, write a paragraph to explain why you have chosen the photos at both ends of the opinion line.

Sustainable   **Unsustainable**

(2·19) 80:20
Niger famine disaster fact file

Fill in the table below to help you answer the activities on page 43 of your textbook.

NIGER FAMINE DISASTER FACT FILE				
Country shown on map C	A	B	C	D
Name of country				
GDP (US$)				
Human Development Index				
Life expectancy (years)				
Causes of poverty				
Most important Millenium Development Goals				

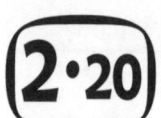

see pages 42–43 in your Horizons Book 3

2·20

80:20

What is the future for Africa?

The cartoon below was produced in 2005 at the time of the G8 world summit in Edinburgh. It is making a clear statement about Africa at this time.

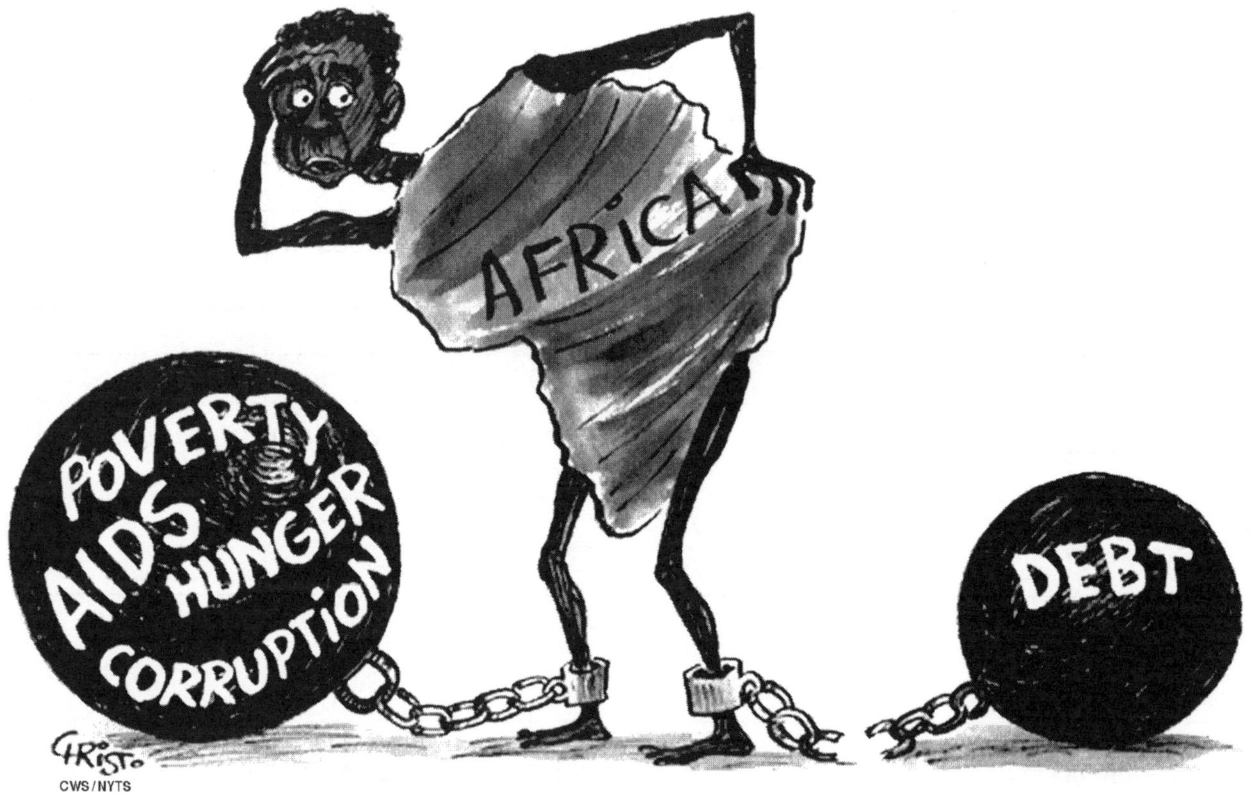

CWS / CARTOONARTS INTERNATIONAL www.cartoonweb.com

1 Study the cartoon.

- **a** What point is the cartoonist making?
- **b** Which details in the cartoon suggest these ideas?
- **c** Which symbols are used by the cartoonist?
- **d** Which things are identified as the causes of poverty in Africa?
- **e** Why is the chain broken on the debt ball?
- **f** In pairs, compare your thoughts on the image and the ideas it portrays.

2
- **a** In small groups, discuss what you have learnt in this unit.
- **b** Identify a group view of what you now think development is.
- **c** Create your own cartoon to portray your group's view of development.

Can aid do more harm than good?

BY HENRI ASTIER

When Niger's president accused aid agencies of exaggerating his country's food crisis for their own gain, Western media reacted with shock.

How dare he bite the hand that feeds his people, commentators asked. Many suggested the president was making excuses for the failings of his own government.

But according to some leading aid experts, Mamadou Tandja had a point.

'I think aid agencies and rich country media do have an incentive to paint too simplistic and bleak a picture, as was the case in Niger's food crisis,' Professor William Easterly of New York University told the BBC News website.

There were localised food shortages this year – but they were not particularly acute, and are now easing.

What Niger is experiencing is not a sudden catastrophe, but chronic malnutrition that makes people vulnerable to rises in food prices.

Glib talk of famine backed by pictures of starving children may help agencies raise funds, but it does nothing to address these basic problems, says Mr Easterly.

'Aid agencies flatter themselves into thinking that they save lives,' says Guy Scott, former Zambian agriculture minister, who finds it 'arrogant of the West to think that without whites, without pop stars, Africans would all be dead'.

DEPENDENCY

The West tends not only to overstate the effectiveness of aid, but also to underestimate its harmful effects.

A bonanza often undermines self-reliance. 'Flooding the market with food drives down the price for local farmers,' Mr Easterly says.

WHAT IS TO BE DONE?

The most effective move would be to focus less on emergencies and more on chronic problems. Mr Easterly says this could be done cheaply in the Sahel.

Improving access to clean water and distributing re-hydration tablets, for instance, would help eradicate diarrhoea, which drains nutrients away and makes children particularly vulnerable.

'When I first joined Oxfam in 1972 there was a famine in the Sahel, exactly like the famine today,' he recalls. Three decades and umpteen appeals later the same emergencies keep recurring, Tony Vaux, author of the book *The Selfish Altruist*, says ruefully.

Adapted from the BBC News website (news.bbc.co.uk), 27 August 2005

1 Why do you think the president of Niger accused aid agencies of exaggerating his country's food crisis?

2 a In pairs, discuss the advantages and disadvantages of emergency aid.

   b Draw a table like the one below and use it to summarise your ideas.

Advantages of emergency aid	Disadvantages of emergency aid

3 How does the article suggest aid could be used more effectively?

4 Read the following quotation by a Niger citizen.

> *I live in Niger. Had the media in the West not reported on the famine, the chronic, gut-wrenching poverty would have gone unnoticed by the world. The challenge is not to rush to Niger to help during a crisis, but to remain here for the long haul to help the wonderful people of my country reach their potential. Will the cameras be back in six months to see if anyone is still helping?*

What kind of support does this Niger citizen think is more suitable for his country?

5 Can aid do more harm than good? Explain your views.

3 Comparing Countries

Unit 3 of the Pupil Book is supported by:

- photocopiable activity sheets and assessment for learning materials in this *Teaching and Learning Resources* guide on pages 121–151

- customisable unit and lesson plans on the accompanying *Planning CD-ROM* attached to the inside front cover of this guide

- visual resources, presentations and interactive activities on the *Electronic Resources CD-ROM* using the Just Click teaching solution.

Just Click!

In this section of the *Teaching and Learning Resources* guide you will find:

Pages 121–122... have a list of opportunities for **Assessment for Learning** in this unit. One example is provided for each double-page spread. These ideas are based on activities in the Pupil Book, but each activity needs some development if it is to be used as an Assessment for Learning opportunity. Most of the suggestions involve pupils in assessment of their own work, in peer- assessment, or in some other form of discussion of the work either before or after it is attempted. All these suggestions are intended to increase pupils' awareness of what characterises good work, and of how their own work can be developed and improved.

The suggestions here are not intended to be prescriptive. Rather they provide teachers with opportunities that we feel fit the best practice of Assessment for Learning, and which target pupils' learning – an increasingly important area of focus under the new Ofsted inspection framework.

Page 123... is a **Learning Plan** for pupils, which gives them a copy of the learning objectives for the unit – copied from page 44 of the Pupil Book – and provides opportunities for pupils to assess their prior learning and set their targets for the whole unit, using the Attainment Targets on pages 124–125 as criteria for success. There is an opportunity at the end of the unit for pupils to re-assess their level against the Attainment Targets before completing the final self-assessment form (How far have I travelled?) on page 131.

Pages 124–125... give pupils a summary of the **Attainment Target** statements, adapted from the National Curriculum level descriptors, which are relevant to their work in this unit. Pupils can use the levels as criteria for success to set themselves learning targets for the unit and check their progress using the Learning Plan on page 123. They have also been divided into two sections, *Places and Environments* and *Enquiry and Skills*. Pupils should be able to see what it is that allows their work to move from one level to the higher level. These Attainment Targets can also be used to provide further support if required for pupils setting and reviewing their targets in the Assessment Opportunity for this unit (see below).

Pages 126–128... are also written for pupils. They describe the **Assessment Opportunity** on pages 60–61 of the Pupil Book. If teachers decide to use this exercise to assess the level at which pupils are working, these pages can be used to help guide pupils through that exercise. They should also help pupils to set targets for the exercise, to assess their own work and to set new targets for subsequent work. This will enable teachers and pupils to benefit from making formative use of the Assessment Opportunity. (Note that this differs from the Learning Plan on page 123 which provides Assessment for Learning support for the whole unit rather than an individual assessment.) Alternatively, teachers can use these pages as a mark scheme to help them to assess the individual performance of pupils and build a portfolio of assessments to track their progress during Key Stage 3 Geography.

Pages 129–130... provide **Model Answers** for the Assessment Opportunity on pages 60–61 of the Pupil Book. These model answers can be used in a variety of ways. Teachers can display them as models of good practice for whole-class discussion, or pupils could look at them before they start to write their own answers. However, they are really intended to support self- or peer-assessment process before pupils analyse their own work. The aim is to demonstrate the need to offer supporting information/explanation for each point made when answering the question as well as the need for balance when constructing an argument. Pupils can identify where the writer has successfully addressed the question and/or where they fail to address it. Pupils will be better able to identify the specific actions they must take to produce better-quality answers. This will help them to assess their own work or the work of peers. This process is further supported by the Assessment Sheets on pages 43–49.

Page 131... is a **Self-Assessment Sheet** (How far have I travelled?) that can be used to complement the Learning Plan on page 123 or as an alternative form of self-review for the unit to be filled in by pupils at the end of the unit. This form is not linked to the Attainment Targets for the unit, but reviews progress against the learning objectives and enables pupils to record their personal impressions and achievements during the unit, providing them with a more subjective opportunity for self-assessment than the levelled approach adopted by the Learning Plan.

Pages 132–151... consist of photocopiable **Activity Sheets** to support the material in the Pupil Book.

*All of these resources and activities are also available on the **Planning CD-ROM** in either Word or PDF for teachers to print out if preferred or to display on whiteboards or projectors for whole-class discussion. They can also be customised to suit individual needs and, if required, saved with the other **electronic resources** for the unit using the facility to 'add your own resources' in the Just Click teaching solution.*

3 Comparing Countries
Assessment for Learning

The following suggestions are intended to show how the material in Unit 3 of **Horizons 3** provides opportunities for teachers and pupils to assess their work as they go along, and to improve their learning as a result of that assessment. It must be stressed that these are only a few of the ways in which the material in the Pupil Book can be used. The techniques could be used as they are outlined here, but teachers will probably find that it is more helpful to use these as starting points and to develop their own ideas to suit their own circumstances.

Before you get started

There is an integral Assessment for Learning framework provided for Unit 3 (and every unit in **Horizons**):

- The unit opens on pages 44–45 of the Pupil Book with the learning objectives for the unit (Where are we going?). The lesson plans on the *Planning CD-ROM* then include learning objectives and outcomes for each spread in turn (supported by pupil-friendly versions in PowerPoint on the *Electronic Resources CD-ROM*).

- The unit ends on pages 62–63 of the Pupil Book with a plenary spread to review and evaluate the unit (Where are we now?), particularly in light of the learning objectives from the opening spread.

- The Learning Plan and Attainment Targets for the unit on pages 123–125 in this *Teaching and Learning Resources* guide provide pupils with the opportunity to set individual learning targets at the start of the unit and to review their progress against these targets at the end. The final self-assessment sheet (How far have I travelled?) on page 131 then offers pupils a more subjective review of their progress during the unit.

Teachers can use or adapt all or some of these resources to set and review goals and involve pupils in their own learning. Further resources on the *Electronic Resources CD-ROM* provide activities for initial assessment of prior learning at the start of the unit to help teachers to diagnose strengths and weaknesses for each topic and for checking and testing knowledge and understanding during and at the end of the unit. All these resources will provide teachers with further evidence to help structure and focus the learning programme.

Pages 44–45

Pupils can share and then compare their ideas on why they think the images provided are most like Mexico or the USA (activities 1–5), identifying any similarities and differences in their current perceptions (also supported by Activity Sheet 3.2). They should come back to these questions at the end of the unit to see if their ideas have changed. The starter based on Activity Sheet 3.1 helps pupils establish their level of prior knowledge and to question their preconceptions.

Pages 46–47

The starter exercise based on activities 1–3 requires pupils to ask questions about Mexico and the USA prior to starting their major investigation throughout the rest of the unit. This is supported further by Activity Sheet 3.3.

By asking which are the big questions and which are the smaller, less searching questions, a class consensus can be derived and pupils can begin to plan their route to enquiry. Activity 5 could be introduced by asking groups to come up with the possible headings for an investigation and to justify their choices and order. This activity is supported further by Activity Sheet 3.4.

Pages 48–49

The starter in the lesson plan suggests that the keywords in diagram B should be reproduced on A4 cards and pinned along an opinion 'washing line'. The left-hand side should be captioned 'Low population' and the right-hand side 'High population'. Pupils should volunteer to place a card on the line and then explain their relative choice of position. This helps pupils recall ideas from earlier work on settlement in **Horizons 1** Unit 2 People.

Pupils can share their thoughts on activities 1 and 2 by peer-assessing their initial work to check their descriptions do have the points outlined in the success criteria (e.g. 1a–c). Activity 3 could be used by pairs of pupils to identify their best sentences relating to the criteria indicated in the hints section. Activity Sheets 3.5 and 3.6 add another aspect to their comparisons as annotated versions of these maps could form the basis of group analysis, e.g. using the naming method of formative assessment.

Pages 50–51

Pupils can peer-assess their initial work on activities 1 and 2 by using the hints section as simple success criteria or a checklist. Activities 4 and 5 require pupils to draw and annotate their graphs. These could be presented as part of pupil-led plenaries to help summarise their understanding of population change in the USA. This could be augmented by plotting and annotating population distribution on Activity Sheet 3.9. Alternatively, use Activity Sheets 3.7 and 3.8 as an extension exercise or homework activity, allowing pupils to prepare a piece of work to act as the starter in the next lesson, thus bridging the topics of population and economic activity.

Pages 52–53

Pupils can peer-assess their initial work on activities 1 and 2 after devising success criteria by considering what a good description should contain. Activity Sheet 3.10 supports activity 4 and pupils can compare their plots. Pupil-led plenaries can be set up based on activity 5, with personal justifications being tested against class opinion.

Pages 54–55

Activities 1, 2 and 3 are suited to pupils sharing their choices of information to explain the differences between the states. Peer-assessment of the presentations based on either state (activity 4) will allow for oral and ICT skills to be assessed as well as providing an opportunity to suggest possible improvements. This is an example of persuasive writing and speaking. The comparisons recommended in activity 5 could provide homework and a starter for the next lesson.

Pages 56–57

The starter involves comparing the items in photos A. Pupils could use the 'thumbometer' to indicate if they think the products are:

- always made in the USA (thumbs up)
- sometimes made in Mexico as well (thumbs level)
- only made in Mexico (thumbs down).

Activity 2 based on timeline B could be replicated on the board by using the CD-ROM version of the image and asking pupils to come to the whiteboard to select and explain which factors reflect land, war, population or trade links. Peer-assessment of the answers to activities 3, 4 and 5 are faciliatated by presenting a contentious statement such as 'All Mexican immigrants live in the extreme south of the USA' and asking pupils to find map information to prove or disprove the hypothesis. The same can be done for table E by stating 'The USA imports raw materials only from Mexico' and asking pupils to find information to prove or disprove it.

Pages 58–59

The starter involves comparing the photos in A and B, which show images of US and Mexican influences on the UK. Pupils could use the 'thumbometer' to indicate if they think the products are:

- very important to UK culture/economy (thumbs up)
- fairly important to UK culture/economy (thumbs level)
- not important to UK culture/economy (thumbs down).

Activity 1 is best accomplished in groups. Activity Sheet 3.16 encourages pupils to consider how diverse relationships in international trading can be. By replicating the Venn diagram on the board and asking pupils to classify the statements on the board, their peers can concur or suggest alternative categorisations.

Pages 60–61

The mystery 'Why is John Doe staying in Tucson, Arizona?' based on Mexican migration to the USA offers many opportunities for pupils to peer- and self-assess their work. In particular, the plenary should concentrate on which factors make for a strong oral argument and which factors should be included in the criteria for success for the follow-up written answer (supported by Activity Sheet 3.19). Pupils should be encouraged to look beyond the immediate reason for his staying and consider the broader issues of why John left his own country and made such a hazardous trip in the first place. Emphasis should also focus on how their thinking changed as they worked on the mystery.

Pages 62–63

This spread allows for pupil reflection on the work they have done in this unit and as such is entirely devoted to peer- and self-assessment. In the unit, review misconceptions to challenge pupils by asking pairs or small groups to find evidence to disprove and attempt to correct the seven wrong statements. The review of final perceptions is supported further by Activity Sheet 3.20.

3 Comparing Countries
Learning plan

What are my learning objectives for this unit?

I aim to learn to:

✓ ask geographical questions about Mexico and the USA

✓ develop a sequence for investigation

✓ select relevant information in order to aid comparison of two countries

✓ present data effectively to highlight similarities and differences

✓ consider the interdependence of nations.

Read the Attainment Targets for this unit on pages 124–125 and tick any statements that you feel refer to you. *Places and Environments* covers *what you know* about the topic and *Enquiry and Skills* covers *what you can do.*

Using these statements for this unit, decide what level you are overall at this stage:

Level ⬚

What level do you think you can achieve by the end of this unit?

Level ⬚

What are you going to concentrate on to achieve this level? A good place to start might be any statements on pages 124–125 that you have not ticked:

At the end of the unit, read the Attainment Targets again and tick in a different colour any *new* statements that refer to you. Then decide what level you are now:

Level ⬚

If you have improved, well done! What evidence can you show for this improvement? What or who do you think particularly helped you to improve your level?

If you have stayed the same, better luck next time! What do you think you could have done differently to help improve your levels? What will you do next time to progress further?

3 Comparing Countries

My Attainment Targets for this unit

Level 3

Places and Environments

☐ I can describe some physical and human features of Mexico and the USA.

☐ I can describe some of the similarities and differences between Mexico and the USA.

☐ I can describe some of the ways nations depend on each other.

Enquiry and Skills

☐ I can select and use some information from maps, photographs and written sources to find out about Mexico and the USA.

☐ I can draw maps and graphs of Mexico and the USA.

☐ I can use some appropriate geographical vocabulary to describe the geography of Mexico and the USA.

Level 4

Places and Environments

☐ I can describe and begin to explain some physical and human features of Mexico and the USA.

☐ I can describe and begin to explain some of the similarities and differences between Mexico and the USA.

☐ I can describe and begin to explain some of the ways nations depend on each other.

Enquiry and Skills

☐ I can select and use information from maps, photographs and written sources to find out about Mexico and the USA.

☐ I can draw and annotate maps and graphs of Mexico and the USA with some accuracy.

☐ I can use appropriate geographical vocabulary to describe the geography of Mexico and the USA.

Level 5

Places and Environments

☐ I can describe accurately and explain the physical and human features of Mexico and the USA.

☐ I can describe accurately and explain some of the similarities and differences between Mexico and the USA.

☐ I can explain how nations are interdependent and give some reasons why they are linked.

Enquiry and Skills

☐ I can collect data from a range of sources to investigate Mexico and the USA.

☐ I can select appropriate skills and ways of presenting to help me compare Mexico and the USA.

☐ I can suggest geographical questions to investigate Mexico and the USA.

☐ I can present my findings with a conclusion.

3 Comparing Countries
My Attainment Targets for this unit

Level 6

Places and Environments

☐ I can use a range of examples from local to national level to describe and explain the physical and human features of Mexico and the USA.

☐ I can describe and explain some of the similarities and differences between Mexico and the USA in physical, human and economic terms.

☐ I can explain a variety of ways in which nations are interdependent on one another and give reasons why.

☐ I can explain why people may hold different views on the way countries develop and their influence in the world.

Enquiry and Skills

☐ I can suggest geographical questions as part of my investigations of Mexico and the USA.

☐ I can collect data from a wide range of sources to investigate countries.

☐ I can select an appropriate range of skills to compare and contrast Mexico and the USA.

☐ I can present the findings of my investigations in a logical way and reach conclusions consistent with the evidence.

Level 7

Places and Environments

☐ I can use a wide range of examples from local to national level to describe and explain the physical and human features of Mexico and the USA.

☐ I can describe how physical, human and economic factors interact to determine the similarities and differences between Mexico and the USA.

☐ I can explain a wide variety of ways in which nations are interdependent on one another and give reasons why.

☐ I can explain why people may hold different views on the way countries develop and their influence in the world, and how these views may conflict.

Enquiry and Skills

☐ I can show independence to identify issues to investigate Mexico and the USA, ask geographical questions, and establish and follow my own sequence of enquiry.

☐ I can use accurately a wide range of skills and sources of evidence.

☐ I can select an appropriate range of skills to compare and contrast Mexico and the USA.

☐ I can evaluate critically most sources of evidence, present well-argued summaries of my investigations and begin to reach conclusions that are clearly based on evidence.

Level 8

Places and Environments

☐ I can use a wide range of examples at all scales to describe and explain the physical and human features of Mexico and the USA.

☐ I can offer explanations for the interactions within physical, human and economic factors that determine the similarities and differences between Mexico and the USA.

☐ I can explain a wide variety of ways in which nations are interdependent on one another and give reasons why.

☐ I can understand a range of views and attitudes on the way countries develop and their influence in the world, and appreciate how these views may conflict.

Enquiry and Skills

☐ I can show a high level of independence to identify issues, ask geographical questions, and establish and follow my own sequence of enquiry.

☐ I can independently select a wide range of techniques and skills to collect and analyse data.

☐ I can select an appropriate wide range of skills to compare and contrast Mexico and the USA.

☐ I can evaluate critically most sources of evidence, present well-argued summaries of my investigations and reach conclusions that are clearly based on evidence.

On page 61 in activities 1–3 you are asked: Why is John Doe staying in Tucson, Arizona?

1. Use the statements in resource C on page 61 to work out why John Doe is staying in Tucson. There is no one true answer and it may be a combination of factors. Your teacher may provide the cards to sort into groups.

2. Try to sort them into 3 to 5 categories according to the similarities and links you see between the evidence on the cards. *Remember*: When you have worked out why you think he is staying in Tucson, Arizona, you will have to justify your story by explaining how the facts support your argument. The more facts you can use, the stronger your answer will be. If you think some facts are less important, be prepared to say why.

3. Write your answer in less than 500 words.

Before you start these activities, look at the **Criteria for success** sheet. Set yourself a target level to aim for in this Assessment Opportunity. Write this level in the box on the target setting sheet. Explain how you intend to obtain this level.

Once you have finished the activities, look again at the Criteria for success and assess your answers. You could also compare your answers with model answers. Write your level in the box and explain how you achieved this level.

Then set yourself a target for improvement in your next assessment. Explain what you need to do to improve next time. Try to set yourself specific tasks to work on.

3 Comparing Countries

Criteria for success

A **Level 3** answer may	• give some general reasons but not linked to each other.
A **Level 4** answer may	• give some general reasons in a sequence but not all linked to each other • include some evidence from the cards to support your arguments.
A **Level 5** answer may	• give a range of reasons with most items justified • suggest an overall solution that shows a logical sequence but not all the ideas are linked to each other or the big picture.
A **Level 6** answer may	• give evidence to justify a range of reasons which are presented in a logical sequence • explain how most factors are linked to each other and how they relate to the big picture (e.g. economic migration, push and pull factors, disparities in wealth).
A **Level 7** answer may	• give evidence to justify a range of reasons that are presented in a logical order • explain how many factors are interlinked and how they relate to the big picture (e.g. economic migration, push and pull factors, disparities in wealth) • show evidence of having prioritised reasons and explain why some aspects are more important than others.
A **Level 8** answer may	• give evidence to justify a range of reasons which are presented in a logical order • explain how many factors are interlinked and how they relate to the big picture (e.g. economic migration, push and pull factors, disparities in wealth) • show evidence of having prioritised reasons and explain why some aspects are more important than others • show how you have considered alternative solutions.

3 Comparing Countries

My target setting

I want to make progress in geography, in my solution to the John Doe mystery.

When I do activities 1–3 on page 61, I aim to obtain:

Level ☐

To do this I will need to:

☐

Answer these questions when you have completed activities 1–3 on page 61:

In this Assessment Opportunity I obtained:

Level ☐

Explain how you obtained this level:

☐

When I do my next Assessment Opportunity, I aim to obtain:

Level ☐

To do this I will need to:

☐

3 Comparing Countries

Model answers

A This is a good basic answer that was written by a pupil who had completed activities 1–3 on page 61.

I think the reason John Doe is staying in Tucson is because he is either too ill to move or dead. He has been out in the desert and will probably have been dehydrated. One card says it was over 40°C in the desert. This will mean he could be mentally damaged and confused. Assuming this is true, I don't see how the police or border guards could shift him without a big fuss in the news or from the Mexican government.

Another answer is that he could be dead, so he is 'staying' in a different sense, i.e. he's buried in Tucson because they don't really know who he is or where to send him. He could have died from the heat or he might have been shot by the Minutemen vigilantes (but they aren't admitting it). Also the border guards said they shot at someone.

There are other reasons as well. He was trying to get into the USA illegally I think. Perhaps he was trying to get away from a poor life in farming and earn some money for his family. He could send money back to them like loads of others do. So that explains what he was doing there in the first place. He was not the only one to die: a woman and her kids also died and there will be thousands more as long as illegal guides take their money.

B This is a better answer, which achieves a higher level than the first one (A).
- Read it carefully, and try to see why this is better than the first answer.
- Try to see how it meets new parts of the criteria for success.
- Try to see how you could use ideas from this work to improve your own work.

John Doe might be staying in Tucson for several reasons. Some of these are to do with the state he is in and some are to do with bigger issues outside of his control.

The immediate reason he is staying in Tucson is probably to do with his medical state. He appears to have been dehydrated after having seemingly got lost in the desert. Although someone from the 'No More Deaths' group tried to revive him, the dead bodies around (perhaps his wife and child?) and the 41°C heat in the Sonora Desert would mean that he would be in a bad way. There is a suggestion of brain damage. That could be permanent and John Doe might not be in any state to be sent back to Mexico or be sent on elsewhere if he has any friends in the USA (other migrants?).

The real reason why he was in the desert is the key to mystery I think. He was most likely trying to enter illegally through this 80 km wide desert, probably with the help of an illegal migrant guide for money. Without support, his chances of being caught are high as half a million illegals are arrested each year near Tucson thanks to the border guards and the Minutemen vigilantes. To take such a risk must mean he was desperate.

I think it's possible that John Doe was a poor Mexican farmer losing his livelihood as prices for his crops fell. Perhaps with a wife and kids to support he would have joined the millions of others on the dangerous journey across the only state border that isn't covered by a huge fence. Unfortunately, he may have become permanently damaged by the effort. But he won't be the last unidentified poor person trying to get to the 'promised land'.

C This is an even better answer, which achieves a higher level than (A) or (B).
- Read it carefully, and try to see why this is better than the previous answer.
- Try to see how it meets new parts of the criteria for success.
- Try to see how you could use ideas from this work to improve your own work.

There are several linked reasons why John Doe is in Tucson and unlikely to leave. The immediate reasons are to do with his having been captured by the border guards but the mystery began much earlier.

It is likely that he comes from Mexico and possibly from the town of Pueblo as it seems his phone was bought there. There is a lot of evidence about Mexican farmers and industry going through a lean time with prices in some crops falling and industry losing jobs as competition from abroad takes its toll.

If John had lost his job, he would have some difficult choices to make: stay and starve with his family or try to follow the millions of others who have crept illegally into the USA. Here, he would hope to be one of the people who sends dollars home – a fact the American and Mexican governments secretly know about.

It is likely, given where he was found, that he used a guide to get him – and his wife and child, perhaps – across the border at the weakest point: Arizona, Sonora.

Half a million Mexicans a year are caught here and sent home. But 300 a year die in the 80 km wide Sonora Desert alone. I think he ran out of water and collapsed in the extreme heat. During the day he must have suffered from the heat and during the night extreme cold in a trackless wilderness. Despite being given water by the Samaritan group, he would have been dehydrated, perhaps to the point of brain damage. In that state he could not give any details about himself. Migrants remove personal details from their person in case they are caught, so he will not be traceable. Although he is probably from Mexico, it cannot be proven by the border guards and the Mexicans cannot send him home as they don't know where to send him to. He may even be too ill to travel.

In conclusion, it is my belief that John Doe is staying in Tucson because, ironically, although it may be where he wanted to be, he is in no state to leave and cannot even recall who he is. But the real reason he is there is because he is an economic migrant, so desperate to get a better life that he ultimately may have nearly lost his own life. The gap in wealth highlighted by the American ambassador says it all. While hardship in Mexico pushes and wealth in the USA pulls, there will always be migrants and casualties like John Doe.

3 Comparing Countries

How far have I travelled?

In this unit my **Learning Objectives** were to learn to:

- ask geographical questions about Mexico and the USA
- develop a sequence for investigation
- select relevant information in order to aid comparison of two countries
- present data effectively to highlight similarities and differences
- consider the interdependence of nations.

My progress in this unit

How well have I achieved my objectives?	Okay							Excellent

Enquiry and Skills:

to ask questions about Mexico and the USA

to annotate photographs, diagrams and maps and present work effectively

to choose sources and use the internet to investigate Mexico and the USA

Places and Environments:

to know how the physical nature of Mexico and the USA has similarities and differences

to be able to explain why some places in Mexico and the USA have denser populations and different land uses than others

to explain how different levels of development can present opportunities and conflict

to understand how different nations can be linked and interdependent

Shade the bars to show how far you think you have made progress in this unit.

The part of this unit that I enjoyed the most was …

because …

The part of this unit that I needed most help with was …

because …

The piece of work that I am most pleased with is …

because …

The aspect of this unit that will be most useful to me in future is …

because…

Any other comments?_____

3·1  Reading pictures

By making links between what we see in a picture and what we know about the place, we have a much better chance of understanding the 'bigger picture'. For example, imagine you are asked to study a photo of your local high street jammed with traffic in the early evening. Possible responses might be:

- *What can I see in the picture?* Many cars, stationary buses, pedestrians waiting to cross the road.

- *What do I know about the 'bigger picture'?* It is rush hour, the busiest time of the day. Many journeys are made at this time – accident figures are a concern for the council. Some people want the street to be pedestrianised.

- *What links explain the connection between the factors shown in the photo or suggest solutions to the problems?* Congestion is a result of many journeys being made at the same time, so staggering work and school times could ease congestion. Pedestrianising the street would reduce accident figures for school pupils.

Study the picture below and write notes around it to help you see the 'bigger picture'.

What do I know about the 'bigger picture'?

What can I see in the picture?

3·2 Comparing Countries
The USA and Mexico

Many of us form opinions of places before we really know anything about them. What impressions do you have of the USA and Mexico?

1 Answer 'the USA' or 'Mexico' to the following questions.
   a In which country are you more likely to be murdered?
   b In which country are most gun crimes committed?
   c Which country has the most televisions?
   d In which country are you more likely to find women working?
   e In which country is your child most more likely to be born underweight?
   f In which country are you more likely to go to prison?
   g In which country are you more likely to find an active or dormant volcano?
   h Which country is bigger?
   i Which country emits more carbon dioxide per person?
   j In which country are you more likely to be Catholic?
   k In which country are you more likely to get divorced?
   l In which country are you more likely to find wilderness?
   m Which country uses more electricity per person?
   n Which country was ranked best at football in the August 2005 FIFA rankings?

2 Answer 'true' or 'false' to the following questions.
   a New York is the capital of the USA.
   b Spain has more Spanish speakers than Mexico.
   c The Mississippi is the longest river in the USA.
   d Chocolate originates from Mexico.
   e Mexico City is the highest city in North America.
   f 'Mexico' means 'bellybutton of the moon'.
   g In the USA, Thanksgiving is held on 4 July.
   h The Rio Grande is Mexico's second longest river.
   i You are more likely to meet descendants of Native American Indians in the USA.
   j The state of Hawaii belongs to Mexico.

3·3 Comparing Countries
What questions do we need to ask?

1 On the diagram below, write the letter for each question A–F where you think it best fits. A possible answer for question A has been done for you.

2 Write your own questions G–K and add each letter in the appropriate place on the diagram.

- **N for Natural:** these are questions about the natural environment – climate, landscape, relief, water – and how people interact with it

- **E for Economic:** these are questions about how people are making a living, money, wealth, poverty, trade, aid

- **S for Social:** these are questions about people, their relationships, traditions, culture and the way they live

- **W for Who decides?:** these are questions about who is in charge, who is the decision maker, who is making decisions about changes

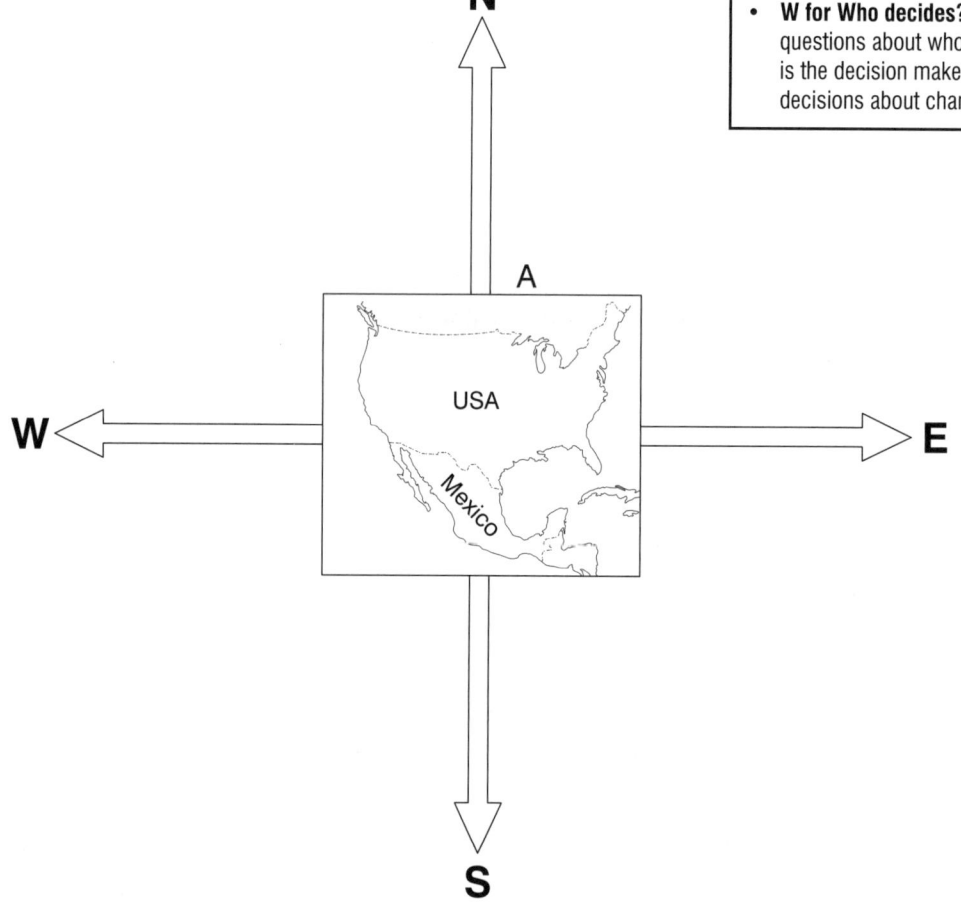

A	Where does the high temperature make farming difficult?
B	Who lives along the border?
C	Which country has the most oil?
D	How high are the highest mountains?
E	Which country has the most rivers?
F	What kind of industry does each country specialise in?
G	
H	
I	
J	
K	

(3·4) Comparing countries advanced organiser

Use this organiser to compare and contrast the USA and Mexico. You need to visit a number of websites to collect information about each country. Some areas to compare are given in the organiser below. Add extra categories you feel are relevant.

WEBLINKS You will find a link to the websites you need at www.nelsonthornes.com/horizons

COMPARING COUNTRIES – ADVANCED ORGANISER			Notes
TASK: To compare and contrast the USA and Mexico			
Category	**USA**	**Mexico**	
Physical and climatic factors			
Population distribution and composition			
Economic aspects			
Differences within each country			
Connections between the two countries			
Connections with the UK			

CONTENTS CHECKLIST – the final report must contain these things:
1
2
3
4
5

STAGES – the different parts of this report must be ready by these dates:			
1	2	3	Final

SELF-EVALUATION – the strengths of this piece of work are:			
1	2	3	4

SELF-ASSESSMENT – my report could be improved by:			
1	2	3	4

DATA SOURCES – record where you obtained your information:			
Web addresses	Texts	Papers	Other

Use these base maps in your report to show patterns in the physical geography of the USA and Mexico.

A Physical map, USA

B Physical map, Mexico

Comparing Countries

see pages 48–49 in your Horizons Book 3

Precipitation maps: the USA and Mexico

Use these base maps in your report to show patterns in the climatic geography of the USA and Mexico.

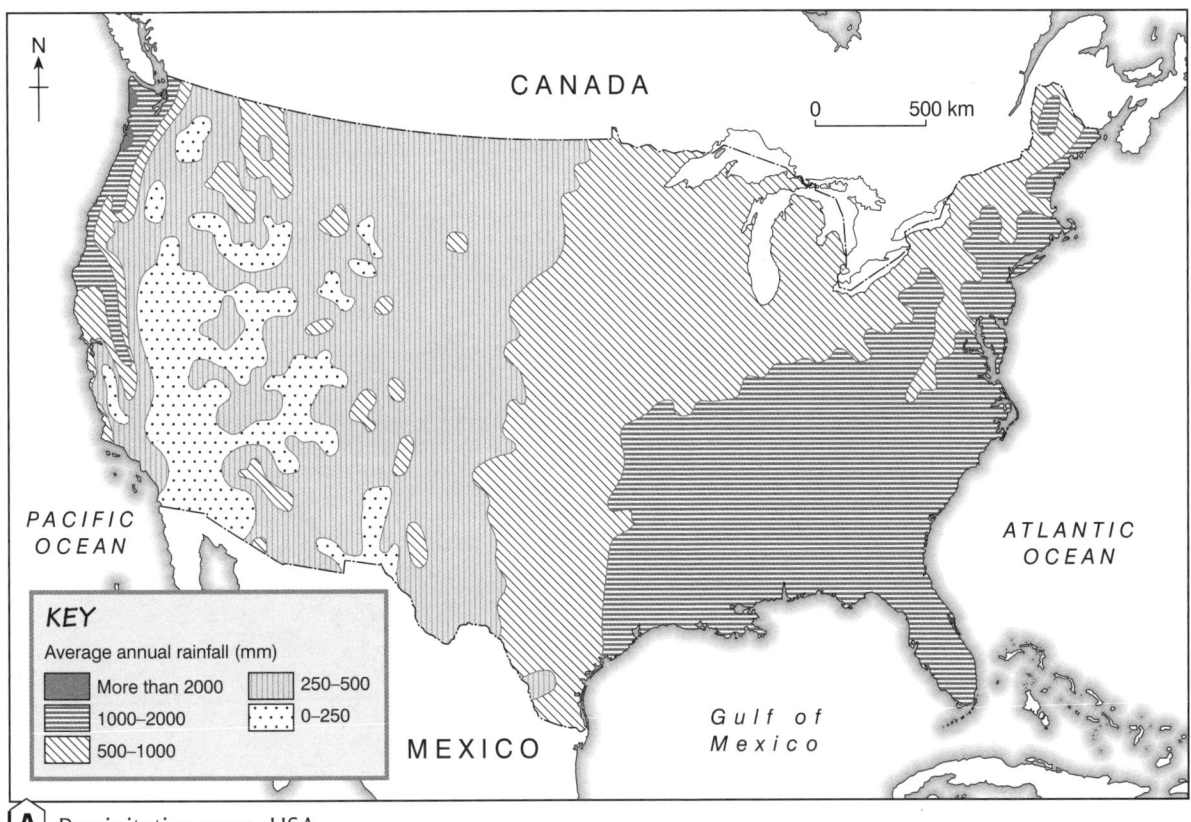

KEY

Average annual rainfall (mm)

More than 2000	250–500
1000–2000	0–250
500–1000	

A Precipitation map, USA

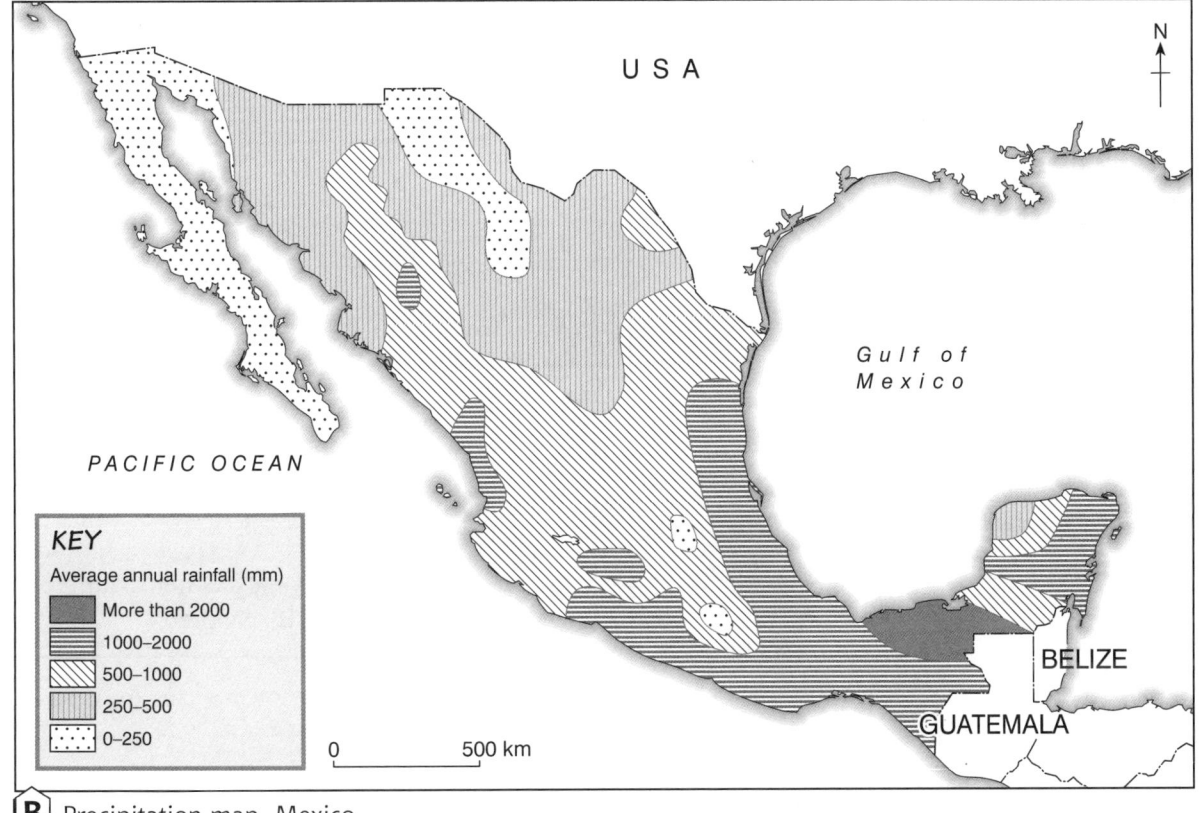

KEY

Average annual rainfall (mm)

- More than 2000
- 1000–2000
- 500–1000
- 250–500
- 0–250

B Precipitation map, Mexico

1 On graph A, write the letter for each statement in box C where you think it best fits.

2 Study graph B.

  a Find evidence to prove that the statements in box D are true, false or unproven. Remember that if you cannot tell something from the graph, you cannot say it is true.

  b Write three statements of your own about graph B.

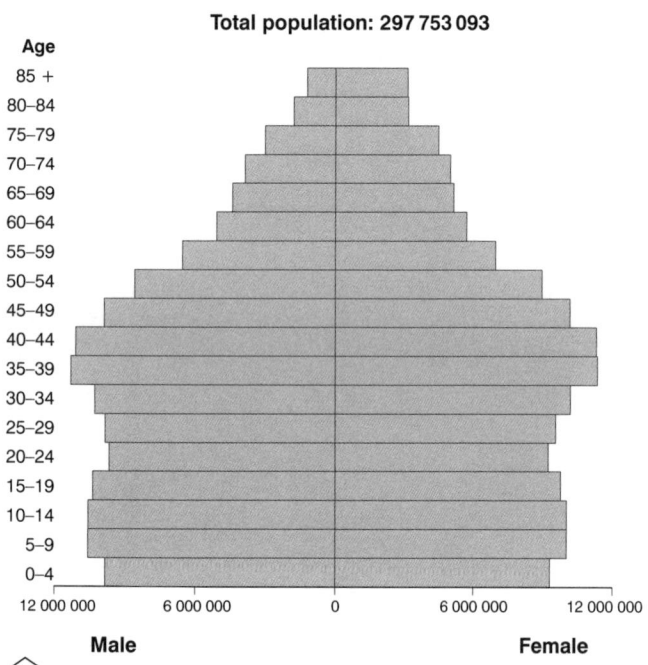

A Population pyramid, USA

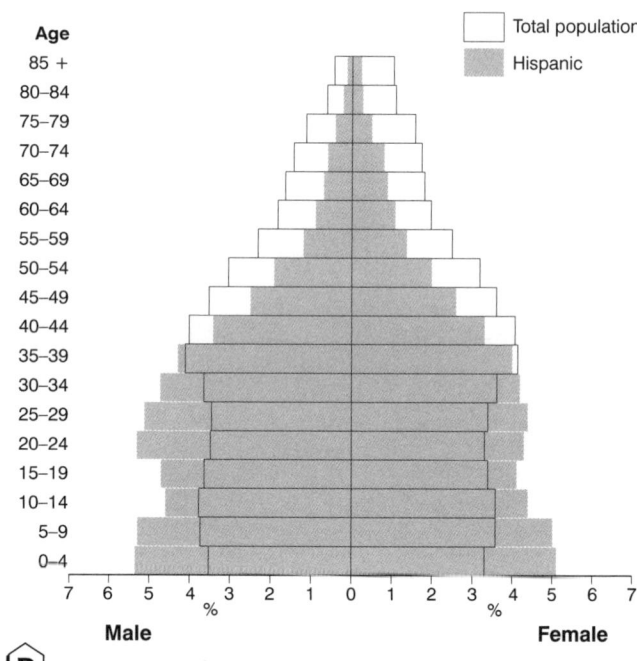

B Percentage of Hispanic population, USA

A There are very few men to talk to in this rest home.

B I leave college next year, but marriage is out until I'm established in my career.

C I guess 38 sounds quite old but I'm having my first baby next year.

D The numbers in elementary school are going to drop soon.

E I can retire now but there must be 5 million other guys saying the same thing.

F We're the baby boomers born in the swinging 60s!

G They say the 1980s recession depressed birth rates.

H Actually there are slightly more male than female children born here.

C

I Most Hispanics are young men coming here to work.

J Overall, there are more Hispanic men than women.

K Hispanic men die younger than Hispanic women.

L Some Hispanic men may be migrant workers.

M Few Hispanic adults have children.

N Most Hispanic children are working in the fields.

O The number of Hispanic children is far greater than the number of US children.

D

Comparing Countries

(3·8) Political maps: the USA and Mexico

Use these base maps in your report to show patterns in the human and economic geography of the USA and Mexico.

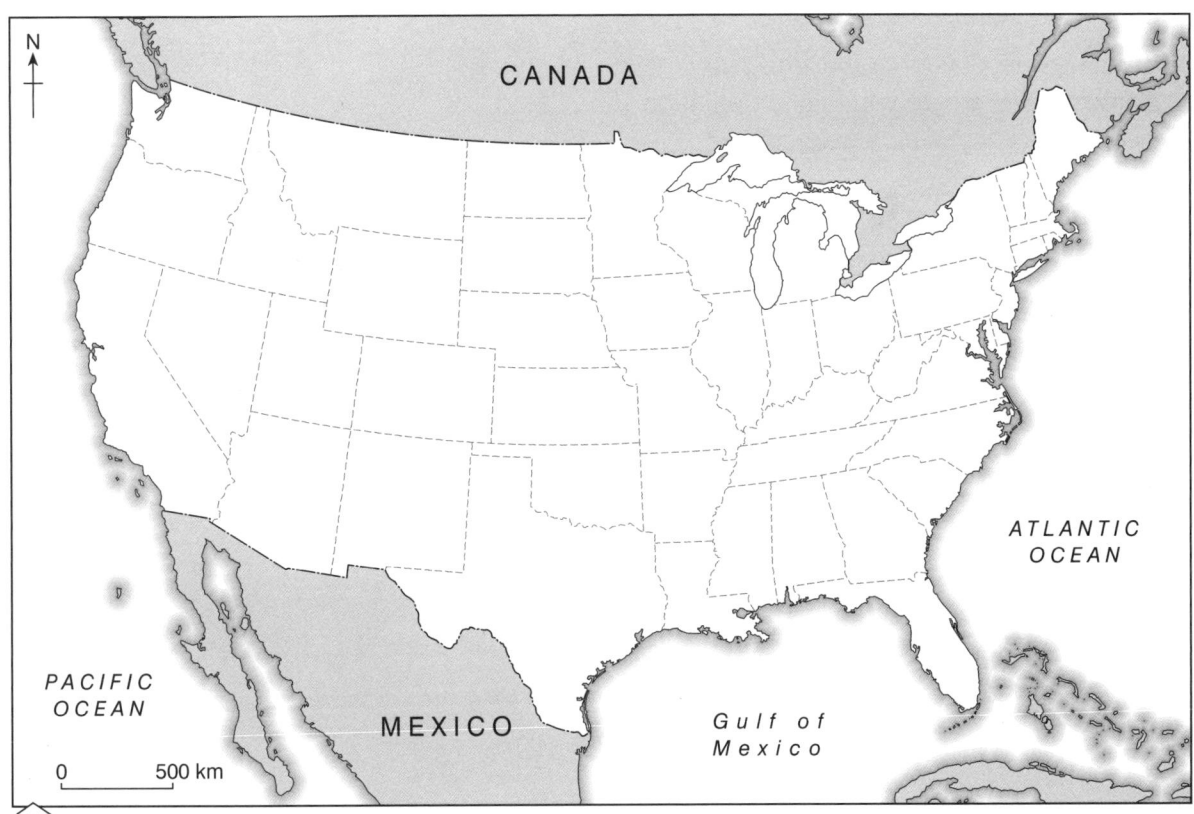

A Outline political map, USA

B Outline political map, Mexico

1 Use the figures in the table below to draw a total population line graph showing how both countries have changed over time.

2 Add a title and label your graph, and pinpoint at least two places where you think population changed significantly in either country.

3 Annotate your graph to explain why you think these changes are significant.

	1900	1930	1960	1990	1995	2000	2005
Mexico	13 607 259	16 552 722	30 000 000	81 249 645	91 158 290	97 483 412	105 000 000
USA	76 094 000	123 076 741	180 671 158	249 438 712	262 764 948	281 421 906	297 753 093

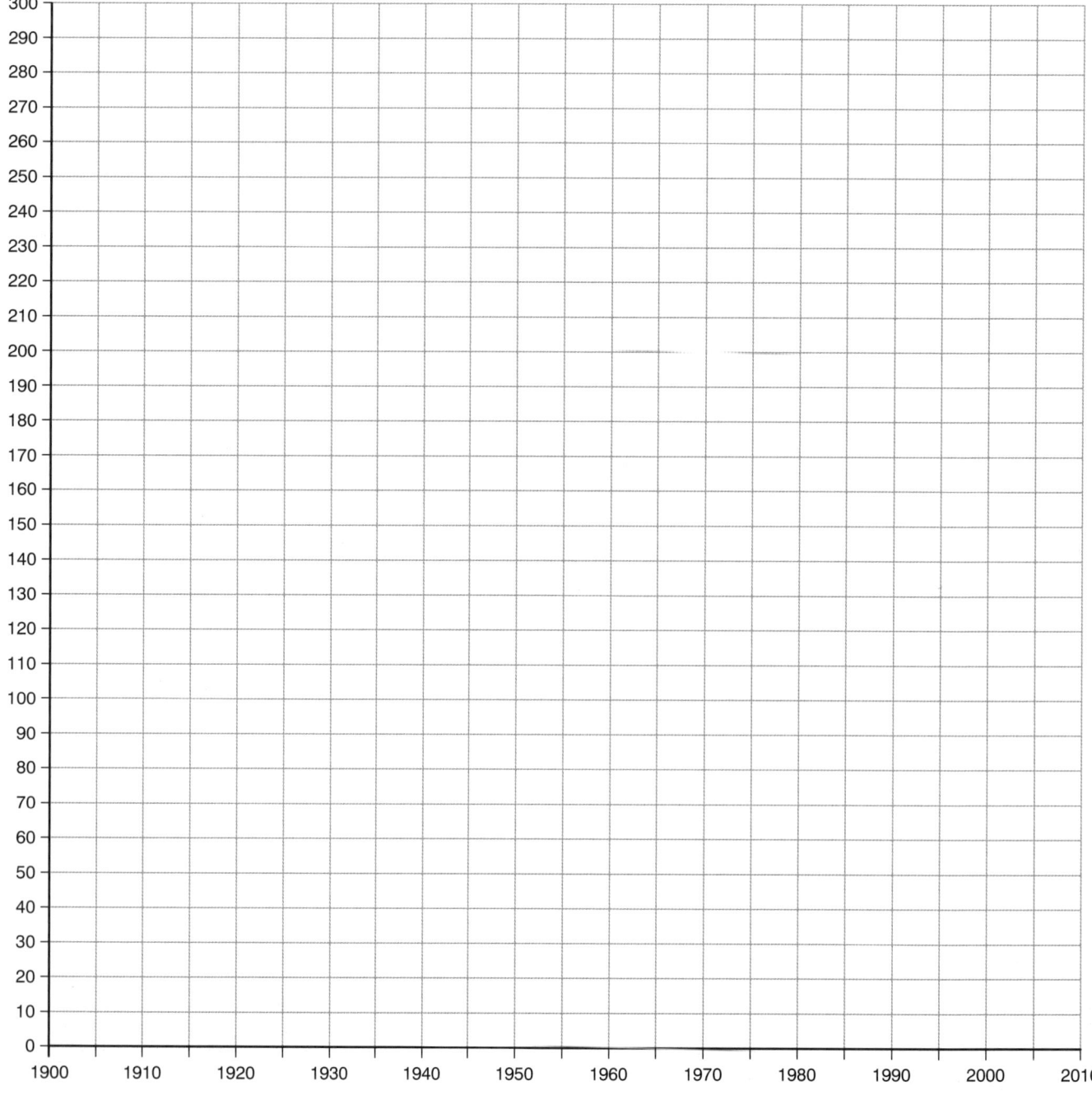

(3·10) Using triangular graphs

1 a Use graph outline A to show the employment data for the countries in table B.

  b Label the graph to show which areas represent the most developed and which the least developed countries. Explain your decisions.

  c Which countries do not fit into the pattern you expected? Explain why this might be the case.

2 a Work out the employment data for the country shown in graph C.

  b How would you describe this country in terms of development?

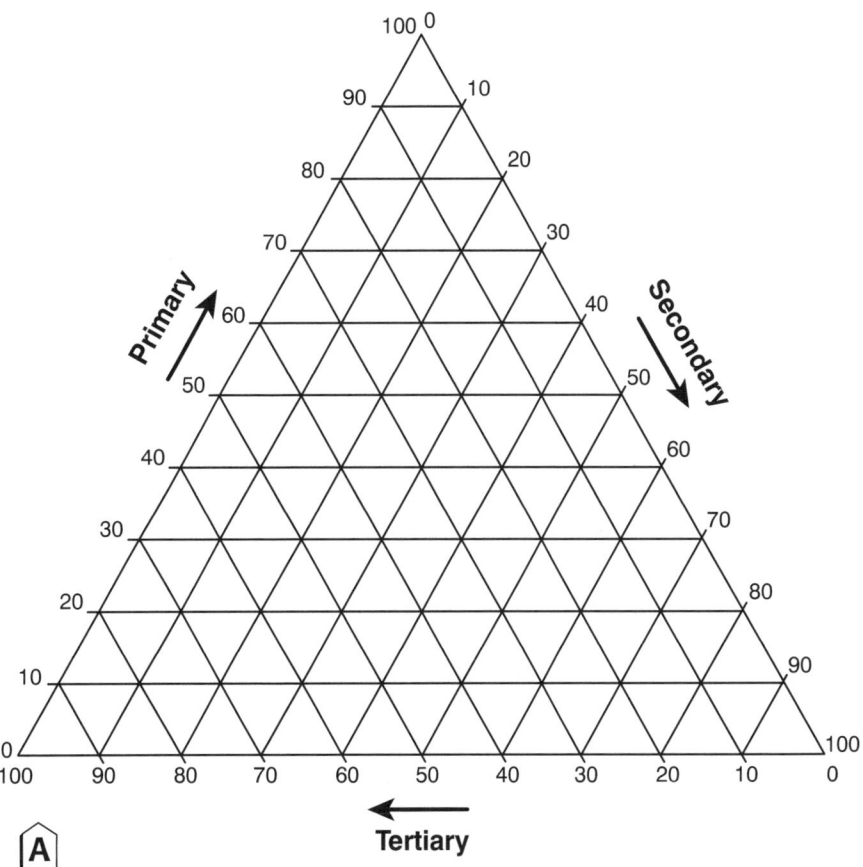

A

	Country	Primary (%)	Secondary (%)	Tertiary (%)
A	Australia	4	26	70
B	Brazil	20	14	66
C	China	49	22	29
D	Germany	3	33	64
E	India	60	17	23
F	Italy	5	32	63
G	Jordan	5	13	82
H	Mexico	18	24	58
I	Poland	16	29	55
J	Russia	12	23	65
K	Spain	6	30	64
L	UK	1	19	80
M	USA	1	24	75
N	Zimbabwe	66	10	24

B Employment data

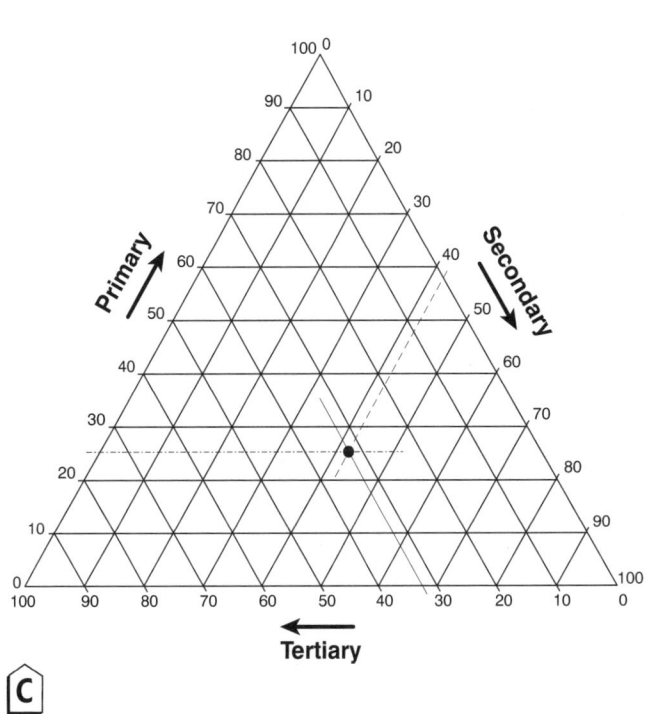

C

3·11 Maps: Arizona and Illinois

Use these base maps in your report to show patterns in the human, physical and economic geography of Arizona and Illinois.

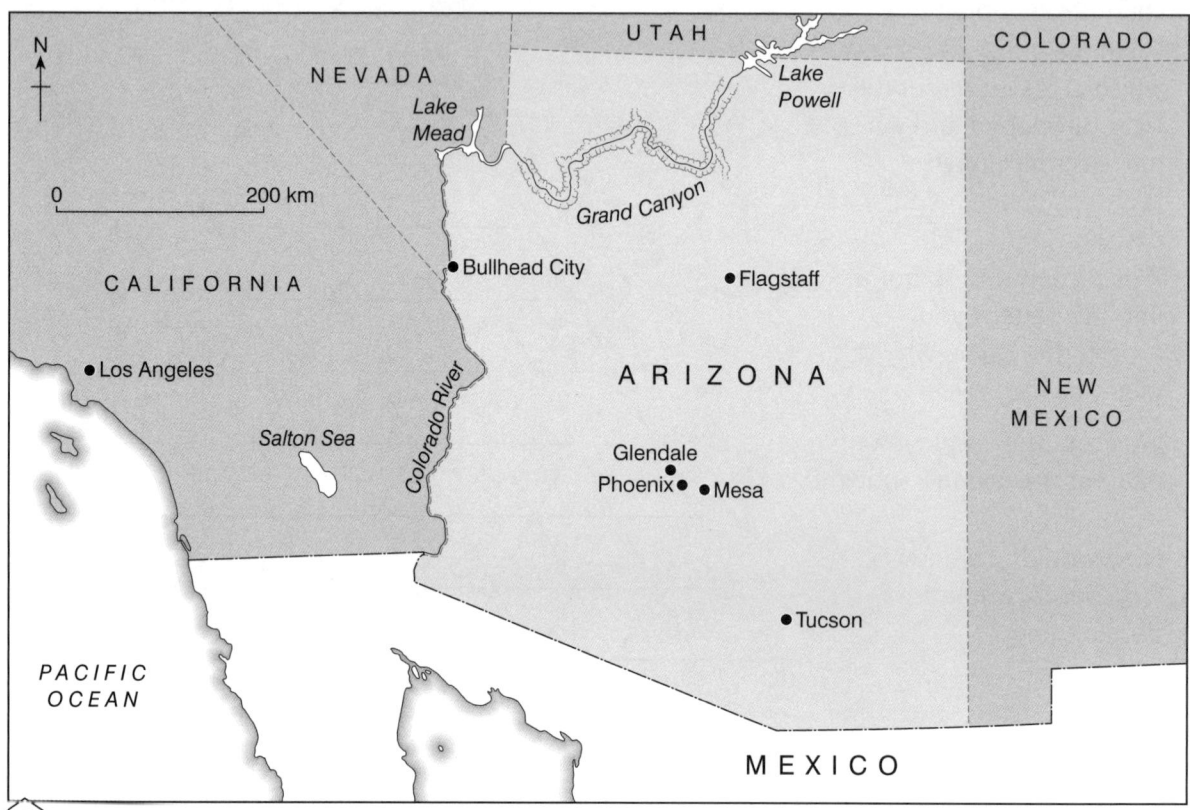

A Map of Arizona

B Map of Illinois

3·12 Maps: Yucatán and Sonora

Use these base maps in your report to show patterns in the human, physical and economic geography of Yucatán and Sonora.

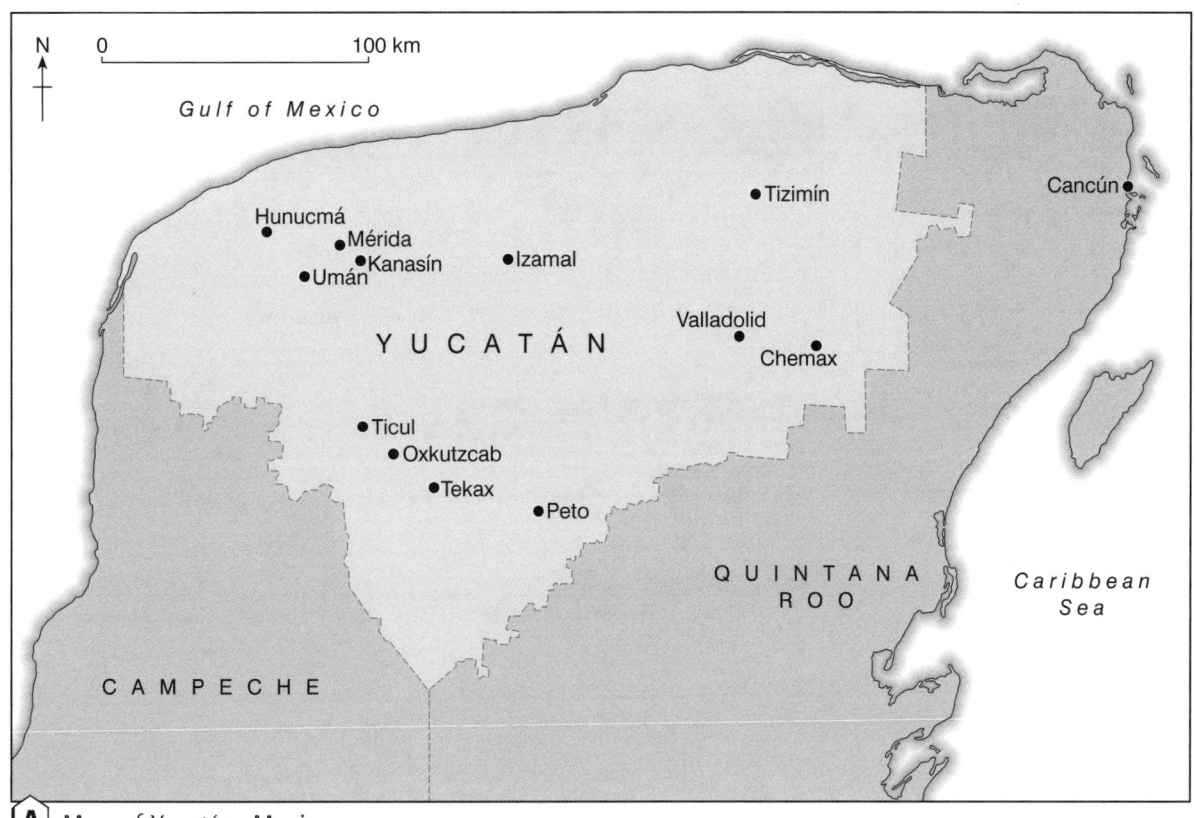

A Map of Yucatán, Mexico

B Map of Sonora, Mexico

3·13 Yucatán and Sonora

Use these base maps in your report to show patterns
in the climatic geography of Yucatán and Sonora.

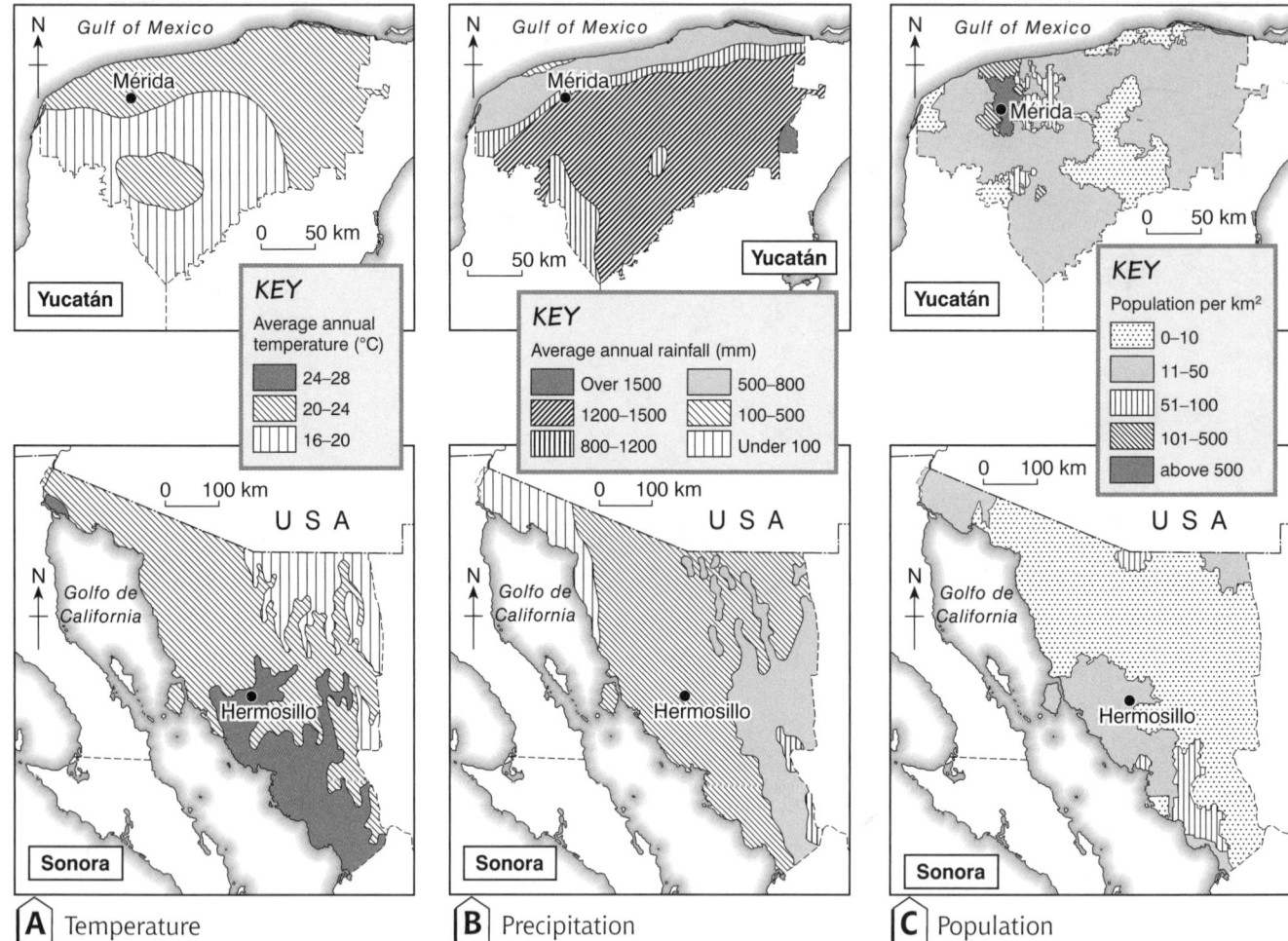

A Temperature   **B** Precipitation   **C** Population

FACT FILE		
Category	**Yucatán**	**Sonora**
Area	38 402 km²	181 052 km²
Peaks < 2000 m	0	7
Population (people)	1 658 210	2 216 969
Population density (people/km²)	42	12
Average temperature (°C)	26	21
Average precipitation (mm/year)	1290	400
Births vs deaths	38 006 vs 8681	57 435 vs 10 995
Top three industries	**1** Hotels and restaurants: 21%	**1** Services (community, social and personal): 22%
	2 Services (community, social and personal): 19%	**2** Hotels and restaurants: 21%
	3 Manufacturing: 18%	**3** Financial services: 19%

D Yucatán and Sonora fact file

(3·14) Comparing Countries
Climate data for Arizona and Illinois

Use the figures in the table below to draw a climate data graph for Arizona and Illinois. Use different colours for Arizona and Illinois.

1 Draw the lines for temperature using the right-hand side y axis.

2 Draw the bars for precipitation using the left-hand side y axis.

3 Identify four points on the graph where you think climate could have a positive or a negative effect on the following aspects of life in either state:
   a farming
   b transport
   c leisure and recreation
   d business

| Month | Arizona | | Illinois | |
	Temperature (°C)	Precipitation (mm)	Temperature (°C)	Precipitation (mm)
January	12.0	28	−4.1	50
February	14.3	26	−1.1	51
March	16.8	30	4.8	82
April	21.1	14	10.9	97
May	26.0	9	16.9	109
June	31.2	7	22.0	105
July	34.2	47	24.1	100
August	33.1	53	22.9	94
September	29.8	34	18.8	82
October	23.6	27	12.3	73
November	16.6	25	5.3	85
December	12.3	33	−1.2	69

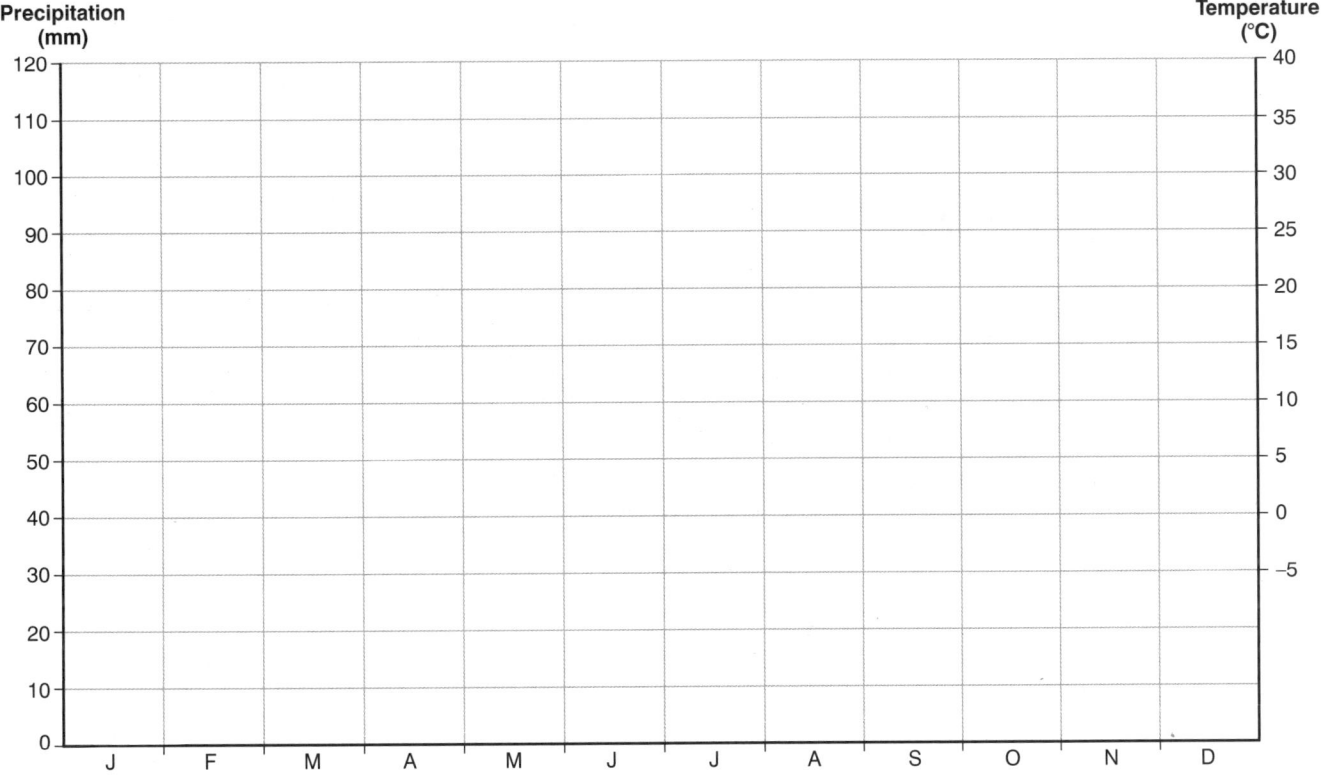

3•15

Comparing Countries

see pages 56–57 in your Horizons Book 3

The message behind the picture

Study the cartoon.

1 What point do you think the cartoonist is trying to make?

2 Do you think the cartoon tells the whole truth?

3 From which of the following groups do you think the message is conveyed?

- **a** US anti-immigration groups.
- **b** Mexican migrants.
- **c** US businesses.
- **d** Human rights sympathisers in the USA.

4 Draw your own cartoon from an opposing point of view and suggest which group's views it might represent.

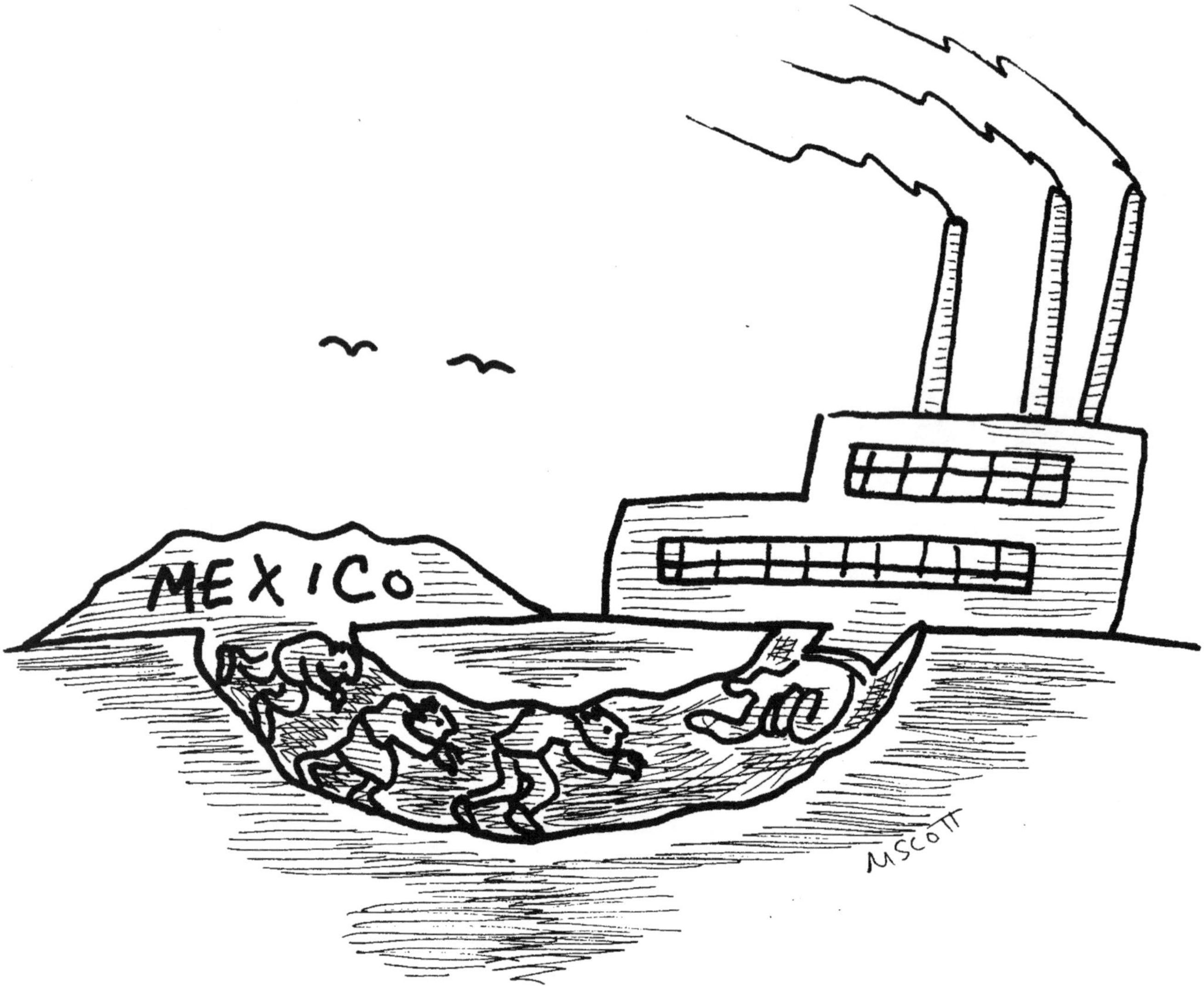

3·16 Comparing Countries
Trading places

Mexico, the USA and the UK are connected in many different ways.

1 Read the statements below and try to assign each letter to one part of the Venn diagram.

2 Add five more statements of your own.

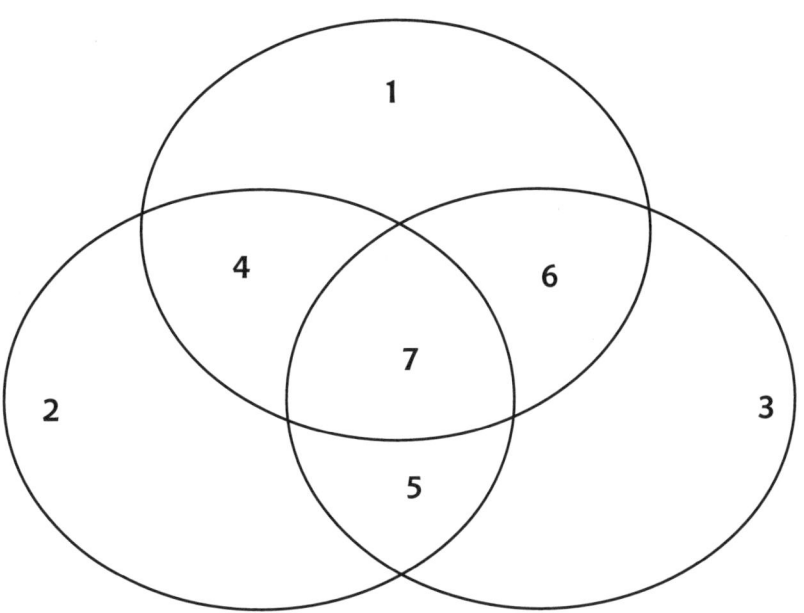

KEY

1 Mexico	**2** USA
3 UK	**4** Mexico and USA
5 USA and UK	**6** Mexico and UK
7 Mexico, USA and UK	

A GuitarWorld in Southampton requires 20 more Fender Mexican telecasters.

B The Tasty Taco, Milwaukee has been voted the best restaurant for enchiladas.

C This holiday in Cancun has been brilliant and it's a direct flight from Heathrow.

D I buy all my Levis direct from the web. They're here in Glasgow with three days.

E He was returned to his own country at the border crossing in Ciudad Juarez.

F I've got a visa to work as a lecturer in geography in Pasadena, California for two years but will then have to return to Leeds.

G The plane on the Manchester to Naples flight was a Boeing 737.

H This Sunfire Pontiac was built by General Motors Mexico and sells all over the USA, South and Central America.

I BBC Gardeners' World special offer on new dahlias, the national flower of Mexico.

J Most people in Yucatán have Mayan connections in some way.

K Illinois gets its name from the Illiniwek Indians who were part of the Algonquin tribes.

L I love baseball and football so I see most home games by the Diamondbacks and Cardinals.

M I'm not too happy about Manchester United being bought out by Americans.

N The only time I get to enjoy the 'American Dream' is when I'm at my holiday home in Baja.

O Well, we're really a Tijuana-based band but our gigs go down well in Tampa, Florida and we get fan mail from Cape Town to Cardiff.

P The student exchange trip just got better. I've got tickets for Green Day in Monterrey!

The articles below and on sheet 3.18 offer different perspectives on the problem of illegal immigration.

1 As you read the articles, underline evidence that may help you to answer questions on the following topics. Use the colours given.

a Living conditions and opportunities: *red*.
b Earnings and taxation: *green*.
c Healthcare and education: *blue*.
d Borders and security: *black*.

2 Select evidence you have underlined to help you write an essay of no more than 300 words discussing one of the following statements:

a Until the gap in wealth between the USA and Mexico narrows, people will continue to flood north.
b Although many Americans are unhappy about illegal immigrants, they might find life harder with Mexican labour.
c Sealing the border treats the symptoms of the problem, not the cause.

A

Immigration, the United States and Mexico

By Ambassador Jeffrey Davidow

Any discussion of the US–Mexico illegal immigration scene should take into consideration certain basic assumptions:

● Outflow from Mexico to the US – 'the push' – will continue at high rates until the Mexican economy can provide sufficient work opportunities and decent standards of living to a far greater percentage of its population.

● The attraction of the US – 'the pull' – as a society in which working for wages well above those available in Mexico and with a way of life that offers greater economic security, personal opportunities, and the rule of law will continue.

● The severe measures necessary to 'seal the border' are unlikely to be acceptable to the American public, industry or politicians.

● The Mexican government cannot and will not use force to prevent its citizens from leaving the country.

Adapted from the Mexidata.info website (www.mexidata.info)

B

Migrant workers aid growth at home

By Alberto Souviron, BBC News business reporter

Three years after arriving in Los Angeles, Mexican labourer Antonio Villalobos is still keeping a close eye on his home town of Nochistlan. That is where his family is, and they still rely heavily on the $150 he sends them each week. Development projects in Mr Villalobos's home state of Zacatecas receive support from the Mexican migrant association he is a member of – the Zacatecan Federation of Southern California. Last year, Mexicans abroad sent back $16.6 bn (£8.9 bn), making it the second largest source of income after oil. Mexico's government is backing the so-called 3x1 initiative, under which every $1 injected by migrants is matched by a further $3 by local, state and federal governments to improve facilities in Mexico.

Adapted from the BBC News website (news.bbc.co.uk), 28 March 2005

C

Mexico's tips to enter US safely

Mexicans thinking of crossing illegally into the USA can now get a book of tips on how to make the journey safely. A 32-page comic guide with advice on surviving the hazards of the trip is published by Mexico's foreign ministry. Would-be migrants are told to add salt to water to avoid dehydration in the Arizona desert, and where to swim across the Rio Grande. US pressure groups have accused the Mexican government of encouraging illegal migration with the 'manual'. Each day thousands of Mexicans enter the US on foot via the Arizona desert in the hope of finding work. Mexico says it has a duty to protect its citizens, many of whom die each year crossing the long and dangerous border.

Adapted from the BBC News website (news.bbc.co.uk), 6 January 2005

D

Proposition 200

BY CBS NEWS CORRESPONDENT JERRY BOWEN

Opinion in Arizona is split over the controversial Proposition 200 – a new law to try to address the flood of illegal immigrants into the USA.

'These people just flood across and they're ruining our healthcare system and they're ruining our schools,' says Arizona resident Walter Kolbe. 'The people are just fed up with it.' From Kolbe's backyard one can see Mexico and the backpacks and water bottles abandoned by the nightly wave of illegals crossing over. 'We are saying to our politicians, "If you're against it then do something and stop this raping of our country,"' Kolbe said. 'I'm afraid it's going to turn violent if someone doesn't listen to us.'

It was ten years ago that Angelita sneaked across to work as a housekeeper. Now she's afraid to show her face. 'Ten years have passed and I live in fear in a country that can at any moment send me back to Mexico,' Angelita said. Angelita is still illegal. So is her oldest daughter. Only her youngest girl was born in the United States. 'The oldest asks "Why? Why can't we be accepted as Americans?"'

Adapted from the CBS News website (www.cbsnews.com), 22 December 2004

Mystery: Why is John Doe staying in Tucson, Arizona?

1 Cut out the cards and rearrange them to help you organise your thinking about this question. It may help to arrange them into similar or related groups or into columns. Try to think of headings for these groups or columns.

2 When you have sorted the facts and worked out why John Doe is staying in Tucson, Arizona, you will have to justify your story by explaining how the facts support your viewpoint. You may need to ignore some pieces of evidence if you think they are not relevant to your explanation.

A Jobs in some areas of Mexico are declining as transnational firms switch production to China.	**B** Governor of California Arnold Schwarzenegger says he thinks the Minutemen are 'doing a great job'.	**C** A Samaritan from a Christian group 'No More Deaths' found John and tried to revive him with water.	**D** The severe measures necessary to 'seal the border' are unlikely to be acceptable to the American voters.
E Border patrol guards looking for drug dealers opened fire on a man who ran when challenged.	**F** When he was picked up he muttered a friend's name and repeated the word 'Tucson'.	**G** John Doe is a name given to any unidentified person in the USA.	**H** The temperature hit 41 °C for at least 5 days in the desert that week.
I A Mexican woman and a child of 5 were found dead in the same desert area the next day. 300 died there in 2004.	**J** Minutemen are vigilantes who go armed into the desert of Arizona and California to find 'illegals'.	**K** The American Border Action Group aims to help the 'illegals' get to safety.	**L** Arizona is seen as the easiest place to cross the border now that California and Texas have tightened security.
M John cannot remember his name. He carried a mobile phone bought in Pueblo, Mexico.	**N** The Mexican government has produced a comic-book-style guide to staying alive in the desert for migrants.	**O** The ambassador says that the wealth of the USA will always 'pull' and Mexican poverty will always 'push' migrants.	**P** A border crossing guide costs about $1500, including rooms and transport.
Q With coffee selling at only 60 cents a pound, many Mexican farmers have sold up.	**R** The Border Action Group keeps water tanks in the desert to help dehydrated people.	**S** The Sonora Desert in Arizona is 80 km wide and has high mountains (2000+ metres) which have to be crossed.	**T** Illegal immigrants are deported back to Mexico when they are found by the border patrol guards.
U 500 000 'illegals' were arrested in the Tucson sector in 2004.	**V** A Minutemen patriot thought he 'spooked' someone like John Doe in the Sonora Desert.	**W** Doctors at Tucson hospital say heat exhaustion and dehydration can lead to permanent brain damage.	**X** In 2004, Mexicans abroad sent back $16.6 bn (£8.9 bn), making it the second largest source of income for Mexico after oil.

3·20 Mexico/USA: opinion line

1 The statements below give suggestions for some of the key differences between Mexico and the USA. Write the letter for each statement along the opinion line below. Arrange each letter according to its importance.

2 When you have chosen which statement is the most important, write a paragraph to explain why, in your opinion, it is the most important difference between the USA and Mexico.

Not important   **Important**

◁ ☐ ☐ ☐ ☐ ☐ ☐ ☐ ☐ ☐ ▷

A The USA is a far wealthier country than Mexico. People earn around four times as much on average.

B Mexico began its development later than the USA.

C The USA has far more farmable land and natural resources than Mexico.

D Mexico spends 60 times less on its military forces than the USA.

E Both countries have great extremes of climate but the USA has a greater percentage of land with mild climatic conditions.

F The USA has greater imports and exports than Mexico and a bigger trade deficit.

G American culture affects a far greater number of people than Mexican culture.

H People live longer in the USA, with an average life expectancy of 77.71 years compared to 75.19 years in Mexico.

I The gap between rich and poor is greater in the USA but there is a higher proportion of poor people in Mexico.

J The population of Mexico is growing faster than that of the USA.

_____

_____

_____

_____

_____

_____

_____

_____

_____

4 Ecosystems

Unit 4 of the Pupil Book is supported by:

- photocopiable activity sheets and assessment for learning materials in this *Teaching and Learning Resources* guide on pages 153–185

- customisable unit and lesson plans on the accompanying *Planning CD-ROM* attached to the inside front cover of this guide

- visual resources, presentations and interactive activities on the *Electronic Resources CD-ROM* using the Just Click teaching solution.

(Just Click)

In this section of the *Teaching and Learning Resources* guide you will find:

Pages 153–154... have a list of opportunities for **Assessment for Learning** in this unit. One example is provided for each double-page spread. These ideas are based on activities in the Pupil Book, but each activity needs some development if it is to be used as an Assessment for Learning opportunity. Most of the suggestions involve pupils in assessment of their own work, in peer-assessment, or in some other form of discussion of the work either before or after it is attempted. All these suggestions are intended to increase pupils' awareness of what characterises good work, and of how their own work can be developed and improved.

The suggestions here are not intended to be prescriptive. Rather they provide teachers with opportunities that we feel fit the best practice of Assessment for Learning, and which target pupils' learning – an increasingly important area of focus under the new Ofsted inspection framework.

Page 155... is a **Learning Plan** for pupils, which gives them a copy of the learning objectives for the unit – copied from page 64 of the Pupil Book – and provides opportunities for pupils to assess their prior learning and set their targets for the whole unit, using the Attainment Targets on pages 156–157 as criteria for success. There is an opportunity at the end of the unit for pupils to re-assess their level against the Attainment Targets before completing the final self-assessment form (How far have I travelled?) on page 165.

Pages 155–156... give pupils a summary of the **Attainment Target** statements, adapted from the National Curriculum level descriptors, which are relevant to their work in this unit. Pupils can use the levels as criteria for success to set themselves learning targets for the unit and check their progress using the Learning Plan on page 155. They have also been divided into two sections, *Places and Environments* and *Enquiry and Skills*. Pupils should be able to see what it is that allows their work to move from one level to the higher level. These Attainment Targets can also be used to provide further support if required for pupils setting and reviewing their targets in the Assessment Opportunity for this unit (see below).

Pages 158–161... are also written for pupils. They describe the **Assessment Opportunity** on pages 82–83 of the Pupil Book. If teachers decide to use this exercise to assess the level at which pupils are working, these pages can be used to help guide pupils through that exercise. They should also help pupils to set targets for the exercise, to assess their own work and to set new targets for subsequent work. This will enable teachers and pupils to benefit from making formative use of the Assessment Opportunity. (Note that this differs from the Learning Plan on page 155 which provides Assessment for Learning support for the whole unit rather than an individual assessment.) Alternatively, teachers can use these pages as a mark scheme to help them to assess the individual performance of pupils and build a portfolio of assessments to track their progress during Key Stage 3 Geography.

Pages 162–164... provide **Model Answers** for the Assessment Opportunity on pages 82–83 of the Pupil Book. These model answers can be used in a variety of ways. Teachers can display them as models of good practice for whole-class discussion, or pupils could look at them before they start to write their own answers. However, they are really intended to support the self- or peer-assessment process before pupils analyse their own work. The aim is to demonstrate the need to offer supporting information/explanation for each point made when answering the question as well as the need for balance when constructing an argument. Pupils can identify where the writer has successfully addressed the question and/or where they fail to address it. Pupils will be able to identify the specific actions they must take to produce better-quality answers. This will help them assess their own work or the work of peers. This process is further supported by the Assessment Sheets on pages 43–49.

Page 165... is a **Self-Assessment Sheet** (How far have I travelled?) that can be used to complement the Learning Plan on page 155 or as an alternative form of self-review for the unit to be filled in by pupils at the end of the unit. This form is not linked to the Attainment Targets for the unit, but reviews progress against the learning objectives and enables pupils to record their personal impressions and achievements during the unit, providing them with a more subjective opportunity for self-assessment than the levelled approach adopted by the Learning Plan.

Pages 166–185... consist of photocopiable **Activity Sheets** to support the material in the Pupil Book.

All of these resources and activities are also available on the **Planning CD-ROM** *in either Word or PDF for teachers to print out if preferred or to display on whiteboards or projectors for whole -class discussion. They can also be customised to suit individual needs and, if required, saved with the other* **electronic resources** *for the unit using the facility to 'add your own resources' in the Just Click teaching solution.*

The following suggestions are intended to show how the material in Unit 4 of **Horizons 3** provides opportunities for teachers and pupils to assess their work as they go along, and to improve their learning as a result of that assessment. It must be stressed that these are only a few of the ways in which the material in the Pupil Book can be used. The techniques could be used as they are outlined here, but teachers will probably find that it is more helpful to use these as starting points and to develop their own ideas to suit their own circumstances.

Before you get started

There is an integral Assessment for Learning framework provided for Unit 4 (and every unit in **Horizons**):

- The unit opens on pages 64–65 of the Pupil Book with the learning objectives for the unit (Where are we going?). The lesson plans on the *Planning CD-ROM* then include learning objectives and outcomes for each spread in turn (supported by pupil-friendly versions in PowerPoint on the *Electronic Resources CD-ROM*).

- The unit ends on pages 82–83 of the Pupil Book with a plenary spread to review and evaluate the unit (Where are we now?), particularly in light of the learning objectives from the opening spread.

- The Learning Plan and Attainment Targets for the unit on pages 157–159 in this *Teaching and Learning Resources* guide provide pupils with the opportunity to set individual learning targets at the start of the unit and to review their progress against these targets at the end. The final self-assessment sheet (How far have I travelled?) on page 165 then offers pupils a more subjective review of their progress during the unit.

Teachers can use or adapt all or some of these resources to set and review goals and involve pupils in their own learning. Further resources on the *Electronic Resources CD-ROM* provide activities for initial assessment of prior learning at the start of the unit to help teachers to diagnose strengths and weaknesses for each topic and for checking and testing knowledge and understanding during and at the end of the unit. All these resources will provide teachers with further evidence to help structure and focus the learning programme.

Pages 64–65

All the activities on this spread could be used in pair work. Pupils could discuss the answers to all the questions, and may well stimulate each other by asking questions and spotting different things on the photos. When two pairs have completed one activity, or the whole group of activities, they can compare their answers. Once again, this might allow all those involved to see more in the photos and deduce more from their observations.

Activity 5 is probably the most difficult of the set. Pupils need to assess the degree of interest in each area from a point of view that may be different from their own. Therefore, it is even more important to have different opinions on the photos. A group has more chance of seeing the positive attractions of the areas than an individual would have.

Pages 66–67

All pupils can plan the lesson that Kamel might teach in activity 5, then some pupils can present their lesson to the rest of the class. The presenter and the rest of the class can assess the presentation using the Presentation Activity Assessment Sheet on page 46 of this *Teaching and Learning Resources* guide.

This could then be followed up by other members of the class taking on the role of Kamel and making a presentation based on their answers to activity 6. These pupils should learn from the comments made about the original presentation.

Pages 68–69

Pupils can do the soil experiment on Activity Sheet 4.5. This sheet can be presented in two ways: either with the questions attached or without them. More-able pupils should be able to decide which questions to ask about their experiment's outcome without needing the full version of the sheet, but some pupils might not be confident to think of their own questions.

After completing the experiment, allow the class two minutes to write down a list of questions that they would like to ask about the result. Pupils take it in turns to read out a question and to explain why it is significant. As the questions are discussed, each pupil develops his or her own list of questions. At the end of this process, pupils' lists can be compared with the list that was removed from the activity sheet – their lists may well be better!

Pages 70–71

Activity 3 appears to be fairly open-ended and yet the second part of the activity will not work unless certain, specific answers have been reached. Therefore, all pupils need to come up with the answers – rapid decay of plant material; rapid uptake of the nutrients by the roots of the vegetation; deep weathering; rapid weathering; some erosion of top soil; some loss of minerals or nutrients by water running down through the soil. With these answers, their labelling of the soil diagram will then be very useful.

To ensure that these answers are reached, pupils' thinking about the mind maps needs to be well structured. Allow pupils three or four minutes to think about their answers to the questions in mind maps C and D, then discuss them around the class. Hopefully, the right answers for labelling the diagram will come from the pupils working as a group. If they do not appear to be doing so, the teacher will need to move the discussion towards the desired outcome.

Pages 72–73

As part of activity 2, ask pupils to work in groups to produce posters showing how vegetation adapts to the tropical wet and dry climate. The layout can be similar to that on the page, with annotations on the diagrams to help explain the links between the different parts of the ecosystem.

At the end of the lesson, ask pupils to display their work. Each group assesses their own work, using the Poster

Activity Assessment Sheet on page 45 of this guide. They should pay particular attention to the last column on the sheet: 'How will you improve next time?'

Pages 74–75

Use Activity Sheet 4.9 to help complete activities 1 and 2.

When pupils have completed the first graph in activity 1, ask them to compare their graphs with a partner. Each pair should discuss the strengths and weaknesses of their two graphs and decide how both of them could improve the second graph.

When both graphs have been completed and cut out, pupils should place (but not stick) their graphs in the best locations on their maps. They should then discuss why they put them in that place and why they linked each of the graphs to particular map locations.

When they are both sure that they have got the right locations for the correct reasons, they should stick their graphs in place.

Pages 76–77

Activity 9 is designed to be a testing activity for all pupils and to allow the most able to have an opportunity to work at a high level, helping towards their final Level of Attainment. The most able should be allowed to work at this without help, in order to allow them an opportunity to achieve at a high level. Less-able pupils might be able to achieve good results on the activity, if they are given the opportunity with a well-structured support system in place.

Ask pupils to work in pairs and to look back through their work on pages 72–73 and on the current spread. Ask them to list all the separate pieces of evidence showing what causes the nature of the savanna vegetation. Next to each piece of evidence, they should write a brief explanation to show whether that aspect of the vegetation is affected by:

- climate
- soil
- animals
- people
- fire (either natural or started by people)
- any combination of these.

They should then discuss which of the factors they have listed seems to be the most important. Through discussion, they should reach a ranking of the factors. The discussion is important, because it allows everyone to put forward ideas that others can respond to and test, build on, or reject.

Having completed the discussion, each pupil should then try to reach a conclusion, working individually but taking into account all that was discussed.

Pages 78–79

Before pupils start to write their diary for activity 7, ask them what they are trying to achieve in their piece of work. Ask the class to make a list of criteria for success in this work. Criteria might include:

- it is interesting to read
- the illustrations are good
- the diary includes a lot of good geography ideas
- the work is original and imaginative.

When completed, pupils should swap their work with a colleague and the pair should assess each other's work, judging against the criteria that the class established.

Pages 80–81

At the end of the debate in activity 3, ask pupils to assess their own contribution to the debate and to assess the work of the class as a whole. They could use the Oral Discussion Assessment Sheet on page 48 of this guide, but it is not ideal for the debate format. You could ask the class how the sheet could be adapted to fit the class's needs in this lesson or the teacher could adapt it for them.

Pages 82–83

Activity 5 can be used as a summative assessment opportunity for this unit. However, the Assessment Opportunity on pages 158–164 in this *Teaching and Learning Resources* guide provides criteria for success, model answers and a process for target setting and use of this assessment.

4 Ecosystems
Learning plan

What are my learning objectives for this unit?

I aim to learn about:
- ✓ the interactions that take place in all ecosystems
- ✓ the coral reef ecosystem – how it is threatened, and how it can be conserved
- ✓ the rainforest ecosystem
- ✓ the savanna grassland ecosystem and the farming systems that use it
- ✓ population and food supply in the human ecosystem.

Read the Attainment Targets for this unit on pages 156–157 and tick any statements that you feel refer to you. *Places and Environments* covers *what you know* about the topic and *Enquiry and Skills* covers *what you can do*.

Using these statements for this unit, decide what level you are overall at this stage:

Level ☐

What level do you think you can achieve by the end of this unit?

Level ☐

What are you going to concentrate on to achieve this level? A good place to start might be any statements on pages 156–157 that you have not ticked:

☐

At the end of the unit, read the Attainment Targets again and tick in a different colour any *new* statements that refer to you. Then decide what level you are now:

Level ☐

If you have improved, well done! What evidence can you show for this improvement? What or who do you think particularly helped you to improve your level?

☐

If you have stayed the same, better luck next time! What do you think you could have done differently to help improve your levels? What will you do next time to progress further?

☐

4 Ecosystems
My Attainment Targets for this unit

Level 3

Places and Environments

- ☐ I can describe and compare some physical and human features of different places, and offer explanations for the location of some of these features.
- ☐ I can show that I am aware that different places may show both similarities and differences.
- ☐ I can give reasons for some of my observations and judgements about places and environments.
- ☐ I can recognise how people seek to improve and sustain environments.

Enquiry and Skills

- ☐ I can use my skills and sources of evidence to answer a range of geographical questions.
- ☐ I am beginning to use the correct words to communicate my findings.

Level 4

Places and Environments

- ☐ I can show knowledge, understanding and skills in studies of a range of places in different parts of the world.
- ☐ I am beginning to recognise and describe patterns, and to see the importance of geographical location in understanding places.
- ☐ I can recognise and describe physical and human processes.
- ☐ I am beginning to understand how processes can change the features of places, and how these changes can affect the lives and activities of people living there.
- ☐ I can understand how people can both improve and damage the environment.
- ☐ I can explain how my own views, and the views of other people, about an environment can change.

Enquiry and Skills

- ☐ I can suggest suitable geographical questions for study.
- ☐ I can use a range of geographical skills to help me investigate places and environments.
- ☐ I can communicate my findings using appropriate vocabulary.

Level 5

Places and Environments

- ☐ I can show my knowledge, understanding and skills in relation to studies of a range of places and environments in different parts of the world.
- ☐ I can describe and begin to explain geographical patterns and physical and human processes.
- ☐ I can describe how these processes can lead to similarities and differences in the environments of places and in the lives of people who live there.
- ☐ I can recognise some of the links and relationships that make places dependent on each other.
- ☐ I can suggest explanations for ways in which human activities cause changes in the environment, and the different views that people hold about those changes.
- ☐ I can recognise how people try to manage environments sustainably.

Enquiry and Skills

- ☐ I can select and use appropriate skills and ways of presenting evidence to help me investigate places and environments.
- ☐ I can explain my own views and begin to suggest relevant geographical questions and issues.
- ☐ I can select information and sources of information, suggest sensible conclusions to investigations and present my findings both in writing and with maps and diagrams.

4 Ecosystems

My Attainment Targets for this unit

Level 6

Places and Environments

- [ ] I can show my knowledge, understanding and skills in studies at various scales in different parts of the world.
- [ ] I can describe and explain a range of physical and human processes and recognise that these processes interact to produce the distinctive characteristics of places.
- [ ] I can describe ways in which processes operating at different scales create geographical patterns and lead to changes in places.
- [ ] I can appreciate the links and relationships that make places dependent on each other.
- [ ] I can recognise how conflicting demands on the environment may arise, and I can describe and compare different approaches to its management.
- [ ] I can recognise that different values and attitudes, including my own, result in different approaches that have different effects on people and places.

Enquiry and Skills

- [ ] I can suggest relevant geographical questions and issues and appropriate sequences of investigation.
- [ ] I can select a range of skills and sources of evidence and use them effectively in my investigations.
- [ ] I can present my findings coherently and reach conclusions that are consistent with the evidence.

Level 7

Places and Environments

- [ ] I can show knowledge and understanding in studies at various scales in different parts of the world.
- [ ] I can describe interactions within/between physical and human processes and show how these interactions create geographical patterns and help change places and environments.
- [ ] I can understand that many factors, including people's values and attitudes, influence decisions and can use this understanding to explain the resulting changes.
- [ ] I can appreciate that the environment in a place, and the lives of the people who live there, are affected by actions and events in other places.
- [ ] I can recognise that human actions, including my own, may have unintended environmental consequences and that change can cause conflict.
- [ ] I can appreciate that considerations of sustainable development affect the planning and management of environments and resources.

Enquiry and Skills

- [ ] With growing independence, I can identify geographical questions and issues and establish my own sequence of investigation.
- [ ] I can select and use a wide range of skills.
- [ ] I can evaluate sources of evidence in a critical way, present well-argued summaries of my investigations, and reach substantiated conclusions.

Level 8

Places and Environments

- [ ] I can show knowledge, understanding and skills in studies at various scales in different places.
- [ ] I can offer explanations for interactions within and between physical and human processes.
- [ ] I can explain changes in characteristics of places over time, in terms of location, physical and human processes, and interactions with other places.
- [ ] I can begin to account for disparities in development and understand some of the range and complexity of factors that contribute to the quality of life in different places.
- [ ] I can recognise the causes and consequences of environmental issues and understand a range of views and approaches to tackling them.
- [ ] I can understand how sustainable development can affect planning and management of resources, and use examples to illustrate this.

Enquiry and Skills

- [ ] I can independently identify appropriate geographical questions and issues, and use an effective sequence of investigation.
- [ ] I can select a range of skills and use them accurately.
- [ ] I can evaluate sources of evidence in a critical way, before using them in my investigations.
- [ ] I can present full, well-argued summaries of investigations and reach substantiated conclusions.

4 Ecosystems
Assessment opportunity

On page 83 in activity 5 you are asked to make a display to illustrate the ecosystems that you have studied in this unit.

It is suggested that you could:

- make a display on a large world map outline
- use the statistics in the Pupil Book to draw a climate graph
- use photos from the book
- ask further questions of your own to take your enquiry further.

The key questions are:

1 How can the ecosystem be described?

2 Could the desert in photo B be developed as an area for the tourist industry?

3 If this area were developed, could the industry be sustainable?

4 What rules would have to be put in place if the area were to be used for sustainable tourism?

Before you start this activity, look at the **Criteria for success** sheet. Set yourself a target level to aim for in this Assessment Opportunity. Write this level in the box on the target setting sheet. Explain how you intend to obtain this level.

Once you have finished the activity, look again at the Criteria for success and assess your answers. You could also compare your answers with model answers. Write your level in the box and explain how you achieved this level.

Then set yourself a target for improvement in your next assessment. Explain what you need to do to improve next time. Try to set yourself specific tasks to work on.

4 Ecosystems
Criteria for success

A **Level 2** answer may	• describe physical and/or human features of an ecosystem and make observations about those features that give the area its character
	• show awareness of places beyond your own locality
	• express views on the environment and recognise how people affect the environment
	• carry out simple tasks and select information from resources provided
	• use this information and personal observations to respond to questions about places.
A **Level 3** answer may	• describe and compare physical and other features of different places and offer explanations for the locations of some of these features
	• offer reasons for some observations and judgements about places and environments
	• recognise how people seek to improve and sustain environments
	• use skills and evidence to answer a range of geographical questions.
A **Level 4** answer may	• show knowledge, understanding and skills in studies of places and environments
	• begin to recognise and describe patterns and to appreciate the importance of wider geographical location in understanding places
	• recognise and describe physical and human processes
	• begin to understand how these processes can change the features of places, and how these changes can affect the lives and activities of people living there
	• understand how people can improve and damage environments
	• explain your and other people's views about an environmental change
	• drawing on knowledge and understanding, suggest suitable geographical questions for study
	• use a range of skills to help investigate places and environments.
A **Level 5** answer may	• show knowledge, skills and understanding in relation to places
	• describe and begin to explain geographical patterns and physical and human processes
	• describe how processes cause differences in the environments of different places and in the lives of people who live there
	• recognise some of the links and relationships that make places dependent on each other
	• suggest explanations for ways in which human activities cause changes in the environment
	• recognise how people try to manage environments sustainably
	• begin to suggest relevant geographical questions and issues
	• select information and evidence, suggest plausible conclusions to investigations and present findings graphically and in writing.

A **Level 6** answer may	• show knowledge, skills and understanding in relation to places
	• describe and explain a range of physical and human processes and recognise that these processes interact to produce the distinctive characteristics of places
	• describe ways in which processes operating at different scales create geographical patterns and lead to changes in places
	• recognise how conflicting demands on the environment arise and describe and compare approaches to managing environments
	• drawing on knowledge and understanding, suggest geographical questions and issues and appropriate sequences of investigation
	• present findings in a coherent way and reach conclusions that are consistent with the evidence.
A **Level 7** answer may	• describe interactions within and between physical and human processes and show how these interactions create geographical patterns and help change places and environments
	• understand that people's values and attitudes influence decisions about places, and explain the resulting changes
	• appreciate that considerations of sustainable development affect the planning and management of environments and resources
	• with growing independence, draw on knowledge and understanding to identify geographical questions and issues and establish a sequence of investigation
	• evaluate evidence critically, present well-argued summaries of investigations and begin to reach substantiated conclusions.
A **Level 8** answer may	• offer explanations for interactions within and between physical and human processes
	• explain changes in places over time, in terms of location, physical and human processes and interactions with other places
	• begin to account for disparities in development and understand that complex factors contribute to the quality of life in different places
	• recognise the causes and consequences of environmental issues and understand a range of different approaches to tackling them
	• understand how consideration of sustainable development can affect the management of environments
	• show independence in identifying appropriate geographical questions and issues, and in using effective sequences of investigation
	• evaluate critically sources of evidence before using them in investigations
	• present full and coherently argued summaries of investigations and reach substantiated conclusions.

4 Ecosystems
My target setting

I want to make progress in geography, working on my part of the group activity on the world's ecosystems.

When I do activity 5 on page 83, I aim to obtain:

Level ⎯⎯⎤

To do this I will need to:

Answer these questions when you have completed activity 5 on page 83:

In this Assessment Opportunity I obtained:

Level ⎯⎯⎤

Explain how you obtained this level:

When I do my next Assessment Opportunity, I aim to obtain:

Level ⎯⎯⎤

To do this I will need to:

Model answers

A   This is a good basic answer that was written by a pupil who had asked some extra questions as a follow-up to activity 5 on page 83.

This pupil took the desert ecosystem as her part of the group work. She drew a climate graph and shaded the areas of deserts on the world map.

She annotated this picture of Wadi Rum in Jordan. She drew an arrow to the world map to show where Wadi Rum is located.

There is hardly any vegetation on the steep slopes. When it does rain, the water runs off this steep slope so that the soil cannot soak up any water to help the vegetation grow.

There are some tussocks of grass. They are spread quite evenly apart. This is so their roots can spread out and collect water from a wide area.

Rain washes sand down to the bottom of the slope. This sand can form soil and it can hold some water for the plants to survive. The leaves die back during the dry season then they grow up again when it rains.

You can just see a small group of ibex (a kind of goat) that lives here. They graze on the grass and can just survive with the amount of vegetation. They attract tourists who come to see the ecosystem in this area.

B The pupil who had done example (A) decided that she could improve her Level of Attainment if she wrote more about links between the physical environment and the human environment. She found another photo, taken in the same area, and annotated this one too.

The Bedouin hire out some of their camels to tourists who want to go trekking in the desert.

The clouds show that it rains sometimes in the desert.

Here you can see tyre tracks. These can damage the vegetation. Once the vegetation has been destroyed, it takes a long time to grow again because of the shortage of rainfall and the way that the sand blows around when there are no roots to hold it together.

This is a Bedouin camp in the desert. They keep flocks of goats and camels, which can survive by grazing on the sparse grass. The Bedouin also make some money from the tourists who come to see the scenery and the ecosystems.

C

Another pupil had also written about the desert ecosystem in Wadi Rum. He wanted to make sure that he explained how the physical and human processes interacted in that area, but he wanted to go on and explain about disparities in development and different ways of tackling environmental issues.

He annotated some photos of the area, but then added this explanation after his annotations.

The Bedouin people have lived in this ecosystem for many generations. They have adapted their way of life to surviving in a difficult environment. In the last few years there has been an increase in tourists going to the area from more developed countries. This has caused a problem for the local people. They could do one of three things:

1 Encourage as many tourists to come as they can, and make as much money as they can from them. This will make them much richer, but it may destroy the environment. For example, they may want to drive across the desert in 4x4 vehicles and destroy the vegetation.

2 Encourage a smaller number of tourists to come, but control what they can do and where they can go. This means that the Bedouin can make some money to spend on better healthcare, better education and some luxuries, such as mobile phones. This can lead to sustainable development, with tourists staying in camps with Bedouin tents and trekking on camels to see the scenery.

3 They could discourage tourists from coming and keep things as they are. This might be a sustainable way of looking after the ecosystem, but it is not development. On the other hand, it might not be sustainable. If the Bedouin increase their population, they will not be able to survive by just grazing their animals.

In fact, the people of Wadi Rum have followed suggestion number 2, as you can see from the photo of Alan on page 124 of the Pupil Book. It shows a tourist who is in Wadi Rum to try to experience the Bedouin way of life without damaging the ecosystem of the area.

4 Ecosystems
How far have I travelled?

In this unit my **Learning Objectives** were to learn about:

- the interactions that take place in all ecosystems
- the coral reef ecosystem – how it is threatened, and how it can be conserved
- the rainforest ecosystem
- the savanna grassland ecosystem and the farming systems that use it
- population and food supply in the human ecosystem.

My progress in this unit

How well have I achieved my objectives?	Okay							Excellent
Enquiry and Skills:								
to interpret photos of ecosystems								
to interpret climate graphs								
to label a living graph								
to complete my part of a group display								
Places and Environments:								
to understand the links in ecosystems								
to understand how soil develops								
to understand the formation of at least one world ecosystem								
to understand how people use ecosystems sustainably								

Shade the bars to show how far you think you have made progress in this unit.

The part of this unit that I enjoyed the most was …

because …

The part of this unit that I needed most help with was …

because …

The piece of work that I am most pleased with is …

because …

The aspect of this unit that will be most useful to me in future is …

because …

Any other comments?

Stick a picture of an ecosystem in the box in the middle of this page. Use the boxes around the picture to help you complete the activities on page 65 of your textbook.

Vegetation

Soil

Climate

Human activities

Great Barrier Reef returns to life

Australia's Great Barrier Reef has recovered from the severe bleaching that was taking place a few years ago and is now one of the healthiest reefs in the world – as well as being the biggest. This was stated in the Report from the Australian Institute of Marine Science.

The Reef, 1920 km long, is listed as a World Heritage Site. It is one of Australia's most popular tourist attractions and is made up of more than 2600 individual reefs and 300 islands.

Coral on almost 60% of the reef was dying because the water was becoming too warm, but the coral is recovering. Now only about 6% of the reef is affected. A living coral reef is usually a mass of pinks, blues, yellows – all the colours of the rainbow and then some more. When coral dies, it turns a ghostly white (bleaching). The death can happen when the water gets too warm or when the coral is affected by over-fishing, pollution or run-off of sediments from nearby land masses.

The death of corals on the Great Barrier Reef was mainly caused by the El Niño event of 1997–98. This was caused by changes in the way warm currents circulated in the Pacific Ocean, which warmed the water off the eastern coast of Australia. Some people thought that the reefs would not recover, but the fear was misplaced.

'Reefs, if they are left alone and not stressed, can recover quite rapidly,' said Dr Clive Wilkinson, head of the Global Coral Reef Monitoring Network.

The report praised the Great Barrier Marine Park Authority for preserving the reef by ensuring that its water was unpolluted, controlling tourists, protecting fish stocks and setting up marine sanctuaries.

However, the situation was not as good in south-east Asia, which has a very high proportion of the world's reefs. Here, 88% of reefs are at medium or high risk because of the impact of humans. The most serious threat is destructive over-fishing. Some fishermen even use

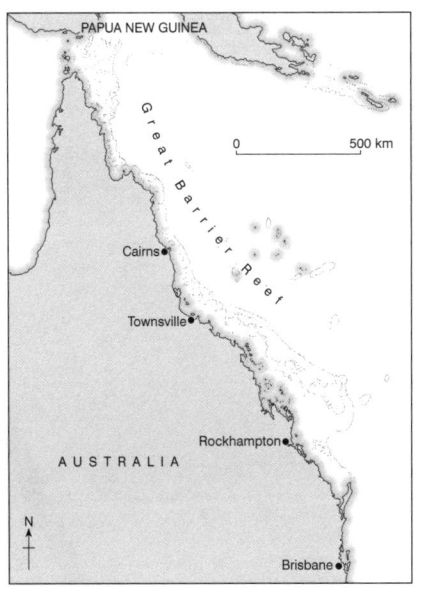

explosives, which stun the fish but destroy the reefs which are their habitat. Other reefs are threatened by coastal development that releases pollution and causes increased sedimentation.

The report says that development often takes priority over environmental conservation, but this can be seen as a short-term view of development. In the world as a whole, £62 million per year is spent on conserving reefs, but their direct value in terms of food, tourism and bio-diversity is £250 billion.

---

1 Name the world's biggest group of coral reefs and describe its location.

2 What happens to the appearance of coral reefs when the corals die?

3 List three major threats to the world's coral reefs.

4 What, according to the article, was the main threat to the Great Barrier Reef in the period from 1997 to 2000?

5 Explain how the Australian authorities are managing to conserve the Great Barrier Reef.

6 a Explain why the coral reefs in many of the countries of south-east Asia are being damaged or destroyed.

b Suggest why the authorities in these countries are not able to conserve their reefs as well as the Australians can.

7 Some people might say that LEDCs cannot afford to protect and conserve their reefs. Other people might say they cannot afford not to protect them.

a In small groups, discuss these two points of view.

b Which viewpoint do you agree with? Explain your answer.

4·3 Ecosystem links

Use the diagram below to help you complete
activities 1 and 2 on page 69 of your textbook.

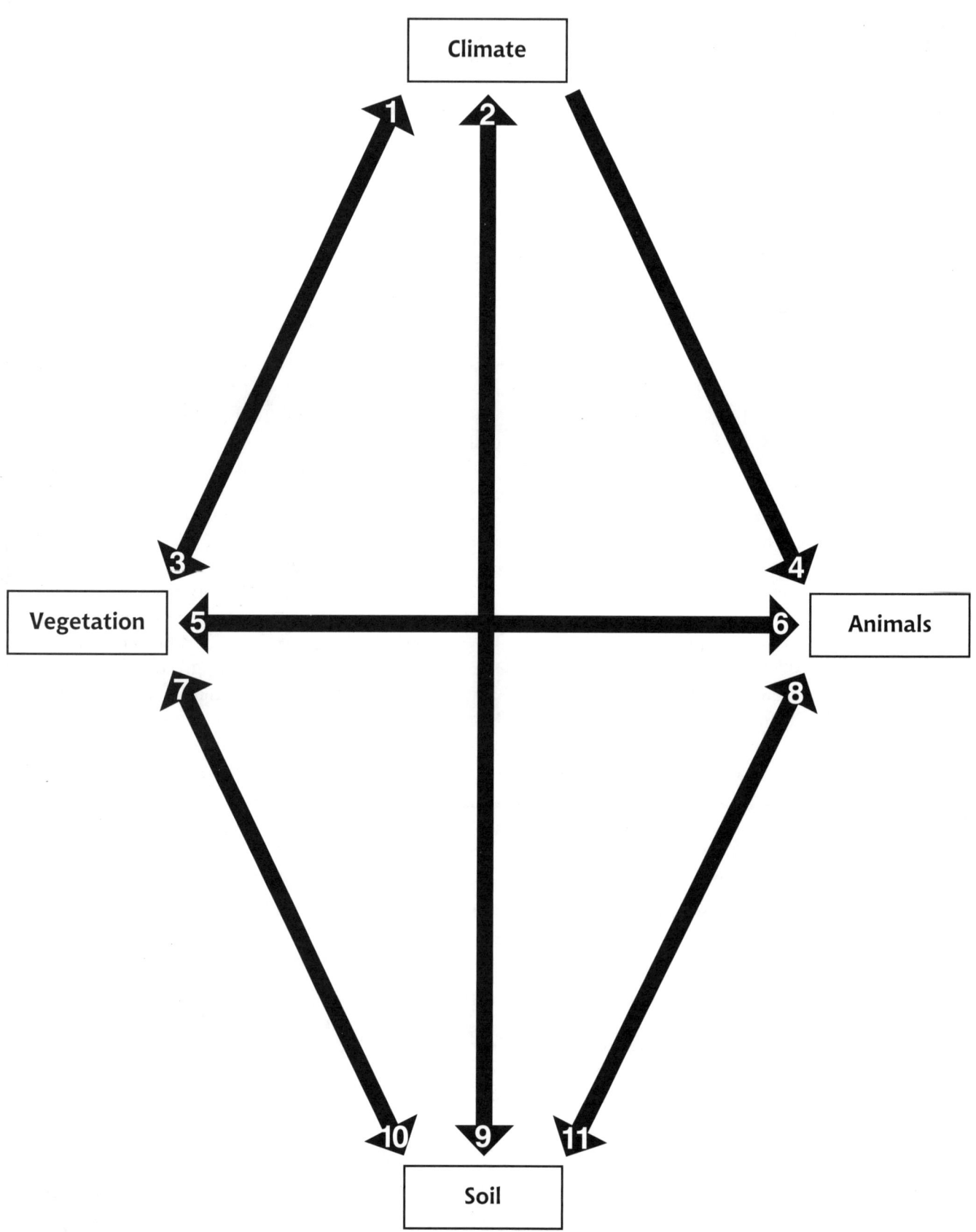

4·4 Soil systems

Use the diagram below to help you complete
activity 3 on page 69 of your textbook.

4·5 Soil experiment 1

1 You will need a screw-top jar, a trowel and some water.

2 Use the trowel to dig some soil from the ground and put it in the jar. If you see worms or other creatures in the soil, make sure you take them out before you put the soil inside.

3 Collect enough soil to fill the jar so that it is about a quarter full.

4 Top up the jar with water so that it is almost full, and then screw on the top tightly.

5 Shake the jar well, so that the soil and the water become completely mixed together.

6 Leave the jar so that the soil settles.

7 Observe what happens:
   a after 30 seconds
   b after five minutes
   c by the end of the lesson or at the start of the next lesson.

8 Sketch the jar and label the interesting features that you have observed. Hold a ruler next to the jar so that you can draw your experiment to the correct scale.

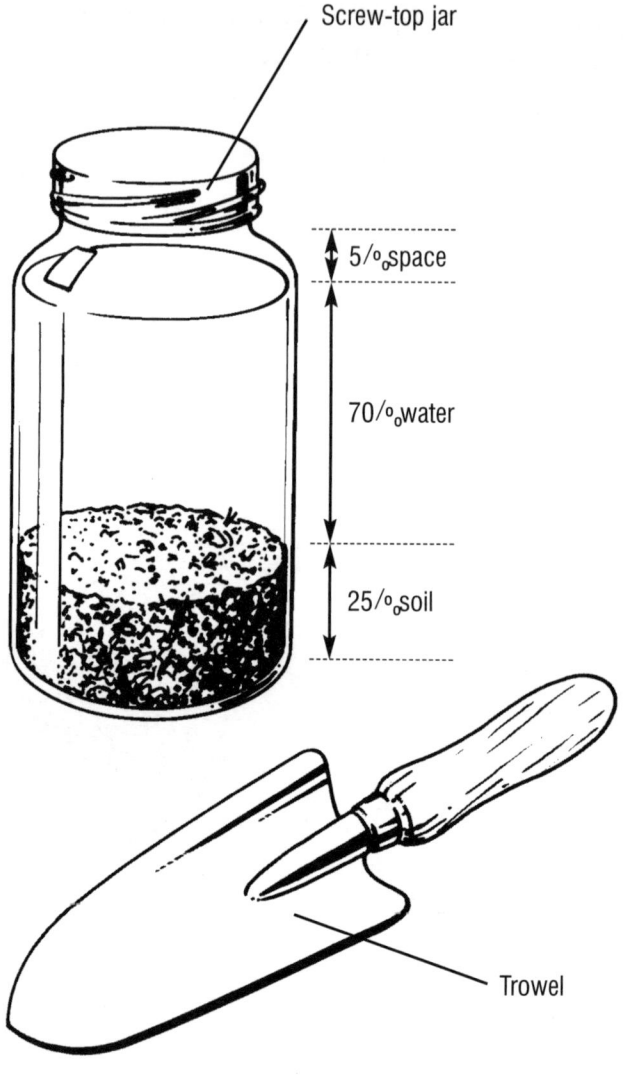

Screw-top jar

5% space

70% water

25% soil

Trowel

✂

Questions to ask when observing and drawing the experiment:
- Does the soil form layers in the bottom of the jar?
- What type of material settles in the first layer?
- How long did it take for this layer to form?
- What other layers formed in the jar?
- How deep was each layer?
- What was the colour of each layer? What was its texture (coarse, fine, sandy, silty, mixed)?
- Was any material left floating in the water? If so, what was this material like?
- What changes happened at each stage of the settling process?

Ecosystems

4·6 Soil experiment 2

1. You will need a clean tin can with the top and bottom removed, a container with enough water to fill the can exactly, and a stopwatch.

2. Place the can on an area of exposed soil. Choose your soil type carefully. Press it down firmly so that water will not be able to leak out between the base of the tin and the soil.

3. Carefully and quickly pour the water into the tin so that it comes just level with the top of the tin.

4. Start the stopwatch as soon as the tin is full.

5. Watch as the water sinks into the soil and stop the watch as soon as all the water has soaked away.

6. Record the time taken.

7. Repeat the experiment on another soil surface. For example, you could compare soil from the middle of a field where few people walk with soil on a footpath, which has been compressed by people walking over it. Alternatively, you could compare well-cultivated garden soil that has been worked well and dug over by a gardener with uncultivated soil that has not been looked after.

8. Compare the infiltration rates at the two sites.

9. Suggest reasons for any differences.

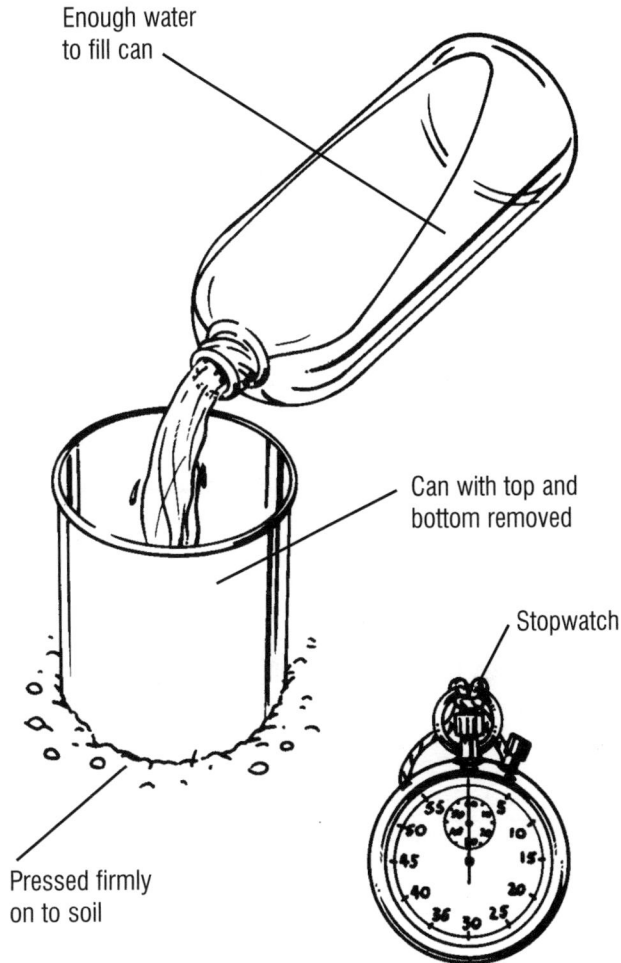

Enough water to fill can

Can with top and bottom removed

Stopwatch

Pressed firmly on to soil

Questions to ask when explaining the results of the experiment:
- Was infiltration speeded up or slowed down by the presence of pore spaces?
- Were pore spaces affected by people, animals or walking on the soil?
- Were pore spaces affected by gardeners digging and cultivating the soil?
- Had pores been affected by recent weather, particularly the amount of rainfall?
- Does vegetation cover affect pores in the soil? Think about roots and dead vegetation decaying to form humus in the soil.
- Was there any evidence of animal life affecting the soil? Think about worms and other small creatures, which are more likely to have affected the soil than rabbits, etc.
- In conclusion, is air an important part of soil structure?

Use the sketch of the photo below to help you complete activity 2 on page 70 of your textbook.

① Sun's rays allow plants to photosynthesise.

② Trees grow upwards very quickly,

③ It is hot and wet at all seasons,

④ Climbing plants and lianas use the trees for support,

⑤ Heat evaporates water from land surface,

⑥ There are few branches in the middle layers,

⑦ Branches spread out to catch maximum sunlight.

⑧ Heat and evaporation produce thick cumulus clouds,

a This produces new plant material.

b and transpires water from leaves.

c which bring rain storms.

d so plants grow all year round.

e so that they can compete for the light.

f to help them reach the light more quickly.

g They form a continuous canopy.

h because the canopy traps most of the sunlight.

4·8 Savanna grasslands

1 Cut out the six sketches below. Each one shows how a plant adapts to the savanna climate.

2 Cut out the 'heads' and the 'tails' below.

3 Match the heads and tails to make sentences to describe the sketches.

4 Use the completed sentences to label the sketches.

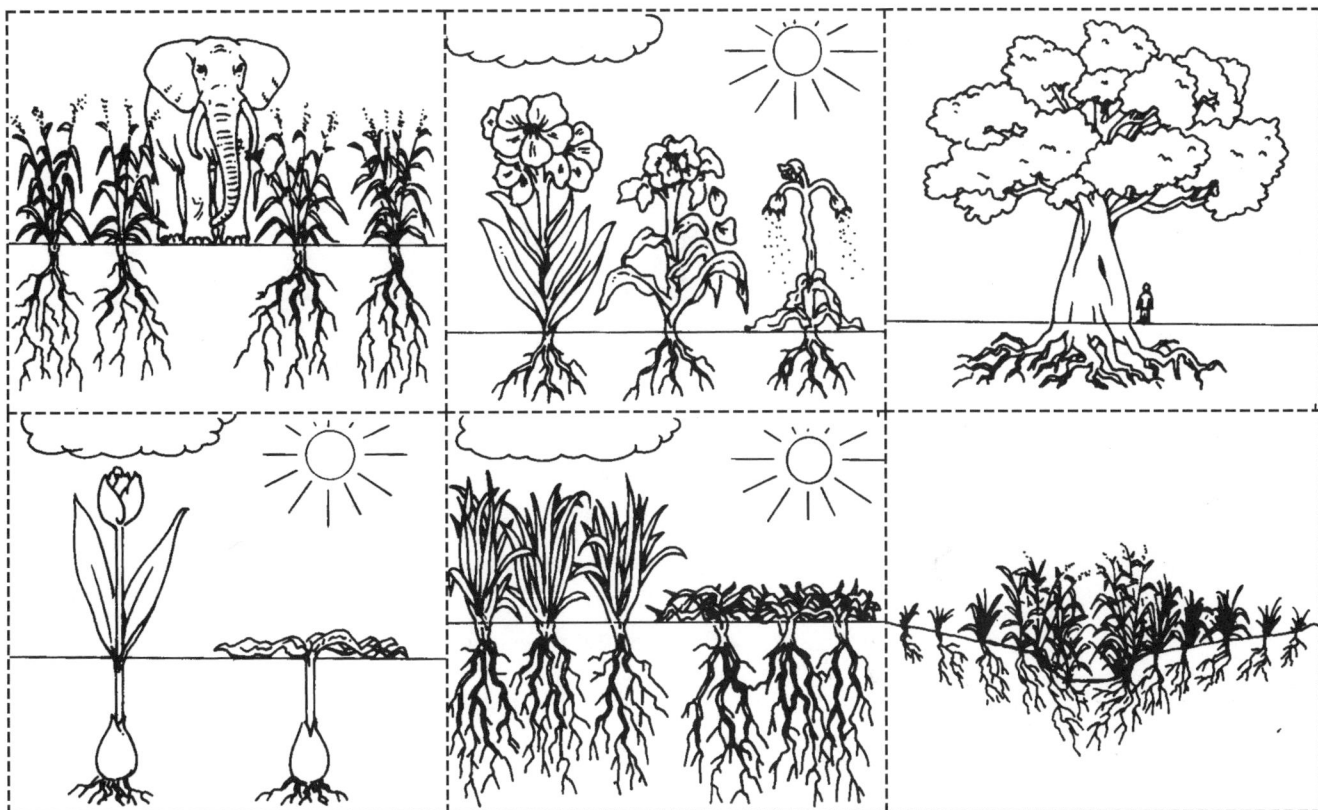

Heads

Grasses have deep roots
Flowers die and scatter their seeds
Trees like the baobab have thick trunks
Some flowers grow from bulbs
There is denser vegetation by the river courses because
Grasses die back in the dry season

Tails

that store food and water deep in the soil.
and protect the roots from heat and evaporation.
to seek for water deep in the ground.
to store water for the dry season.
that lie dormant then germinate when the next rains come.
even when the river dries up there may be water in the sediment on the bed.

Ecosystems

4·9 Timbuktu and Lusaka climates

1 a Use graphs A and B to help you complete activity 1 on page 75 of your textbook.

b When you have completed the graphs, cut them out.

2 a Cut out outline map C of Africa.

b Mark the positions of Timbuktu and Lusaka on the map.

3 a Stick the two graphs and the map on a large sheet of paper.

b Draw arrows from your two graphs to show the places they represent on the map.

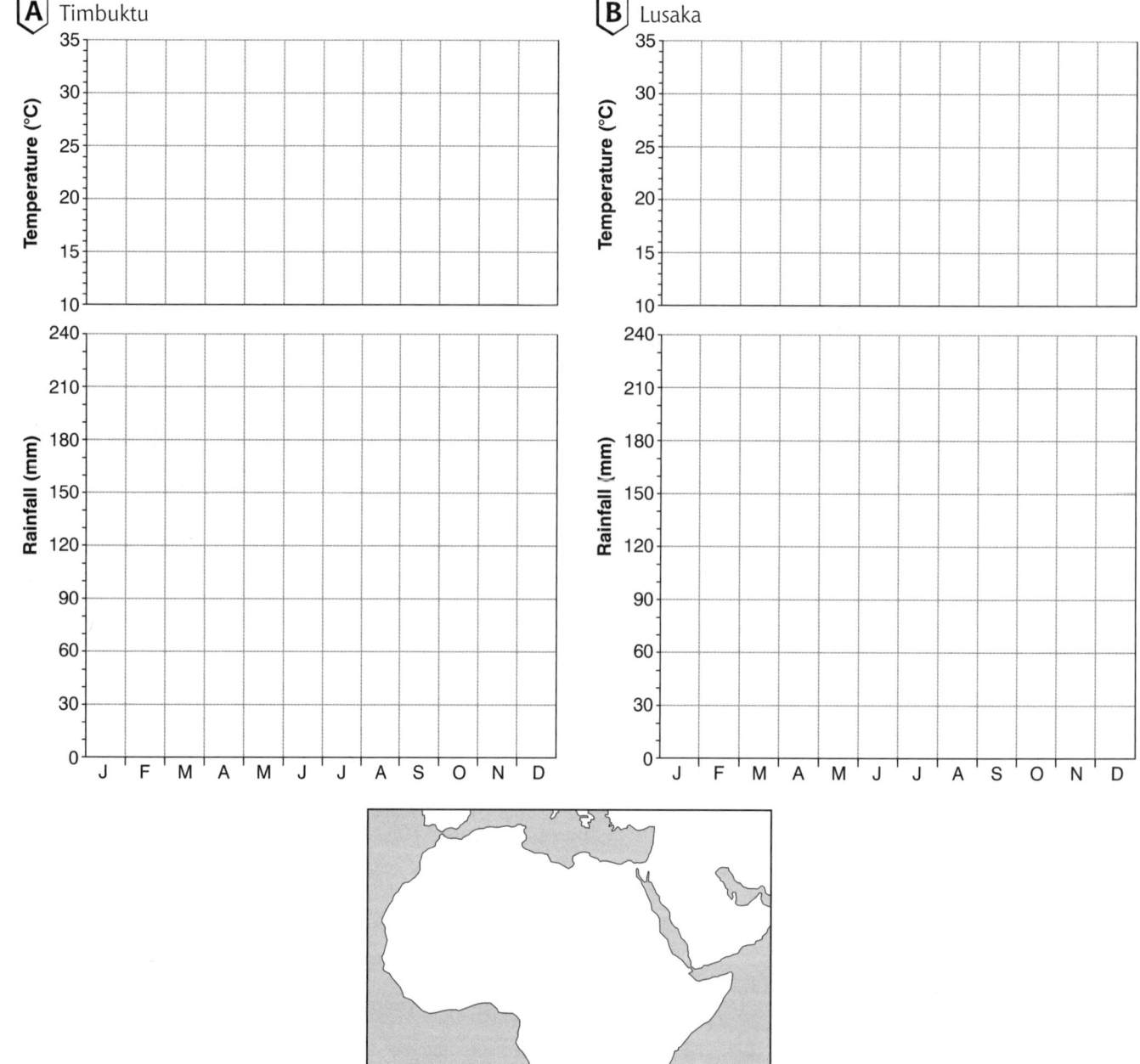

A Timbuktu

B Lusaka

C

4·10 Serengeti living graph

Use the graph below to help you complete activity 1 on page 77 of your textbook.

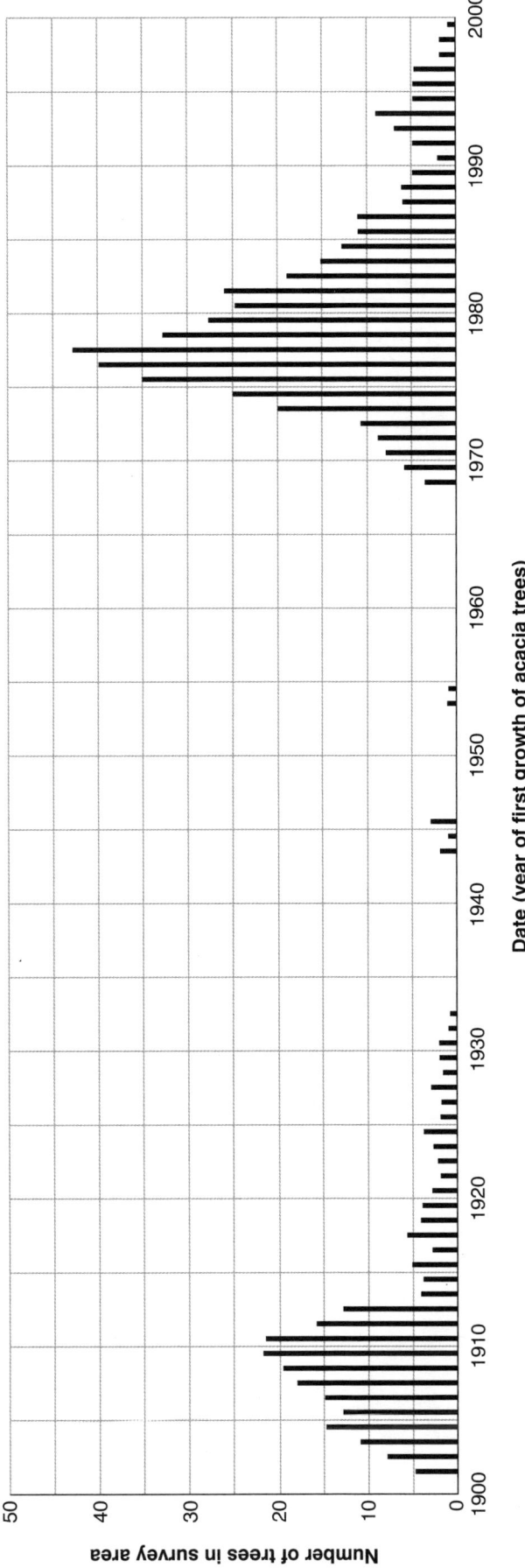

Number of trees in survey area

Date (year of first growth of acacia trees)

(4·11) The Serengeti ecosystem 1

Godwin is an elder in a tribe of herdsmen in northern Tanzania. He is puzzled about several odd things that have happened recently.

He thought that he understood the environment and its ecosystem after living here for over 60 years, but it has been behaving strangely.

He is also worried about the youth of the tribe becoming lazy and disrespectful, although his wife tells him that he ought to listen carefully to what they have to say rather than blaming them for everything that goes wrong.

Read the cards below and on sheet 4.12
- Can you help him to explain the things that are worrying him?
- What has happened to the ecosystem?
- What has happened to the youth of the tribe?

The area of white, where snow covers the top of Mt Kilimanjaro, has grown much smaller over the last ten years.	The streams running down from Mt Kilimanjaro usually start to flow faster when the weather gets warmer at the end of the cold season. That faster flow has come earlier in the last few years.
The higher flow of the rivers at the start of the warm season does not seem to last as long as it used to do.	The youths who take the cattle to the watering places are taking much longer than we did when it was my job to water the cattle. I think they are getting lazy and wasting time.
The rains at the start of the warm season come earlier than they used to, but then they finish earlier.	The pasture that our cattle graze on does not last into the dry season like it used to. We have to take the cattle further to find pasture, which can bring us into conflict with neighbouring groups also seeking pasture.

My friend told me he went to watch the youths while they watered the cattle and he said they were digging holes in the sand on the stream bed. Time wasting, I call it.	I sometimes wonder if the tourists in their big vehicles are damaging the pasture. They leave tracks in the ground, but the pasture is getting poorer even where the tourists never go.
I heard a tourist complain about the smell of cattle dung the other day. How we all laughed! It is their vehicles that smell bad, not our cattle.	The tourists come in big planes that we see flying high in the sky. I wonder if they are upsetting the clouds and altering the rain.
Kilimanjaro is a special, spiritual place. We believe the spirits of the mountain watch over us.	Some of our young men are leaving the traditional way of life and becoming park rangers.
When the young men who work as rangers send money back to us, we can use it to buy more cattle.	During the dry season some of our cattle are dying because there is not enough water or grazing land.
A man from the government is trying to make us cut the number of cattle we keep. He says fewer healthy cattle are better than a lot of weak cattle.	We have always tried to increase the size of our herds. A man's status depends on the number of his cattle.
We graze the cattle close to the village for as much of the time as we can. In the last few years, we have noticed that the grazing close to the village does not last as long as it used to. We have to start moving with our herds sooner each year.	When the rains fall on bare ground they wash away the soil. This is bad because it means the grasses do not grow well the next year.
A vet came to look at our cattle. He said he could vaccinate them to stop them getting diseases, but he would only do it if we would keep the cattle in pens to stop them grazing with our neighbours' cattle. Why would he want to change our whole way of life?	If the pasture and the water supply keep getting worse, it is going to destroy our traditional way of life for ever.

4•13 Ecosystems

see pages 80–81 in your Horizons Book 3

Ask the expert 1

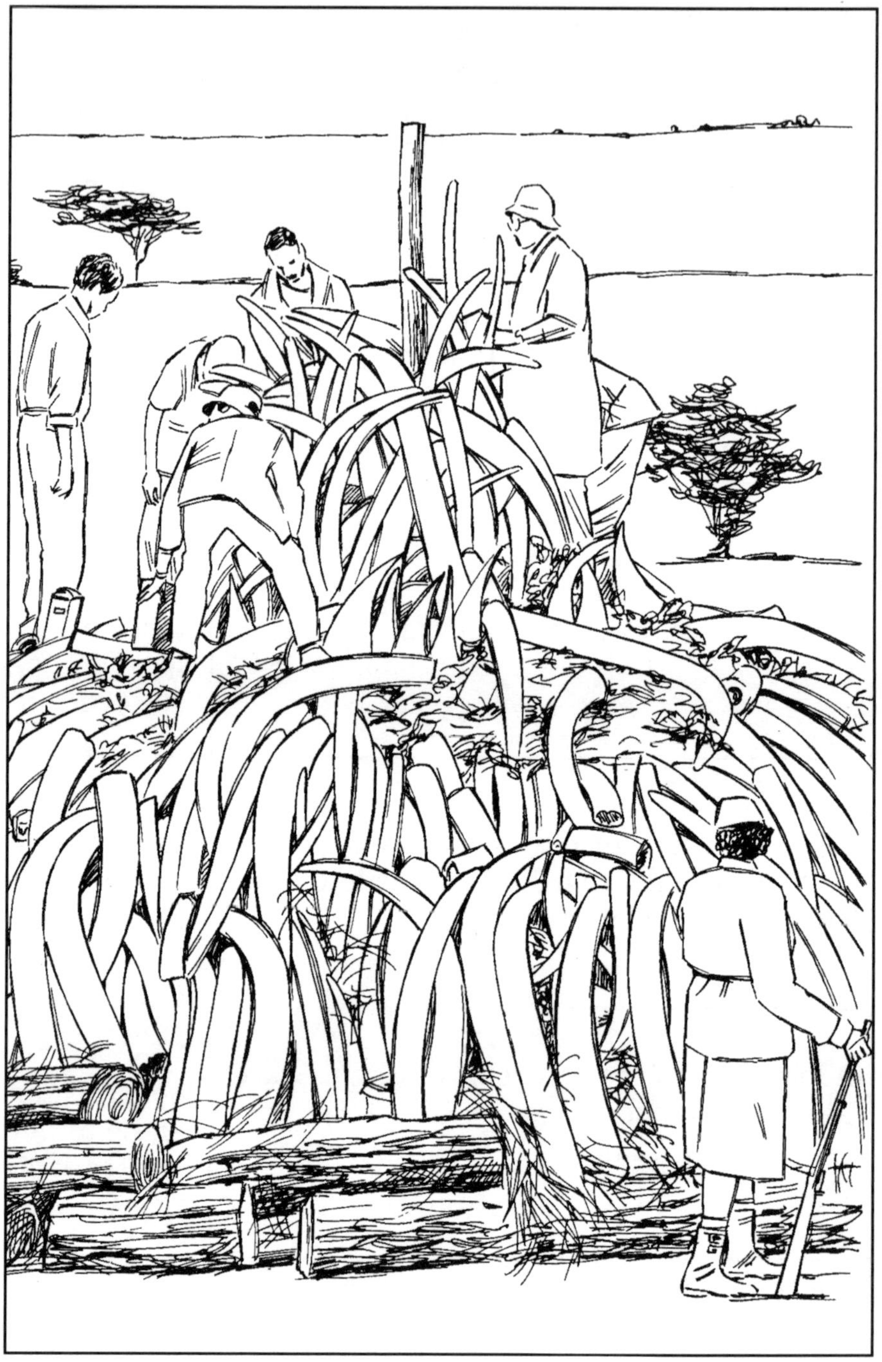

1. One member of your class will leave the room. He or she will be given information to help make them the 'expert' on this picture. Note that there is a copy of the original photo on the *Electronic Resources CD-ROM*.
2. The rest of the class should think of 20 questions to ask the expert. These questions can be answered only 'Yes', 'No' or 'Don't know'.
3. Write down the 20 questions before the expert comes back into the classroom. Ask the questions in the order you have written them down.
4. When you have asked all the questions, retell the story behind the picture in as much detail as possible.

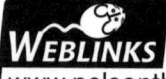

WEBLINKS **You will find a links to websites giving more information about elephants at**
www.nelsonthornes.com/horizons

(**4·14**) Ask the expert 2

You have been chosen to be the 'expert' in this activity.

1. Read the information below so that you know a lot of detail about the picture the rest of the class is looking at.

2. The class will ask you 20 questions to try to find out exactly what the picture is about. When they ask their questions, you can answer only 'Yes', 'No' or 'Don't know'.

3. Afterwards, your teacher might tell the class to ask you some more open-ended questions. Then you will have to give more detailed answers.

This picture shows a pile of confiscated ivory and rhino horns that is about to be burnt. It was taken in the Nairobi National Park in Kenya.

The bonfire consists of 27 tons of elephant ivory and 57 rhino horns that have been confiscated from poachers. These are people who have hunted the animals illegally because of the price they can get for selling the ivory and horn.

The ivory is sold to carve and make ornaments. The rhino horn is sold to make traditional medicines in some countries in the Far East.

The people building the bonfire are park rangers who have helped to track down the poachers. The bonfire is being built to publicise the worldwide ban on the trade in ivory that was introduced in 1989 by the treaty known as Convention on International Trade in Endangered Species of Wild Fauna and Flora (CITES).

CITES is a United Nations-administered agreement to control international trade in wild flora (plants) and fauna (animals) in order to protect against over-exploitation through commercial trade.

Between 1979 and 1989 – a time when there was a legal ivory trade – African elephants were poached at such a rapid rate that the continent-wide population was cut from 1.3 million to approximately 600 000. The scale of poaching was so great that it threatened African economies. If it had been allowed to continue, it could have destroyed the tourist industry. It could also have damaged the grassland ecosystem.

Countries like Kenya and Tanzania were spending a lot of money to fight poachers. Many human lives were lost in these ivory wars, both of poachers and game wardens.

This picture was taken as part of a worldwide publicity campaign about the ban, to discourage illegal poaching and trade in ivory. The ivory came from several captured poaching gangs.

This widely supported ban halted the devastation of elephant populations and African elephants began their slow, but promising, recovery.

(4·15) Tanzania role play 1

Four members of your class will be given role descriptions of four people's viewpoints. These people have thought about the issues of conservation and development in Tanzania.

1. The four people who have been given these roles should read the information carefully and prepare to take these roles in a debate. The rest of the class should read the information and opinions on pages 80–81 in your textbook. This will prepare you for the debate in activity 3 on page 81.

2. In the debate, the four main speakers should introduce themselves to the class. They should each make a speech to give their points of view.

3. When the four main people have spoken, the rest of the class can join in, taking it in turns to give their points of view, supported by facts and logical arguments. Remember that you should think about the sustainable development of the ecosystem at all stages of the debate.

4. At the end of the debate, take a vote on the question: 'Should hunting of wild animals ever be allowed in the Serengeti or Loliondo areas of Tanzania?'

5. When you have voted, you could draw up a list of rules to say either:
   a when, how and where hunting can be permitted, or
   b how poaching should be stopped, and how alternative sources of food and income could be developed for the people who live in the area.

Alternative activity

1. In groups of four, take the four role descriptions and read through them, looking for:
   a arguments against hunting wild animals
   b arguments in favour of hunting wild animals
   c references to links in the ecosystem
   d references to the development of the people and the economy
   e references to sustainability.

2. Underline references to the five ideas using five different colours.

3. Write a summary of the ideas about each of the five points.

4. Write a conclusion about the best way to ensure the sustainable development of the Serengeti National Park and the Loliondo Wildlife Conservation Area.

(4·16) Tanzania role play 2

Role description 1: Maasai tribal elder

My group of Maasai lives in the Serengeti. We try to live like we have always lived. We are herders and our whole life is planned around the care of our herds. To care for them, we have to know and understand the land as well as we understand ourselves.

We have to migrate with the seasons. We look for pasture and water for our herds so we have to follow the rains, and the rains follow the sun. We cannot carry much with us when we move, so most of our food comes from the cattle. We drink their milk and make cheese from it too. We also drink blood from the cattle. We take this from a cut in their necks. It does not damage the cow, but it is good food that makes us strong.

Sometimes when we are travelling we kill a goat for meat. We usually do this when we are celebrating a special day. Why should we not kill wild animals too? When we see the enormous herds of zebra and wildebeest, with lions and hyenas hunting them, it is difficult to understand why the rangers stop us hunting just one or two animals for meat.

I know things are changing in the outside world. I know foreign people come to see the wild animals. I know many of our young men are getting jobs and money from the tourists. But I still don't see how we would harm all this by just taking a few animals for food, like our fathers and grandfathers always did. The Maasai have always known how to live in balance with the natural world. We will not upset it now.

Role description 2: Tanzanian minister for the environment

Tanzania is a poor country. Our average GNP per person is just US$120 a year. Only Ethiopia and Mozambique of the African countries have a lower GNP than us. In the UK, GNP per person is US$18 700, so you must understand that we have to try to find every possible source of income for our people.

One of our biggest resources is our scenery, our wildlife, our ecosystem. We are trying to develop it in a sustainable way, so that it brings new wealth to our people today and yet will be preserved to bring wealth to future generations of Tanzanians. That is why we are developing our tourist industry, and why we are doing all that is within our power to keep it sustainable.

Two types of tourists come to Tanzania: those on camera safari and those who are real hunters. There are far more camera tourists than hunters, so we must look after the needs of the camera tourists first. But the hunters pay much more than the others, and so we have to meet their needs too.

How do we balance their needs? We have completely separate areas for the two groups. The National Parks are areas for conservation, and the only tourists allowed in there are the ones with cameras. But around the edges of the Parks are areas where we allow hunting under very strict conditions. We have to keep the ecosystem in balance, and so we monitor the numbers of each species of animal, issue licences to hunters, and charge them for their kills. That is as well as the basic tour price.

Keeping the animals in balance means that the pastures aren't overgrazed by too many herbivores and the carnivores are kept in balance too. The local farmers and cattle herders aren't threatened by too many predators and their cattle pasture is conserved. Their young men also get work guiding the hunters.

(4·17) Tanzania role play 3

Role description 3: Safari tourist from the UK

This has been a truly spiritual experience, to see the enormous herds of animals moving across the plains drawn by an invisible force of nature. The herds of zebra and wildebeest are tens or hundreds of thousands strong, but they move as if they were controlled by a single mind. It is quite extraordinary to watch and it makes me feel close to a primitive force and I have to wonder about the whole meaning of life.

On other days we have seen smaller groups of bigger animals – lions, elephants, giraffes – and each of them is magnificent and awe-inspiring in its own way. All of them have wonderful adaptations to the environment and they have great dignity as they live their lives.

Dignity is the word that I would use to describe the Maasai too. They live in harmony with their surroundings, surviving on what the environment provides but conserving their environment at the same time.

So how could anyone want to come in to this environment for sport, to kill for the sake of killing, to disrupt and to destroy? I'm opposed to blood sports in my own country but I'm even more strongly opposed here where shooting animals seems such an insult to everything around us.

I know I'm an outsider in the area, but I'm doing all that I can to minimise my effect. All that I'm taking from the area are my photos and my memories. I cannot even begin to understand why people should want to come here to kill and to take life from the area.

Role description 4: National Park warden

I'm a Maasai and a warden in the Loliondo Wildlife Conservation Area. My job is difficult and I have to make some hard choices. I have to help to conserve the ecology of the WCA and I also have to make sure that the people who live here can make a good living. I have to make sure people do not just live well now but that they will still be able to live well here many years from now. That is the Maasai way, because we know we can make use of the land now but that we must also protect it for future generations.

So should the killing of animals be allowed? Everything dies, but I sometimes have to decide when and how an animal should die. There are several reasons for killing an animal. We can kill an animal that threatens our own lives, or that threatens our cattle or the crops of the settled tribes. We can also kill some animals for food. That is allowed in the WCA, but not in the National Park. As wardens, we have to keep a check on how many animals are being killed by local people, but they usually obey the rules. As I said, it's our way to kill only when we need to kill.

However, there are some difficult cases. What do we do when animals threaten the ecosystem? If there are too many animals, they will overgraze and some might die of starvation, or if there are too many predators they might damage the herds and lose their own supplies of food. So we sometimes have to 'cull' animals for the good of the whole group and to keep the ecosystem in balance. We also allow rich foreigners to come and do the culling for us. They get fun from stalking and killing and we get their money.

There are two big problems though. Some people bring in parties of hunters who are not controlled. They just hunt without any controls. They kill whatever they can, whether it needs culling or not. Then there are the ivory poachers. They come to kill elephants for their tusks. They know that they can sell the tusks on the black market and make a huge profit. People like that wouldn't care if they killed all the elephants in Africa. They would probably like it. As the elephants grew scarcer, the price of ivory went up and they made even more money. Those are the people who must be stopped.

The following words and phrases will help you with your descriptions
of photos B–F on pages 82–83 of your textbook.

1 Some of the words and phrases describe the climate, some
describe the vegetation and some describe the soil. Underline the
three sets of words and phrases in different colours.

2 Decide which words and phrases are linked to which photos.

Almost all the land area is covered by
coniferous woodland

Animals here may be hibernating because of
the cold winter

This area looks unsuitable for any animal life
except camels

Birds, squirrels, mice and rabbits are
probably found here

Coniferous woodland (taiga)

Deciduous trees grow in countries with a
moderate climate like the UK

Deciduous trees, such as beech

Desert

Dying grass will help to provide humus for
rich soils

Frost on the trees' branches and patches of
snow in the clearings

The grass is greener in the hollows because
streams probably run there

Grey sky with little winter sunlight

Hardly any soil because there are few plants
to provide humus

Hills of bare, red rock

Leaves decay to help form fertile, brown soil

Marshy plain covered with mosses and low
grass

Most of the land is covered with grasses

New green leaves are growing in spring and
old leaves still lie on the ground

No signs of surface water

Patches of snow on the mountains

Plain looks like it has just thawed out after a
cold winter

Poor soil that is marshy and probably freezes
in river

Prairie

Sand swept into dunes by the wind

Soil will be poor because pine needles decay
slowly, so not much humus

Some trees turning gold and orange in
autumn

Sunlight can reach the ground because leaves
are not fully grown

Temperate deciduous woodland

Tundra

Tussocks of grass growing on the lower land

Two caribou grazing on the mossy plain

---

see pages 82–83 in your Horizons Book 3

4•19 World ecosystems 1

Use this map to help you complete activity 5 on page 83 of your textbook.

It shows the locations of climate graphs a–e on pages 82–83 of your textbook, graph A on page 70 and the figures in tables D and E on page 74. Climate graphs are given on sheet 4.20 for you to use.

The boundaries of the areas with similar ecosystems to those places are also marked.

Tropic of Cancer 23½°N
Equator 0°
Tropic of Capricorn 23½°S
1
2
3
4
5
6
7
8

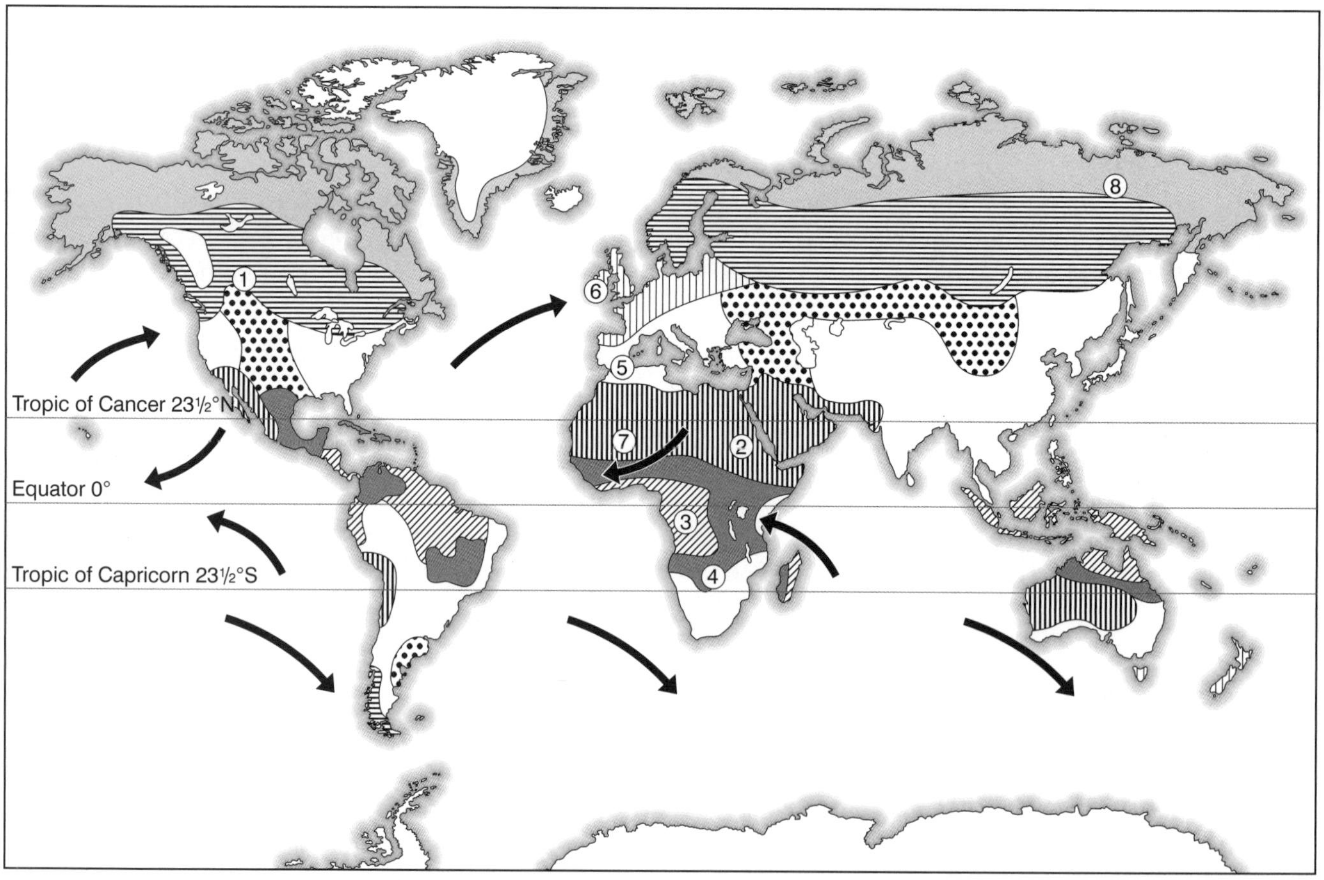

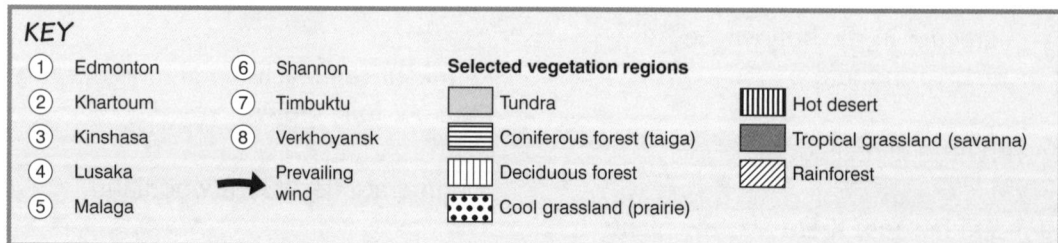

KEY

① Edmonton	⑥ Shannon	**Selected vegetation regions**	
② Khartoum	⑦ Timbuktu	Tundra	Hot desert
③ Kinshasa	⑧ Verkhoyansk	Coniferous forest (taiga)	Tropical grassland (savanna)
④ Lusaka	→ Prevailing wind	Deciduous forest	Rainforest
⑤ Malaga		Cool grassland (prairie)	

4·20 World ecosystems 2

see pages 82–83 in your Horizons Book 3

Use these graphs to help you complete activity 5 on page 83 of your textbook.

Cut out the graphs, stick them around the outside of the world map on sheet 4.19, and draw arrows linking them to the places they represent.

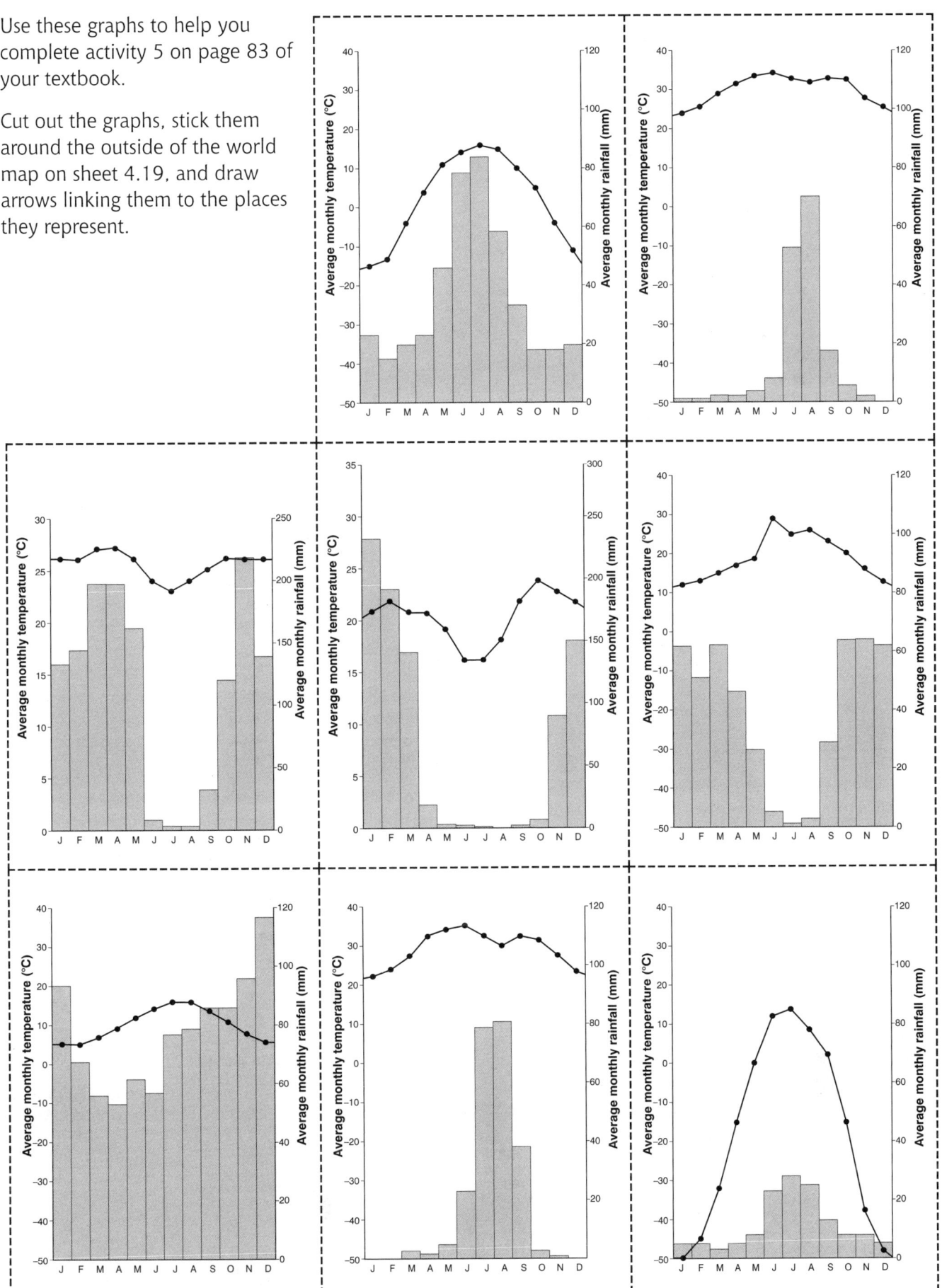

5 Think – Act

In this section of the *Teaching and Learning Resources* guide you will find:

Pages 187–188... have a list of opportunities for **Assessment for Learning** in this unit. One example is provided for each double-page spread. These ideas are based on activities in the Pupil Book, but each activity needs some development if it is to be used as an Assessment for Learning opportunity. Most of the suggestions involve pupils in assessment of their own work, in peer-assessment, or in some other form of discussion of the work either before or after it is attempted. All these suggestions are intended to increase pupils' awareness of what characterises good work, and of how their own work can be developed and improved.

The suggestions here are not intended to be prescriptive. Rather they provide teachers with opportunities that we feel fit the best practice of Assessment for Learning, and which target pupils' learning – an increasingly important area of focus under the new Ofsted inspection framework.

Page 189... is a **Learning Plan** for pupils, which gives them a copy of the learning objectives for the unit – copied from page 84 of the Pupil Book – and provides opportunities for pupils to assess their prior learning and set their targets for the whole unit, using the Attainment Targets on pages 192–193 as criteria for success. There is an opportunity at the end of the unit for pupils to re-assess their level against the Attainment Targets before completing the final self-assessment form (How far have I travelled?) on page 199.

Pages 190–191... give pupils a summary of the **Attainment Target** statements, adapted from the National Curriculum level descriptors, which are relevant to their work in this unit. Pupils can use the levels as criteria for success to set themselves learning targets for the unit and check their progress using the Learning Plan on page 189. They have also been divided into two sections, *Places and Environments* and *Enquiry and Skills*. Pupils should be able to see what it is that allows their work to move from one level to the higher level. These Attainment Targets can also be used to provide further support if required for pupils setting and reviewing their targets in the Assessment Opportunity for this unit (see below).

Pages 192–195... are also written for pupils. They describe the **Assessment Opportunity** on pages 102–103 of the Pupil Book. If teachers decide to use this exercise to assess the level at which pupils are working, these pages can be used to help guide pupils through that exercise. They should also help pupils to set targets for the exercise, to assess their own work and to set new targets for subsequent work. This will enable teachers and pupils to benefit from making formative use of the Assessment Opportunity. (Note that this differs from the Learning Plan on page 189 which provides Assessment for Learning support for the whole unit rather than an individual assessment.) Alternatively, teachers can use these pages as a mark scheme to help them to assess the individual performance of their pupils and build a portfolio of assessments to track their progress during Key Stage 3 Geography.

Pages 196–198... provide **Model Answers** for the Assessment Opportunity on pages 102–103 of the Pupil Book. These model asnwers can be used in a variety of ways. Teachers can display them as models of good practice for whole-class discussion, or pupils could look at them before they start to write their own answers. However, they are really intended to support the self- or peer-assessment process before pupils analyse their own work. The aim is to demonstrate the need to offer supporting information/ explanation for each point made when answering the question as well as the need for balance when constructing an argument. Pupils can identify where the writer has successfully addressed the question and/or when they fail to address it. Pupils will be better able to identify the specific actions they must take to produce better-quality answers. This will help them to assess their own work or the work of peers. This process is further supported by the Assessment Sheets on pages 43–49.

Page 199... is a **Self-Assessment Sheet** (How far have I travelled?) that can be used to complement the Learning Plan on page 189 or as an alternative form of self-review for the unit to be filled in by pupils at the end of the unit. This form is not linked to the Attainment Targets for the unit, but reviews progress against the learning objectives and enables pupils to record their personal impressions and achievements during the unit, providing them with a more subjective opportunity for self-assessment than the levelled approach adopted by the Learning Plan.

Pages 200–219... consist of photocopiable **Activity Sheets** to support the material in the Pupil Book.

*All of these resources and activities are also available on the **Planning CD-ROM** in either Word or PDF for teachers to print out if preferred or to display on whiteboards or projectors for whole-class discussion. They can also be customised to suit individual needs and, if required, saved with the other **Electronic Resources** for the unit using the facility to 'add your own resources' in the Just Click teaching solution.*

The following suggestions are intended to show how the material in Unit 5 of **Horizons 3** provides opportunities for teachers and pupils to assess their work as they go along, and to improve their learning as a result of that assessment. It must be stressed that these are only a few of the ways in which the material in the Pupil Book can be used. The techniques could be used as they are outlined here, but teachers will probably find that it is more helpful to use these as starting points and to develop their own ideas to suit their own circumstances.

Before you get started

There is an integral Assessment for Learning framework provided for Unit 5 (and every unit in **Horizons**):

- The unit opens on pages 84–85 of the Pupil Book with the learning objectives for the unit (Where are we going?). The lesson plans on the *Planning CD-ROM* then include learning objectives and outcomes for each spread in turn (supported by pupil-friendly versions in PowerPoint on the *Electronic Resources CD-ROM*).

- The unit ends on pages 102–103 of the Pupil Book with a plenary spread to review and evaluate the unit (Where are we now?), particularly in light of the learning objectives from the opening spread.

- The Learning Plan and Attainment Targets for the unit on pages 189–191 in this *Teaching and Learning Resources* guide provide pupils with the opportunity to set individual learning targets at the start of the unit and to review their progress against these targets at the end. The final self-assessment sheet (How far have I travelled?) on page 199 then offers pupils a more subjective review of their progress during the unit.

Teachers can use or adapt all or some of these resources to set and review goals and involve pupils in their own learning. Further resources on the *Electronic Resources CD-ROM* provide activities for initial assessment of prior learning at the start of the unit to help teachers to diagnose strengths and weaknesses for each topic and for checking and testing knowledge and understanding during and at the end of the unit. All these resources will provide teachers with further evidence to help structure and focus the learning programme.

Pages 84–85

Activity 5 is ideally suited as an Assessment for Learning activity. In the earlier activities, pupils will have thought about Francesca's, and their own, connections with the environment and the footprints they leave. In activity 5 they start to think about reducing the size of their footprints. Activity 5a asks them to work in pairs. This is deliberate. Reducing our impact on the environment is difficult; working with a 'buddy' can make the task easier – rather like having a 'gym buddy' to spur you on with a programme of training!

From an Assessment for Learning viewpoint, this work also helps focus pupils' minds on their own work, and on improving that work. Activity 5b asks two pairs to evaluate each other's work. Pairs can either spur each other on to greater efforts or maybe make each other think more realistically about what is possible. They can also assess each other's suggestions in terms of their geography work, and help each other to make it even better.

Pages 86–87

Activity 3 is set up as a piece of group work requiring groups of four. Pupils can find the website together or use Activity Sheets 5.2 and 5.3 instead. They can study the site together, working out exactly what the different maps and commentaries are about. Then they can discuss how they should go about the written work, deciding just what is required of each of them.

Having completed their individual pieces of data collection and analysis, pupils can then assess each person's contribution to the finished product. Pupils who are deemed not to have finished the work properly can go back and complete their tasks.

At the end of the activity, pupils could fill in one of the following Assessment Sheets:

- Group Work Activity (page 43 in this *Teaching and Learning Resources* guide)

- Investigation or Enquiry (page 44).

Pages 88–89

Activity 8 is similar to activity 5 on page 85, except now pupils are working with more specific knowledge of how and why they should be changing their lifestyles.

Ask them to complete this activity and then to compare their answers with those that they gave to the previous activity. How do they differ? Why do they differ? Have their answers improved now that they have more knowledge and understanding? What can they learn from this development process?

Pages 90–91

When working on activity 5, all pupils need to know the criteria for the assessment of the posters for the energy-saving campaign. Three criteria are given at the end of the activity, although more could be added or the whole set could be changed if the class felt that a better set could be produced.

At the end of the activity, the posters can be evaluated by the class as a whole against the clearly stated criteria.

Other aspects of the work could also be assessed, maybe using one of the Assessment Sheets from pages 43–46 in this guide.

Pages 92–93

Activity 6 is another (or an alternative) poster activity. This can be assessed using one or more of the techniques suggested above.

Pages 94–95

Activity 5 includes an element of the cognitive dissonance thinking skill. Pupils look at a certain situation from one angle, and then they are forced to change their viewpoint and their second piece of work should contain some elements that contradict their first answer.

To follow up their work, pupils should compare their answers with those of a colleague. Alternatively, perhaps pupils could work in groups of three so that all the people listed in the book are covered.

There are many aspects of the work that could be compared and assessed, but it is usually best to concentrate on assessing a single, clearly defined aspect. In this case, pupils ought to look at how well the pairs of answers manage to establish two different voices, and to look at the same basic set of facts from two different stand points. Pupils could consider:

• whether both statements are factually based
• the way different words and sentence structures are used to indicate the different people
• whether both people are given reasonable points of view, or whether it easy to see that the pupil agrees with one point of view and so makes that person sound sensible and the other person sound silly
• whether there is any suggestion, in either person's statement, of an attempt to find a compromise point of view.

Pages 96–97

Activity 5 is a fieldwork-based enquiry that can be assessed using the Investigation or Enquiry Assessment Sheet on page 44 in this guide.

Pages 98–99

Time may well not allow classes to carry out both the enquiry on pages 96–97 and the one on this spread. However, in an ideal world it should be possible to do one enquiry, to assess it using self- or peer-assessment techniques, and then to do the second enquiry, taking note of any recommendations from the assessment of the previous work.

Given the time constraints, it may well be that only one of these enquiries can be completed. In that case, and if the enquiry on pages 98–99 is the one chosen, it would be sensible to use the Investigation or Enquiry Assessment Sheet on page 44 in this guide.

Pages 100–101

Activity 2 is a small-scale opportunity for Assessment for Learning, with a pair working together to draw up a list of questions before working with another pair and assessing each other's work by trying to answer the questions. A further stage of assessment will be gone through if the foursome presents their results to the class.

Activity 4 is rather more demanding. With a confident group of pupils it would be good for them, as part of their preparation for their written work, to present their thoughts on the bullet-pointed questions to the whole class, and to seek their opinions before going on to complete the written work.

Pages 102–103

Activities 3–5 can be used as a summative assessment opportunity for this unit. The Assessment Opportunity on pages 192–199 in this *Teaching and Learning Resources* guide provides criteria for success, model answers and a process for target setting and use of this assessment.

5 Think – Act

Learning plan

What are my learning objectives for this unit?

I aim to learn about:

✓ the influence I have on the environment when I consume

✓ some of the causes and consequences of global warming

✓ 'food miles' and 'ghost acres'

✓ the problem of rubbish

✓ what we can all do to reduce the size of our footprints on the global environment.

Read the Attainment Targets for this unit on pages 190–191 and tick any statements that you feel refer to you. *Places and Environments* covers *what you know* about the topic and *Enquiry and Skills* covers *what you can do*.

Level [   ]

Using these statements for this unit, decide what level you are overall at this stage:

What level do you think you can achieve by the end of this unit?

Level [   ]

What are you going to concentrate on to achieve this level? A good place to start might be any statements on pages 190–191 that you have not ticked:

[   ]

At the end of the unit, read the Attainment Targets again and tick in a different colour any *new* statements that refer to you. Then decide what level you are now:

Level [   ]

If you have improved, well done! What evidence can you show for this improvement? What or who do you think particularly helped you to improve your level?

[   ]

If you have stayed the same, better luck next time! What do you think you could have done differently to help improve your levels? What will you do next time to progress further?

[   ]

5 Think – Act
My Attainment Targets for this unit

Level 3

Places and Environments

☐ I can show my knowledge, skills and understanding in studies at a local scale.

☐ I can give reasons for some of my observations and judgements about places and environments.

☐ I can recognise how people seek to improve and sustain environments.

Enquiry and Skills

☐ I can use my skills and sources of evidence to answer a range of geographical questions.

☐ I am beginning to use the correct words to communicate my findings.

Level 4

Places and Environments

☐ I can recognise and describe physical and human processes.

☐ I am beginning to understand how processes can change the features of places, and how these changes can affect the lives and activities of people living there.

☐ I can understand how people can both improve and damage the environment

☐ I can explain my own views, and the views of other people, about an environmental change.

Enquiry and Skills

☐ I can suggest suitable geographical questions for study.

☐ I can use a range of geographical skills to help me investigate places and environments.

☐ I can use primary sources in my investigations.

☐ I can communicate my findings using appropriate vocabulary.

Level 5

Places and Environments

☐ I can describe and begin to explain physical and human processes.

☐ I can suggest explanations for ways in which human activities cause changes in the environment, and the different views that people hold about those changes.

☐ I can recognise some of the links and relationships that make places dependent on each other.

☐ I can recognise how people try to manage environments sustainably.

Enquiry and Skills

☐ I can select and use appropriate skills and ways of presenting evidence to help me investigate places and environments.

☐ I can explain my own views and begin to suggest relevant geographical questions and issues.

☐ I can select information and sources of information, suggest sensible conclusions to investigations and present my findings both in writing and with maps and diagrams.

Level 6

Places and Environments

☐ I can describe and explain a range of physical and human processes and recognise that these processes interact.

☐ I can describe ways in which processes operating at different scales create geographical patterns and lead to changes in places.

☐ I can appreciate the many links and relationships that make places dependent on each other.

☐ I can recognise how conflicting demands on the environment may arise, and I can describe and compare different approaches to managing environments.

☐ I can recognise that different values and attitudes result in different approaches that have different effects on people and places.

Enquiry and Skills

☐ I can suggest relevant geographical questions and issues and appropriate sequences of investigation.

☐ I can select a range of skills and sources of evidence and use them effectively in my investigations.

☐ I can present my findings in a coherent way and reach conclusions that are consistent with the evidence.

Level 7

Places and Environments

☐ I can describe interactions within and between physical and human processes, and show how these interactions create geographical patterns and help change places and environments.

☐ I can understand that many factors, including people's values and attitudes, affect decisions about places and environments, and use my understanding to explain the resulting changes.

☐ I can appreciate that the environment is a place and the lives of people who live there are affected by actions and events in other places.

☐ I can recognise that human actions may have unintended environmental consequences and that change sometimes leads to conflict.

☐ I can appreciate that considerations of sustainable development affect the planning and management of environments and resources.

Enquiry and Skills

☐ With growing independence, I can identify geographical questions and issues, and establish my own sequence of investigation.

☐ I can select and use accurately a wide range of skills.

☐ I can evaluate evidence critically, present well-argued summaries of my investigations, and begin to reach substantiated conclusions.

Level 8

Places and Environments

☐ I can offer explanations for interactions within and between physical and human processes.

☐ I can explain changes in the nature of places over time, in terms of location, physical and human processes, and interactions with other places.

☐ I can begin to understand the range and complexity of factors that contribute to the quality of life in different places.

☐ I can recognise the causes and consequences of environmental issues, and I can understand a range of different views about them and different approaches to tackling them.

☐ I can understand how sustainable development can affect the planning and management of resources, and use examples to illustrate this.

Enquiry and Skills

☐ I can show independence in identifying appropriate geographical questions and issues, and in using an effective sequence of investigation.

☐ I can select a wide range of skills and use them accurately.

☐ I can evaluate sources of evidence in a critical way, before using them in my investigations.

☐ I can present full and coherently argued summaries of my investigations and reach substantiated conclusions.

191

5 Think – Act

Assessment opportunity

On page 103 in activities 3–5 you are asked to:

3 List some products that you use every day which might be designed to be recycled through a deconstruction plant in Future World.

4 Explain why deconstruction plants are likely to be common in Future World.

5 Suggest what a deconstruction plant might look like. Describe it in words, or pictures, or both.

The key questions are:

1 Why will products need to be taken apart after they have been used?

2 Can this be done at a profit?

3 Will the parts be sold so they can be reused, or will they be sold for scrap and recycling?

4 How will product design need to change so that old goods can be taken apart and reused or recycled?

5 Will construction plants need to change so that deconstruction plants can work?

6 How will these changes in one area affect other areas of the world?

Before you start these activities, look at the **Criteria for Success** sheet. Set yourself a target level to aim for in this Assessment Opportunity. Write this level in the box on the target setting sheet. Explain how you intend to obtain this level.

Once you have finished the activities, look again at the Criteria for Success and assess your answers. You could also compare your answers with model answers. Write your level in the box and explain how you achieved this level.

Then set yourself a target for improvement in your next assessment. Explain what you need to do to improve next time. Try to set yourself specific tasks to work on.

5 Think – Act
Criteria for success

A **Level 2** answer may	• express views on the environment and show how people affect the environment • use information and your own observations to ask and respond to questions about the environment • use appropriate geographical vocabulary.
A **Level 3** answer may	• offer reasons for some of your observations about the environment • recognise how people seek to improve and sustain the environment • use skills and sources of evidence to respond to a range of geographical questions • use appropriate vocabulary to communicate your ideas.
A **Level 4** answer may	• recognise and describe human processes • begin to understand how these processes can change the lives and activities of people • understand how people can both improve and damage the environment • explain your own views and the views that other people hold about the environment • use a range of geographical skills • communicate your findings using appropriate vocabulary.
A **Level 5** answer may	• describe and begin to explain human processes • describe how these processes can lead to changes in the environment and in the lives of people • recognise some of the links and relationships that make places dependent on each other • recognise how people try to manage the environment sustainably • select and use appropriate skills and ways of presenting evidence • present your conclusions in both writing and diagrams.
A **Level 6** answer may	• describe and explain a range of human processes and recognise that these processes interact to produce the environment • describe the way that human processes lead to changes in the environment • appreciate the many links and relationships in the environment • recognise how conflicting demands on the environment may arise, and describe ways of managing the environment • select a range of skills and use them effectively to present evidence • present your findings in a coherent way that is consistent with the evidence.

A **Level 7** answer may	• describe interactions within and between physical and human processes and show how these interactions help to change the environment
	• show an understanding that many factors influence the decisions made about the environment, and use this understanding to explain changes in the environment
	• appreciate that the lives of people are affected by actions and events in other places
	• appreciate that considerations of sustainable development affect the planning and management of the environment and resources
	• select and use accurately a wide range of skills
	• present a well-argued summary of your investigation and reach substantiated conclusions.
A **Level 8** answer may	• offer explanations for interactions within and between human and physical processes
	• begin to show understanding of the range and complexity of factors that contribute to the quality of life
	• recognise the causes and consequences of environmental issues and understand a range of different views about them and different approaches to tackling them
	• understand how considerations of sustainable development can affect your own life and that there is a need to plan and manage resources
	• select a wide range of skills and use them effectively and accurately
	• present full and coherently argued summaries of your investigations and reach substantiated conclusions.

5 Think – Act

My target setting

I want to make progress in geography, in my study of the Think – Act unit.

When I do activities 3–5 on page 103, I aim to obtain: Level ☐

To do this I will need to:

[ ]

Answer these questions when you have completed activities 3–5 on page 103:

In this Assessment Opportunity I obtained: Level ☐

Explain how you obtained this level:

[ ]

When I do my next Assessment Opportunity, I aim to obtain: Level ☐

To do this I will need to:

[ ]

A   This is a good basic answer that was written by a pupil completing activities 3–5 on page 103. This is not the full answer.

4 A deconstruction plant takes old goods apart so that they can be used again. These plants will become common because the world is running out of resources so that we cannot afford to waste things and just throw them away. We have to make sure that we Reduce! Reuse! Recycle!

5 It is the year 2020 and my job is an inspector of deconstruction plants for the government's Ministry of Rubbish. Today I'm visiting a plant that takes in old computers. From outside, the IBM deconstruction plant looks very well organised, not like the scrap yards in the pictures in the book. We make sure that deconstruction plants do not look as ugly as the old construction plants looked back in the twentieth century.

On one side there are lots of boxes stacked neatly with IBM computers in them. They do not look like they were just thrown away. They look like they were sent off carefully. People have got used to the need to reuse their old goods, and companies know that the Ministry of Rubbish will not let them sell goods if they cannot be reused later.

On the other side there are containers waiting to go on lorries to the port. Some of these contain reconditioned computers and others contain parts for computers. The computers will be sent to India where they can be sold at quite a good price. The parts are sent to Bangladesh where the workforce is skilled but still fairly cheap, so new computers can be made.

When you look inside the plant you are surprised that there are so few people working there. The old computers are all put on 'deconstruction lines'. These are conveyor belts that run past a series of robots. Each robot has a special job to do over and over again on each computer that passes.

One takes apart the case of the computer – remember the computer was made so that it can be deconstructed easily. Then the case is put on a separate line for inspection to see if it can be reused.

The next robot takes out the memory board and sends that for checking. If it is good it will be reused. If it is worn out it is sent for recycling, where all the reusable minerals, plastics and so on are separated out.

There is a bit of waste at the end. This is all burnt to make electricity ... but no carbon is released from the plant. New processes can recycle the carbon so that it does not escape and add to the global warming problem.

B   This is a better answer, which achieves a higher level than the first one (A).
- Read it carefully, and try to see why this is better than the first answer.
- Try to see how it meets new parts of the criteria for success.
- Try to see how you could use ideas from this work to improve your own work.

4   There are several reasons why deconstruction plants will become common in Future World:
- The earth has limited resources and so we should reuse as much as possible.
- Disposing of old products is using up a lot of landfill sites.
- Disposing of products causes pollution, either of the Earth if things are buried or of the atmosphere if things are burned.
- Making products entirely from new materials uses a lot of energy which is in short supply and becoming more expensive.
- Today's generation knows about the need to reuse but our parents' generation did not think about such things. This just shows how attitudes have changed because of education and the government's publicity campaigns.

5   The IBM deconstruction plant cannot be seen from the main road. Of course, it has to be near the main road for easy access, but it has been surrounded by trees and lakes to disguise it.

The lorries that bring in the old computers are all electrically powered, using electricity that is generated from renewable sources that can be stored in batteries. Each day they put in a newly charged battery.

Inside the plant the computers are put on the deconstruction lines, which were designed at the same time as the production lines were being designed for the construction plant in Bangladesh. The whole process of construction was planned so that it could work in reverse. The parts click or screw together so that they can be taken apart without damaging them. The robots that do the work were designed at the same time as the assembly plant robots. They just work the opposite way around.

When the parts have been disassembled, they are all sent off to be checked and tested electronically. Most of this is done by robots. Obviously, with our shrinking population, labour has become very expensive so it is cheaper to use robots and they are better for the repetitive jobs.

The separated parts are sorted into three sections:
- perfectly good, so they can be reused in new or reconditioned computers
- in need of some small repairs, so they are sent to a country with a cheap labour/specialist skill economy, like the new Iraq
- not repairable, so they are sent to a country with a cheap labour/low skill economy, such as Niger, for recycling or disposal.

Of course, the Future World Council will not allow the environment of the disposal countries to be polluted. The waste has to be buried in sealed containers if it is toxic or burnt in a power station that collects all the carbon so that it does not add to global warming. They are working on ways of using the carbon to help restore the coral reefs in places where they have been damaged due to pollution in the Difficult Years around 2011 ad.

C

Finally, the pupil who wrote the second answer (B) thought about his work and decided to develop his answer to activity 5 a little further. He went back through his work and thought in more detail about the interconnections between human and physical processes, about the range and complexity of factors that contribute to the quality of life, and about a variety of different approaches to tackling environmental issues.

5 The IBM deconstruction plant cannot be seen from the main road. Of course it has to be near the main road for easy access, but it has been surrounded by trees and lakes to disguise it. The trees have another function; they act as a carbon sink, taking carbon dioxide out of the air so that the plant is carbon-neutral. The lakes also contain reed beds that help to clean the waste water from the plant so that it can be recycled. The plant is water-neutral as well as carbon-neutral. This is a closed loop system working really well.

The lorries that bring in the old computers are all electrically powered, using electricity that is generated from renewable sources that can be stored in batteries. Each day they put in a newly charged battery and the old ones are recharged.

Inside the plant the computers are put on the deconstruction lines, which were designed at the same time as the production lines were being designed for the construction plant in Bangladesh. The whole process of construction was planned so that it could work in reverse. The parts click or screw together so that they can be taken apart without damaging them. The robots that do the work were designed at the same time as the assembly plant robots. They just work the opposite way around.

When the parts have been disassembled, they are all sent off to be checked and tested electronically. Most of this is done by robots. Obviously, with our shrinking population, labour has become very expensive so it is cheaper to use robots and they are better for the repetitive jobs. The unions were worried about this at first, but they were won round when the company offered retraining schemes for all the old workers. Some were trained in

robotics design and some were trained in estate management so that they could look after the environment around the plant.

The separated parts are sorted into three sections:

• perfectly good, so they can be reused in new or reconditioned computers – in restyled cases to keep up with fashion

• in need of some small repairs, so they are sent to a country with a cheap labour/specialist skill economy, like the new Iraq

• not repairable, so they are sent to a country with a cheap labour/low skill economy, such as Niger, for recycling or disposal.

What has amazed IBM is how this interconnection between countries has helped to boost their sales. They did not realise that in 2020 they would be selling almost as many home computers in newly developing markets such as Bangladesh, Iraq and Niger as they do in the mature markets of Europe and North America. More and more transnational corporations are realising that helping LEDCs to develop (by training the workers and paying them sensible wages) also helps the corporation to grow by giving them an educated market with some disposable income.

Of course, the Future World Council will not allow the environment of the disposal countries to be polluted. The waste has to be buried in sealed containers if it is toxic or burnt in a power station that collects all the carbon so that it does not add to global warming. They are working on ways of using the carbon to help restore the coral reefs in places where they have been damaged due to pollution in the Difficult Years around 2011 AD.

5 Think – Act

How far have I travelled?

In this unit my **Learning Objectives** were to learn about:

- the influence on the environment when I consume
- some of the causes and consequences of global warming
- 'food miles' and 'ghost acres'
- the problem of rubbish
- what we can all do to reduce the size of our footprints on the global environment.

My progress in this unit

How well have I achieved my objectives?	Okay							Excellent
Enquiry and Skills:								
to interpret a sequence of satellite photos								
to design a poster for an energy-saving campaign								
to carry out part of a class survey								
to do my own environmental audit								
Places and Environments:								
to understand how I affect the global environment								
to understand how I can reduce the damage that I do								
to understand the causes, effects and solutions of global warming								
to understand about the problems of waste disposal								

Shade the bars to show how far you think you have made progress in this unit.

The part of this unit that I enjoyed the most was …

because …

The part of this unit that I needed most help with was …

because …

The piece of work that I am most pleased with is …

because …

The aspect of this unit that will be most useful to me in future is …

because …

Any other comments?

5·1 Think – Act
How do I affect the global ecosystem?

Use this sheet to help you complete activity 4 on page 85 of your textbook.

1 Here is an example of a map showing a journey to school, drawn by a boy who walked to the bus stop then took the bus. He has shown the tracks he made on that journey as well as some of the footprints he has left all over the world.

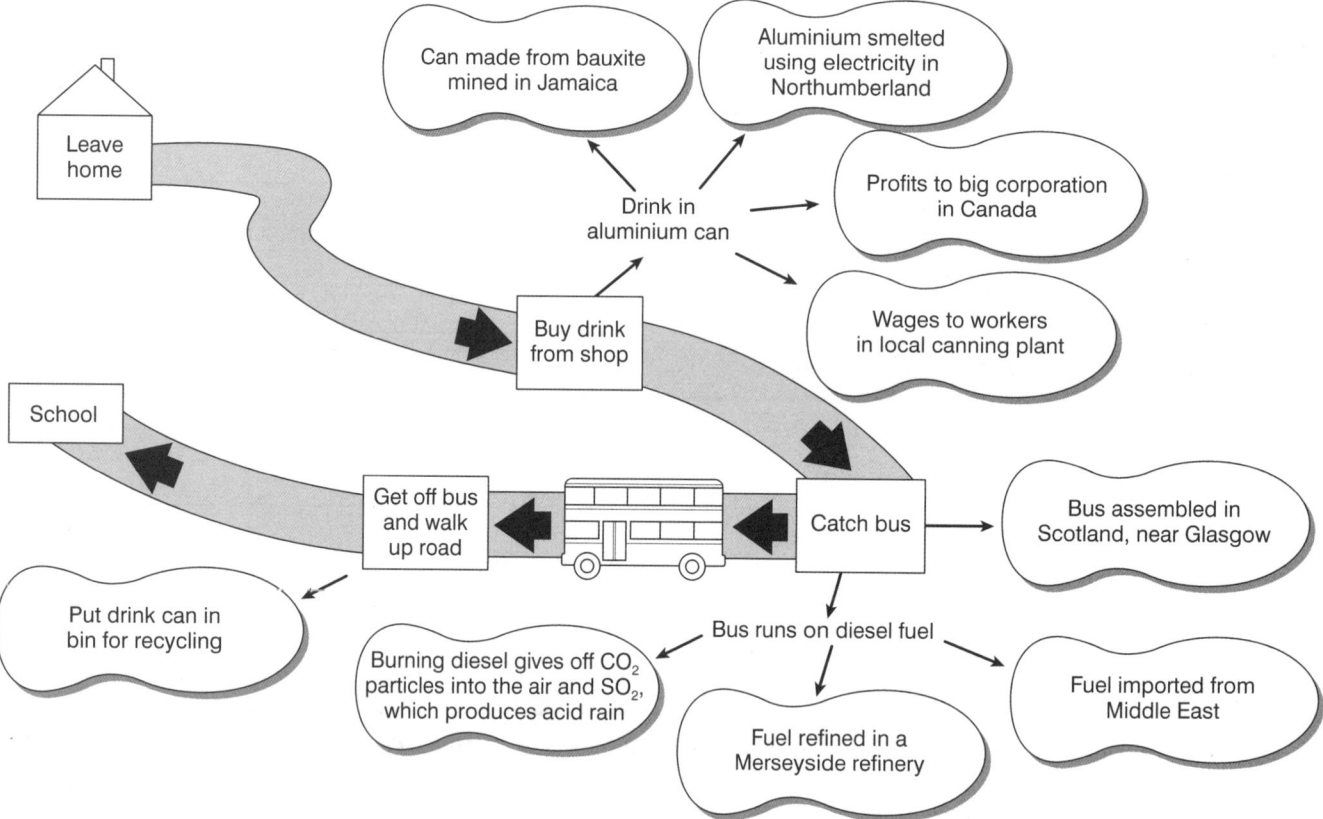

2 If you are going to draw a 'global footprints' diagram for the clothes you wear, you could draw yourself in the middle of the page or use a photo. Show the links spreading out from you describing what the clothes are made from, where they were made, who might have made them, and how all this has affected the world's environment.

3 Perhaps you could show two types of footprints on your diagrams:
- 'bad' footprints that cause damage (draw muddy footprints?)
- 'good' footprints (like prints in the sand that leave no lasting damage?)

Think of the best ways to show these different types of footprints.

4 Ask yourself the following questions:
- I bought this item, but how was it made?
- Where did its raw materials come from?
- How and where were the raw materials processed?
- Are the workers treated fairly?
- What happens to the waste products?

You might like to work with a partner and ask questions about each other's diagrams.

Activity 3 on page 87 of your textbook asks you to use a weblink to find out details of possible climate change in Europe. The weblink gives details for the UK, Spain, Switzerland and Finland. It shows how their climates might change during the next century. The climate graphs for the UK and Spain are shown on sheet 5.3.

The graphs show what meteorologists predict:
* will probably happen
* might possibly happen in an extreme scenario.

Choose either the UK or Spain. For your chosen country:

a summarise the changes that are predicted by filling in the table below.

			UK	Spain
Temperature change (%)	By 2050s	Probable		
		Extreme		
	By 2080s	Probable		
		Extreme		
Rainfall change (%)	By 2050s	Probable		
		Extreme		
	By 2080s	Probable		
		Extreme		

b Explain how these changes might affect:
* farming
* holiday makers
* vegetation
* water supply
* heating/air-conditioning bills
* the chance of forest fires
* the frequency and size of floods
* wildlife
* coastal erosion
* architecture and building design.

5·3 Climate change: the UK and Spain 2

KEY
- ■ Probable change
- ▨ Extreme scenario

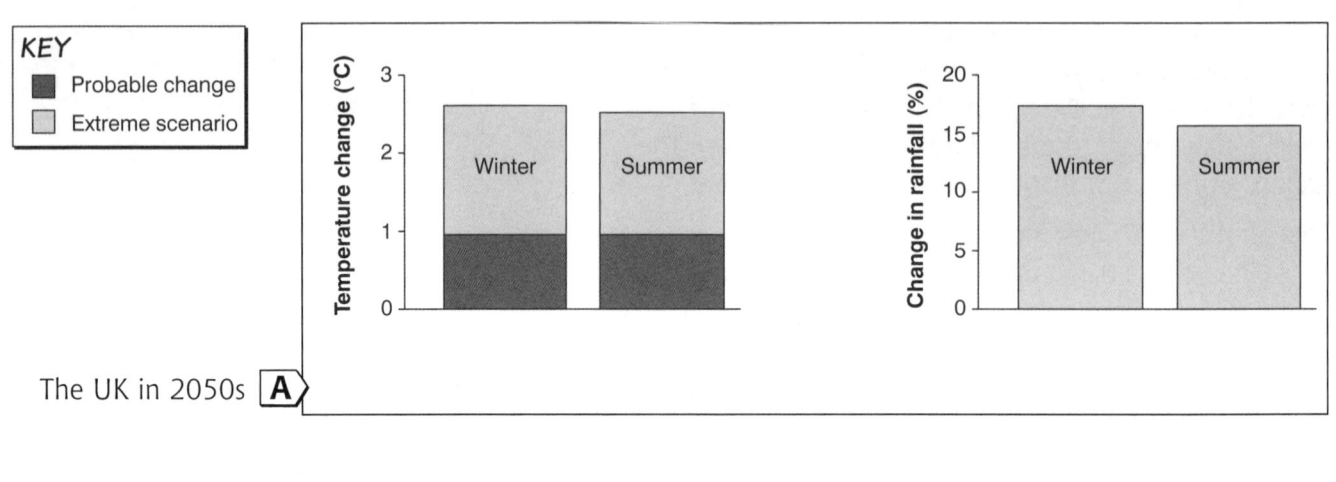

The UK in 2050s **A**⟩

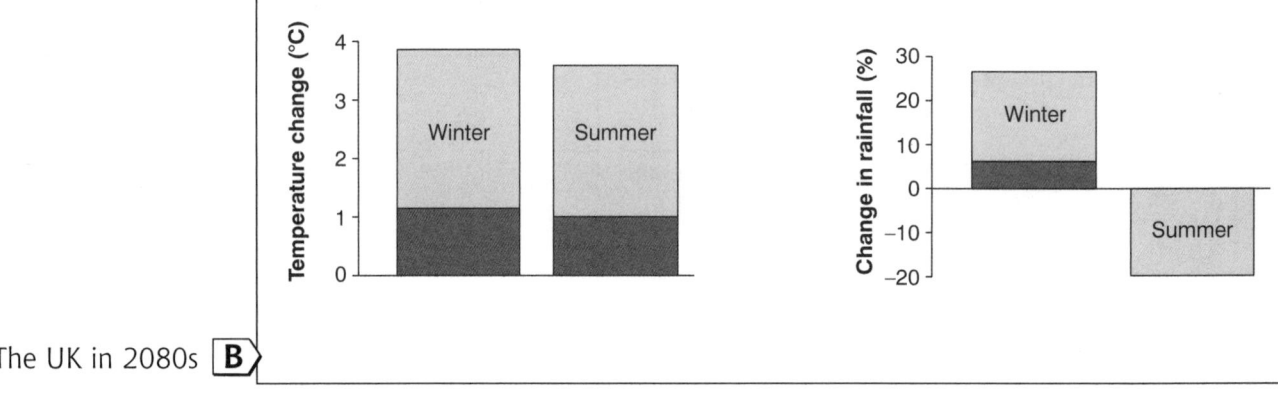

The UK in 2080s **B**⟩

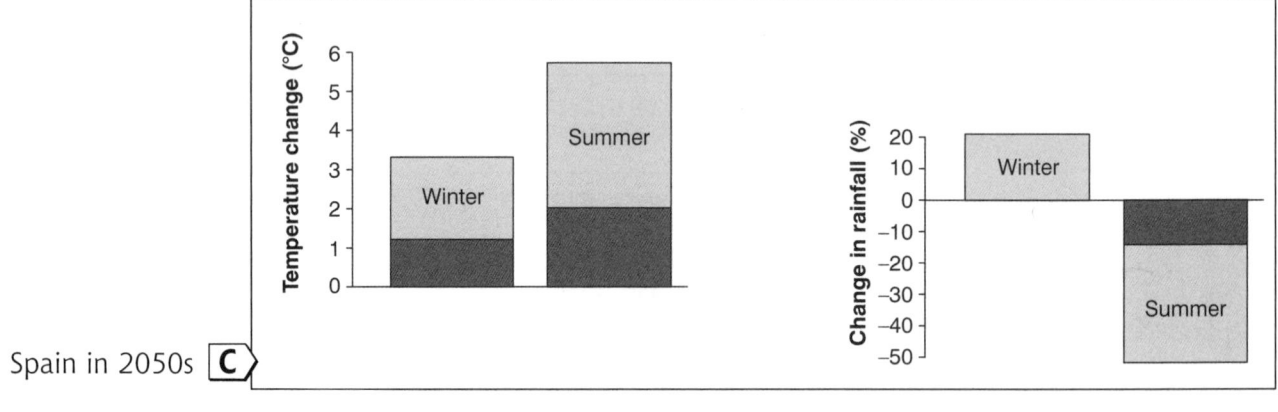

Spain in 2050s **C**⟩

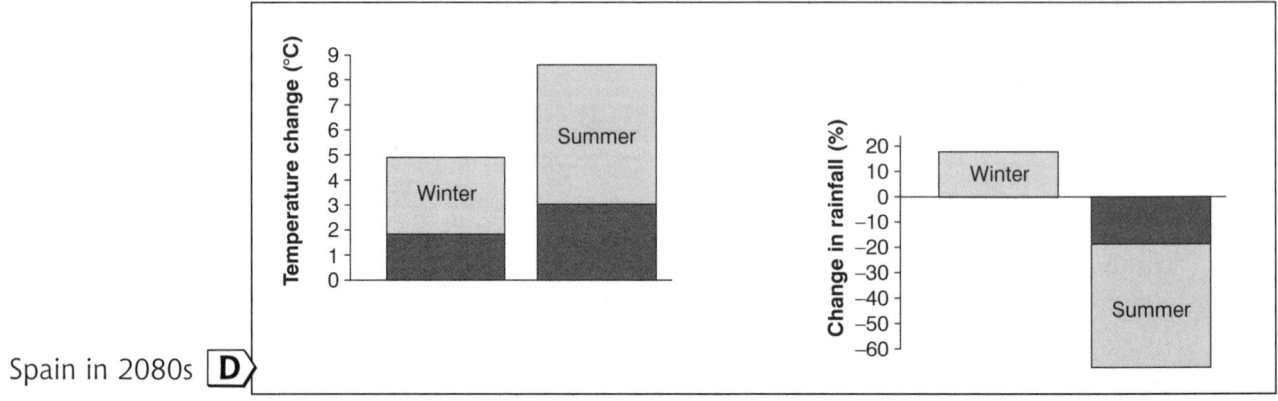

Spain in 2080s **D**⟩

5·4 European climate change 1

Activity 3 on page 87 of your textbook asks you to use a weblink to find out details of possible climate change in Europe. The weblink gives details for the UK, Spain, Switzerland and Finland. It shows how their climates might change during the next century. Sheet 5.5 provides two maps, one to show the change in precipitation and one to show temperature change by the 2080s.

1. In groups of four, each member should choose one country to investigate: the UK, Spain, Switzerland or Finland. Fill in the table below.

Country	Predicted change in precipitation by 2080s	Predicted change in temperature by 2080s
UK		
Spain		
Switzerland		
Finland		

2. Explain how these changes might affect:
   - farming
   - holiday makers
   - vegetation
   - water supply
   - heating/air-conditioning bills
   - the chance of forest fires
   - the frequency and size of floods
   - wildlife
   - coastal erosion
   - architecture and building design.

5·5 European climate change 2

Europe's rainfall in the 2080s

This map shows how total annual rainfall is predicted to change. Almost all of Europe is predicted to see an increase in total annual rainfall. However, many areas will see a big increase in winter and a smaller increase in summer. Some parts of Europe, particularly the south around the Mediterranean, are likely to become much drier in summer.

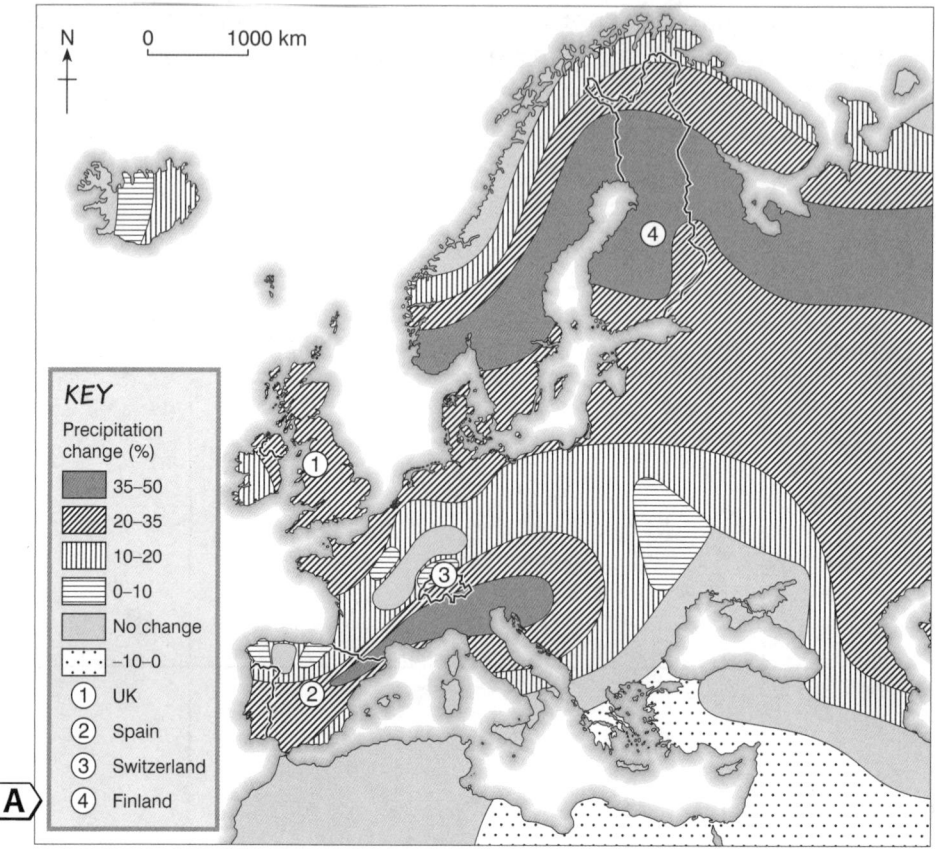

Change in precipitation by 2080s **A**

KEY
Precipitation change (%)
- 35–50
- 20–35
- 10–20
- 0–10
- No change
- −10–0
1. UK
2. Spain
3. Switzerland
4. Finland

Europe's temperature in the 2080s

This map shows how average annual temperatures might change. It does not show seasonal variations. In fact, it is likely that summer temperatures would rise more than winter temperatures in most parts of Europe. In other words, the temperature range would increase and climates would become more extreme.

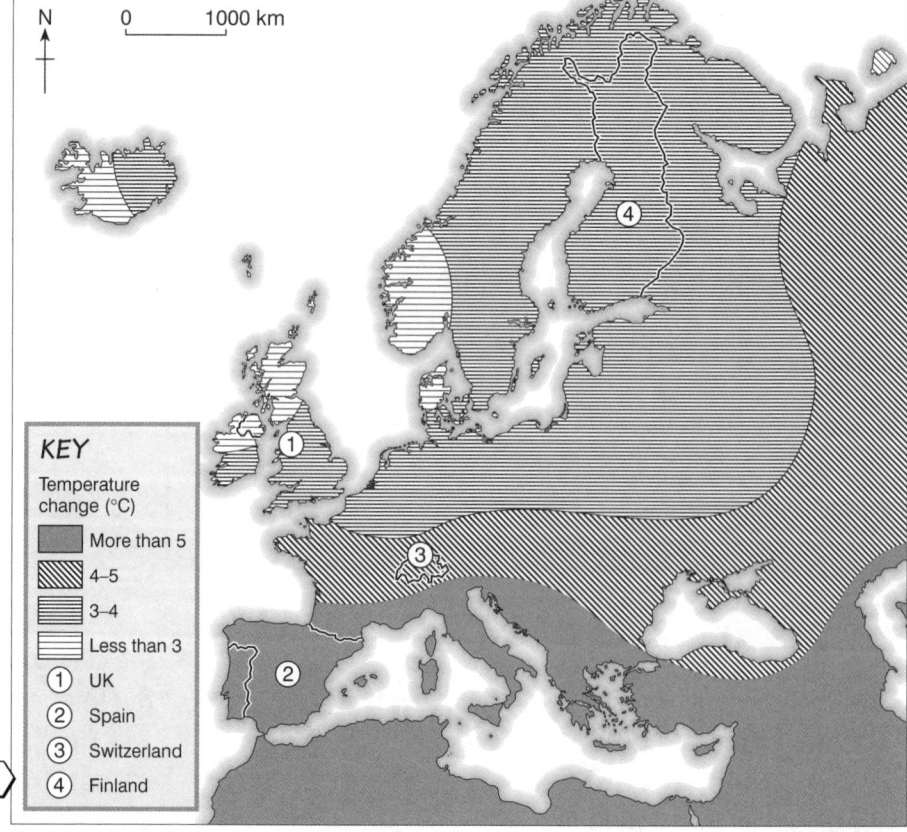

Change in temperature by 2080s **B**

KEY
Temperature change (°C)
- More than 5
- 4–5
- 3–4
- Less than 3
1. UK
2. Spain
3. Switzerland
4. Finland

5·6 Antarctic internet research 1

The text on pages 86–87 of your textbook gives you some information about global warming, how it is affecting the Antarctic ice sheet, and how it might be affecting global sea level. This sheet and sheet 5.7 suggest how you can use the internet to carry out further research into these topics. Log on to the Horizons website and then follow the numbered links to investigate each site.

 **You will find a link to the websites you need at**
WEBLINKS
www.nelsonthornes.com/horizons

1 British Antarctic Survey: *About Antarctica*

This is a detailed site, although it is easy to navigate around. It gives general background information on Antarctica and the pictures are wonderful. The Frequently Asked Questions (FAQs) link is easy to use.

2 British Antarctic Survey: *Environmental protection*

If you are interested in the British Antarctic Survey website on Antarctica (link 1), you will probably also enjoy reading these pages on environmental protection.

3 BBC News: *Antarctic ice shelf breaks apart*

This link will help you to find out more about the Larsen B ice shelf collapse. You could find out:
- where the ice shelf is
- how big it is
- why it collapsed
- what the collapse has produced
- how its collapse might affect the sea and the rest of the Antarctic.

4 BBC News: *Low probability of ice collapse*

This link, which gives an article about the West Antarctic Ice Sheet, will help you to follow up some of the ideas from link 3 in more detail.

5 BBC News: *Antarctic base commander*

This link gives details of an interview with an Antarctic survey base commander. You could use it to find out:
- what life is like living on a survey base, cut off from the rest of the world for many months
- why people go there
- how the base disposes of its waste without polluting the Antarctic environment
- what kinds of research do scientists do there.

6 BBC News: *Antarctica's climate clues*

This link allows you to follow up some of the questions about the type of research that goes on at an Antarctic survey base. It also looks at research on board a ship in the Antarctic Ocean.

7 BBC News: *Warmth puts penguins under pressure*

This page looks in detail at research into the penguins living near the survey base.

8 BBC News: *'Heatwave' stresses penguins*

This page gives an interesting article about penguins and climate change.

9 BBC News: *Rapid Antarctic warming puzzle*

This link investigates the way the climate of the Antarctic is changing. It also suggests that there are several possible causes for these changes.

10 British Antarctic Survey: *Climate change*

This website also includes a statement about climate change in the Antarctic. It is more detailed than the BBC News site (link 9), but is interesting for students who might be developing a really deep interest in the topic of climate change or in the region of Antarctica.

11 British Antarctic Survey: *The Antarctic ice sheet and rising sea levels*

This page is about how the melting of the Antarctic ice sheet might be affecting the rise in sea level throughout the world. This site is British, and cautious in its predictions, but it is written in fairly difficult language.

12 Public Broadcasting Service (PBS): *Water world*

This website is American and contains some superb maps. It is dramatic and, some may think, offers rather frightening predictions about the future.

13 National Snow and Ice Data Center (NSIDC): *Antarctic ice shelf collapses*

Visit this website to see an animation of the photos in B on page 87 of your textbook.

Study the information on sheet 5.9, which was produced by Carbon Trust. The Carbon Trust is a government-sponsored organisation that aims to reduce the UK's output of carbon into the atmosphere. All the articles are aimed at small and medium-sized businesses, although the Trust also works with domestic users and large businesses.

1 What is the Carbon Trust?

2 The government set up the Trust to help the UK meet its commitments under the Kyoto Agreement. What is the Kyoto Agreement?

3 How does the Trust help the UK to meet its Kyoto commitments?

4 Extract A states that the Trust offers 'practical advice that will help you manage issues like increased energy prices, new legislation and consumer pressure'. Suggest why it is important for small businesses to manage the issues of:
  a   energy prices
  b   new legislation
  c   consumer pressure.

5 One businessman reacted like the man in the cartoon below when someone suggested he should contact the Carbon Trust.

Explain to him why he was being:
  a   a bad citizen
  b   a bad businessman.

You could write your answer or draw it as a cartoon.

Call in the Carbon Trust? Do you think I can't run my own business!

6 Imagine that an energy consultant from the Carbon Trust came to visit your school to survey energy efficiency.
  a   Suggest some places where the surveyor should start to look.
  b   Think of which practical steps to save energy the surveyor may suggest.
  c   Imagine the school site manager saw these suggestions and said: 'We're on a very tight budget. We can't afford to invest money in putting these problems right.' What might you say to the site manager to explain how short-sighted this view is?

7 Look at this Carbon Trust energy-saving sticker.
  a   Design your own energy-saving stickers for use in school.
  b   Suggest some good places where your stickers could be placed so that they will have maximum impact.

SWITCH IT OFF!

CARBON TRUST
Making business sense of climate change

A

'When Carbon Trust came to audit our site they were able to point out some very practical changes that helped us to cut our carbon emissions and save ourselves money too.'

Head of Finance
– large company in Edinburgh

CARBON TRUST

Making business sense
of climate change

Climate change is fast rising up the agenda, driven by growing scientific evidence that it is the biggest environmental threat we face. Leading businesses are already taking advantage of the opportunities and managing the risks associated with climate change.

The Carbon Trust offers practical advice that will help you manage issues like increased energy prices, new legislation and consumer pressure. Practical services include energy surveys, interest-free loans for energy-saving projects and a comprehensive Carbon Management Programme.

Every business in the UK can do something to reduce carbon emissions. Every action helps, from the simplest energy-saving measures to exploring new low-carbon business opportunities.

B

Climate change is a business issue

Six ways the Carbon Trust can help your business

(1) Energy Surveys

A free visit by a consultant will identify energy-saving opportunities.

(2) Energy-Efficiency Loans

We offer interest-free loans to help small and medium-sized companies upgrade their premises or replace equipment.

(3) Website

Visit the Carbon Trust website for examples of energy saving in action.
www.thecarbontrust.co.uk

(4) Energy Helpline

A call to our Energy Helpline gives you free advice on any aspect of energy saving. The number to call is 0800 917 30 30.

(5) Posters and Stickers

To help you get the idea of energy saving across to all your employees we have a range of posters and stickers with thought-provoking messages.

(6) Publications

We publish fact sheets, case studies and in-depth guides tailored to your organisation – part of the biggest library of advice on energy efficiency in the UK.

Think – Act

5·10 The greenhouse effect

Use this sheet to help you complete activity 2 on page 88 of your textbook.

Complete diagram B to show how the burning of fossil fuels has led to the greenhouse effect.

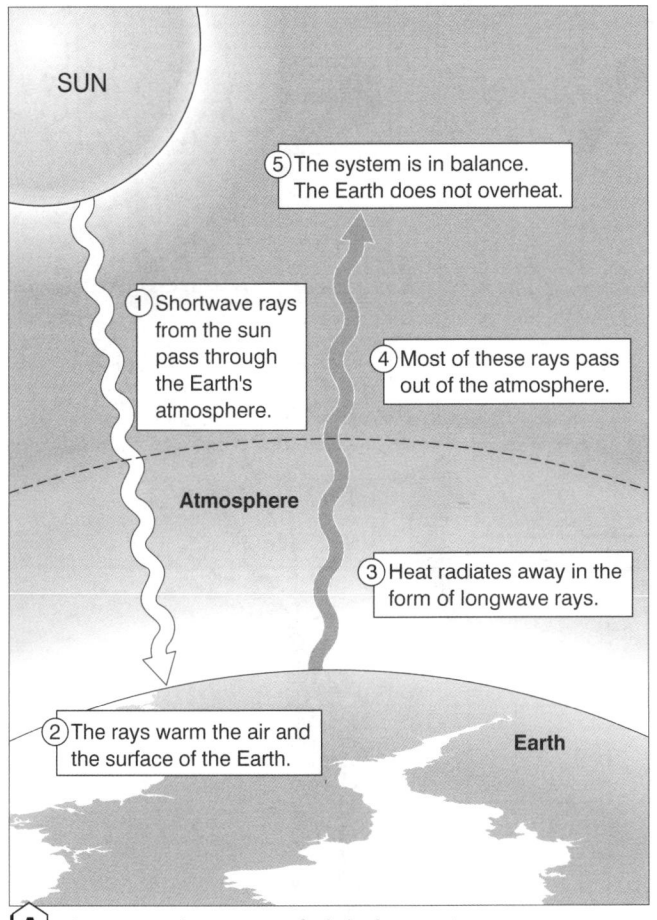

A The natural process of global warming

B Global warming: increased as a result of human activities

- ✂ - -

You may find these labels useful:

| factories burn coal | produce carbon dioxide | trapped by atmosphere |

| vehicles use petrol and diesel | other pollutants | cause global warming |

| burning forests | short-wave rays radiated |

see pages 88–89 in your Horizons Book 3

The carbon cycle

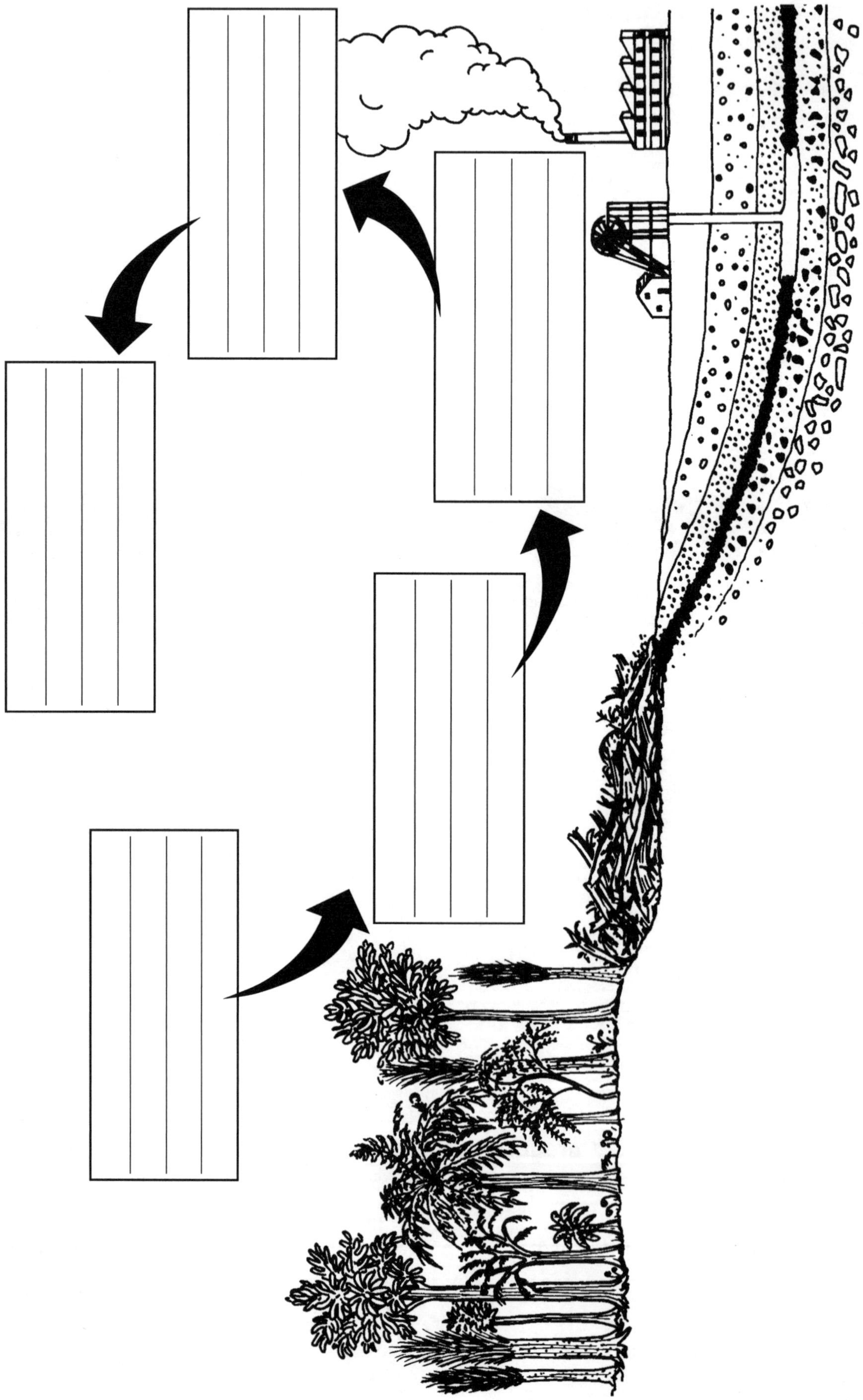

Use this sheet to help you complete activity 4 on page 89 of your textbook.

This diagram shows trees growing and dying during the Carboniferous period and then being burnt today. It covers a period of about three hundred million years!

Think – Act

(5·12) Energy-saving campaign

Use this sheet to help you complete activity 5b on page 91 of your textbook.

The government has set up an organisation called Recycle Now to help people save energy. Recycle Now helps local authorities design and run advertising campaigns. Use this organisation's website to help design your posters.

WEBLINKS You will find a link to the Recycle Now website at
www.nelsonthornes.com/horizons

Once you have registered on this website, click on the links to access the following pages.

1 Planning your campaign

This page contains information on how to plan a successful campaign.

2 Download communication tools

The download area contains all the tools and guidance you need for your campaign.

- PR materials: this page contains links where you can download press release templates.

- Brand artwork: this is a useful page allowing you to download Recycle Now icons and tag lines, 'Recycle for your community' straplines and recycling stickers.

- Advertising templates: this page provides customisable posters, adverts and banners in many sizes.

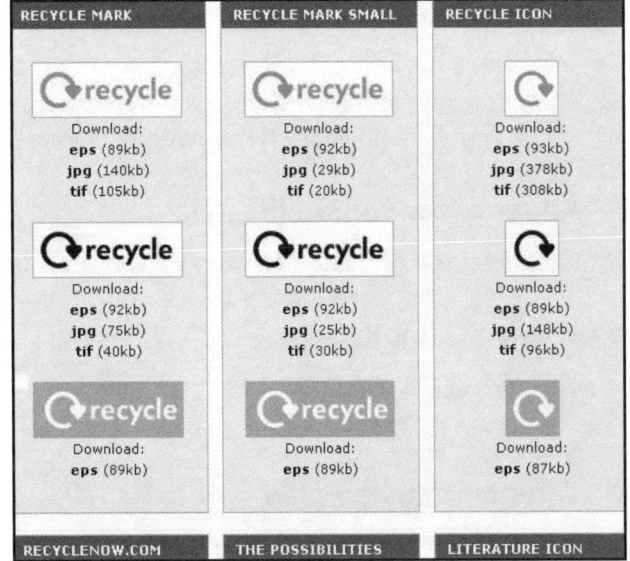

- Guidance documents: here you can download guidance documents to support all areas of your Recycle Now campaign.

3 Evaluating your campaign

This toolkit provides practical, easy-to-use information on how to develop monitoring and evaluation programmes.

211

Think – Act

(5·13) Exploring the Energy Saving Trust website

Log on to the Horizons website and then follow the numbered links to investigate the Energy Saving Trust website.

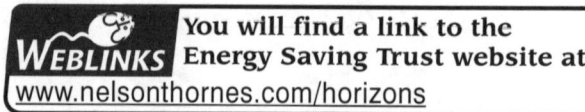

WEBLINKS You will find a link to the Energy Saving Trust website at www.nelsonthornes.com/horizons

1 Climate change explained

Watch the animation that explains what is happening to the world's climate. It might help you to complete sheets 5.4 and 5.5 if you have not done these already.

2 Watch TV ads

Click on the links to watch the adverts. What is the main point that each advert is trying to make? How successfully does it make its point? What changes could you make to fit in with the advice given?

3 'Your home' wastage tour

Take the 'your home' wastage tour. Make a list of all the ways to save energy in your home and underline the things that you can do in *red*. Underline the things that your parents or carers can do in *green*.

4 Adopt a low-carbon lifestyle

Click on link 4 to read about how to adopt a low-carbon lifestyle.

5 Cheap & simple toys

This page gives a number of simple tips that could help you save energy at home.

6 Ten-point energy plan

Read how to make your home cosier in the winter and cooler in summer.

7 Generate your own energy

This link provides information on renewable energy sources. It contains lots of good ideas, mainly aimed at home owners not school pupils! However, you could make a list of possible home-generation schemes.

8 Pupils' base

This link gives information on how to help your school save energy and benefit the environment.

9 Energy certificate for schools

This page gives more details about a scheme to promote energy management and energy efficiency in schools. If you are going to become involved with a scheme like this, you need to work with your teacher. There are lots of good ideas to help you to think about and understand your geography. This scheme could also be an excellent way of starting a citizenship project, which could be useful if you are studying citizenship.

5·14 Think – Act
Farmers' markets

Read this press release, which was produced by the National Farmers' Retail and Markets Association (FARMA). It was designed to give information to journalists and to encourage them to write articles publicising the markets.

January 2006

PRESS RELEASE

Over 2,000 varieties of apples still grown in Britain.

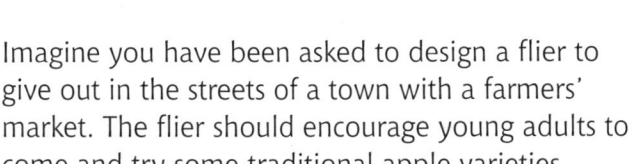

Every autumn, apple producers across Britain take their apples to farmers' markets to give the public the opportunity to taste some of the 2,000 varieties of apples still grown in Britain.

The best choice is available in autumn, with different ones becoming ripe each week and a number here one week and gone the next until the following season. One producer at Stroud Farmers' Market says that each year he has customers eagerly awaiting the return of John Standish – a short-season, local celebrity. The height of the season is celebrated with Apple Day in mid-October. There are also varieties that keep well and are available into the New Year.

Sue Thomson of the National Farmers' Retail and Markets Association (FARMA) said: 'This home-grown seasonal treat is not to be missed – each variety has its own distinct flavour, the more so when fresh and local. There should be something to satisfy every palate. At many markets, you will also find apple juice, some made from a specific variety such as Paynton Codling, which produces a sweet/dry juice, or you may prefer your apple juice mulled – a deliciously warming, spicy drink for a frosty market day. Local ciders are available at some farmers' markets and even cider brandy if you're lucky enough to live in the Dorset area.'

All around the country are 'museum' orchards lovingly conserving what have become traditional British apple varieties. Dave Kaspar, chair of the Gloucestershire Orchard Group, works hard to keep the local varieties in cultivation and grows over a hundred varieties in his own orchard.

'Many counties around Britain grow their own local specialities,' says Dave. 'In Gloucester you will find varieties named after villages along the Severn such as Arlington Schoolboy. For centuries, "graft-wood" has been passed between neighbours and communities to keep these traditional varieties in cultivation.'

Traditional orchards also help British wildlife, with some trees more than 100 years old. As they age, the number of wildlife species living on the trees increases with each passing year. Because the trees are allowed to grow to six foot before branching, wildlife also flourishes beneath them with butterflies, birds and flowers attracted to the dappled shade.

Sue added: 'British apple producers need public support, as do traditional orchards. We are often told that British apples aren't available in supermarkets because there isn't the demand – maybe we need to remind ourselves that they are worth demanding.'

For information about your nearest farmers' markets, farm shops or pick your own, go to www.farma.org.uk and use the link 'Find a farm retailer'.

Imagine you have been asked to design a flier to give out in the streets of a town with a farmers' market. The flier should encourage young adults to come and try some traditional apple varieties.

1. Read the press release and chose four or five key points that might be of interest to your target age group (16–25 year olds). Underline these points.

2. Rewrite these points in your own words. Make sure your text is clear and striking. You have to grab people's attention quickly and make them want to come and see what is going on. You could refer to taste, the novelty value, traditional British culture, the health value of fresh fruit, jobs for local people, etc.

3. Design your flier, paying attention to layout, graphics and type sizes.

Think – Act

5·15 Food miles 1

Work out how many 'food miles' were involved for a meal of your choice. Food miles is a general term meaning the distance food has travelled, but you will be working in kilometres (km) not miles.

1 Draw your meal.

    a Using a sheet of thin card, trace around a plate and cut it out.

    b Draw each item of food in your meal.

2 a Work out where each item of food in your meal is produced. You can do this by looking on labels in supermarkets or by discussing it with your geography teacher, food technology teacher or a parent/carer.

    b Remember that processed foods usually contain a variety of different ingredients. Try to find out what the main ones are, then carry out some research to find out where each ingredient comes from.

3 Use the map on sheet 5.16 to work out the distance that each food item has travelled. To do this, you could make yourself a 'food miles' ruler. Use the scale on the map to help you. Mark your ruler in hundreds, or even thousands, of miles.

4 Work out a figure for the total food miles that your meal has travelled to reach your plate.

5 Think about sourcing your meal using local suppliers.

    a Could any of the ingredients have been replaced with the same product grown locally?

    b Could you have changed your food choices so that you ate only locally produced ingredients? For example, you could change burgers – which are often made from meat reared in South American countries – for burgers made using British beef. British farms have very high standards of animal welfare and food standards that may not exist elsewhere in the world.

6 Create a wall display to show your 'food miles'. You could draw the plate at the top, a map of the world showing where the food came from in the middle and the calculations below.

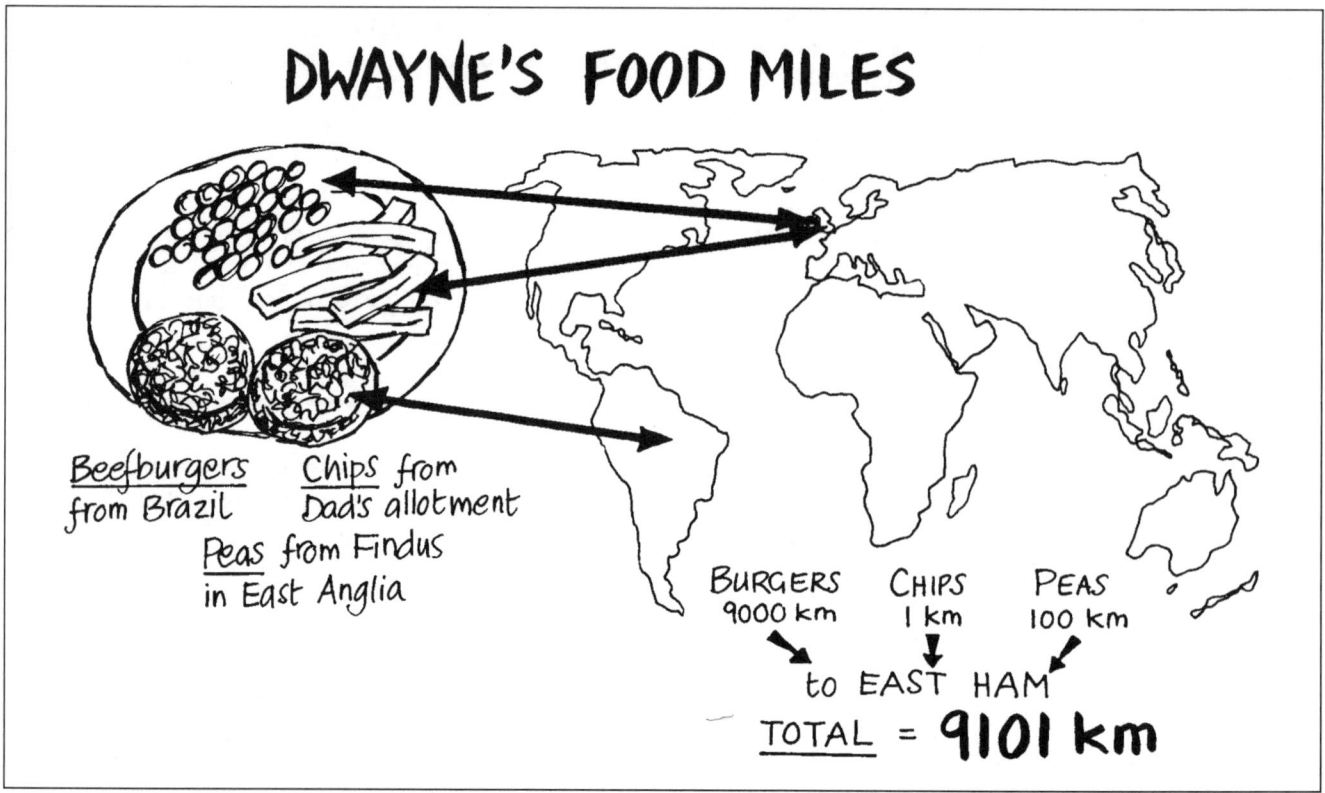

5·16 Food miles 2

Use this map to help you work out how many food miles your meal has travelled.

1 Use the scale on the map to make a 'food miles' ruler.

2 The map is an unusual shape because there is a problem showing the surface of a sphere on a flat map: imagine trying to peel an orange and then flattening out the peel without tearing or distorting it. This map is drawn using a Westermann projection, which means distances on the map are fairly – but not always – accurate. As distances become less accurate near the poles, the top and bottom of the map have been left off.

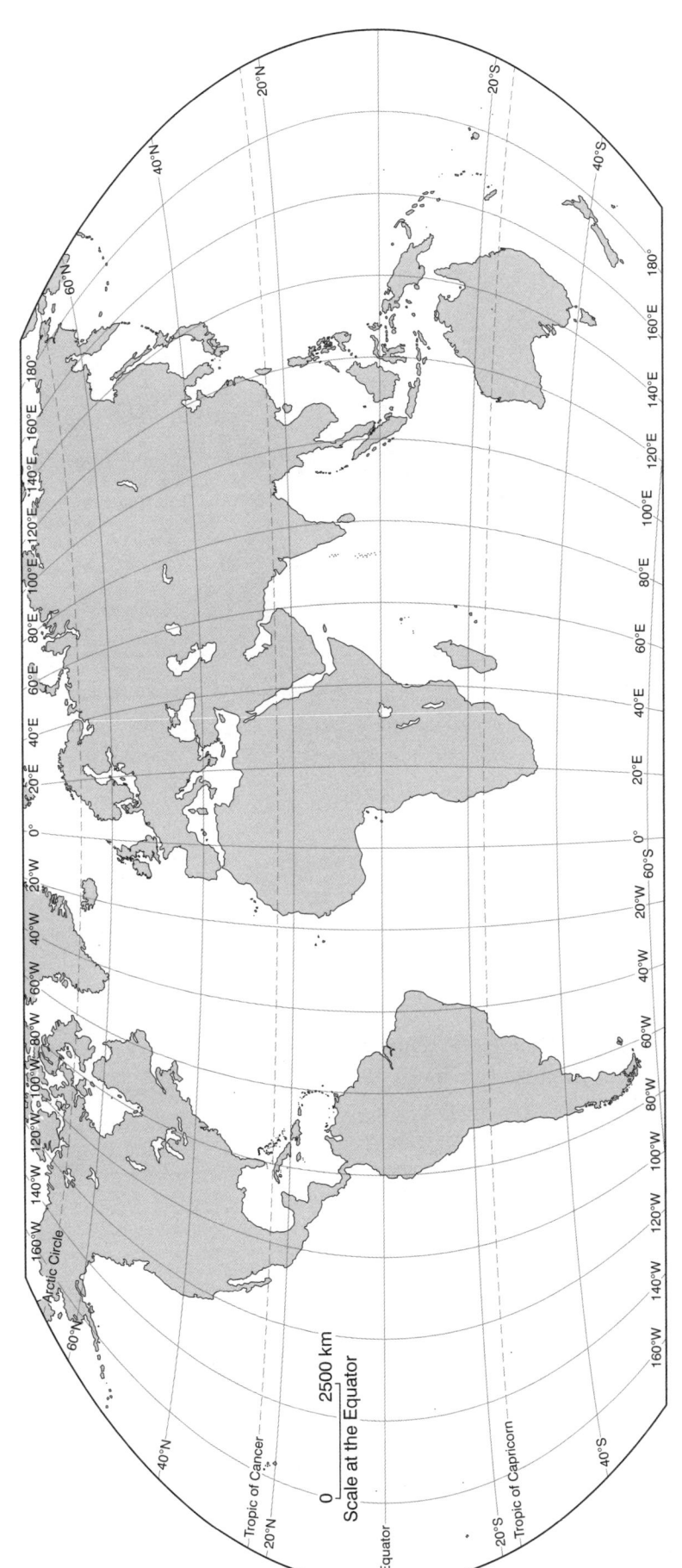

(5·17) How could you recycle a tyre? 1

The nature of used tyres makes them ideal for reclamation. They have elasticity, they are compact and dense, and they are inert (non-decomposable). Read the following information about recycling tyres and then answer the questions on sheet 5.18.

1 In developed countries, tyres are used as:
- weights for silage cover sheets on farms
- erosion protection on dam walls and landscaped slopes
- breakwaters in coastal protection schemes
- artificial reefs to encourage breakers for surfers or as artificial breeding reefs for fish
- bumpers and ship fenders in harbours
- playground equipment.

In Germany, about 10 000 tonnes of old tyres a year are used in these ways. That is about 2.5% of all the country's tyres. Many more are recycled and reused as 'retread' tyres, which are perfectly safe remoulded tyres that are cheaper than new ones.

2 In less developed countries, tyres are also used to make:
- soles for sandals
- cords for tethering animals or tying loads on lorries
- mats for cars or doormats for houses
- pads for handling glass in the building industry
- hinges for gates and doors
- stool and chair seats.

3 Used tyres can be broken up to produce rubber pieces, granules (like sand) or powder.
- Pieces can be mixed with polyurethane to form the floor of an indoor riding school.
- Pieces can be used as insulating material for cold stores.
- Granules are mixed with bitumen or cement in road construction.
- Granules are used for sound insulation.
- Granules are mixed with sand as a basement for all-weather sports pitches.
- Powder is used in the production of new tyres.
- Powder is mixed with PVC to make running tracks, floor tiles, cover sheets, shoe soles, car bumpers, signboards and roadside barriers.

4 As a last resort, tyres can be burnt in specially adapted power stations. Care has to be taken to remove dust from the smoke, but even this 'waste' includes a lot of zinc, which can be recycled by industry.

5·18 How could you recycle a tyre? 2

Read the information about recycling tyres on sheet 5.17.

1. The following words are used in the first paragraph on sheet 5.17:
   - reclamation
   - elasticity
   - dense
   - inert.

   Explain what each word means. Look them up in a dictionary if you are not sure.

2. There are four lists on sheet 5.17. Choose one use from each list. Explain why old tyres are especially suitable for your chosen uses. You might find it helpful to use some of the words you defined in activity 1.

3. What disadvantages are there in using old tyres in the ways you have described in activity 2?

4. In small groups, compare your answers to activities 2 and 3. Do any common themes come out from your answers for the four different groups of uses? Explain your views.

5. When taking a car to have new tyres fitted, a driver has to pay an extra charge to have the old tyres disposed of safely. Why should he or she have to pay this charge when the tyre company may be able to sell them to another company for recycling? (Clues: storage, transport.)

Think – Act

5·19 How much water do you use?

Activity 1 on page 102 of your textbook asks you to work out how much water you/your family use in a week.

1 Can you work out how many times you use the washing machine or the dishwasher? You may never use either of them, but you probably have some things in the dishwasher or the washing machine when they are used, together with items for other members of your family. Therefore, it might be more fair to carry out a survey for your whole family's water use during a typical week.

2 The calculator does not show some water use figures. For example, it does not show water used in cooking or in a washing-up bowl, and it only gives one figure for flushing a toilet (some toilets have a 'water-saving' short flush in addition to the full flush option). You will have to estimate these other uses of water.

3 As a family exercise, find out how much water the whole family uses. Divide the total by the number of people in your family to work out the average use per person per week.

4 When you have worked out your average water use, rate yourself using the water gauge below. Are you a water waster, a water watcher or a water warrior?

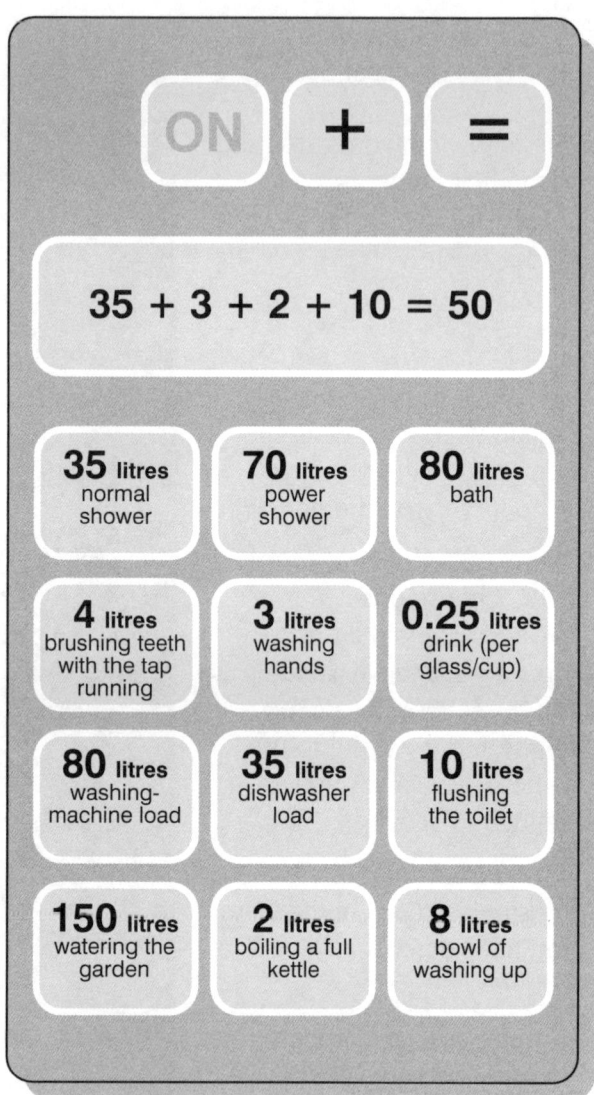

ON	+	=

35 + 3 + 2 + 10 = 50

35 litres normal shower | **70 litres** power shower | **80 litres** bath

4 litres brushing teeth with the tap running | **3 litres** washing hands | **0.25 litres** drink (per glass/cup)

80 litres washing-machine load | **35 litres** dishwasher load | **10 litres** flushing the toilet

150 litres watering the garden | **2 litres** boiling a full kettle | **8 litres** bowl of washing up

Water waster
more than 1200 litres

You're using way more water than you need – about 32 times more than a person in Gambia. Try to cut down on your water wastage to make sure there's enough to go round in the future. Take showers instead of baths, don't leave taps running and make your favourite but dirty item of clothing wait until there's a full load of washing to be done.

Water watcher
750–1200 litres

You're pretty water-friendly. You don't waste a lot of water but you could still do better! Only boil as much water in the kettle as you need. If you're not that thirsty, only pour yourself a small drink. And if you ever see a dripping tap – you know what to do!

Water warrior
fewer than 750 litres

Wow – pretty impressive. You don't waste a drop, do you? Just make sure it's because you're careful with water, not because you go without a shower for weeks on end or are about to faint from dehydration!

5·20 Household rubbish survey

Dear Parents or Carers

Your child and their geography class are studying recycling and waste management in a unit of study on the environment called Think – Act.

We would like to ask for your help and understanding with a rather unusual homework exercise. Class members have been asked to analyse what they and their families throw away during one week. We would like each class member to separate and weigh the different types of rubbish that are produced in the house. We want to reduce the mess, stress and inconvenience that this could cause and so we are asking, in advance, for your co-operation.

The operation will be less messy than you might fear if the pupils plan the operation carefully and if the whole family helps with the exercise. We suggest that:

- *the survey starts on the day your bin is emptied by the council*
- *to make the survey easier and tidier, the week's rubbish is stored in separate bags with a bag for each main component:*
    - *paper*
    - *glass*
    - *metal*
    - *plastic*
    - *food*
    - *fabrics*
    - *others.*
- *when one of these component bags is full, it can be weighed, recorded and binned in the main dustbin or recycling bin*
- *a sheet of old newspaper is put over the pan of the scales for protection while weighing*
- *your child records whether this material could have been recycled, and whether it was put out for recycling*
- *the area is properly cleared and wiped after each weighing operation.*

If this advice is followed, there should be no mess and little inconvenience to your household.

*Please note we are not asking **you** to do this work! We are suggesting how your child can do it without causing too much disruption to the rest of the family. If the class collects this data successfully, we should be able to analyse the data, draw valid conclusions and make some sensible recommendations for further action.*

Many thanks for your co-operation.

Yours sincerely

Horizons Geography Authors

6 Development or Destruction?

Unit 6 of the Pupil Book is supported by:

- photocopiable activity sheets and assessment for learning materials in this *Teaching and Learning Resources* guide on pages 221–255

- customisable unit and lesson plans on the accompanying *Planning CD-ROM* attached to the inside front cover of this guide

- visual resources, presentations and interactive activities on the *Electronic Resources CD-ROM* using the Just Click teaching solution.

In this section of the *Teaching and Learning Resources* guide you will find:

Pages 221–222... have a list of opportunities for **Assessment for Learning** in this unit. One example is provided for each double-page spread. These ideas are based on activities in the Pupil Book, but each activity needs some development if it is to be used as an Assessment for Learning opportunity. Most of the suggestions involve pupils in assessment of their own work, in peer assessment, or in some other form of discussion of the work either before or after it is attempted. All these suggestions are intended to increase pupils' awareness of what characterises good work, and of how their own work can be developed and improved.

The suggestions here are not intended to be prescriptive. Rather they provide teachers with opportunities that we feel fit the best practice of Assessment for Learning, and which target pupils' learning – an increasingly important area of focus under the new Ofsted inspection framework.

Page 223... is a **Learning Plan** for pupils, which gives them a copy of the learning objectives for the unit – copied from page 104 of the Pupil Book – and provides opportunities for pupils to assess their prior learning and set their targets for the whole unit, using the Attainment Targets on pages 224–225 as criteria for success. There is an opportunity at the end of the unit for pupils to re-assess their level against the Attainment Targets before completing the final self-assessment form (How far have I travelled?) on page 235.

Pages 224–225... give pupils a summary of the **Attainment Target** statements, adapted from the National Curriculum level descriptors, which are relevant to their work in this unit. Pupils can use the levels as criteria for success to set themselves learning targets for the unit and check their progress using the Learning Plan on page 223. They have also been divided into two sections, *Places and Environments* and *Enquiry and Skills*. Pupils should be able to see what it is that allows their work to move from one level to the higher level. These Attainment Targets can also be used to provide further support if required for pupils setting and reviewing their targets in the Assessment Opportunity for this unit (see below).

Pages 226–230... are also written for pupils. They describe the **Assessment Opportunity** on pages 122–123 of the Pupil Book. If teachers decide to use this exercise to assess the level at which pupils are working, these pages can help to guide pupils through that exercise. They should also help pupils to set targets for the exercise, to assess their own work and to set new targets for subsequent work. This will enable teachers and pupils to benefit from making formative use of the Assessment Opportunity. (Note that this differs from the Learning Plan on page 223 which provides Assessment for Learning support for the whole unit rather than an individual assessment.) Alternatively, teachers can use these pages as a mark scheme to help them to assess the individual performance of pupils and build a portfolio of assessments to track their progress during Key Stage 3 Geography.

Pages 231–234... provide **Model Answers** for the Assessment Opportunity on pages 122–123 on the Pupil Book. Further exemplars for the other photos are provided on the *Electronic Resources CD-ROM*. These model answers can be used in a variety of ways. Teachers can display them as models of good practice for whole-class discussion or pupils could look at them before they start to write their own answers. However, they are really intended to support the self- or peer-assessment process before pupils analyse their own work. The aim is to demonstrate the need to offer supporting information/explanation for each point made when answering the question as well as the need for balance when constructing an argument. Pupils can identify where the writer has successfully addressed the question and/or where they fail to address it. Pupils will be better able to identify the specific actions they must take to produce better-quality answers. This can help them when assessing their own work or the work of peers. This process is further supported by the Assessment Sheets on pages 43–49.

Page 235... is a **Self-Assessment Sheet** (How far have I travelled?) that can be used to complement the Learning Plan on page 223 or as an alternative form of self-review for the unit to be filled in by pupils at the end of the unit. This form is not linked to the Attainment Targets for the unit, but reviews progress against the learning objectives and enables pupils to record their personal impressions and achievements during the unit, providing them with a more subjective opportunity for self-assessment than the levelled approach adopted by the Learning Plan.

Pages 236–255... consist of photocopiable **Activity Sheets** to support the material in the Pupil Book.

*All of these resources and activities are also available on the **Planning CD-ROM** in either Word or PDF for teachers to print out if preferred or to display on whiteboards or projectors for whole-class discussion. They can also be customised to suit individual needs and, if required, saved with the other electronic resources for the unit using the facility to 'add your own resources' in the Just Click teaching solution.*

6 Development or Destruction?
Assessment for Learning

The following suggestions are intended to show how the material in Unit 6 of **Horizons 3** provides opportunities for teachers and pupils to assess their work as they go along, and to improve their learning as a result of that assessment. It must be stressed that these are only a few of the ways in which the material in the Pupil Book can be used. The techniques could be used as they are outlined here, but teachers will probably find that it is more helpful to use these as starting points and to develop their own ideas to suit their own circumstances.

Before you get started

There is an integral Assessment for Learning framework provided for Unit 6 (and every unit in **Horizons**):

- The unit opens on pages 104–105 of the Pupil Book with the learning objectives for the unit (Where are we going?). The lesson plans on the *Planning CD-ROM* then include learning objectives and outcomes for each spread in turn (supported by pupil-friendly versions in PowerPoint on the *Electronic Resources CD-ROM*).

- The unit ends on pages 122–123 of the Pupil Book with a plenary spread to review and evaluate the unit (Where are we now?), particularly in light of the learning objectives from the opening spread.

- The Learning Plan and Attainment Targets for the unit on pages 223–225 in this *Teaching and Learning Resources* guide provide pupils with the opportunity to set individual learning targets at the start of the unit and to review their progress against these targets at the end. The final self-assessment sheet (How far have I travelled?) on page 235 then offers pupils a more subjective review of their progress during the unit.

Teachers can use or adapt all or some of these resources to set and review goals and involve pupils in their own learning. Further resources on the *Electronic Resources CD-ROM* provide activities for initial assessment of prior learning at the start of the unit to help teachers to diagnose strengths and weaknesses for each topic and for checking and testing knowledge and understanding during and at the end of the unit. All these resources will provide teachers with further evidence to help structure and focus the learning programme.

Pages 104–105

This spread has been designed to get pupils thinking about why the rainforest ecosystem is so important to the planet. These starter activities provide the ideal opportunity for group work. By sharing ideas and experiences, pupils should gain a much better understanding of why this environment is so important. The crucial point to emphasise is provided in the 'Fantastic Facts': the rainforest is such a rich and varied source of life. In activity 4 pupils are required to share the ideas and images of the rainforest they have developed in their presentations. They could play back their presentations to each other and then to groups. They can discuss the strengths and weaknesses of their work. Ultimately, they can select the best work produced by the class and think why it is the best. This work can be celebrated in a classroom display.

Pages 106–107

The activities provide further opportunities to extend pupils' place knowledge. The focus here is on South America and Brazil. The tasks begin with basic location work using the political map and satellite image of South America. Activity Sheet 6.4 provides a more detailed place knowledge assessment. It also encourages pupils to identify any problems they encountered and to suggest actions for future progress. Activity 3 and Activity Sheet 6.5 develop place knowledge and understanding further by encouraging pupils to compare a range of maps of Brazil to analyse the distribution of population. All these activities could be developed as a formal assessment.

Pages 108–109

All of the activities provided on this spread could be developed as group activities involving pupils in discussion and joint analysis of the images of Brazil. The teacher could start this discussion by presenting one of the images on a whiteboard using the *Electronic Resources CD-ROM*. The class could be divided into groups, with each group interpreting a different image and then sharing their ideas with the rest of the class, again perhaps using the images on screen from the CD-ROM. For activity 3, pupils work in groups of three to create their mind movies. In sixes they could play back their mind movies to each other. Activity Sheet 6.6 encourages pupils to share ideas about labelling a photo on this spread.

Pages 110–111

This an important spread in the development of pupils' understanding of a complex global issue. People in MEDCs often overlook or underestimate the development needs of LEDCs, which see clearing areas of rainforest as a necessary aspect of economic development. The spread links development projects in the Amazon to Unit 2 80:20. This should emphasise that Brazil is an LEDC attempting to improve the quality of life of its people. The spread also extends understanding of how development is measured, demonstrating through map A that wealth can vary within a country. Pupils could look back at map A on pages 26–27 and reassess their answers to activity 6. They could also work in groups to compare map A showing the GDP for each region and state in Brazil with the population distribution map and satellite image on pages 106–107. Pupils could compare their 100-word summaries from activity 5, and the class could create a list of views outlining the benefits of development projects in the Amazon.

Pages 112–113

Activity 6 provides an opportunity for further research about tribal peoples using the internet. Pupils could also use ICT to design the poster; this activity is an ideal opportunity to use DTP software to present these. The activity encourages pupils to comment on each other's posters. They could develop their own criteria for what makes a good campaign poster. Before pupils start to design their posters, ask them what they are trying to achieve. Ask the class to make a list of criteria for success in this work. Criteria might include:

- it is interesting to read
- the illustrations are good
- the poster includes a lot of good geography ideas
- the work is original and imaginative.

When the work is completed, pupils should swap their work with a colleague and the pair should assess each other's work, judging against the criteria the class has established for the work.

They could select the best posters to be displayed either in the geography classroom or in a more public space in the school such as the school hall or library as part of a whole-school raising awareness exercise of the plight of tribal peoples linked to citizenship. Pupils could assess how successful they have been in this poster activity by using the Assessment Sheets on pages 43–49 of this *Teaching and Learning Resources* guide.

Pages 114–115

This spread is another important milestone towards the level of understanding required in the debate conducted in the plenary spread of this unit. Two different users of the rainforest are introduced, one using it sustainably and the other unsustainably. Pupils can also be reminded of this spread as part of the lesson developed from pages 120–121. Activity 1 requires pupils to work in groups to determine what the people feel about their life in the rainforest. Initially working with a partner and later in larger groups, pupils share ideas before summarising opinions about the lifestyle of the poor farmer and rubber tapper.

Pages 116–117

This spread introduces the environmentalist perspective about what is happening in rainforests. Previous spreads have predominantly focused on the development aspect in the unit title. This spread introduces the term 'deforestation' linked to the destruction aspect in the unit title. It is worth emphasising this point with pupils. This spread is linked to the next two, which focus on the consequences of deforestation and possible sustainable development options for the Amazon. Activity Sheet 6.13 involves pupils working with a partner to prioritise the main causes of deforestation.

Pages 118–119

Photo A is a dramatic image depicting the impact of deforestation. This image (without the labels) could be used as a starter activity projected on an interactive whiteboard using the *Electronic Resources CD-ROM*.

Pupils could share their feelings about the image, labelling words using the whiteboard tools. Activity Sheet 6.16 can then be used by pupils to summarise feelings before going on to activity 3 to consider how a rubber tapper and a logger might feel. Again, this provides an opportunity for group discussion. The photo of the rubber tapper on page 115 could be projected on the interactive whiteboard. Activities 5 and 6 introduce views of Brazilians that challenge the stereotypical views of people in MEDCs that deforestation is wrong and solely the responsibility of LEDCs. The final question on the spread could be the basis for small group discussion. This will form another important milestone leading to the plenary debate for this unit.

Pages 120–121

Having emphasised the environmental consequences of deforestation, this spread outlines examples of sustainable projects that offer possibilities for developing the rainforest without cutting down the trees. Pupils could work together and share ideas in activity 6 to determine how successful each sustainable project would be in helping Brazil to become more developed. If pupils are to access the higher national curriculum levels in the major Assessment Opportunity for this unit, it is important that they consider the merits of sustainable development projects in the rainforest.

Pages 122–123

All the activities on this spread can be used as a summative assessment opportunity for the Development or Destruction? unit. However, the Assessment Opportunity on pages 226–230 in this *Teaching and Learning Resources* guide provides criteria for success, model answers and a process for target setting and use of this assessment. The model answers in this section focus on steps 5 and 6 of the enquiry process: reaching a conclusion and evaluation. Activity 9 requires pupils to produce a piece of extended writing summarising their view presented in the class debate, adding a conclusion where they present their own views. This unit of work has developed the QCA citizenship geography unit plan Unit 10, 'Debating a global issue'. The geography department could take responsibility for this aspect of citizenship and contribute to the end of Key Stage 3 summative statement for citizenship.

Pupils could then assess their own contribution to the debate, and the conduct of the debate as a whole, using one of the Assessment Sheets on pages 43–49 of this guide. Note that some of the questions may need to be modified slightly for use in the debate situation.

6 Development or Destruction?

Learning plan

What are my learning objectives for this unit?

I aim to learn:

✓ about the global importance of rainforests

✓ what Brazil is like

✓ about the location and size of Brazil

✓ about development in Brazil

✓ about deforestation in the Amazon and how it affects different groups of people and the environment

✓ about sustainable development projects in the Amazon

✓ to conduct an enquiry using ICT, ending with a mock public debate.

Read the Attainment Targets for this unit on pages 224–225 and tick any statements that you feel refer to you. *Places and Environments* covers *what you know* about the topic and *Enquiry and Skills* covers *what you can do.*

Using these statements for this unit, decide what level you are overall at this stage:

Level

What level do you think you can achieve by the end of this unit?

Level

What are you going to concentrate on to achieve this level? A good place to start might be any statements on pages 224–225 that you have not ticked:

At the end of the unit, read the Attainment Targets again and tick in a different colour any *new* statements that refer to you. Then decide what level you are now:

Level

If you have improved, well done! What evidence can you show for this improvement? What or who do you think particularly helped you to improve your level?

If you have stayed the same, better luck next time! What do you think you could have done differently to help improve your levels? What will you do next time to progress further?

6 Development or Destruction?

My Attainment Targets for this unit

Level 3

Places and Environments

- [ ] I can describe and compare the physical and human features of different localities in South America.
- [ ] I can offer explanations for the locations of some of these features.
- [ ] I am aware that different places may have both similar and different characteristics.
- [ ] I can offer reasons for some of my observations and for my views and judgements about places and environments.
- [ ] I can recognise how people try to improve and sustain environments.

Enquiry and Skills

- [ ] I can collect some data from maps, photographs and satellite images.
- [ ] I can describe and label satellite images, charts and graphs showing human and physical features.
- [ ] I can use simple geographical vocabulary to describe images and maps.

Level 4

Places and Environments

- [ ] I can show my knowledge of a range of places in South America.
- [ ] I am beginning to recognise and describe geographical patterns and to appreciate the importance of wider geographical location in understanding places.
- [ ] I can recognise and describe physical and human processes.
- [ ] I am beginning to understand how these processes can change the features of rainforests, and how these changes affect the lives and activities of people living there.
- [ ] I can understand how people can both improve and damage the rainforest environment.
- [ ] I can explain my own views and the views that other people hold about an environmental change in the rainforest.

Enquiry and Skills

- [ ] I can collect data from maps and photographs and display it clearly, using several techniques.
- [ ] I can use maps, satellite images, photographs and cartoons to describe places.
- [ ] I can communicate clearly, using geographical vocabulary.

Level 5

Places and Environments

- [ ] I can describe and begin to explain geographical patterns and physical and human processes.
- [ ] I can describe how these processes can lead to similarities and differences in the environments of different places and in the lives of people who live there.
- [ ] I can recognise some of the links and relationships that make places dependent on each other.
- [ ] I can suggest explanations for the ways in which human activities cause changes to the rainforest environment and the different views people hold about them.
- [ ] I can recognise how people try to manage rainforest environments sustainably.
- [ ] I can explain my own views and begin to suggest relevant geographical questions and issues.

Enquiry and Skills

- [ ] I can suggest relevant geographical questions to investigate.
- [ ] I can select a variety of types of data and can explain that data.
- [ ] I can use a range of geographical vocabulary and can communicate conclusions clearly.

6 Development or Destruction?

My Attainment Targets for this unit

Level 6

Places and Environments

- [ ] I can show my knowledge, understanding and skills in my studies of a range of places in Brazil at different scales and in greater depth.

- [ ] I can describe and explain a range of physical and human processes and recognise that these processes interact to produce the distinctive characteristics of rainforests.

- [ ] I can describe ways in which physical and human processes operating at local to global scales create geographical patterns and lead to changes in rainforests.

- [ ] I can recognise how conflicting demands on the rainforest may arise and describe and compare different approaches to managing it.

- [ ] I can appreciate that different values and attitudes, including my own, result in different approaches that have different effects on people and places such as rainforests.

Enquiry and Skills

- [ ] I can suggest relevant geographical questions to investigate.

- [ ] I can collect data to investigate these questions with some independence.

- [ ] I can use a range of techniques to present the data and draw conclusions that are clearly based on that data.

- [ ] I can communicate conclusions well, with the support of relevant evidence.

Level 7

Places and Environments

- [ ] I can describe interactions within and between physical and human processes, and show how they create geographical patterns and help change environments such as rainforests.

- [ ] I can understand that many factors, including people's values and attitudes, influence the decisions made about places and environments, and use this understanding to explain the resulting changes in rainforests.

- [ ] I can appreciate that the rainforest and the lives of the people who live there are affected by actions and events in other places.

- [ ] I can recognise that human actions, including my own, may have unintended environmental consequences and that change sometimes leads to conflict.

- [ ] I can appreciate that considerations of sustainable development affect the planning and management of environments and resources.

Enquiry and Skills

- [ ] I can identify questions to investigate and independently collect and research appropriate data.

- [ ] I can use accurately a wide range of techniques to present the data and draw conclusions that are clearly based on that data.

- [ ] I can communicate the conclusions well, with the support of relevant evidence that has been clearly evaluated.

Level 8

Places and Environments

- [ ] I can offer explanations for interactions within and between physical and human processes.

- [ ] I can explain changes in the characteristics of the rainforest over time, in terms of location, physical and human processes, and interactions with other places.

- [ ] I can begin to account for differences in development and understand the range and complexity of factors that contribute to the quality of life in different places in Brazil.

- [ ] I can recognise the causes and consequences of environmental issues in the rainforest and understand a range of views about them and different approaches to tackling them.

- [ ] I can understand how considerations of sustainable development can affect the planning and management of the rainforest environment.

Enquiry and Skills

- [ ] I can show independence in identifying appropriate geographical questions and issues and using an effective sequence of investigation.

- [ ] I can select a wide range of skills and use them effectively and accurately.

- [ ] I can evaluate critically sources of evidence before using them in my investigations.

- [ ] I can present full and coherently argued summaries of my investigations and reach substantiated conclusions.

On page 123 in activities 8–11 you are asked to reach a conclusion and evaluate your work.

Step 5 Reaching a conclusion

8 At the end of the debate, vote on the motion, ideally in character. If each of the groups has presented their views well, your vote might not be as straightforward as you thought!

9 Produce a piece of extended writing summarising the views presented in the meeting. Add a conclusion giving your own views on what is happening in the rainforest, and what should happen in the future.

Step 6 Evaluating your work

10 Once you have finished your writing, share your own views about the rainforest with a partner.

11 Why is it important to approach websites on the internet critically and to consider the motives of the information providers?

Before you start this activity, look at the **Criteria for success** sheet. Set yourself a target level to aim for in this Assessment Opportunity. Write this level in the box on the target setting sheet. Explain how you intend to obtain this level.

Once you have finished the activities, look again at the Criteria for success and assess your answers. You could also compare your answers with model answers. Write your level in the box and explain how you achieved this level.

Then set yourself a target for improvement in your next assessment. Explain what you need to do to improve next time. Try to set yourself specific tasks to work on.

6 Development or Destruction?

Criteria for success

A **Level 3** answer may	• offer reasons for some of your observations and for your views and judgements about places and environments
	• involve collecting some data from maps, photographs and satellite images
	• use simple geographical vocabulary to describe images and maps.
A **Level 4** answer may	• begin to understand how human and physical processes can change the features of rainforests, and how these changes affect the lives and activities of people living there
	• understand how people can both improve and damage the rainforest environment
	• explain your own views, and the views that other people hold, about an environmental change in the rainforest
	• involve collecting data from maps and photographs and displaying it clearly, using several techniques
	• communicate clearly, using geographical vocabulary.
A **Level 5** answer may	• recognise some of the links and relationships that make places dependent on each other
	• suggest explanations for the ways in which human activities cause changes to the rainforest environment and the different views people hold about them
	• recognise how people try to manage rainforest environments sustainably
	• explain your own views and begin to suggest relevant geographical questions and issues
	• suggest relevant geographical questions to investigate
	• select a variety of types of data, and explain that using a range of geographical vocabulary and communicating conclusions clearly.
A **Level 6** answer may	• describe and explain a range of physical and human processes and recognise that these processes interact to produce the distinctive characteristics of rainforests
	• describe ways in which physical and human processes operating at local to global scales create geographical patterns and lead to changes in rainforests
	• recognise how conflicting demands on the rainforest environment may arise and describe and compare different approaches to managing it

- appreciate that different values and attitudes result in different approaches that have different effects on people and places such as rainforests

- suggest relevant geographical questions to investigate

- collect data to investigate these questions with some independence

- use a range of techniques to present the data and draw conclusions that are clearly based on that data

- communicate conclusions well, with the support of relevant evidence.

A **Level 7** answer may

- describe interactions within and between physical and human processes, and show how these interactions create geographical patterns and help change places and environments such as rainforests

- understand that many factors, including people's values and attitudes, influence the decisions made about places and environments, and use this understanding to explain the resulting changes in rainforests

- appreciate that the rainforest and the lives of the people who live there are affected by actions and events in other places

- recognise that human actions may have unintended environmental consequences and that change sometimes leads to conflict

- appreciate that considerations of sustainable development affect the planning and management of environments and resources

- identify questions to investigate and independently collect and research appropriate data

- use accurately a wide range of techniques to present the data and draw conclusions that are clearly based on that data

- communicate the conclusions well, with the support of relevant evidence that has been clearly evaluated.

A **Level 8** answer may

- explain changes in the characteristics of the rainforest over time, in terms of location, physical and human processes, and interactions with other places

- begin to account for differences in development and understand the range and complexity of factors that contribute to the quality of life in different places in Brazil

- recognise the causes and consequences of environmental issues in the rainforest and understand a range of views about them and different approaches to tackling them

- understand how considerations of sustainable development can affect the planning and management of the rainforest environment

- show independence in identifying appropriate geographical questions and issues, and in using an effective sequence of investigation

- select a wide range of skills and use them effectively and accurately

- evaluate critically sources of evidence before using them in the investigations

- present full and coherently argued summaries of your investigations and reach substantiated conclusions.

6 Development or Destruction?

My target setting

I want to make progress in geography, in my extended writing about the debate.

When I do activities 8–11 on page 123, I aim to obtain: Level ___

To do this I will need to:

[ ]

Answer these questions when you have completed activities 8–11 on page 123:

In this Assessment Opportunity I obtained: Level ___

Explain how you obtained this level:

[ ]

When I do my next Assessment Opportunity, I aim to obtain: Level ___

To do this I will need to:

[ ]

6 Development or Destruction?

Model answers

A This is a good basic answer that was written by a pupil who had completed activities 8–11 on page 123.

My class had a debate about the Amazon rainforest. We conducted research for a point of view and then presented our findings in a mock public meeting. The motion that we debated was: Amazonia – development or destruction?

My group researched the views of tribal people. These groups of people have lived in the rainforest for a very long time. New tribes are discovered regularly as the rainforest is developed. Studies estimate that over 2000 indigenous tribes with more than seven million people lived in the Amazon before the arrival of the Europeans. Today this number is down to less than 400 tribes and between 1 and 1.5 million people. Development has affected tribal people badly.

Tribal people live in harmony with the rainforest. They do not cut down all the trees. They use the rainforest resources in a sustainable way so future generations of tribal people can live the same way. They hunt wildlife, grow small areas of crops and harvest plants for medicines. Their way of life is changing, however, due to other groups of people moving into the rainforest and cutting down the trees. Many tribal people were killed in the 1970s when the Brazilian military government attempted to open up the Amazon to gold speculators and cattle barons. They were killed by infections, such as yellow fever, brought by the road builders. Some 45 000 gold miners have poured on to their land, polluting their rivers with mercury, blowing up villages and shooting children (they call them 'monkeys') out of the trees for sport. Tribal people want to be left alone. They are happy with their life and appreciate the importance of the rainforest environment for their way of life. They are concerned for their future and the future of the rainforest. My group did some research on the internet and we found the following view of a tribe on the Survival International website: 'We

live in the depths of the forest and we are getting cornered as the whites close in on us. They're always advancing and now they are on top of us. We are always fleeing. We love the forest because we were born here and we know how to live off the forest. Without the forest we are nobody and we have no way of surviving. We don't know about agriculture and commerce and we can't speak Portuguese. We depend on the forest. Without the forest we'll be gone, we'll be extinct.'

The Kayapo have been fighting to protect their lands, forests and traditions, both physically and politically. A fight that began with war clubs has evolved into a war with words. Chief Raoni of the Kayapo Nation, having learned the language of politicians, went to the Brazilian capital to explain to the government how his environment was being destroyed. He said to them: 'Since the beginning of the world, we Indians began to love the forest and the land. Because of this, we have learned how to preserve it. We are trying to protect our lands, our traditions, our knowledge. We defend not to destroy. If there was no forest, there would be no Indians. I had to come out [of the forest] to tell you that by destroying our environment, you are destroying your own. If I didn't come out, you wouldn't know what you're doing.'

In our class debate other groups presented the views of the Brazilian government and poor farmers. I don't agree with them: I think like the environmentalists that the Amazon is being destroyed not developed. Why should the tribal people be forced to leave the rainforest and change their lifestyle? They were happy and they used the rainforest well without destroying it. Their way of life is much more sustainable than ours. We should learn from tribal people to see if we can adapt their approaches so that more people can benefit from rainforest resources.

B This is a better answer, which achieves a higher level than the first one (A).

- Read it carefully, and try to see why this is better than the first answer.
- Try to see how it meets new parts of the criteria for success.
- Try to see how you could use ideas from this work to improve your own work.

Amazonia is the largest area of rainforest in the world. Sixty-two per cent of the Amazon rainforest lies in Brazil, the rest lies in eight surrounding countries. All these countries are attempting to develop and see the rainforest as an area to be opened up or developed. Environmentalists – many of whom live in developed countries such as the UK and USA – think the Amazon rainforest is being destroyed and this has implications for everyone on the planet.

The Brazilian government has a duty to improve the quality of life of all Brazilians. The Amazon rainforest represents a vast empty area rich in mineral resources. Brazilian politicians coined a slogan when Amazonia was first being opened up: 'Land without people. For people without land.' This clearly shows their view of the rainforest. In many areas of Brazil, particularly the north-east which suffers from drought, people suffer from extreme poverty. The government saw that they could improve life for the poor by giving land in the rainforest to them to farm. The first thing the government had to do was make the rainforest more accessible, so they began to build a series of major roads in the 1970s and then land on either side of the road was cleared for people to farm. Money could be made abroad from the trees that were cut down. Tropical hardwoods are scarce and a high-value product often purchased on the world market by developed countries like UK and USA. The high rainfall and emptiness of the rainforest made it ideal for the development of hydro-electric power stations but building dams leads to flooding vast areas of rainforest. Many power stations that are planned for development will power the major industrial areas in the south-east of Brazil focused on the cities of Belo Horizonte, Rio de Janerio and São Paulo. This is an important source of energy for a country short on oil. This is therefore an important part of the Brazilian government's programme for development. Their 'Avança Brasil' (Advance Brazil) launched in 2001 proposes to build many more HEP schemes in the Amazon rainforest.

Images and a flyer produced by the group to represent the views of the Brazilian government were included here.

Environmentalists see the rainforest as a vitally important ecosystem that should be protected for the benefit of future generations of people on the planet. They point out that rainforests cover only 2% of the Earth's surface, or 6% of its land mass, and yet they house over 50% of the plant and animal species on Earth. It is thought to be the most diverse ecosystem on Earth, supporting around 60 000 plant species, 1000 bird species and more than 300 mammal species. Fifteen per cent of the Amazon rainforest has already been destroyed. Since the 1970s, an area of rainforest the size of France has been lost. In 2000 alone, almost two million hectares of rainforest in the Brazilian Amazon were lost to logging, mining, farming and road building.

Environmentalists predict that the planned developments of the Brazilian government will lead to the damage or loss of between 33% and 42% of Brazil's remaining Amazon forest. The range of plant and animal species in the Amazon remains largely unknown. Only 40% of all insect species have so far been identified. Over 300 000 species of plants have been identified, but an estimated 20 000 remain undiscovered. In the 1990s alone, seven species of monkeys, two species of birds and dozens of species of frogs and fish were discovered.

A labelled satellite image showing levels of deforestation researched on the internet was included here.

Environmentalists believe that we should be using the potential of the rainforest rather than destroying it. They acknowledge that some development is necessary for the benefit of the people already living in the rainforest and also to the benefit of Brazil as a whole. They believe that development need not lead to the destruction of rainforest, but it should be developed sustainably, thus preserving this precious ecosystem for the future. The medical potential of plants of the Amazon has only just begun to be realised internationally. At present, close to 650 species of plant with pharmaceutical properties and economic value from the Amazon have been assessed. Forty-eight native fruits of the Amazon have been identified as having the potential for sale on the international market. The fruits of the Acai palm found in the Amazon are traditionally used to make a type of juice that is rich in minerals. A single palm tree produces up to 20 kg of fruit per year. In 1995, almost 106 000 tonnes of juice were produced at a value of US$40 million. Eco-tourism has the potential to guarantee minimal environmental impact on the Amazon rainforest through the application of environmentally friendly technologies and environmentally sympathetic accommodation for visitors. It could also guarantee that the income received from such activities would directly benefit the local communities.

Tribal people have lived sustainably in the Amazon rainforest for many generations. They have learnt how to use rainforest resources and have evolved effective ways of living in this environment. Development has often meant moving tribal people from their lands, sometimes using violence or purposely infecting tribes with diseases that they have no immmunity against, resulting in the death of whole tribal groups. Environmentalists and increasingly tribal people believe that there is much to be learnt from the way tribal groups live sustainably in the forest. Tribal leaders are beginning to realise that there is a world beyond the rainforest and they need to warn developers what damage they are doing. One of the most famous tribal campaigners is Chief Raoni of the Kayapo Nation. Having learned the language of politicians, he went to the Brazilian capital to explain to the government how his environment was being destroyed. He said to them: 'Since the beginning of the world, we Indians began to love the forest and the land. Because of this, we have learned how to preserve it. We are trying to protect our lands, our traditions, our knowledge. We defend not to destroy. If there was no forest, there would be no Indians. I had to come out [of the forest] to tell you that by destroying our environment, you are destroying your own. If I didn't come out, you wouldn't know what you're doing.'

There are other groups who currently live in the rainforest and earn a living in a sustainable way without doing long-term damage to the ecosystem, most notably rubber tappers who collect latex from rubber trees which grow naturally in the rainforest. They also collect brazil nuts. It is possible to earn a higher income from this than cutting down the forest for farming. The poor farmers that have flooded into the rainforest were attracted by the offer of free land from the government. They came from the drought-stricken north-east where life was hard farming on poor-quality land they did not own. Once in the rainforest, however, they have had to cope with inaccessibility, a hostile environment and attacks from tribal people trying to hold on to their lands.

When I started this work I thought the issues would be obvious, in that the rainforest is being destroyed by the Brazilian government's schemes and other developers. However, as a result of our class debate where different viewpoints were presented, I have realised that the issues are not as clear-cut as I first thought. Brazil is one of the largest countries in the world and like all LEDCs is trying hard to develop and improve the life of its people. The government has a responsibility to improve the quality of life of Brazilians. The Amazon represents a large part of the country and is currently underused. I think the government is right to exploit the resources of this vast area, and encourage people to move into it from other areas of Brazil like the drought-affected north-east. I also agree with environmentalists and tribal people, however, that the trees should not be chopped down unnecessarily. This is an important ecosystem for the whole planet and it should be developed sustainably. We need to learn more about the plants and animals in this environment rather than just chopping down or burning the forest.

C

Finally, the pupil who wrote the second answer (B) thought about his work and decided to develop his answer further by adding the following text at the end.

The Brazilian government also has a responsibility to develop the rainforest sustainably. Governments ideally need to consider the quality of life of future generations of people, not just the current population. Short-term economic gains should not lead to long-term economic damage. The Amazon rainforests are vital to the world's future; burning trees only adds to the amount of carbon dioxide in the atmosphere, increasing the impact of global warming. Many rich countries have polluted the atmosphere in the name of economic development. MEDCs have seriously damaged their own environments, and it's often MEDCs that are involved in deforesting the Amazon either by funding government projects or by purchasing tropical hardwoods. However, it is also MEDC environmentalists who preach to Brazil and other LEDCs with rainforest areas, trying to stop them cutting down the forest in order to develop. Many LEDCs probably see this as an attempt by MEDCs like the USA and the UK to keep them poor. Rich countries should work with LEDCs to help them develop rainforests sustainably. Fairtrade projects could be developed to collect and market crops and products that grow naturally in the rainforest.

Help could be given to tribal groups and people like the rubber tappers to share and develop their sustainable approaches for other groups of people.

The mock public meeting was useful in helping us consider different points of view about an issue. I now think the rainforest should be developed but not destroyed. People can live in the rainforest and use its resources without cutting down the trees. It is important that knowledge of how to do this is shared. Tribal people have an important role to play in this – they need to be studied carefully and their knowledge of the rainforest riches shared.

It was interesting investigating different websites about the Amazon rainforest as they often provide conflicting information. The Brazilian government website, for example, presented different views about what is happening in the Amazon than, say, the Rainforest Action Network website. This has made me realise that I cannot always believe views portrayed on websites. I need to question these views carefully and consider who has produced a website and what their reasons are for developing the site in the first place.

6 Development or Destruction?

How far have I travelled?

In this unit my **Learning Objectives** were to learn:

- about the global importance of rainforests
- what Brazil is like
- about the location and size of Brazil
- about development in Brazil
- about deforestation in the Amazon and how it affects different groups of people and the environment
- about sustainable development projects in the Amazon
- to conduct an enquiry using ICT, ending with a mock public debate.

My progress in this unit

How well have I achieved my objectives?	Okay							Excellent

Enquiry and Skills:

to use satellite images to describe environmental change								
to analyse data on maps								
to collect and present data using ICT								
to conduct an enquiry leading to a mock public meeting								

Places and Environments:

to improve my place knowledge of South America								
to understand and identify how features of an ecosystem are interlinked								
to identify the causes and effects of deforestation								
to consider different points of view about environmental change								
to identify sustainable approaches to developing rainforests								

Shade the bars to show how far you think you have made progress in this unit.

The part of this unit that I enjoyed the most was …

because …

The part of this unit that I needed most help with was …

because …

The piece of work that I am most pleased with is …

because …

The aspect of this unit that will be most useful to me in future is …

because …

Any other comments?

N

0   500 km

Development or Destruction?   *see pages 104–105 in your Horizons Book 3*

Where are the world's rainforests?

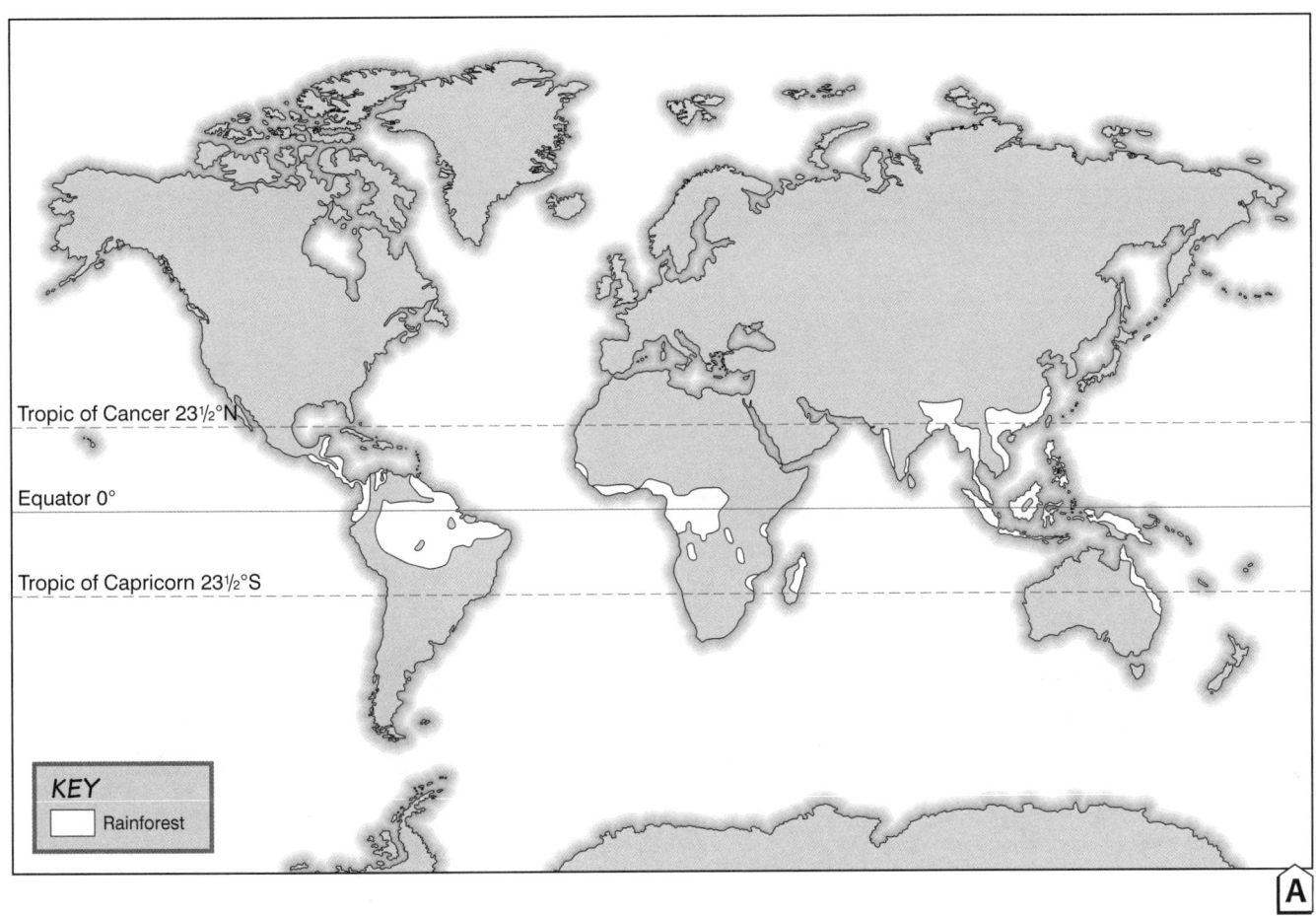

Tropic of Cancer 23½°N

Equator 0°

Tropic of Capricorn 23½°S

KEY
☐ Rainforest

A

Countries with rainforest	Share of world's tropical rainforest (%)	**B**
Brazil	33	
Rest of South America	25	
Zaire	10	
Rest of Africa	9	
Indonesia	10	
Rest of Southeast Asia and Oceania	13	

1 **a** Using map A, colour in *green* the areas of rainforest.

b Describe the world distribution of rainforests.

2 The data shown in table B shows the percentage share of rainforests.

a Draw a pie chart to present this data.

b Again, describe the world distribution of rainforests. This time, identify which countries have the most rainforests.

3 Compare map A and your pie chart with map A on pages 26–27 of your textbook.

a What do you notice about most of the countries that have rainforests?

b Why might this be a problem for the world's rainforests in the future?

6•3 Development or Destruction?

see pages 104–105 in your Horizons Book 3

What are rainforests like?

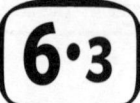

1 Look carefully at the information about rainforests on pages 104–105 of your textbook.

2 Annotate the sketch below to show key features of the rainforest.

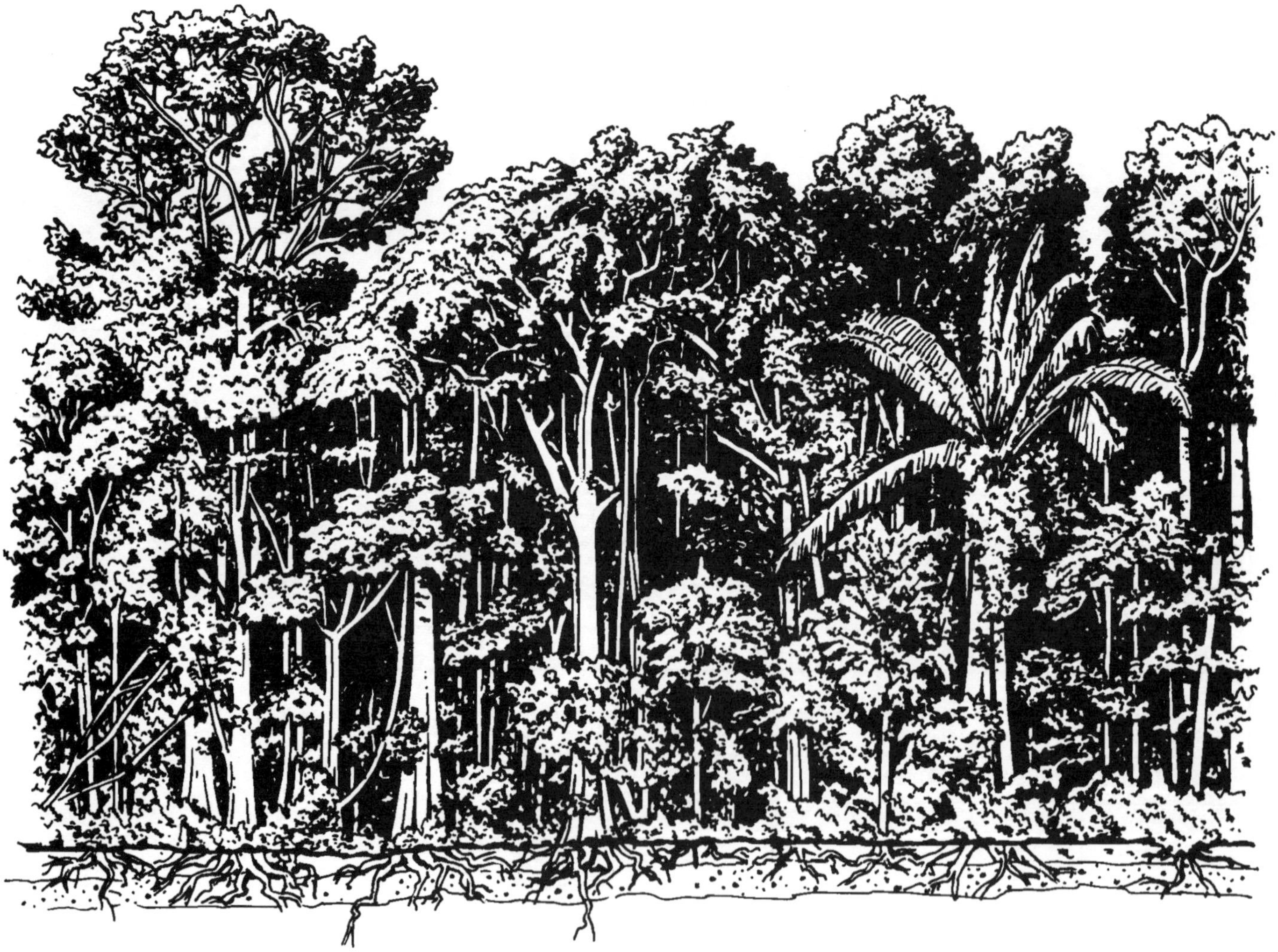

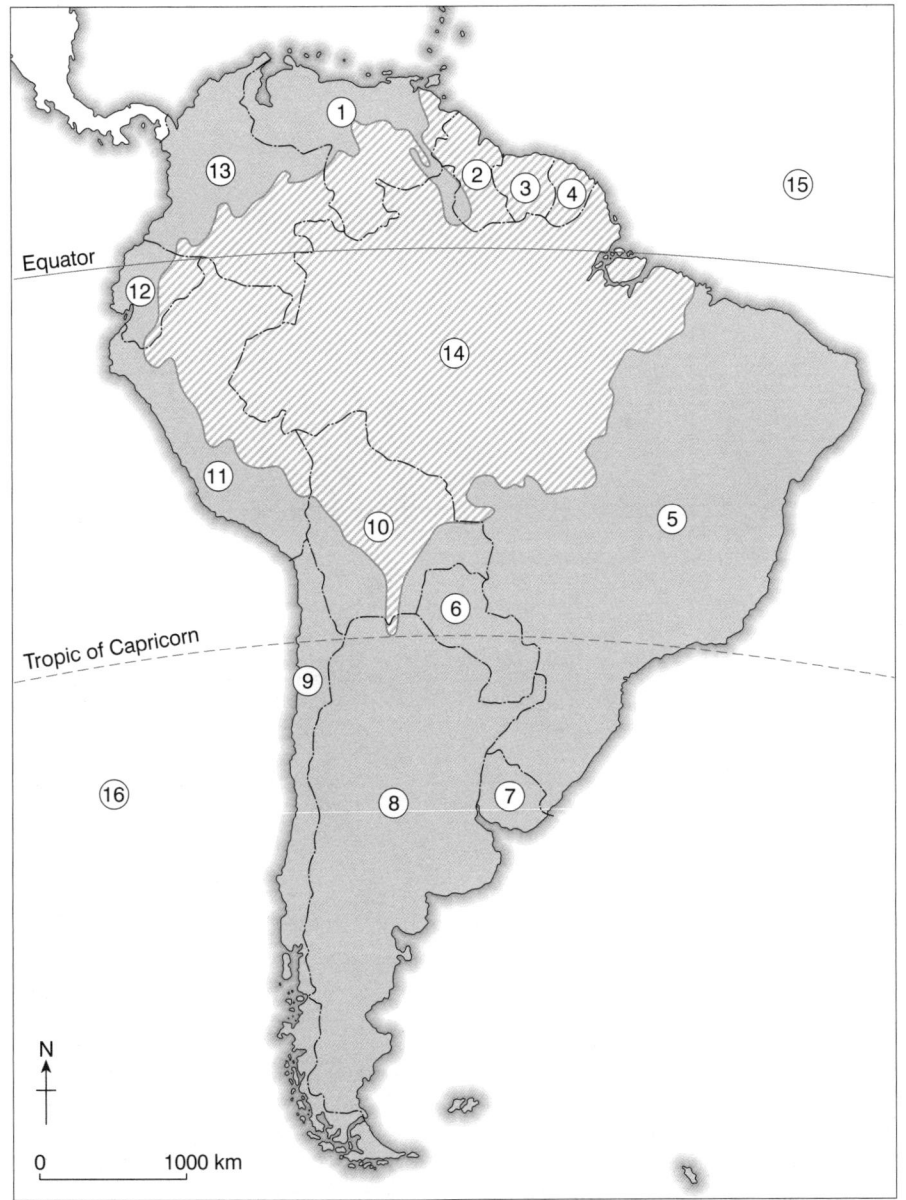

Countries

1 _____
2 _____
3 _____
4 _____
5 _____
6 _____
7 _____
8 _____
9 _____
10 _____
11 _____
12 _____
13 _____

Physical areas

14 _____
15 _____
16 _____

1 Name the countries of South America in the spaces provided next to the map.

2 Name the physical areas in the spaces provided next to the map.

3 Complete the table below by adding Y for Yes and N for No to show whether each country has land in the rainforest.

Country	Land in rainforest?	Country	Land in rainforest?
Argentina		Guyana	
Bolivia		Paraguay	
Brazil		Peru	
Chile		Suriname	
Colombia		Uruguay	
Ecuador		Venezuela	
French Guiana			

Use this sheet to help you complete activity 3 on page 106 of your textbook.

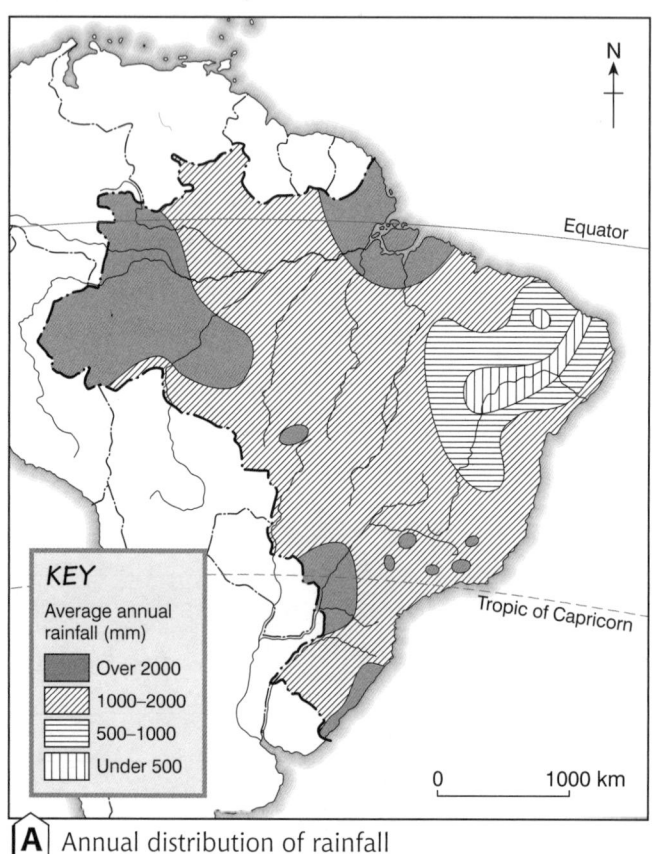

A Annual distribution of rainfall

KEY

Average annual rainfall (mm)

- Over 2000
- 1000–2000
- 500–1000
- Under 500

0   1000 km

B Physical features

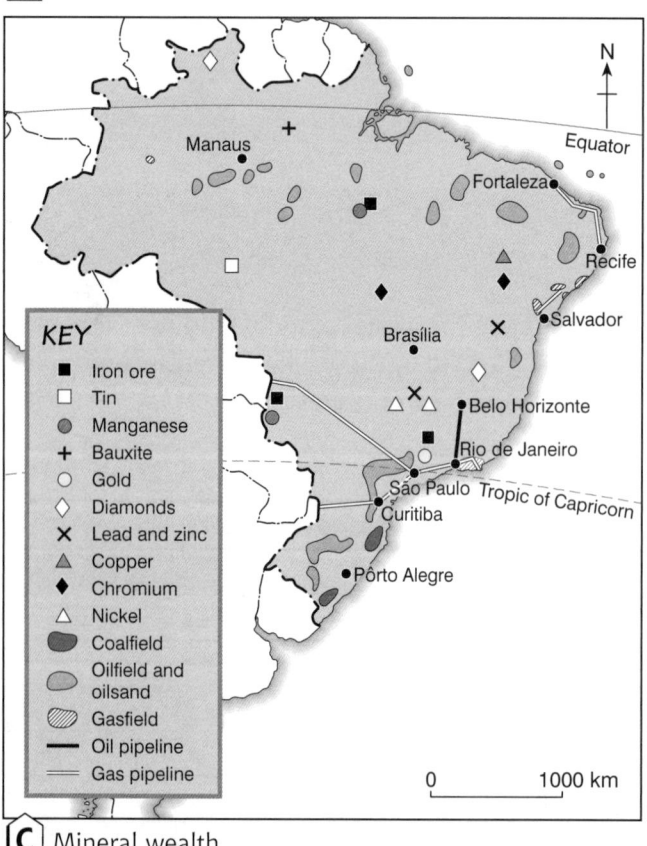

C Mineral wealth

KEY

- ■ Iron ore
- □ Tin
- ● Manganese
- + Bauxite
- ○ Gold
- ◇ Diamonds
- ✕ Lead and zinc
- △ Copper
- ◆ Chromium
- △ Nickel
- Coalfield
- Oilfield and oilsand
- Gasfield
- Oil pipeline
- Gas pipeline

0   1000 km

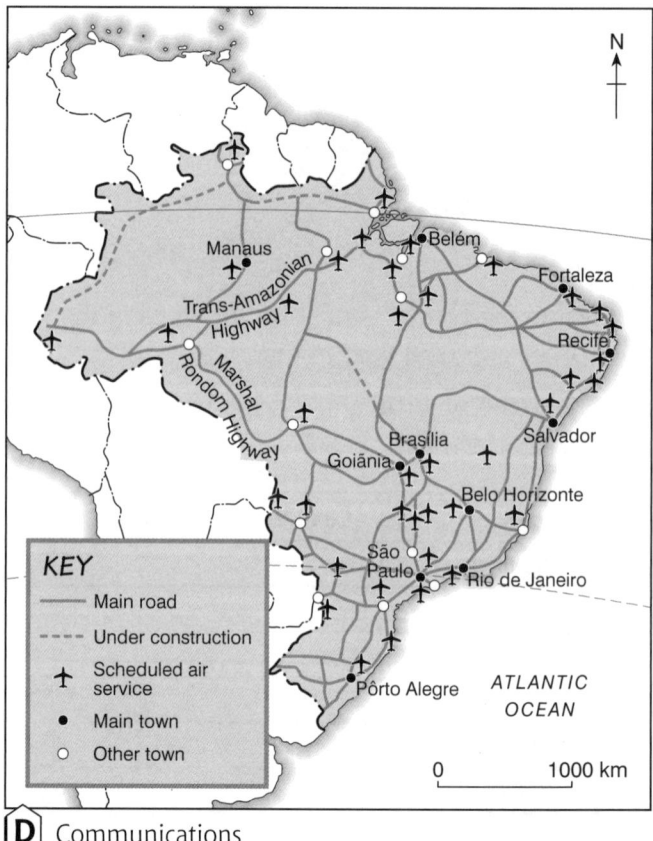

D Communications

KEY

- Main road
- Under construction
- ✈ Scheduled air service
- ● Main town
- ○ Other town

0   1000 km

Development or Destruction?

see pages 108–109 in your Horizons Book 3

5Ws

What?	**Where?**	**When?**

Why?	**Who?**

1 Answer the 5Ws questions around the photo.

2 In pairs, swap sheets and compare your answers.

6·7 Amazon development projects

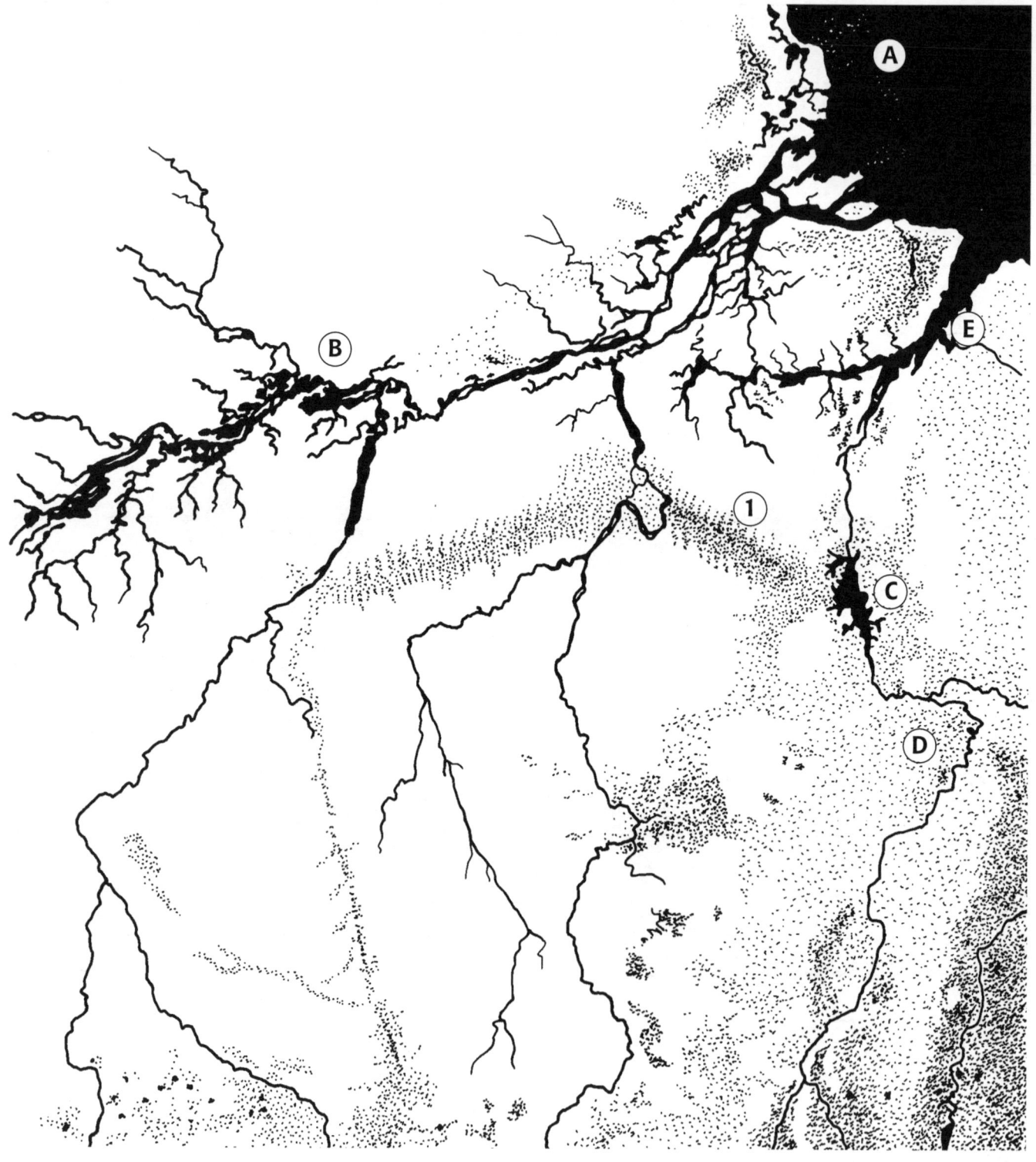

1. Compare this sketch map with back cover resource D and map C on page 110 of your textbook.

2. Add labels to the sketch for the following places and features:
   - Ocean A
   - River B
   - Lake C
   - Mining town D
   - City E

3. Explain what has happened to the area marked ① on the sketch map.

1   Using the ranges in the key on the map on sheet 6.9, shade each state to show population change in Brazil between 1991 and 2003. You will need to use four coloured pencils. The greater the population change, the darker the colour you should use.

2   Which type of map have you drawn to show population change in Brazil?

3   Describe the distribution of states with **a** the highest population change between 1991 and 2003; **b** the lowest population change between 1991 and 2003. Try to give reasons for these changes.

4   In January 2001 the Brazilian government announced its plans for 'Avança Brasil' (Advance Brazil). What does the pattern of population change suggest about its campaign?

State	Area (km²)	Population in 1991	Population in 2003	Population change (%)
Acre	153 149	417 100	600 595	31
Alagoas	27 933	2 512 661	2 917 664	14
Amapá	143 453	289 041	534 835	46
Amazonas	1 577 820	2 102 771	3 031 068	31
Bahia	567 295	11 867 328	13 435 612	12
Ceará	146 348	6 366 117	7 758 441	18
Distrito Federal	5 822	1 601 095	2 189 789	27
Espírito Santo	46 184	2 600 624	3 250 219	20
Goiás	341 289	4 017 510	5 306 459	24
Maranhão	333 365	4 929 687	5 873 655	16
Mato Grosso	906 806	2 026 078	2 651 335	24
Mato Grosso do Sul	358 158	1 780 370	2 169 688	18
Minas Gerais	588 383	15 743 561	18 553 312	15
Pará	1 253 164	4 949 217	6 574 993	25
Paraíba	56 584	3 201 319	3 518 595	9
Paraná	199 709	8 448 600	9 906 866	15
Pernambuco	98 937	7 127 942	8 161 862	13
Piauí	252 378	2 582 077	2 923 725	12
Rio de Janeiro	43 909	12 807 220	14 879 118	14
Rio Grande do Norte	53 306	2 415 092	2 888 058	16
Rio Grande do Sul	282 062	9 138 453	10 510 992	13
Rondônia	238 512	1 133 268	1 455 907	22
Roraima	225 116	217 584	357 302	39
Santa Catarina	95 442	4 542 044	5 607 233	19
São Paulo	248 808	31 588 801	38 709 320	18
Sergipe	22 050	1 491 871	1 874 613	20
Tocantins	278 420	918 387	1 230 181	25

Use this map for the activities on sheet 6.8.

N

Roraima

Amapá

Amazonas

Pará

Rio Grande
do Norte

Maranhão

Ceará

Paraíba

Piauí

Pernambuco

Acre

Rondônia

Tocantins

Alagoas

Sergipe

Mato Grosso

Bahia

Goiás

Distrito
Federal

Minas Gerais

Mato Grosso
do Sul

Espírito Santo

São Paulo

Rio de Janeiro

Paraná

Santa
Catarina

Rio Grande
do Sul

KEY

% population change, 1991–2003

Over 30

21–29

13–20

Under 13

0   500 km

see pages 112–113 in your Horizons Book 3

6•10 Development or Destruction?

Think Yanomami!

A

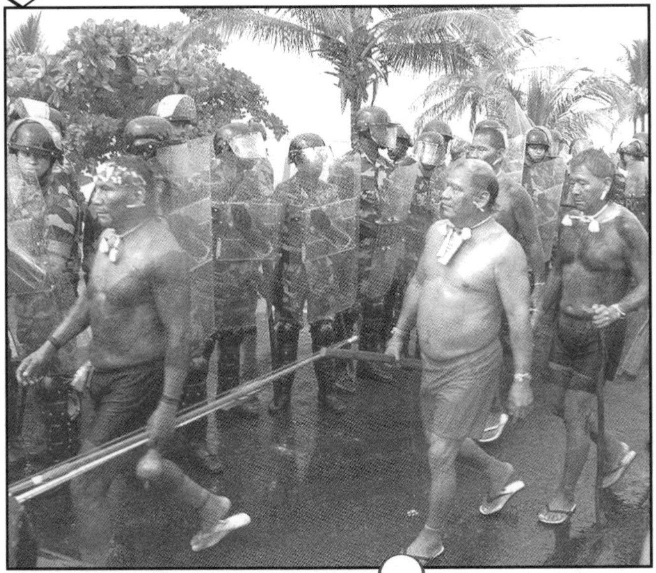

B

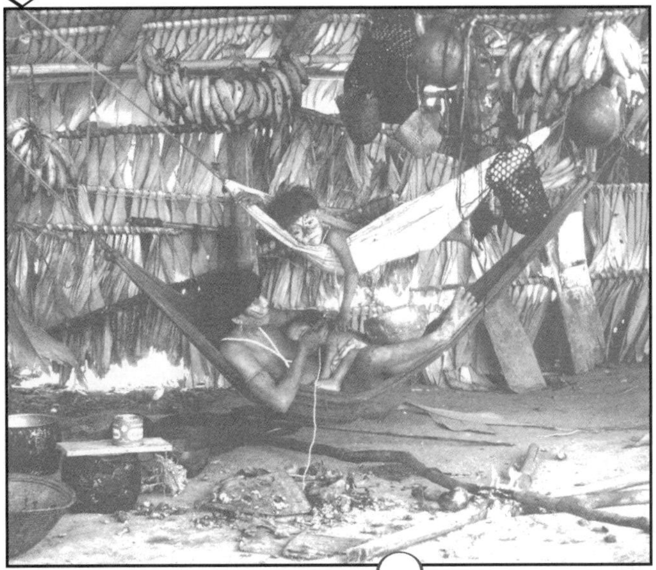

1 Photos A and B show different images of Yanomami people. Look carefully at the images and discuss them with a partner. Your teacher may display colour versions to help you.

2 Imagine each photo is to be used on the front page of a newspaper. Discuss with your partner a suitable headline for each photo and write them in the boxes above each one.

3 Discuss what the Yanomami people in the photos might be thinking. Write your ideas in the think bubbles.

4 Join up with another pair and swap your headlines and thought bubbles. Which headlines and thoughts do you think are the best? Share your views with the rest of the class.

1 Imagine you are a graphic designer. You have won a contract from Survival International, an organisation committed to campaigning on behalf of tribal groups around the world. Your brief is to design a poster for a new campaign to promote the lifestyle of tribal peoples in the Amazon.

Things to include in your poster

- Photos of tribal peoples to illustrate their lifestyle. Use the photos on pages 112–113 of your textbook as a starting point.

- Sketches to explain their way of life.

- A catchy title to draw attention to your ideas.

- The Survival International logo and website address to tell people how to find further information.

- Your name.

2 Use the internet to carry out research and download resources to include in your poster.

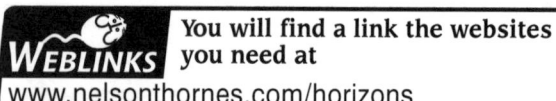

WEBLINKS You will find a link the websites you need at www.nelsonthornes.com/horizons

3 You can draw your poster or produce it using desktop publishing software.

4 Produce a draft design for homework before working on the final version.

5 Your posters will make a colourful classroom display and can be used by pupils next year to better understand the way of life of tribal peoples.

I've come to the rainforest from Pernambuco in the north-east of Brazil, where I was a 50–50 sharecropper growing sugar cane – 50% of what I earned went to the landowner. There was regular drought and my crops were destroyed. I had no money or future there. Then I heard that the government would give me my own land and a house in the Amazon. I jumped at the chance to get a decent life for me and my family. I now have my own land to farm, although we're frightened of the tribal people who sometimes attack us. My small plot of land doesn't make much difference – the rainforest is so huge.

Poor farmer

I walk along trails containing up to 200 rubber trees. At each tree I make a diagonal cut in the bark to make the latex run into a small metal cup that I place at the end of the cut. I return later to each tree to pick up the latex that has collected in the tins. On the trail I also collect Brazil nuts, which I can sell. It's back-breaking work – the cutting and collecting can take me up to 10 hours. I spend a further 2 hours processing the rubber into a ball for sale. I don't earn a lot. Life has become more difficult since the government encouraged people from the south of Brazil to buy land here. They want to clear forest for cattle ranching. They've tried to move us off the land, sometimes resorting to violence.

Rubber tapper

1 Read why the poor farmer and the rubber tapper moved into the rainforest in search of a better quality of life.

2 Underline the text that explains:
  a the reasons why they moved to the Amazon in *yellow*.
  b how they make a living in *blue*.
  c what they think about the rainforest in *green*.
  d any dangers or conflicts they are facing in *red*.

3 Use this sheet to help you answer the activities on page 115 of your textbook.

6·13 Causes of deforestation

So far you have investigated many causes for the deforestation of the Amazon. You need to consider the relative importance of these causes.

1 Read the text on pages 116–117 of your textbook and choose seven to ten causes of deforestation that you think are important.

2 Write each cause on a separate piece of card.

3 Arrange your cards in order of importance in a triangle shape similar to the one below.

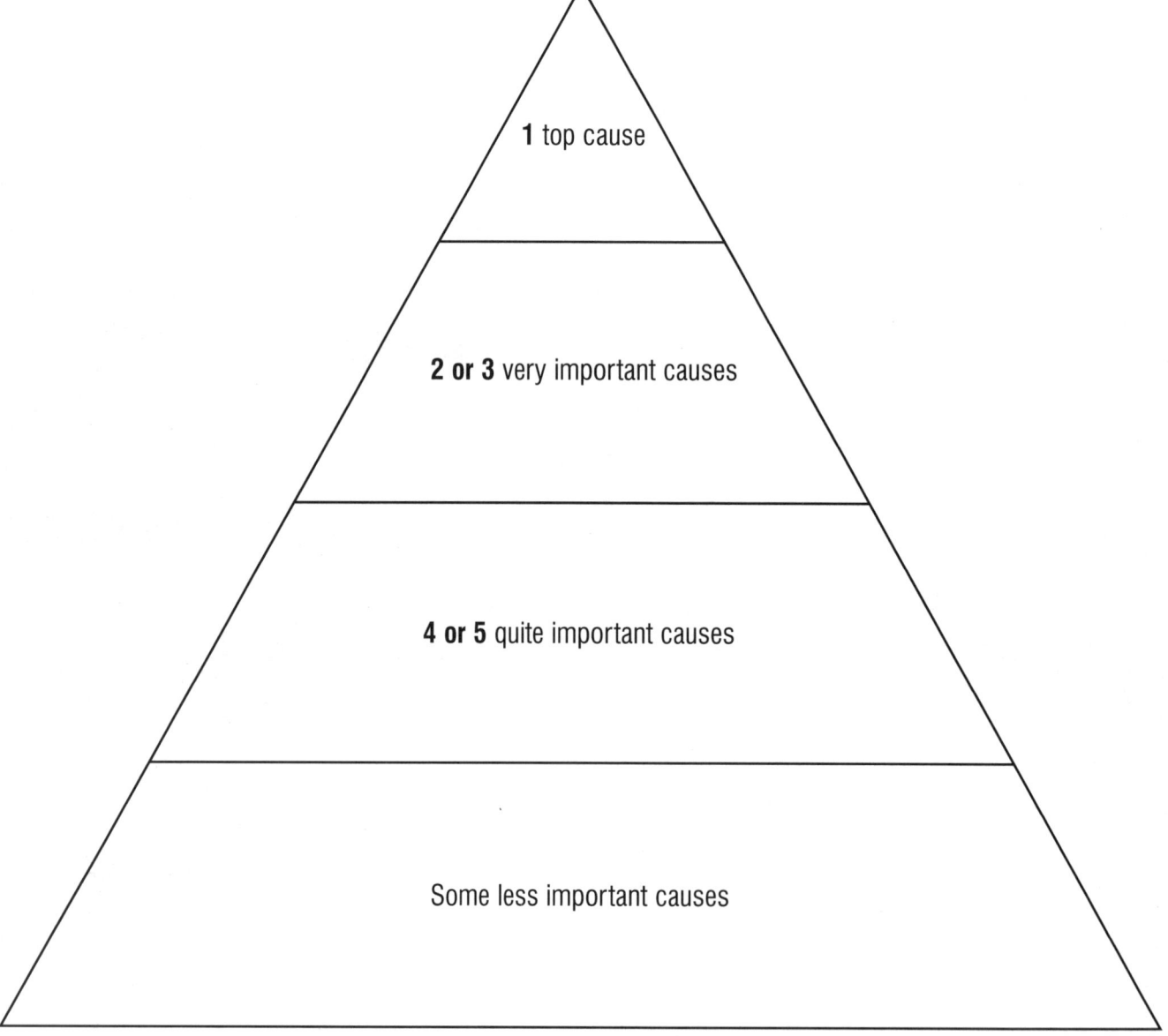

1 top cause

2 or 3 very important causes

4 or 5 quite important causes

Some less important causes

4 You may be able to arrange your cause cards quickly at first, but then you should think hard about your order and rearrange them if necessary. Keep moving the cards until you are happy with the order.

5 In pairs, compare your cards and discuss any difference you may have. You can move your cards again if you wish.

6 Make a list of what you think are the most important causes of deforestation.

7 Write a paragraph to explain the most important causes of deforestation in the Amazon.

Development or Destruction?

see pages 116–117 in your Horizons Book 3

Analysing satellite images

☐1 Look at satellite images B and C on page 116 of your textbook and below.

1990

A Satellite photo of the Amazon rainforest in 1990

2000

B The same area ten years later

☐2 Identify how the images are similar and label these similarities on the images.

☐3 Identify how the images are different and label these differences on the images.

☐4 How do you think image B might change by 2010?

Look at photo A and read the text on pages 118–119 of your textbook. Complete the mind map below to summarise the consequences of deforestation in the rainforest.

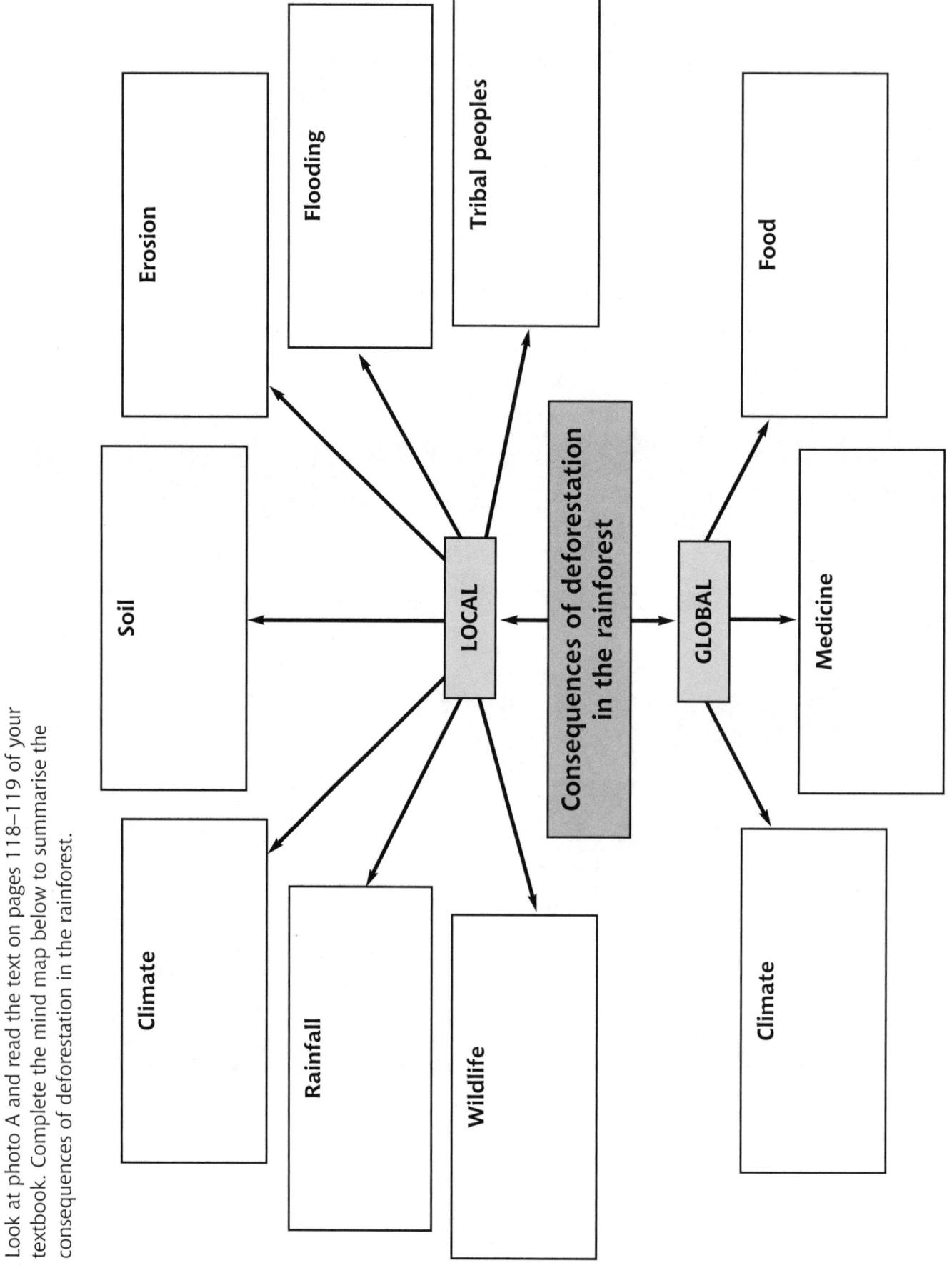

Erosion

Flooding

Tribal peoples

Food

Soil

LOCAL

Consequences of deforestation in the rainforest

GLOBAL

Medicine

Climate

Rainfall

Wildlife

Climate

Look at photo A on page 118 of your textbook.
Using the sketch below, add any words you think of
when you look at the picture.

Use this sheet as a starting point for the development of your group's presentation as part of the class mock public meeting.

The people who want our land do not respect us. Thousands of us have been killed: shot, bombed or poisoned. We catch diseases against which we have no immunity: flu, measles and TB can be fatal for us. Sometimes people known to have these diseases are sent into our villages to wipe us out.

We have a lot to teach about what you call sustainable living. Our medicine men may hold the key to curing many of the world's as yet incurable diseases by using undocumented chemical compounds found in some species of rainforest plants.

We've lived in the rainforest for thousands of years. The land is rightfully ours. We've learnt how to live in harmony with the forest. We get all we need from it without damaging it.

We're happy and content with our way of life. We wish to continue our life in peace, in harmony with the rainforest.

We love the forest because we were born here and we know how to live off the land. Without it, we're nobody and we have no way of surviving. We don't know about agriculture and commerce and we can't speak Portuguese. We depend on the forest. Without it, we'll be gone, extinct.

Farmers are taking our land and clearing the trees. Dams destroy our world by flooding the forest, killing the animals and plants. Trees are cut down, water polluted, soils ruined. They don't care for the forest.

Use this sheet as a starting point for the development of your group's presentation as part of the class mock public meeting.

> I used to live in north-east Brazil. Life was tough with frequent droughts. We had to queue for drinking water and my crops were destroyed. I had no money or land and no future.

> The government has given me my own land and a house in the Amazon. There is now a future for me and my family.

> I clear areas of land to farm each year so we can earn a living. My small plot of land doesn't make much difference – the rainforest is so huge.

> Ninety per cent of the 'environmental' groups engaged in saving the Amazon are scams. They do nothing and help nobody. They are nothing but fancy websites, cute words, overpaid non-profit executives and stupid ideas.

> We Brazilians are developing the resources of our country to earn a living. We try to live in peace with the tribal peoples but they often attack us. We must stop them!

> I am a subsistence farmer mainly growing enough crops to feed my family. I clear the understory shrubbery and then cut the forest trees. I leave the area to dry for a few months and then burn it. I can plant crops such as bananas, palms, manioc, maize and rice. After a year or two, as the yields decrease, I press a little deeper, clear new forest and start again. I make a better living than in the north-east of Brazil.

6·19 Debating briefing 3: environmentalists

Use this sheet as a starting point for the development of your group's presentation as part of the class mock public meeting.

The rainforest ecosystem is very fragile. It has taken millions of years to evolve. The diversity of life in the rainforest is important to everyone. Deforestation has major consequences at local and global scales.

Rainforests are a major natural resource providing a wide variety of products needed by people worldwide. We're losing the Earth's greatest biological treasures just as scientists are beginning to appreciate their true value.

Rainforests currently provide the sources for 25% of today's medicines, and 70% of the plants found to have anti-cancer properties are found only in the rainforest. This immense undiscovered biodiversity could hold the key to unlocking cures for devastating diseases.

Rainforests play a critical role in the atmosphere because they hold vast reserves of carbon in their vegetation. When rainforests are burned, or if trees are cut and left to decay, carbon is released into the atmosphere as carbon dioxide.

In fewer than 50 years more than half of the world's tropical rainforests have been lost.

Scientists now agree that by leaving the rainforests intact and harvesting their many natural resources such as nuts, fruits, oil-producing plants and medicinal plants, they have more economic value than if they were cut down for timber or for grazing cattle. Research shows that rainforest land converted to cattle operations yields $150 per hectare, and if timber is harvested the land yields $988 per hectare.

Without the roots of trees to hold the soil together, bare slopes are eroded by rainstorms, sediments clog up rivers and increase flooding. Nutrients are no longer replaced by the dense vegetation, and what are left are soon used up by farming or washed out by rain. Rainwater that was trapped on the dense vegetation in the rainforest was evaporated in the hot temperatures to provide the next day's rain, but this cycle has been broken by deforestation and the climate begins to become drier.

Use this sheet as a starting point for the development of your group's presentation as part of the class mock public meeting.

'Land without people. For people without land.'

The Amazon rainforest as an untapped resource, ripe for development to help improve the quality of life of all Brazilian people.

Wealth is unevenly spread across our country. We must open up this vast empty area. The first stage is building a major road network to make the region more accessible.

Our resettlement schemes along the new Amazon highways are very popular. We are giving the drought-stricken landless poor farmers of the north-east their own land and a fresh start in life.

Our plan for 'Avança Brasil' (Advance Brazil) is an exciting US$40 billion scheme. Our vast country needs the potential energy resources of the Amazon region if we are to develop. We have 30 new dam projects planned in the Amazon by 2010. They will have the potential to meet 60% of our energy needs – crucial as we are short of oil.

The Grande Carajás project is a major success. It produces export earnings for our country and much-needed jobs for our workers.

You from the developed world are in Brazil to stop us exploiting the wealth of the Amazon. What arrogance! You've already destroyed all the forests in your own nations and so you come and lecture us about the environment.

Horizons has helped you to develop skills that are an asset in any job situation and are highly valued by employers.

- **Numeracy and literacy**: you have written reports and used data. This encourages clarity and preciseness in the use of language.

- **Problem solving**: you have posed questions and investigated the answers, which helps you in complex decision making.

- **Spatial awareness**: extensive map reading helps develop a sense of place.

- **Analytical skills**: geographical investigations test hypotheses and involve data analysis.

- **Social and environmental awareness**: being world-aware and being able to link ideas together are valuable skills.

- **Team work**: fieldwork, an essential part of your geography course, develops team work and leadership skills.

- **Self-management**: the preparation of enquiries has encouraged you to manage yourself and your time.

- **Computer literacy**: **Horizons** has encouraged you to use ICT extensively – vital skills in any business environment.

1. Identify examples in your work with **Horizons** where you have developed each of these geographical skills.

2. Which skills do you feel you are best at?

3. Which skills have you enjoyed the most? Explain why.